THE GOURMAN REPORT

A Rating of Undergraduate Programs in American and International Universities

THE GOURMAN REPORT

A Rating of
Undergraduate
Programs in American
and International
Universities

TENTH EDITION

Dr. Jack Gourman

Random House, Inc. 1998

Princeton Review Publishing, L.L.C.
2315 Broadway
New York, NY 10024
E-mail: info@review.com

ISBN 0-679-77780-6

Editor: Jonathan Spaihts
Production Editor: Kristen Azzara
Design: Meher Khambata and Carmine Raspaolo

Manufactured in the United States of America on partially recycled paper.

9 8 7 6 5 4 3 2 1

Tenth Edition

This book is dedicated to the memory of
Blanka Gourman,
a kind and generous spirit.

ACKNOWLEDGMENTS

I am grateful to many people for their contributions to this text. Paul Gregory Gourman again gave unstintingly of his time for research and technical assistance.

I must also express my obligation and appreciation to those college and university faculty members, presidents, administrators and trustees/regents without whom our survey would be impossible. While I cannot recognize these individuals by name, I know that all readers of my book will join me in thanking them for their anonymous, and therefore selfless, contribution to the cause of quality in higher education.

FOREWORD

If every institution of higher education did its utmost to provide a superior educational experience, and frankly informed the public of its strengths and weaknesses, then there might be no need for *The Gourman Report*. The reality is, however, that colleges and universities too often fall short of this ideal.

At many institutions, decisions about faculty, curriculum and physical resources are made for reasons that have little to do with education. Internal and external political pressures influence much of what happens in academia, and these same pressures often prevent faculty members and administrators from making comments critical of their own institutions. As a result, colleges and universities often fall short in their task of education, and yet their shortcomings are rarely publicized; indeed, they are often deliberately concealed.

At even the best institutions, quality and reputation do not always coincide. Public-relations efforts by universities naturally emphasize strong programs and ignore weak ones. In the worst cases, genuinely fraudulent institutions exist in the interest of profit, and not in the interest of education. Such profit-driven "universities" may fail to maintain even basic standards of education, and yet to the educational consumer they may project an image as impressive as those of more worthy institutions. Distinguishing fact from fiction in the matter of academic quality can be difficult.

It is true that systems of accreditation exist to ensure quality in institutions of higher education. But accreditation has proven all too easy to acquire; it seems to be mainly a finding that an institution is not conspicuously defective in physical and staff resources. Such minimum standards are not sufficient. There are clusters of accredited institutions lacking in essential elements, and institutions that differ greatly in quality and yet receive identical certifications. The conventions of accreditation are not enough to guide the public in making educational choices.

Institutions do differ by quality, and *The Gourman Report* can be used as a basis to distinguish between them. It should also serve to alert the reader to the erratic standards of American education. If the following pages can make a contribution, however slight, toward raising awareness of the need for better educational standards, then the purpose of *The Gourman Report* is well served.

Jack Gourman
Los Angeles, California
December, 1997

TABLE OF CONTENTS

Part II: Rating of American Undergraduate Institutions 143

Part III: Rating of Undergraduate Programs 161

INTRODUCTION

Since 1967, *The Gourman Report* has made an intensive effort to determine what constitutes academic excellence or quality in American colleges and universities. The result of that research and study is found within this book.

The Gourman Report is the only qualitative guide to institutions of higher education that assigns a precise, numerical score to each school and program. This score is derived from a comprehensive assessment of each program's strengths and shortcomings. This method makes it simple to examine the effectiveness of a given educational program, or compare one program to another.

These deceptively simple numerical ratings take into account a wide variety of empirical data. *The Gourman Report* is not a popularity contest or an opinion poll, but an objective evaluation of complex information drawn from the public record, private research foundations, and universities themselves. Many of the resources employed in this research, while public, are not easily accessible. Individual researchers attempting to collect this data in order to compare institutions or programs would face a daunting task.

This book is intended for use by:
- Young people and parents wishing to make informed choices about higher education.
- Educators and administrators interested in an independent evaluation of their programs.
- Prospective employers who wish to assess the educational qualifications of college graduates.
- Schools wishing to improve undergraduate programs
- Foundations involved in funding colleges and universities.
- Individuals interested in identifying fraudulent or inferior institutions.
- Citizens concerned about the quality of today's higher education.

For all of these researchers, the breadth and convenience of the data in *The Gourman Report* can greatly facilitate the study of higher education.

Method of Evaluation
Much of the material used in compiling *The Gourman Report* is internal—drawn from educators and administrators at the schools themselves. These individuals are permitted to evaluate only their own programs—as they know them from daily experience—and not the programs of other institutions. Unsolicited appraisals are

occasionally considered (and weighed accordingly), but the bulk of our contributions come from people chosen for their academic qualifications, their published works, and their interest in improving the quality of higher education. It attests to the dedication of these individuals (and also to the serious problems in higher education today) that over 90% of our requests for contributions are met with a positive response.

In addition, *The Gourman Report* draws on many external resources which are a matter of record, such as funding for public universities as authorized by legislative bodies, required filings by schools to meet standards of non-discrimination, and material provided by the institutions (and independently verified) about faculty makeup and experience, fields of study offered, and physical plant.

Finally, *The Gourman Report* draws upon the findings of individuals, associations and agencies whose business it is to make accurate projections of the success that will be enjoyed by graduates from given institutions and disciplines. While the methods employed by these resources are proprietary, their findings have consistently been validated by experience, and they are an important part of our research.

The Gourman Report's rating of educational institutions is analogous to the grading of a college essay examination. What may appear to be a subjective process is in fact a patient sifting of empirical data by analysts who understand both the "subject matter" (the fields of study under evaluation), and the "students" (the colleges and universities themselves). The fact that there are virtually no "tie" scores indicates the accuracy and effectiveness of this methodology. So does the consistent affirmation of the ratings in *The Gourman Report* by readers who are in a position to evaluate certain programs themselves.

The following criteria are taken into consideration in the evaluation of each educational program and institution. It should be noted that, because disciplines vary in their educational methodology, the significance given each criterion will vary from the rating of one discipline to the next; however, our evaluation is consistent for all schools listed within each field of study.

1. Auspices, control and organization of the institution;
2. Number of educational programs offered and degrees conferred (with additional attention to "sub-fields" available to students within a particular discipline);
3. Age (experience level) of the institution and of the individual discipline or program and division;
4. Faculty, including qualifications, experience, intellectual interests, attainments, and professional productivity (including research);
5. Students, including quality of scholastic work and records of graduates both in graduate study and in practice;

6. Basis of and requirements for admission of students (overall and by individual discipline)
7. Number of students enrolled (overall and for each discipline);
8. Curriculum and curricular content of the program or discipline and division;
9. Standards and quality of instruction (including teaching loads);
10. Quality of administration, including attitudes and policy toward teaching, research and scholarly production in each discipline, and administration research;
11. Quality and availability of non-departmental areas such as counseling and career placement services;
12. Quality of physical plant devoted to undergraduate, graduate and professional levels;
13. Finances, including budgets, investments, expenditures and sources of income for both public and private institutions;
14. Library, including number of volumes, appropriateness of materials to individual disciplines, and accessibility of materials;
15. Computer facility sufficient to support current research activities for both faculty and students;
16. Sufficient funding for research equipment and infrastructure;
17. Number of teaching and research assistantships;
18. Academic-athletic balance.

Specific information about the data used to rank institutions and programs is available in Appendix A and Appendix B.

HOW TO USE THIS BOOK

The Gourman Report is of use both to those investigating a specific institution and to those investigating a specific discipline.

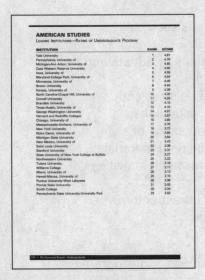

For prospective students, parents, guidance counselors, and others researching a certain discipline, *The Gourman Report* has been a valuable resource for many years. More than 140 fields of study are rated and ranked in the pages that follow, giving the reader a convenient synopsis of the best American institutions in each discipline.

In each table, institutions are listed in order of descending quality. An institution's name is followed by its score, which is compiled from *The Gourman Report's* comprehensive research, and a ranking, which denotes the institution's standing with respect to its fellow institutions in that discipline (e.g., a ranking of 3 indicates the third-best institution in that field).

For students and others investigating specific institutions, the newly expanded Part I offers unprecedented convenience. The top 100 American schools according to Overall Academic score are listed here.

An informational panel for each school provides basic institutional information, including all that a researcher might need to request further information from the school itself. This informational panel is followed by a listing of all programs at the school ranked by *The Gourman Report*. These programs are divided into the following categories: Arts, Humanities, Social Sciences, Sciences, Engineering, Technical, and Professional.

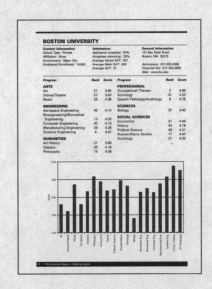

Beneath this listing appears a bar-graph representing the scores of these ranked programs, again arranged by category. This allows the researcher to form a general impression of the university's strengths and weaknesses—its "academic profile."

The breadth of information in *The Gourman Report* obviously supports a great number of research objectives. Its contents may be used to supplement the investigation of a multitude of issues. The expanded table of contents makes it a simple matter to locate specific data within the book.

Because the data within this book are presented without extraneous commentary, the following explanations may be helpful to both the first-time reader and the experienced reader of *The Gourman Report*.

Part I contains overall academic ratings and program rankings for the top 100 undergraduate institutions in the United States. These institutions have distinguished themselves by their commitment to a leadership position in quality education; it is only appropriate that their achievement be recognized in a separate section.

The overall academic rankings are presented in table-form in order of descending quality. Thereafter the program-rankings for individual schools appear alphabetically by school name. The program scores listed here may also be found in Part III.

Part II lists every undergraduate institution approved by *The Gourman Report*, together with the overall academic score for each institution. Institutions are listed by state. This section is included primarily for use by readers who desire information about a particular institution. By no means should a school's mere presence on this list be taken as an endorsement or an indication of quality, as ratings vary from "strong" (4.41 to 4.99) to "marginal" (2.01 to 2.99).

Part III lists program-by-program rankings of institutions in over 140 fields of study. Fields of study are listed in alphabetical order; for each field, rated institutions are listed in order of descending quality.

Part IV contains a ranking of undergraduate engineering schools in the United States. Institutions are listed with Gourman score and Gourman ranking, and appear in order of descending quality.

Part V contains a ranking of undergraduate schools of business administration in the United States. Institutions are listed with Gourman score and Gourman ranking, and appear in order of descending quality.

Part VI contains rankings of undergraduate premedical and prelegal programs in the United States. Institutions are listed with Gourman score and Gourman ranking, and appear in order of descending quality.

Part VII evaluates institutions in eleven administrative areas: administration, alumni associations, athletic-academic balance, comparative competition for fellowships/scholarships, counseling centers, curriculum, intercollegiate athletic departments, libraries, public relations, and trustees/regents of the following private colleges and universities on the approved list of *The Gourman Report*.

Part VIII lists Canadian undergraduate institutions approved by *The Gourman Report*, with score and ranking. Institutions appear in order of descending quality.

Part IX includes ratings of Canadian programs in engineering, listed for the nation in total and also grouped by province.

Part X provides a rating of leading international universities, ranked by curriculum, faculty, and overall academic quality.

Part XI

Appendix A lists, in table form, the total number of areas which were evaluated in preparing each part of *The Gourman Report*.

Appendix B provides a listing of all international universities considered by this Tenth Edition.

Appendix C contains a comparative rating of selective university administrations, regents and trustees for four public university systems.

The Tenth Edition

The Gourman Report now examines more than 140 separate disciplines.

For the Tenth Edition, the chapters of *The Gourman Report* have been re-ordered. In the new format, comprehensive information about American institutions of higher education is followed by information about Canadian and international institutions.

The Gourman Report's former list of the Top 50 Undergraduate Schools in the U.S. has been expanded to include the Top 100 schools. This list of top schools has been supplemented with a school-by-school listing of programs rated by *The Gourman Report*. For the first time, it is now possible to look up a certain institution and see at a glance the score of every program ranked by *The Gourman Report* at that institution.

Part X, Rating of International Universities, does not currently include institutions within the republics of the former Soviet Union, due to upheaval and instability in those regions.

The basic content of *The Gourman Report* is otherwise unchanged from previous editions.

Note: *The Gourman Report* does not approve of undergraduate programs in criminal justice or forensic science. Undergraduate programs in these fields are not ranked. *The Gourman Report* further does not approve of any undergraduate program in education. Undergraduate programs in education and the sub-disciplines of education are not ranked.

Part I

THE TOP 100
UNDERGRADUATE SCHOOLS
IN THE U.S.

INSTITUTION	Rank	Score
PRINCETON UNIVERSITY	1	4.95
HARVARD AND RADCLIFFE COLLEGES	2	4.94
MICHIGAN-ANN ARBOR, UNIVERSITY OF	3	4.93
YALE UNIVERSITY	4	4.92
STANFORD UNIVERSITY	5	4.91
CORNELL UNIVERSITY	6	4.90
CALIFORNIA-BERKELEY, UNIVERSITY OF	7	4.89
CHICAGO, UNIVERSITY OF	8	4.88
WISCONSIN-MADISON, UNIVERSITY OF	9	4.87
CALIFORNIA-LOS ANGELES, UNIVERSITY OF	10	4.86
MASSACHUSETTS INSTITUTE OF TECHNOLOGY	11	4.85
CALIFORNIA INSTITUTE OF TECHNOLOGY	12	4.84
COLUMBIA UNIVERSITY	13	4.83
NORTHWESTERN UNIVERSITY	14	4.82
PENNSYLVANIA, UNIVERSITY OF	15	4.81
NOTRE DAME, UNIVERSITY OF	16	4.80
DUKE UNIVERSITY	17	4.79
BROWN UNIVERSITY	18	4.78
JOHNS HOPKINS UNIVERSITY	19	4.77
DARTMOUTH COLLEGE	20	4.76
ILLINOIS,URBANA-CHAMPAIGN, UNIVERSITY OF	21	4.75
MINNESOTA, UNIVERSITY OF	22	4.74
RICE UNIVERSITY	23	4.73
CARNEGIE MELLON UNIVERSITY	24	4.72
CALIFORNIA-SAN DIEGO, UNIVERSITY OF	25	4.71
WASHINGTON, UNIVERSITY OF	26	4.70
INDIANA UNIVERSITY-BLOOMINGTON	27	4.69
NORTH CAROLINA-CHAPEL HILL, UNIVERSITY OF	28	4.68
WASHINGTON UNIVERSITY IN SAINT LOUIS	29	4.67
STATE UNIVERSITY OF NEW YORK COLLEGE AT BUFFALO	30	4.66
TUFTS UNIVERSITY	31	4.65
VANDERBILT UNIVERSITY	32	4.64
OHIO STATE UNIVERSITY-COLUMBUS	33	4.62
VIRGINIA, UNIVERSITY OF	34	4.61
CALIFORNIA-IRVINE, UNIVERSITY OF	35	4.60
PENNSYLVANIA STATE UNIVERSITY-UNIVERSITY PARK	36	4.59
NEW YORK UNIVERSITY	37	4.58
CALIFORNIA-DAVIS, UNIVERSITY OF	38	4.57
ROCHESTER, UNIVERSITY OF	39	4.56
IOWA, UNIVERSITY OF	40	4.55
GEORGIA INSTITUTE OF TECHNOLOGY	41	4.54
MICHIGAN STATE UNIVERSITY	42	4.53
PURDUE UNIVERSITY-WEST LAFAYETTE	43	4.52
TULANE UNIVERSITY	44	4.50
RUTGERS UNIVERSITY, NEW BRUNSWICK	45	4.48
STATE UNIVERSITY OF NEW YORK AT STONY BROOK	46	4.46
CALIFORNIA-SANTA BARBARA, UNIVERSITY OF	47	4.45

INSTITUTION	Rank	Score
BRANDEIS UNIVERSITY	48	4.44
UNITED STATES AIR FORCE ACADEMY	49	4.43
CASE WESTERN RESERVE UNIVERSITY	50	4.39
MISSOURI-COLUMBIA, UNIVERSITY OF	51	4.38
RENSSELAER POLYTECHNIC INSTITUTE	52	4.38
EMORY UNIVERSITY	53	4.36
UNITED STATES NAVAL ACADEMY	54	4.36
PITTSBURGH, UNIVERSITY OF	55	4.36
KANSAS, UNIVERSITY OF	56	4.34
CALIFORNIA-RIVERSIDE, UNIVERSITY OF	57	4.33
IOWA STATE UNIVERSITY	58	4.30
COLORADO SCHOOL OF MINES	59	4.20
GEORGETOWN UNIVERSITY	60	4.15
AMHERST COLLEGE	61	4.14
TEXAS-AUSTIN, UNIVERSITY OF	62	4.14
CALIFORNIA-SANTA CRUZ, UNIVERSITY OF	63	4.11
WAYNE STATE UNIVERSITY	64	4.11
COLGATE UNIVERSITY	65	4.11
ARIZONA, UNIVERSITY OF	66	4.08
ARIZONA STATE UNIVERSITY	67	4.03
BOSTON UNIVERSITY	68	4.03
STATE UNIVERSITY OF NEW YORK AT BINGHAMTON	69	4.03
FORDHAM UNIVERSITY	70	4.02
UNITED STATES MILITARY ACADEMY	71	4.02
BRYN MAWR COLLEGE	72	4.02
POMONA COLLEGE	73	4.01
MARYLAND-COLLEGE PARK, UNIVERSITY OF	74	4.01
STATE UNIVERSITY OF NEW YORK AT ALBANY	75	4.01
CLAREMONT MCKENNA COLLEGE	76	4.00
COLORADO-BOULDER, UNIVERSITY OF	77	3.99
TEXAS A&M UNIVERSITY-COLLEGE STATION	78	3.99
FLORIDA, UNIVERSITY OF	79	3.98
LOUISIANA STATE UNIVERSITY AND A&M COLLEGE	80	3.98
ALABAMA, UNIVERSITY OF	81	3.97
ARKANSAS, UNIVERSITY OF	82	3.97
CATHOLIC UNIVERSITY OF AMERICA, THE	83	3.97
GEORGIA, UNIVERSITY OF	84	3.97
AUBURN UNIVERSITY	85	3.96
GEORGE WASHINGTON UNIVERSITY	86	3.96
SOUTHERN CALIFORNIA, UNIVERSITY OF	87	3.95
DELAWARE, UNIVERSITY OF	88	3.95
NEBRASKA-LINCOLN, UNIVERSITY OF	89	3.95
CONNECTICUT, UNIVERSITY OF	90	3.94
LEHIGH UNIVERSITY	91	3.94
KANSAS STATE UNIVERSITY	92	3.93
ALABAMA-BIRMINGHAM, UNIVERSITY OF	93	3.92
YESHIVA UNIVERSITY	94	3.92

INSTITUTION	Rank	Score
FLORIDA STATE UNIVERSITY	95	3.91
MASSACHUSETTS-AMHERST, UNIVERSITY OF	96	3.91
WILLIAMS COLLEGE	97	3.91
POLYTECHNIC UNIVERSITY	98	3.91
OREGON, UNIVERSITY OF	99	3.91
SWARTHMORE COLLEGE	100	3.91

ALABAMA, UNIVERSITY OF

Contact Information
School Type: Public
Affiliation: None
Environment: Suburban
Undergrad Enrollment: 14,195

Admissions
Applicants accepted: 78%
Acceptees attending: 44%
Average Verbal SAT: NR
Average Math SAT: NR
Average ACT: 24

General Information
Box 870132
Tuscaloosa, AL 35487

Admissions: 205-348-5666
Financial Aid: 205-348-6756
Web: www.ua.edu

Program	Rank	Score	Program	Rank	Score
ENGINEERING			**TECHNICAL**		
Metallurgical Engineering	25	4.48	Dietetics	12	4.50
Mining & Mineral Engineering	24	4.45	Food Sciences	13	4.51
Petroleum Engineering	21	4.42	Food Services Management	11	4.51
SCIENCES			Home Economics	20	4.43
Nutrition	17	4.61			

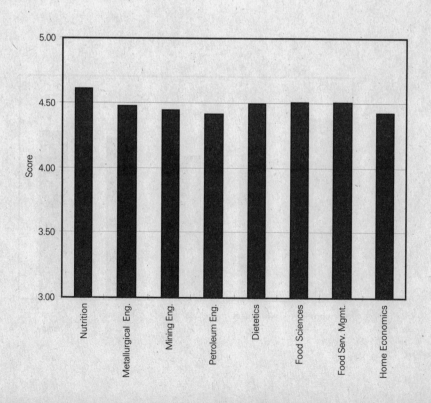

ALABAMA-BIRMINGHAM, UNIVERSITY OF

Contact Information
School Type: Public
Affiliation: None
Environment: Major City
Undergrad Enrollment: 10,692

Admissions
Applicants accepted: 88%
Acceptees attending: 60%
Average Verbal SAT: NR
Average Math SAT: NR
Average ACT: 21

General Information
UAB Station
Birmingham, AL 35294

Admissions: 205-934-8221
Financial Aid: 205-934-8223
Web: www.uab.edu

Program	Rank	Score
ENGINEERING		
Aerospace Engineering	35	4.22
Materials Engineering/Materials Science & Engineering	32	4.28
HUMANITIES		
Information Science	7	4.63

Program	Rank	Score
PROFESSIONAL		
Nursing	19	4.44
Occupational Therapy	22	4.50

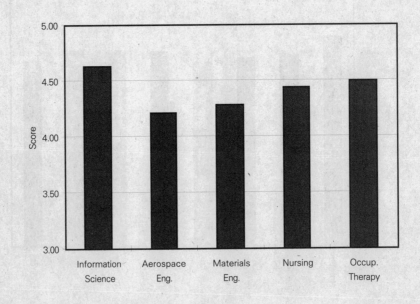

ARIZONA STATE UNIVERSITY

Contact Information
School Type: Public
Affiliation: None
Environment: Suburban
Undergrad Enrollment: 31,859

Admissions
Applicants accepted: 78%
Acceptees attending: 38%
Average Verbal SAT: 540
Average Math SAT: 544
Average ACT: 23

General Information
P.O. Box 870112
Tempe, AZ 85287-0112

Admissions: 602-965-7788
Financial Aid: 602-965-3355
Web: www.asu.edu

Program	Rank	Score	Program	Rank	Score
ARTS			Journalism and Mass		
Drama/Theatre	40	3.13	Communications	30	4.20
ENGINEERING			Management	36	4.28
Bioengineering/			Marketing	34	4.25
Biomedical Engineering	15	4.16	Urban and Regional Planning	12	4.58
Computer Engineering	30	4.46	**SCIENCES**		
Electrical Engineering	74	4.11	Zoology	11	4.59
Mechanical Engineering	55	4.12	Geology/Geosciences	30	4.37
HUMANITIES			**SOCIAL SCIENCES**		
Religious Studies	14	4.59	Anthropology	34	4.27
Spanish	33	4.29	Radio/Television Studies	5	4.77
PROFESSIONAL			**TECHNICAL**		
Accounting	39	4.06	Home Economics	17	4.50
Business Administration	33	4.28			
Finance	33	4.28			

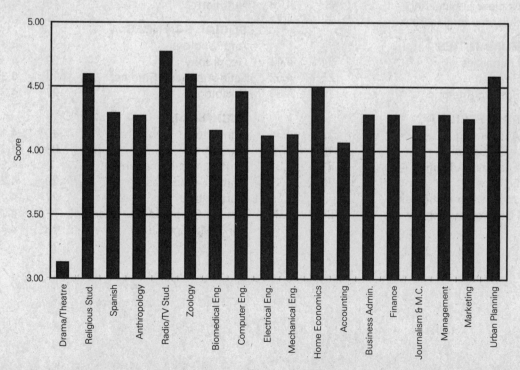

ARIZONA, UNIVERSITY OF

Contact Information
School Type: Public
Affiliation: None
Environment: City
Undergrad Enrollment: 26,468

Admissions
Applicants accepted: NR
Acceptees attending: 34%
Average Verbal SAT: 463
Average Math SAT: 532
Average ACT: 23

General Information
Tucson, AZ 85721

Admissions: 520-621-3237
Financial Aid: 520-621-1858
Web: www.arizona.edu

Program	Rank	Score	Program	Rank	Score
ARTS			Landscape Architecture	16	4.60
Art	36	3.28	Management	34	4.32
Drama/Theatre	34	3.30	Marketing	30	4.32
			Nursing	25	4.36
ENGINEERING			Sociology	27	4.38
Aerospace Engineering	10	4.68	Speech Pathology/Audiology	20	4.55
Agricultural Engineering	34	4.25			
Chemical Engineering	61	4.17	**SCIENCES**		
Civil Engineering	53	4.04	Astronomy	7	4.59
Computer Engineering	38	4.21	Atmospheric Sciences	2	4.85
Electrical Engineering	47	4.46	Cell Biology	17	4.24
Geological Engineering	11	4.73	Earth Science	10	4.49
Industrial Engineering	44	4.18	Ecology/Environmental Studies	11	4.57
Materials Engineering/Materials			Entomology	18	4.47
Science & Engineering	33	4.25	Geology/Geoscience	15	4.66
Mechanical Engineering	53	4.15	Mathematics	53	4.15
Mining & Mineral Engineering	3	4.87	Molecular Biology	17	4.52
Nuclear Engineering	8	4.70	Nutrition	10	4.73
Systems Engineering	5	4.71			
			SOCIAL SCIENCES		
HUMANITIES			Anthropology	5	4.86
Linguistics	24	4.41	Geography	20	4.37
Spanish	21	4.52	Latin American Studies	13	4.30
Speech/Rhetoric	12	4.60	Sociology	27	4.38
PROFESSIONAL			**TECHNICAL**		
Accounting	28	4.34	Agriculture	40	4.15
Architecture	18	3.70	Agronomy	30	4.30
Business Administration	31	4.33	Farm/Ranch Management	7	4.59
Finance	23	4.47	Home Economics	29	4.23
Journalism and Mass			Horticulture	27	4.42
Communications	24	4.35	Natural Resource Management	4	4.72
			Parks Management	13	4.46

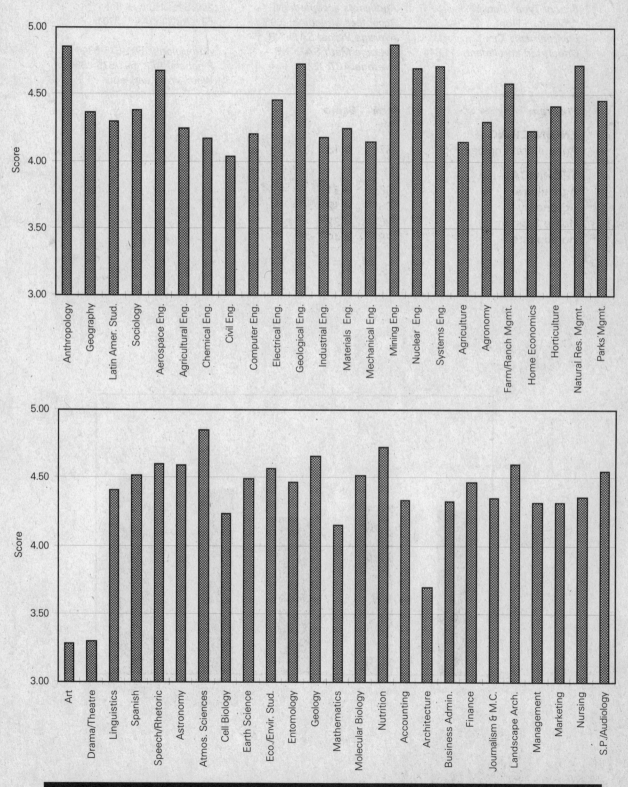

ARKANSAS, UNIVERSITY OF

Contact Information
School Type: Public
Affiliation: None
Environment: City
Undergrad Enrollment: 11,844

Admissions
Applicants accepted: NR
Acceptees attending: 69%
Average Verbal SAT: NR
Average Math SAT: NR
Average ACT: 23

General Information
200 Silas Hunt Hall
Fayetteville, AR 72701

Admissions: 501-575-5346
Financial Aid: 501-575-3806
Web: www.uark.edu

Program	Rank	Score
ENGINEERING		
Agricultural Engineering	37	4.18
TECHNICAL		
Agriculture	36	4.21
Agronomy	38	4.12
Home Economics	26	4.32
Horticulture	28	4.40

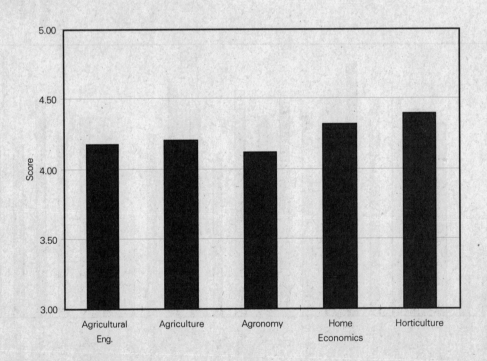

AUBURN UNIVERSITY

Contact Information
School Type: Public
Affiliation: None
Environment: City
Undergrad Enrollment: 18,396

Admissions
Applicants accepted: 89%
Acceptees attending: 40%
Average Verbal SAT: 569
Average Math SAT: 574
Average ACT: 24

General Information
Auburn University
Montgomery, AL 36849

Admissions: 334-844-4080
Financial Aid: 334-844-4723
Web: www.auburn.edu

Program	Rank	Score
ENGINEERING		
Aerospace Engineering	36	4.21
Agricultural Engineering	27	4.37
Industrial Engineering	34	4.30
Materials Engineering/Materials Science And Engineering	30	4.34
SCIENCES		
Entomology	23	4.36
Fish/Game Management	22	4.48

Program	Rank	Score
TECHNICAL		
Agriculture	24	4.36
Agronomy	24	4.40
Fish/Game Management	22	4.48
Forestry	15	4.55
Home Economics	14	4.56
Horticulture	23	4.50
Ornamental Horticulture	7	4.69
Poultry Sciences	11	4.68

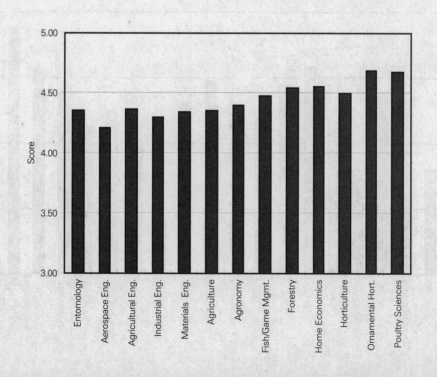

BOSTON UNIVERSITY

Contact Information
School Type: Private
Affiliation: None
Environment: Major City
Undergrad Enrollment: 14,892

Admissions
Applicants accepted: 53%
Acceptees attending: 29%
Average Verbal SAT: 631
Average Math SAT: 630
Average ACT: 27

General Information
121 Bay State Road
Boston, MA 02215

Admissions: 617-353-2300
Financial Aid: 617-353-2965
Web: www.bu.edu

Program	Rank	Score	Program	Rank	Score
ARTS			**PROFESSIONAL**		
Art	21	3.80	Occupational Therapy	2	4.88
Drama/Theatre	27	3.60	Sociology	31	4.32
Music	29	4.36	Speech Pathology/Audiology	9	4.76
ENGINEERING			**SCIENCES**		
Aerospace Engineering	40	4.14	Biology	37	3.40
Bioengineering/Biomedical					
Engineering	13	4.25	**SOCIAL SCIENCES**		
Computer Engineering	40	4.13	Economics	31	4.44
Manufacturing Engineering	29	4.38	History	43	4.18
Systems Engineering	9	4.57	Political Science	49	4.21
HUMANITIES			Russian/Slavic Studies	17	4.47
Art History	21	3.80	Sociology	31	4.32
Classics	20	4.16			
Philosophy	15	4.58			

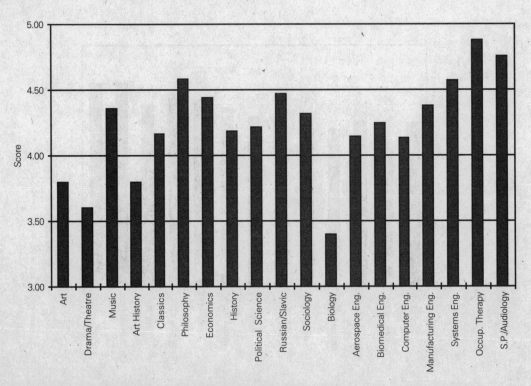

BRANDEIS UNIVERSITY

Contact Information
School Type: Private
Affiliation: None
Environment: Suburban
Undergrad Enrollment: 2,968

Admissions
Applicants accepted: 53%
Acceptees attending: 26%
Average Verbal SAT: 650
Average Math SAT: 650
Average ACT: NR

General Information
415 South Street
Waltham, MA 02254

Admissions: 617-736-3500
Financial Aid: 617-736-3700
Web: www.brandeis.edu

Program	Rank	Score	Program	Rank	Score
ARTS			**SCIENCES**		
Drama/Theatre	28	3.55	Biochemistry	15	4.50
Music	18	4.61	Biology	43	3.25
			Mathematics	57	4.11
HUMANITIES					
Comparative Literature	21	4.24	**SOCIAL SCIENCES**		
English	37	4.20	American Studies	12	4.15
Hebrew	8	4.76	Anthropology	35	4.26
			History	41	4.23
PROFESSIONAL			Political Science	30	4.52
Sociology	32	4.30	Sociology	32	4.30

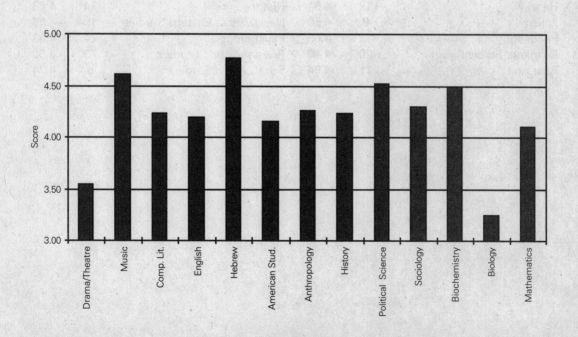

BROWN UNIVERSITY

Contact Information
School Type: Private
Affiliation: None
Environment: City
Undergrad Enrollment: 5,992

Admissions
Applicants accepted: 22%
Acceptees attending: 45%
Average Verbal SAT: 620
Average Math SAT: 680
Average ACT: 28

General Information
45 Prospect Street, Box 1876
Providence, RI 02912

Admissions: 401-863-2378
Financial Aid: 401-863-2721
Web: www.brown.edu

Program	Rank	Score	Program	Rank	Score
ARTS			Slavic Languages	8	4.66
Art	14	4.35	Spanish	14	4.63
ENGINEERING			**SCIENCES**		
Bioengineering/Biomedical			Applied Mathematics	4	4.80
Engineering	3	4.87	Biology	30	4.35
Civil Engineering	16	4.59	Biophysics	11	4.51
Electrical Engineering	44	4.50	Cell Biology	9	4.62
Materials Engineering/Materials			Chemistry	25	4.52
Science And Engineering	8	4.77	Computer Science	16	4.61
Mechanical Engineering	7	4.83	Geology/Geoscience	17	4.62
			Geophysics/Geoscience	9	4.75
HUMANITIES			Marine Biology	6	4.50
Art History	14	4.46	Mathematics	12	4.73
Classics	9	4.64	Physics	25	4.60
Comparative Literature	13	4.47			
English	12	4.74	**SOCIAL SCIENCES**		
French	20	4.42	American Studies	8	4.44
German	26	4.45	Anthropology	47	4.06
Greek	3	4.80	Economics	18	4.69
Hebrew	19	4.51	History	14	4.68
Italian	9	4.50	Near/Middle Eastern Studies	15	4.55
Philosophy	12	4.65	Psychology	24	4.38
Religious Studies	20	4.46	Russian/Slavic Studies	13	4.58
Russian	11	4.64	South Asian Studies	6	4.74

BROWN UNIVERSITY (CONTINUED)

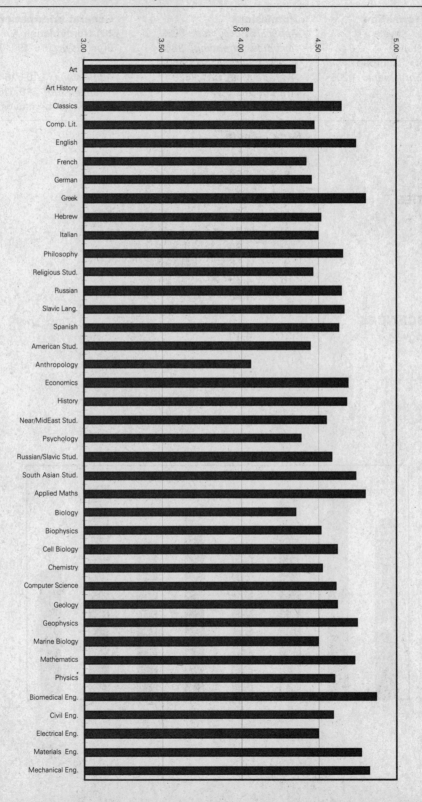

Score

BRYN MAWR COLLEGE

Contact Information
School Type: Private
Affiliation: None
Environment: Suburban
Undergrad Enrollment: 1,205

Admissions
Applicants accepted: 58%
Acceptees attending: 38%
Average Verbal SAT: 660
Average Math SAT: 620
Average ACT: NR

General Information
101 North Merion Avenue
Bryn Mawr, PA 19010-2899

Admissions: 610-526-5152
Financial Aid: 610-526-5245
Web: www.brynmawr.edu

Program	Rank	Score
ARTS		
Art	8	4.54
HUMANITIES		
Art History	8	4.75
Classics	7	4.71
French	23	4.33
Greek	9	4.56
Italian	15	4.35
Latin	3	4.83
SOCIAL SCIENCES		
Anthropology	43	4.10

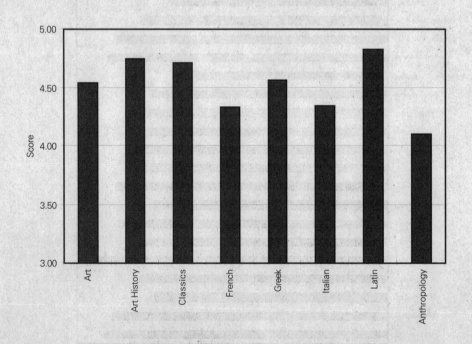

CALIFORNIA INSTITUTE OF TECHNOLOGY

Contact Information
School Type: Private
Affiliation: None
Environment: Suburban
Undergrad Enrollment: 893

Admissions
Applicants accepted: 25%
Acceptees attending: 43%
Average Verbal SAT: 725
Average Math SAT: 767
Average ACT: NR

General Information
1200 East California Boulevard
Pasadena, CA 91125

Admissions: 818-395-6341
Financial Aid: 818-395-6280
Web: www.caltech.edu

Program	Rank	Score
ENGINEERING		
Chemical Engineering	5	4.85
SCIENCES		
Applied Mathematics	9	4.63
Astronomy	1	4.92
Astrophysics	2	4.81
Biology	1	4.92
Cell Biology	2	4.90
Chemistry	1	4.95
Computer Science	8	4.79
Geology/Geoscience	1	4.92
Geophysics/Geoscience	1	4.92
Mathematics	16	4.66
Molecular Biology	2	4.88
Physics	1	4.92

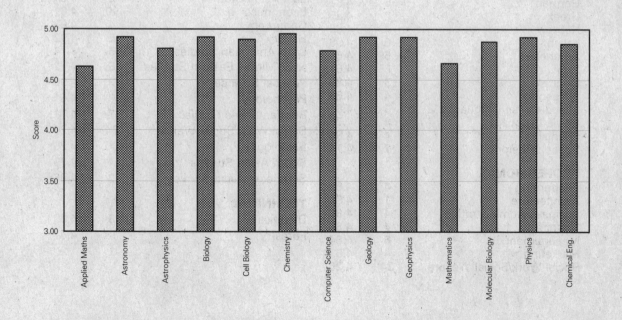

CALIFORNIA-BERKELEY, UNIVERSITY OF

Contact Information
School Type: Public
Affiliation: None
Environment: City
Undergrad Enrollment: 21,358

Admissions
Applicants accepted: 31%
Acceptees attending: 39%
Average Verbal SAT: 664
Average Math SAT: 632
Average ACT: NR

General Information
Office of Undergraduate
Admission and Relations with
Schools, 110 Sproul Hall #5800
Berkeley, CA 94720-5800
Admissions: 510-642-3175
Financial Aid: 510-642-6442
Web: www.berkeley.edu

Program	Rank	Score	Program	Rank	Score
ARTS			**SCIENCES**		
Art	5	4.67	Applied Mathematics	3	4.83
Drama/Theatre	15	4.39	Astronomy	2	4.86
Film	6	4.65	Bacteriology/Microbiology	3	4.88
Music	1	4.92	Biochemistry	3	4.90
			Biology	7	4.84
ENGINEERING			Cell Biology	6	4.74
Chemical Engineering	3	4.88	Chemistry	2	4.94
Civil Engineering	1	4.92	Computer Science	3	4.89
Computer Engineering	2	4.90	Ecology/Environmental Studies	3	4.84
Electrical Engineering	3	4.88	Entomology	1	4.91
Industrial Engineering	3	4.85	Environmental Sciences	4	4.82
Manufacturing Engineering	1	4.42	Geology/Geoscience	10	4.74
Mechanical Engineering	3	4.91	Geophysics/Geoscience	3	4.89
Nuclear Engineering	3	4.83	Mathematics	2	4.91
			Molecular Biology	4	4.82
HUMANITIES			Nutrition	9	4.75
Art History	6	4.80	Physics	6	4.87
Chinese	5	4.68	Statistics	1	4.91
Classics	2	4.89			
Comparative Literature	1	4.81	**SOCIAL SCIENCES**		
English	2	4.91	Anthropology	3	4.90
French	9	4.77	Asian/Oriental Studies	2	4.78
German	5	4.82	East Asian Studies	2	4.83
Greek	2	4.85	Economics	10	4.81
Hebrew	4	4.85	Geography	4	4.82
Italian	6	4.58	History	2	4.92
Japanese	5	4.64	Latin American Studies	3	4.74
Latin	8	4.61	Near/Middle Eastern Studies	6	4.72
Linguistics	3	4.88	Political Science	3	4.90
Philosophy	4	4.83	Psychology	6	4.61
Scandinavian Languages	3	4.82	Russian/Slavic Studies	7	4.71
Slavic Languages	4	4.78	Social Work/Social Welfare	34	4.26
Spanish	4	4.84	Sociology	30	4.26
Speech/Rhetoric	7	4.74	South Asian Studies	4	4.79
			Southeast Asian Studies	2	4.85
PROFESSIONAL					
Accounting	4	4.86	**TECHNICAL**		
Architecture	1	4.89	Dietetics	8	4.69
Business Administration	4	4.85	Forestry	18	4.47
Finance	4	4.86			
Management	5	4.84			
Marketing	4	4.83			
Social Work/Social Welfare	34	4.26			

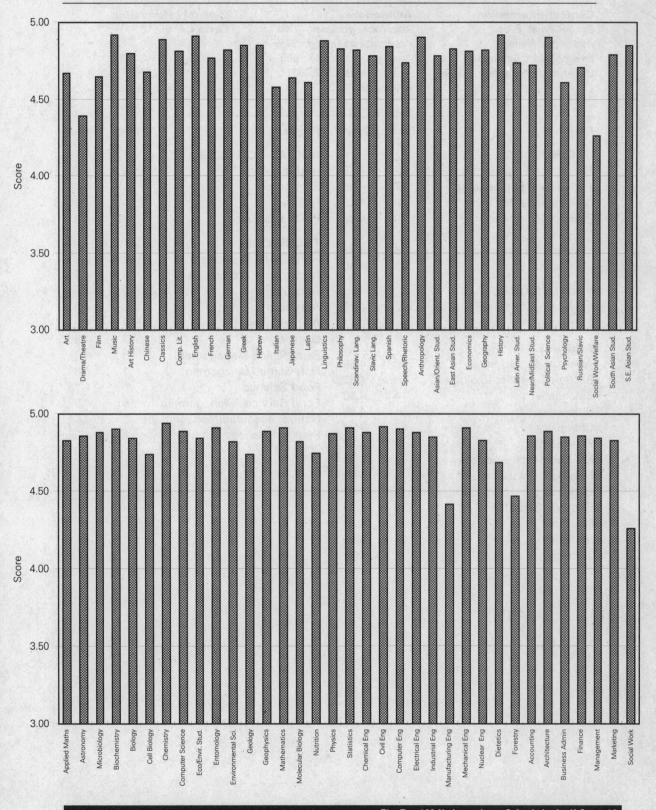

CALIFORNIA-DAVIS, UNIVERSITY OF

Contact Information
School Type: Public
Affiliation: None
Environment: Suburban
Undergrad Enrollment: 16,699

Admissions
Applicants accepted: 73%
Acceptees attending: 27%
Average Verbal SAT: 565
Average Math SAT: 601
Average ACT: 24

General Information
Davis, CA 95616

Admissions: 916-752-1011
Financial Aid: 916-752-2390
Web: www.ucdavis.edu

Program	Rank	Score	Program	Rank	Score
ENGINEERING			**SOCIAL SCIENCES**		
Aerospace Engineering	39	4.15	Anthropology	36	4.23
Agricultural Engineering	17	4.65	Economics	24	4.58
Civil Engineering	22	4.48	History	44	4.15
Electrical Engineering	70	4.18	Political Science	48	4.23
Materials Engineering/Materials					
Science & Engineering	28	4.38	**TECHNICAL**		
Mechanical Engineering	23	4.60	Agricultural Business	10	4.45
			Agricultural Economics	8	4.73
PROFESSIONAL			Agriculture	7	4.74
Environmental Design	5	4.78	Agronomy	12	4.67
Landscape Architecture	4	4.81	Animal Science	2	4.89
			Dietetics	3	4.85
SCIENCES			Farm/Ranch Management	5	4.65
Atmospheric Sciences	5	4.69	Fish/Game Management	1	4.83
Bacteriology/Microbiology	7	4.82	Food Sciences	6	4.76
Biochemistry	14	4.53	Food Services Management	9	4.57
Botany	1	4.90	Natural Resource Management	6	4.61
Chemistry	42	4.27	Poultry Sciences	2	4.85
Entomology	4	4.82			
Environmental Sciences	5	4.79			
Fish/Game Management	1	4.83			
Genetics	1	4.91			
Geology/Geoscience	26	4.45			
Nutrition	4	4.83			
Statistics	19	4.56			
Zoology	6	4.73			

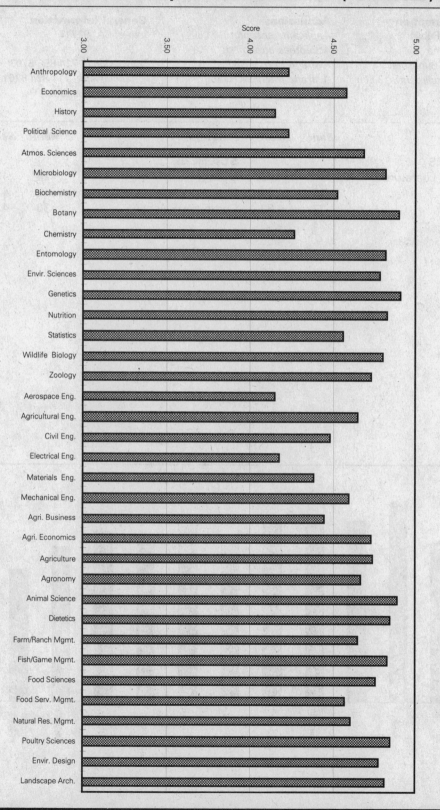

Score

CALIFORNIA-IRVINE, UNIVERSITY OF

Contact Information
School Type: Public
Affiliation: None
Environment: Suburban
Undergrad Enrollment: 13,390

Admissions
Applicants accepted: 71%
Acceptees attending: 27%
Average Verbal SAT: 520
Average Math SAT: 585
Average ACT: NR

General Information
Irvine, CA 92717

Admissions: 714-856-6703
Financial Aid: 714-824-6261
Web: www.uci.edu

Program	Rank	Score
HUMANITIES		
Comparative Literature	17	4.35
English	15	4.69
French	17	4.53
German	24	4.49
Information Science	9	4.55
Linguistics	26	4.35
Spanish	20	4.53

Program	Rank	Score
SCIENCES		
Biology	26	4.43
Chemistry	40	4.30
Computer Science	30	4.11
SOCIAL SCIENCES		
Anthropology	28	4.40

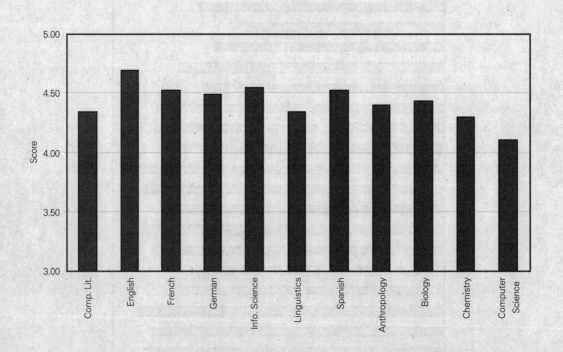

CALIFORNIA-LOS ANGELES, UNIVERSITY OF

Contact Information
School Type: Public
Affiliation: None
Environment: Suburban
Undergrad Enrollment: 23,914

Admissions
Applicants accepted: 39%
Acceptees attending: 35%
Average Verbal SAT: 603
Average Math SAT: 633
Average ACT: 25

General Information
405 Hilgard Avenue
Los Angeles, CA 90024

Admissions: 310-825-3101
Financial Aid: 310-206-0400
Web: www.ucla.edu

Program	Rank	Score	Program	Rank	Score
ARTS			**PROFESSIONAL**		
Art	16	4.27	Sociology	9	4.68
Drama/Theatre	2	4.90	**SCIENCES**		
Film	1	4.86	Applied Mathematics	8	4.66
Music	10	4.78	Astronomy	10	4.46
ENGINEERING			Atmospheric Sciences	7	4.59
Aerospace Engineering	32	4.26	Bacteriology/Microbiology	5	4.84
Chemical Engineering	64	4.13	Biochemistry	6	4.81
Civil Engineering	18	4.55	Biology	15	4.67
Computer Engineering	36	4.31	Chemistry	9	4.82
Electrical Engineering	6	4.82	Computer Science	6	4.82
Materials Engineering/ Materials			Geology/Geoscience	8	4.79
Science & Engineering	15	4.60	Geophysics/Geoscience	5	4.82
Mechanical Engineering	10	4.77	Mathematics	14	4.69
HUMANITIES			Physics	14	4.76
Art History	12	4.59	**SOCIAL SCIENCES**		
Classics	18	4.23	Anthropology	8	4.80
English	11	4.76	Economics	14	4.74
French	30	4.17	Geography	9	4.62
German	12	4.67	History	16	4.66
Hebrew	16	4.55	Latin American Studies	10	4.44
Italian	16	4.33	Near/Middle Eastern Studies	12	4.60
Linguistics	1	4.91	Political Science	12	4.76
Philosophy	8	4.73	Psychology	12	4.52
Russian	17	4.48	Radio/Television Studies	2	4.86
Spanish	8	4.77	Sociology	9	4.68

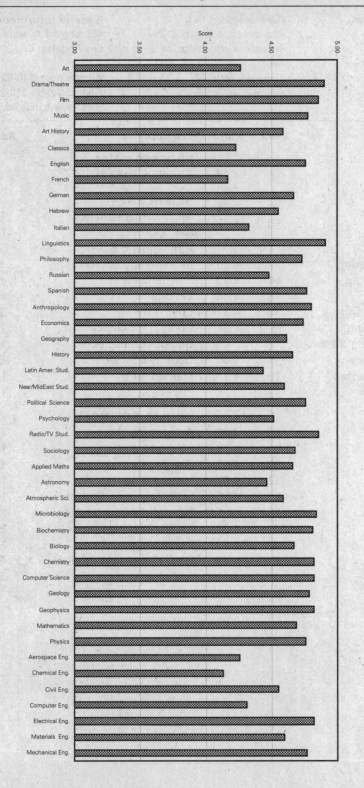

Score

Art	
Drama/Theatre	
Film	
Music	
Art History	
Classics	
English	
French	
German	
Hebrew	
Italian	
Linguistics	
Philosophy	
Russian	
Spanish	
Anthropology	
Economics	
Geography	
History	
Latin Amer. Stud.	
Near/MidEast Stud.	
Political Science	
Psychology	
Radio/TV Stud.	
Sociology	
Applied Maths	
Astronomy	
Atmospheric Sci.	
Microbiology	
Biochemistry	
Biology	
Chemistry	
Computer Science	
Geology	
Geophysics	
Mathematics	
Physics	
Aerospace Eng.	
Chemical Eng.	
Civil Eng.	
Computer Eng.	
Electrical Eng.	
Materials Eng.	
Mechanical Eng.	

CALIFORNIA-RIVERSIDE, UNIVERSITY OF

Contact Information
School Type: Public
Affiliation: None
Environment: City
Undergrad Enrollment: 7,433

Admissions
Applicants accepted: 78%
Acceptees attending: 32%
Average Verbal SAT: 562
Average Math SAT: 547
Average ACT: 21

General Information
900 University Avenue
Riverside, CA 92521
Admissions: 909-787-1012
Financial Aid: 909-787-3878 or 3879
Web: www.ucr.edu

Program	Rank	Score
SCIENCES		
Biochemistry	30	4.14
Biology	45	3.63
Botany	9	4.70
Chemistry	37	4.35
Entomology	6	4.76
SOCIAL SCIENCES		
Anthropology	45	4.08

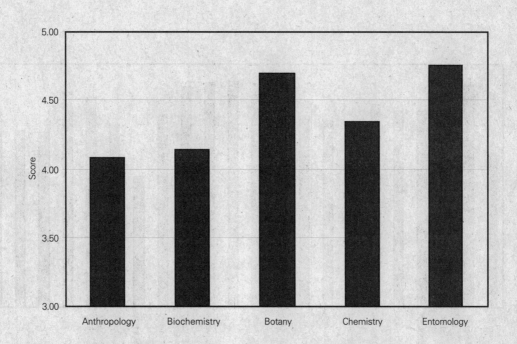

CALIFORNIA-SAN DIEGO, UNIVERSITY OF

Contact Information
School Type: Public
Affiliation: None
Environment: City
Undergrad Enrollment: 14,623

Admissions
Applicants accepted: 50%
Acceptees attending: 23%
Average Verbal SAT: 593
Average Math SAT: 632
Average ACT: 25

General Information
9500 Gilman Drive, 0337
La Jolla, CA 92093-0337

Admissions: 619-534-4831
Financial Aid: 619-534-4480
Web: admissions.ucsd.edu

Program	Rank	Score	Program	Rank	Score
ENGINEERING			Biochemistry	8	4.75
Bioengineering/Biomedical			Biology	6	4.86
Engineering	11	4.44	Biophysics	3	4.85
Electrical Engineering	50	4.45	Cell Biology	4	4.81
Systems Engineering	7	4.65	Chemistry	21	4.58
			Computer Science	31	4.08
HUMANITIES			Mathematics	27	4.51
English	34	4.28	Molecular Biology	7	4.73
Information Science	2	4.83	Physics	13	4.77
Linguistics	6	4.81			
Spanish	15	4.62	**SOCIAL SCIENCES**		
			Anthropology	17	4.62
SCIENCES			Economics	19	4.67
Applied Mathematics	11	4.55	History	29	4.47
Bacteriology/Microbiology	2	4.90	Psychology	11	4.54

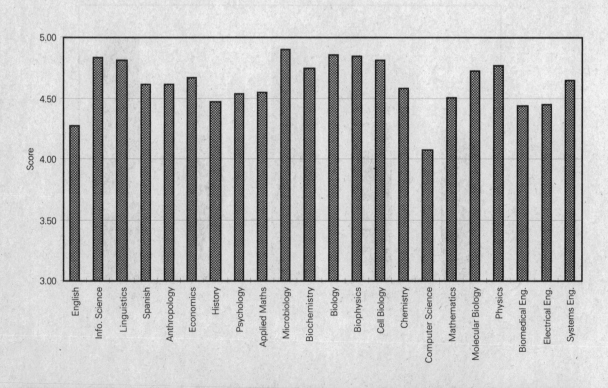

CALIFORNIA-SANTA BARBARA, UNIVERSITY OF

Contact Information
School Type: Public
Affiliation: None
Environment: City
Undergrad Enrollment: 16,281

Admissions
Applicants accepted: 78%
Acceptees attending: 23%
Average Verbal SAT: 549
Average Math SAT: 569
Average ACT: NR

General Information
Santa Barbara, CA 93106

Admissions: 805-893-2485
Financial Aid: 805-893-2432
Web: www.ucsb.edu

Program	Rank	Score	Program	Rank	Score
ARTS			**SCIENCES**		
Drama/Theatre	25	3.66	Biology	28	4.38
			Chemistry	39	4.32
ENGINEERING			Computer Science	36	3.81
Electrical Engineering	37	4.57	Geology/Geoscience	16	4.64
Nuclear Engineering	20	4.46	Marine Biology	2	4.75
			Mathematics	48	4.20
HUMANITIES			Physics	20	4.68
Comparative Literature	28	4.08	Statistics	15	4.62
English	41	4.12			
French	21	4.40	**SOCIAL SCIENCES**		
German	28	4.43	Anthropology	16	4.64
Linguistics	30	4.22	Economics	42	4.13
Religious Studies	9	4.68	History	28	4.48
Spanish	26	4.41	Political Science	36	4.44

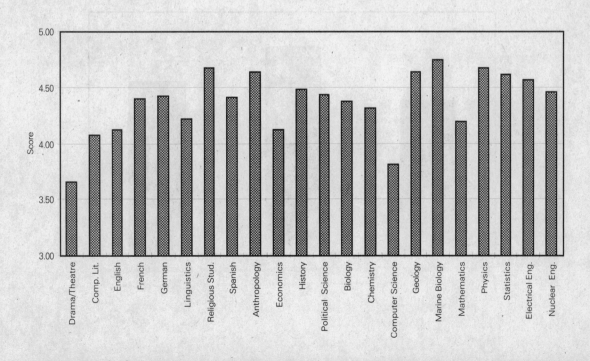

CALIFORNIA-SANTA CRUZ, UNIVERSITY OF

Contact Information
School Type: Public
Affiliation: None
Environment: Suburban
Undergrad Enrollment: 8,629

Admissions
Applicants accepted: 83%
Acceptees attending: 21%
Average Verbal SAT: 570
Average Math SAT: 565
Average ACT: 23

General Information
1156 High Street, Cook House
Santa Cruz, CA 95064

Admissions: 408-459-0111
Financial Aid: 408-459-2963
Web: www.ucsc.edu

Program	*Rank*	*Score*
HUMANITIES		
Italian	18	4.27
SCIENCES		
Geophysics/Geoscience	11	4.71
Molecular Biology	22	4.42

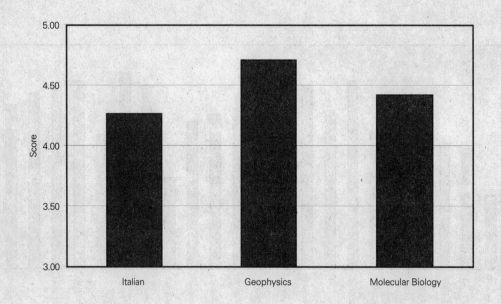

CARNEGIE MELLON UNIVERSITY

Contact Information
School Type: Private
Affiliation: None
Environment: Major City
Undergrad Enrollment: 4,823

Admissions
Applicants accepted: 47%
Acceptees attending: 22%
Average Verbal SAT: 641
Average Math SAT: 688
Average ACT: 29

General Information
5000 Forbes Avenue
Pittsburgh, PA 15213
Admissions: 412-268-2082
Financial Aid: 412-268-2068
Web: www.cmu.edu/enrollment/
admission

Program	Rank	Score	Program	Rank	Score
ARTS			**SCIENCES**		
Ceramic Art/Design	2	4.83	Applied Mathematics	13	4.48
Drama/Theatre	9	4.66	Biophysics	10	4.56
			Cell Biology	12	4.49
ENGINEERING			Chemistry	27	4.50
Chemical Engineering	31	4.60	Computer Science	2	4.91
Civil Engineering	20	4.50	Mathematics	30	4.47
Computer Engineering	21	4.60	Molecular Biology	11	4.66
Electrical Engineering	15	4.74	Physics	22	4.64
Engineering/General	4	4.76			
Mechanical Engineering	19	4.66	**SOCIAL SCIENCES**		
Metallurgical Engineering	5	4.85	Behavioral Sciences	3	4.79
			Child Psychology	7	4.37
HUMANITIES			Economics	17	4.71
Information Science	6	4.66	Labor and Industrial Relations	3	4.82
			Psychology	15	4.48
PROFESSIONAL					
Architecture	3	4.62			
Management	6	4.82			
Operations Research	3	4.79			

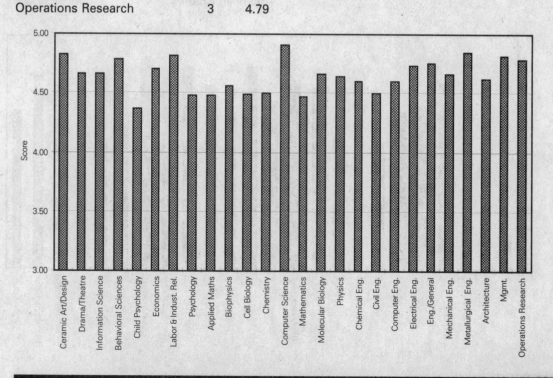

CASE WESTERN RESERVE UNIVERSITY

Contact Information
School Type: Private
Affiliation: None
Environment: Major City
Undergrad Enrollment: 3,679

Admissions
Applicants accepted: 79%
Acceptees attending: 22%
Average Verbal SAT: 655
Average Math SAT: 690
Average ACT: 29

General Information
University Circle
10900 Euclid Avenue
Cleveland, OH 44106
Admissions: 216-368-4450
Financial Aid: 216-368-4530
Web: www.cwru.edu

Program	Rank	Score	Program	Rank	Score
ARTS			**PROFESSIONAL**		
Art	34	3.30	Accounting	17	4.59
Drama/Theatre	29	3.53	Finance	15	4.66
			Management	18	4.60
ENGINEERING			Marketing	15	4.58
Bioengineering/			Operations Research	7	4.65
Biomedical Engineering	7	4.62	Speech Pathology/Audiology	28	4.36
Chemical Engineering	46	4.44			
Computer Engineering	8	4.74	**SCIENCES**		
Electrical Engineering	58	4.35	Astronomy	12	4.40
Engineering Science	8	4.58	Biochemistry	21	4.34
Materials Engineering/ Materials			Biology	49	3.53
Science & Engineering	10	4.74	Chemistry	51	4.09
Mechanical Engineering	21	4.63	Computer Science	52	3.26
Systems Engineering	2	4.82	Mathematics	54	4.14
			Physics	30	4.55
HUMANITIES					
Art History	34	3.27	**SOCIAL SCIENCES**		
			American Studies	4	4.60

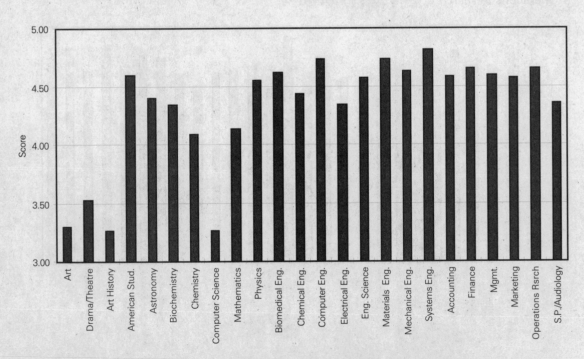

CATHOLIC UNIVERSITY OF AMERICA, THE

Contact Information
School Type: Private
Affiliation: Roman Catholic
Church
Environment: Major City
Undergrad Enrollment: 2,380

Admissions
Applicants accepted: 67%
Acceptees attending: 31%
Average Verbal SAT: 605
Average Math SAT: 580
Average ACT: 26

General Information
Cardinal Station
Washington, DC 20064

Admissions: 202-319-5305
Financial Aid: 202-319-5307
Web: www.cua.edu

Program	Rank	Score
ARTS		
Drama/Theatre	17	4.25
HUMANITIES		
Classics	21	4.14
Italian	11	4.46
Latin	5	4.75

Program	Rank	Score
PROFESSIONAL		
Nursing	8	4.75
Social Work/Social Welfare	33	4.28
Sociology	24	4.40
SOCIAL SCIENCES		
Medieval Studies	10	4.60
Social Work/Social Welfare	33	4.28

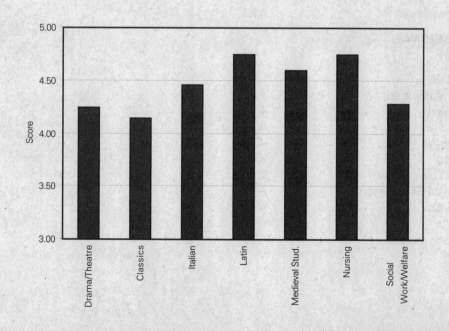

CHICAGO, UNIVERSITY OF

Contact Information
School Type: Private
Affiliation: None
Environment: Major City
Undergrad Enrollment: 3,515

Admissions
Applicants accepted: 58%
Acceptees attending: 31%
Average Verbal SAT: 690
Average Math SAT: 685
Average ACT: 29

General Information
1116 East 59th Street
Chicago, IL 60637

Admissions: 773-702-8650
Financial Aid: 773-702-8666
Web: www.uchicago.edu

Program	Rank	Score	Program	Rank	Score
ARTS			**SOCIAL SCIENCES**		
Art	11	4.46	American Studies	16	3.80
Music	2	4.91	Anthropology	2	4.91
			Asian/Oriental Studies	3	4.73
HUMANITIES			Behavioral Sciences	4	4.74
Arabic	1	4.84	East Asian Studies	5	4.73
Art History	13	4.55	Economics	2	4.91
Chinese	3	4.82	History	8	4.81
Classics	14	4.47	Latin American Studies	11	4.38
Comparative Literature	5	4.71	Medieval Studies	4	4.74
English	4	4.87	Near/Middle Eastern Studies	1	4.82
French	15	4.62	Political Science	5	4.87
Greek	13	4.40	Psychology	9	4.56
Hebrew	10	4.70	Russian/Slavic Studies	1	4.85
Italian	17	4.30	Sociology	2	4.78
Japanese	2	4.80	South Asian Studies	5	4.78
Latin	10	4.51	Southeast Asian Studies	4	4.81
Linguistics	2	4.90			
Philosophy	5	4.80			
Russian	3	4.85			
Slavic Languages	1	4.85			
PROFESSIONAL					
Sociology	2	4.78			
SCIENCES					
Applied Mathematics	2	4.85			
Biochemistry	9	4.71			
Biology	12	4.70			
Cell Biology	5	4.77			
Chemistry	8	4.85			
Geology/Geoscience	7	4.80			
Geophysics/Geoscience	7	4.78			
Mathematics	5	4.85			
Physics	8	4.83			
Statistics	7	4.78			

CHICAGO, UNIVERSITY OF (CONTINUED)

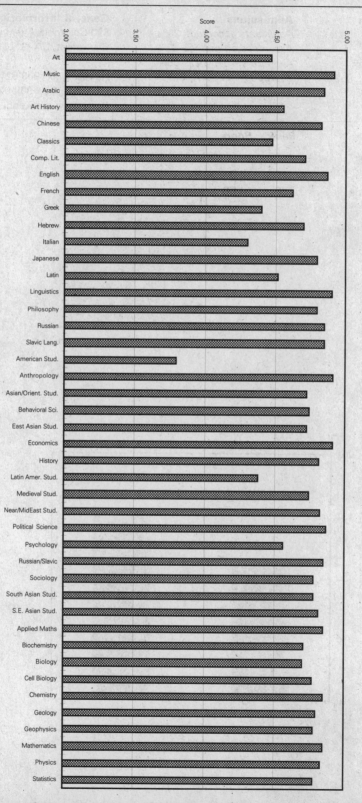

CLAREMONT MCKENNA COLLEGE

Contact Information
School Type: Private
Affiliation: None
Environment: Suburban
Undergrad Enrollment: 952

Admissions
Applicants accepted: 29%
Acceptees attending: 32%
Average Verbal SAT: 665
Average Math SAT: 675
Average ACT: 29

General Information
890 Columbia Avenue,
Claremont, CA 91711

Admissions: 909-621-8088
Financial Aid: 909-621-8356
Web: www.mckenna.edu

Program	Rank	Score
SOCIAL SCIENCES		
Economics	45	4.08
International Relations	15	4.50

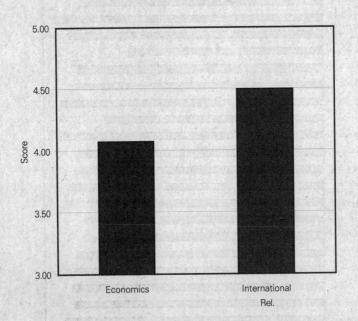

COLORADO SCHOOL OF MINES

Contact Information
School Type: Public
Affiliation: None
Environment: Suburban
Undergrad Enrollment: 2,400

Admissions
Applicants accepted: 80%
Acceptees attending: 36%
Average Verbal SAT: 575
Average Math SAT: 640
Average ACT: 26

General Information
Weaver Towers
1811 Elm Street
Golden, CO 80401
Admissions: 303-273-3220
Financial Aid: 303-273-3301
Web: www.mines.edu

Program	Rank	Score
ENGINEERING		
Engineering Physics	13	4.44
Engineering/General	5	4.75
Geological Engineering	1	4.91
Metallurgical Engineering	8	4.81
Mining & Mineral Engineering	1	4.89
Petroleum Engineering	9	4.73

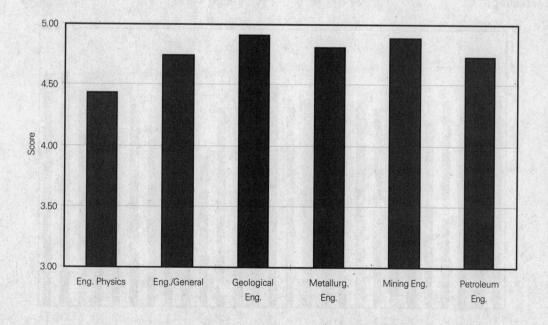

COLORADO-BOULDER, UNIVERSITY OF

Contact Information
School Type: Public
Affiliation: None
Environment: City
Undergrad Enrollment: 20,006

Admissions
Applicants accepted: NR
Acceptees attending: 37%
Average Verbal SAT: 505
Average Math SAT: 590
Average ACT: 25

General Information
Campus Box 30,
Boulder, CO 80309

Admissions: 303-492-6301
Financial Aid: 303-492-5091
Web: www.colorado.edu

Program	Rank	Score	Program	Rank	Score
ENGINEERING			Operations Research	10	4.56
Aerospace Engineering	20	4.50	Speech Pathology/Audiology	13	4.68
Architectural Engineering	4	4.61	Urban and Regional Planning	9	4.66
Chemical Engineering	47	4.43			
Civil Engineering	23	4.47	**SCIENCES**		
Electrical Engineering	52	4.43	Applied Mathematics	16	4.32
			Biology	8	4.82
HUMANITIES			Cell Biology	7	4.71
Religious Studies	18	4.50	Chemistry	32	4.44
			Ecology/Environmental Studies	10	4.60
PROFESSIONAL			Geology/Geoscience	27	4.42
Accounting	38	4.08	Mathematics	39	4.34
Business Administration	39	4.16	Molecular Biology	5	4.79
Environmental Design	8	4.67	Physics	35	4.50
Finance	38	4.20			
Journalism and Mass			**SOCIAL SCIENCES**		
Communications	19	4.45	Anthropology	37	4.20
Management	41	4.16	Geography	12	4.53
Marketing	37	4.16	Psychology	14	4.49

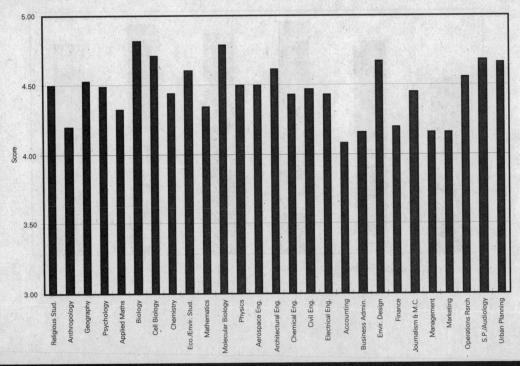

COLUMBIA UNIVERSITY

Contact Information
School Type: Private
Affiliation: None
Environment: Major City
Undergrad Enrollment: 3,570

Admissions
Applicants accepted: NR
Acceptees attending: 45%
Average Verbal SAT: 620
Average Math SAT: 680
Average ACT: NR

General Information
212 Hamilton Hall
New York, NY 10027

Admissions: 212-854-2522
Financial Aid: 212-854-3711
Web: www.columbia.edu

Program	Rank	Score	Program	Rank	Score
ARTS			**PROFESSIONAL**		
Art	6	4.60	Nursing	13	4.59
Music	8	4.80	Operations Research	2	4.83
			Sociology	4	4.74
ENGINEERING					
Chemical Engineering	60	4.18	**SCIENCES**		
Civil Engineering	15	4.60	Applied Mathematics	6	4.74
Electrical Engineering	26	4.66	Biochemistry	11	4.63
Industrial Engineering	12	4.68	Biology	9	4.80
Materials Engineering/Materials			Chemistry	5	4.91
Science And Engineering	16	4.58	Computer Science	23	4.42
Mechanical Engineering	17	4.68	Geology/Geoscience	4	4.87
Mining and Mineral Engineering	14	4.75	Geophysics/Geoscience	13	4.68
			Mathematics	10	4.76
HUMANITIES			Physics	10	4.80
Arabic	8	4.33	Statistics	3	4.84
Art History	5	4.83			
Chinese	6	4.67	**SOCIAL SCIENCES**		
Classics	10	4.62	Anthropology	15	4.67
Comparative Literature	3	4.76	East Asian Studies	4	4.77
English	8	4.81	Economics	13	4.75
French	3	4.90	History	7	4.84
Greek	4	4.77	Latin American Studies	6	4.60
Hebrew	3	4.86	Medieval Studies	1	4.83
Italian	1	4.82	Near/Middle Eastern Studies	4	4.77
Japanese	4	4.71	Political Science	15	4.73
Latin	1	4.89	Psychology	10	4.55
Philosophy	13	4.62	Russian/Slavic Studies	6	4.73
Russian	1	4.89	Sociology	4	4.74
Slavic Languages	15	4.50			
Spanish	17	4.58			

COLUMBIA UNIVERSITY (CONTINUED)

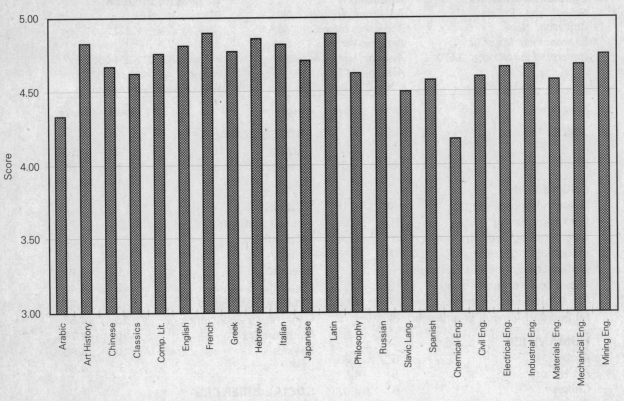

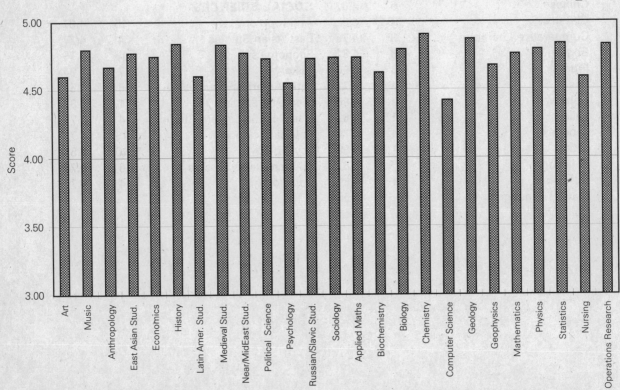

CONNECTICUT, UNIVERSITY OF

Contact Information
School Type: Public
Affiliation: None
Environment: Rural
Undergrad Enrollment: 11,336

Admissions
Applicants accepted: 67%
Acceptees attending: 32%
Average Verbal SAT: 553
Average Math SAT: 559
Average ACT: NR

General Information
Storrs, CT 06269

Admissions: 860-486-3137
Financial Aid: 860-486-2819
Web: www.uconn.edu

Program	Rank	Score	Program	Rank	Score
ENGINEERING			**SOCIAL SCIENCES**		
Electrical Engineering	84	4.00	Anthropology	42	4.12
PROFESSIONAL			**TECHNICAL**		
Physical Therapy	24	4.35	Agricultural Economics	17	4.35
			Agriculture	46	4.03
SCIENCES			Agronomy	44	4.04
Bacteriology/Microbiology	28	4.35	Animal Science	27	4.10
Biology	44	3.67	Horticulture	36	4.26
Computer Science	43	3.54			

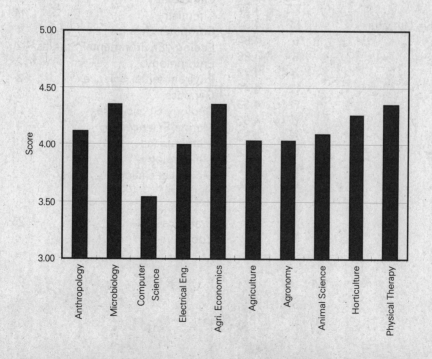

CORNELL UNIVERSITY

Contact Information
School Type: Private
Affiliation: None
Environment: City
Undergrad Enrollment: 13,512

Admissions
Applicants accepted: 33%
Acceptees attending: 45%
Average Verbal SAT: 650
Average Math SAT: 685
Average ACT: NR

General Information
410 Thurston Avenue
Ithaca, NY 14850

Admissions: 607-255-5241
Financial Aid: 607-255-5145
Web: www.cornell.edu

Program	Rank	Score	Program	Rank	Score
ARTS			**PROFESSIONAL**		
Art	12	4.41	Architecture	5	4.53
Drama/Theatre	3	4.88	Environmental Design	3	4.85
Music	5	4.87	Hotel, Restaurant,		
			Institutional Management	1	4.90
ENGINEERING			Landscape Architecture	1	4.90
Agricultural Engineering	1	4.91	Operations Research	1	4.87
Chemical Engineering	23	4.65	Sociology	17	4.55
Civil Engineering	6	4.80	Urban and Regional Planning	5	4.74
Electrical Engineering	8	4.81			
Engineering Physics	4	4.77	**SCIENCES**		
Industrial Engineering	10	4.72	Astronomy	4	4.75
Materials Engineering/Materials			Atmospheric Sciences	1	4.90
Science & Engineering	1	4.91	Bacteriology/Microbiology	12	4.77
Mechanical Engineering	8	4.81	Biochemistry	7	4.79
			Biology	17	4.64
HUMANITIES			Biophysics	9	4.61
Art History	16	4.33	Botany	2	4.89
Chinese	2	4.85	Cell Biology	14	4.37
Classics	12	4.57	Chemistry	11	4.78
Comparative Literature	11	4.54	Computer Science	4	4.87
English	6	4.84	Ecology/Environmental Studies	2	4.87
French	5	4.86	Entomology	2	4.90
German	8	4.73	Environmental Sciences	3	4.85
Greek	12	4.42	Genetics	2	4.90
Hebrew	17	4.53	Geology/Geoscience	11	4.72
Japanese	6	4.62	Marine Sciences	1	4.82
Linguistics	5	4.83	Mathematics	13	4.71
Philosophy	10	4.68	Meteorology	1	4.89
Russian	12	4.60	Molecular Biology	12	4.62
Spanish	13	4.66	Nutrition	1	4.89
			Physics	3	4.90
			Statistics	25	4.45
			Zoology	4	4.80

CORNELL UNIVERSITY (CONTINUED)

Program	Rank	Score	Program	Rank	Score
SOCIAL SCIENCES			**TECHNICAL**		
American Studies	11	4.26	Agricultural Business	1	4.83
Anthropology	13	4.70	Agricultural Economics	4	4.83
Asian/Oriental Studies	4	4.70	Agriculture	1	4.93
Behavioral Sciences	1	4.86	Agronomy	1	4.90
Child Psychology	3	4.52	Animal Science	1	4.91
East Asian Studies	7	4.68	Dairy Sciences	2	4.90
Economics	21	4.65	Dietetics	1	4.90
History	11	4.75	Farm/Ranch Management	1	4.85
International Relations	7	4.72	Food Sciences	1	4.91
Labor and Industrial Relations	1	4.91	Food Services Management	1	4.86
Medieval Studies	2	4.80	Horticulture	1	4.92
Near/Middle Eastern Studies	14	4.56	Natural Resource Management	1	4.84
Political Science	10	4.80	Ornamental Horticulture	1	4.87
Psychology	21	4.41	Poultry Sciences	1	4.89
Russian/Slavic Studies	8	4.69			
Sociology	17	4.55			
Southeast Asian Studies	6	4.76			

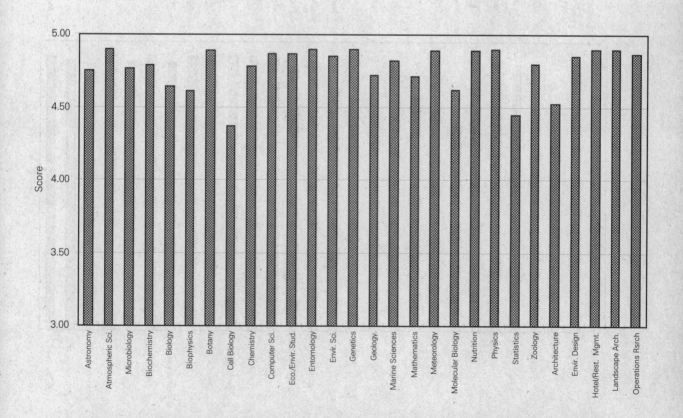

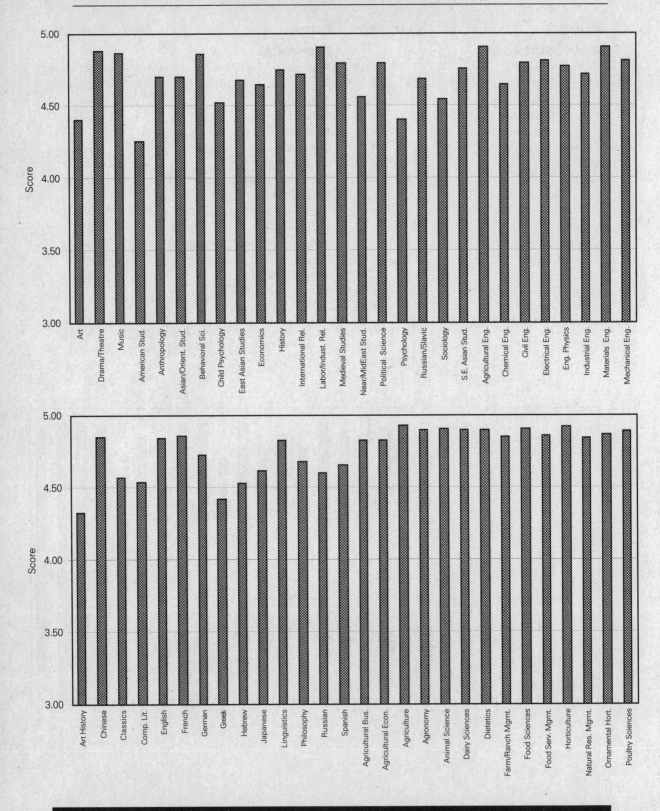

DARTMOUTH COLLEGE

Contact Information
School Type: Private
Affiliation: None
Environment: Rural
Undergrad Enrollment: 4,285

Admissions
Applicants accepted: 20%
Acceptees attending: 48%
Average Verbal SAT: 704
Average Math SAT: 711
Average ACT: NR

General Information
6016 McNutt Hall
Hanover, NH 03755

Admissions: 603-646-2875
Financial Aid: 603-646-2451
Web: www.dartmouth.edu

Program	Rank	Score	Program	Rank	Score
ARTS					
Drama/Theatre	42	3.09	**SCIENCES**		
			Chemistry	38	4.34
ENGINEERING			Earth Science	5	4.70
Engineering/General	8	4.66	Mathematics	42	4.30
HUMANITIES			**SOCIAL SCIENCES**		
English	32	4.32	History	40	4.27
Religious Studies	8	4.70	Political Science	45	4.28

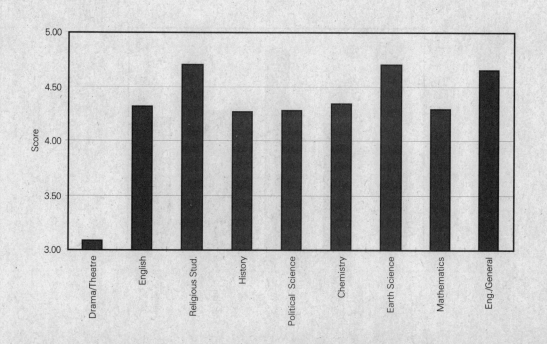

DELAWARE, UNIVERSITY OF

Contact Information
School Type: Public
Affiliation: None
Environment: City
Undergrad Enrollment: 14,829

Admissions
Applicants accepted: 66%
Acceptees attending: 31%
Average Verbal SAT: 575
Average Math SAT: 585
Average ACT: NR

General Information
U.S.P.S. 077580
Newark, DE 19716

Admissions: 302-831-8123
Financial Aid: 302-831-8761
Web: www.udel.edu

Program	Rank	Score
ARTS		
Art	19	3.89
ENGINEERING		
Chemical Engineering	9	4.80
Mechanical Engineering	46	4.25
HUMANITIES		
Art History	19	4.14
TECHNICAL		
Animal Science	24	4.19

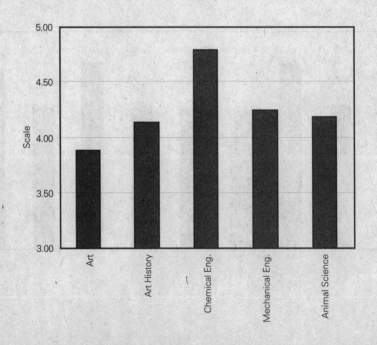

DUKE UNIVERSITY

Contact Information
School Type: Private
Affiliation: United Methodist
Church
Environment: City
Undergrad Enrollment: 6,272

Admissions
Applicants accepted: 30%
Acceptees attending: 41%
Average Verbal SAT: 685
Average Math SAT: 700
Average ACT: 30

General Information
2138 Campus Drive
Box 90586
Durham, NC 27708
Admissions: 919-684-3214
Financial Aid: 919-684-6225
Web: www.duke.edu

Program	Rank	Score	Program	Rank	Score
ENGINEERING			**SCIENCES**		
Bioengineering/Biomedical			Biology	13	4.69
Engineering	4	4.84	Botany	6	4.78
Civil Engineering	36	4.23	Chemistry	45	4.20
Electrical Engineering	71	4.17	Computer Science	26	4.28
			Mathematics	51	4.17
HUMANITIES					
Classics	16	4.33	**SOCIAL SCIENCES**		
Comparative Literature	26	4.13	Anthropology	24	4.48
English	26	4.45	Economics	20	4.66
French	14	4.64	History	26	4.51
German	29	4.39	Medieval Studies	9	4.63
Religious Studies	6	4.74	Political Science	17	4.70
Slavic Languages	17	4.44	Psychology	28	4.34
Spanish	32	4.31	Sociology	22	4.47
PROFESSIONAL					
Sociology	22	4.47			

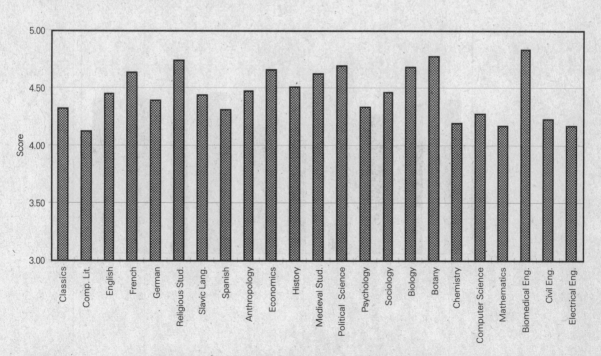

EMORY UNIVERSITY

Contact Information
School Type: Private
Affiliation: United Methodist Church
Environment: Major City
Undergrad Enrollment: 5,736

Admissions
Applicants accepted: 44%
Acceptees attending: 27%
Average Verbal SAT: 570
Average Math SAT: 650
Average ACT: 28

General Information
1380 South Oxford Road, NE
Atlanta, GA 30322

Admissions: 404-727-6036
Financial Aid: 800-727-6039
Web: www.emory.edu

Program	Rank	Score	Program	Rank	Score
HUMANITIES			**SCIENCES**		
English	30	4.38	Biology	42	3.27
PROFESSIONAL			**SOCIAL SCIENCES**		
Accounting	41	4.02	History	36	4.35
Business Administration	40	4.14	Political Science	47	4.25
Finance	25	4.44			
Management	39	4.20			
Marketing	26	4.39			
Nursing	22	4.39			

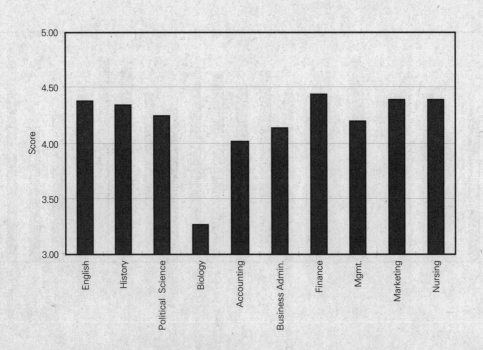

FLORIDA STATE UNIVERSITY

Contact Information
School Type: Public
Affiliation: None
Environment: City
Undergrad Enrollment: 23,051

Admissions
Applicants accepted: 73%
Acceptees attending: 30%
Average Verbal SAT: 576
Average Math SAT: 571
Average ACT: 24

General Information
2249 University Center
Tallahassee, FL 32306

Admissions: 904-644-2525
Financial Aid: 904-644-0539
Web: www.fsu.edu

Program	Rank	Score	Program	Rank	Score
ARTS			**SCIENCES**		
Art	40	3.10	Biology	41	3.77
Drama/Theatre	19	4.18	Chemistry	49	4.14
Film	10	4.49	Nutrition	18	4.60
Music	28	4.40	Statistics	20	4.53
HUMANITIES			**SOCIAL SCIENCES**		
Art History	39	3.13	American Studies	31	3.05
			Child Psychology	16	4.05
PROFESSIONAL			Communication	10	4.54
Hotel, Restaurant, Institutional			Radio/Television Studies	6	4.75
Management	13	4.43	Social Work/Social Welfare	28	4.38
Social Work/Social Welfare	28	4.38			
Speech Pathology/Audiology	24	4.46	**TECHNICAL**		
			Dietetics	13	4.46
			Home Economics	7	4.71

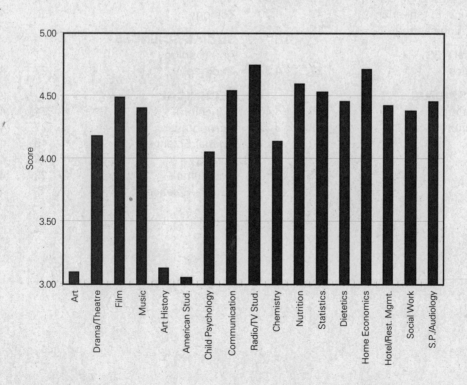

FLORIDA, UNIVERSITY OF

Contact Information
School Type: Public
Affiliation: None
Environment: City
Undergrad Enrollment: 30,008

Admissions
Applicants accepted: 59%
Acceptees attending: 44%
Average Verbal SAT: 615
Average Math SAT: 630
Average ACT: 27

General Information
Undergraduate Admissions
201 Criser Hall
Gainesville, FL 32611
Admissions: 352-392-1365
Financial Aid: 352-392-1275
Web: www.ufsa.ufl.edu/sfa/sfa.html

Program	Rank	Score	Program	Rank	Score
ARTS			Business Administration	28	4.39
Ceramic Art/Design	11	4.46	Finance	22	4.54
Drama/Theatre	35	3.23	Journalism and Mass		
			Communications	22	4.38
ENGINEERING			Landscape Architecture	12	4.68
Aerospace Engineering	26	4.37	Management	26	4.44
Agricultural Engineering	30	4.32	Marketing	20	4.50
Chemical Engineering	41	4.51	Nursing	27	4.34
Civil Engineering	31	4.32	Occupational Therapy	8	4.76
Computer Engineering	25	4.54	Physical Therapy	21	4.40
Electrical Engineering	38	4.56			
Engineering Science	5	4.68	**SCIENCES**		
Environmental Engineering	4	4.80	Botany	22	4.32
Industrial Engineering	39	4.24	Chemistry	36	4.37
Materials Engineering/Materials			Entomology	17	4.49
Science And Engineering	12	4.69	Nutrition	22	4.50
Mechanical Engineering	43	4.30	Zoology	8	4.69
Nuclear Engineering	11	4.63			
			SOCIAL SCIENCES		
HUMANITIES			Anthropology	21	4.52
Linguistics	27	4.32	Geography	27	4.23
PROFESSIONAL			**TECHNICAL**		
Accounting	25	4.40	Agriculture	34	4.25
Architecture	32	3.22	Agronomy	27	4.37
			Animal Science	15	4.50
			Forestry	23	4.33
			Horticulture	22	4.52
			Poultry Sciences	8	4.73

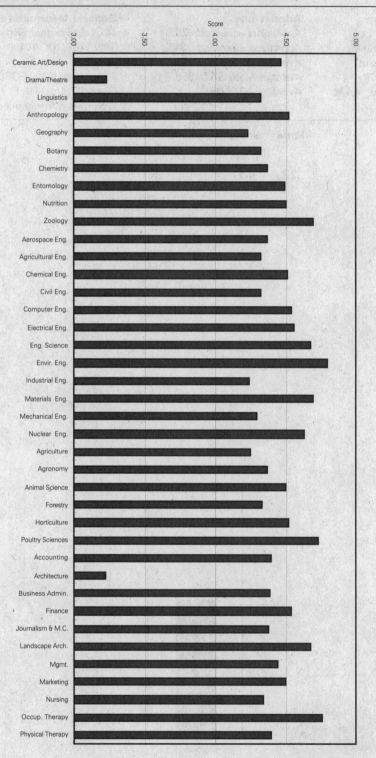

Score

Ceramic Art/Design
Drama/Theatre
Linguistics
Anthropology
Geography
Botany
Chemistry
Entomology
Nutrition
Zoology
Aerospace Eng.
Agricultural Eng.
Chemical Eng.
Civil Eng.
Computer Eng.
Electrical Eng.
Eng. Science
Envir. Eng.
Industrial Eng.
Materials Eng.
Mechanical Eng.
Nuclear Eng.
Agriculture
Agronomy
Animal Science
Forestry
Horticulture
Poultry Sciences
Accounting
Architecture
Business Admin.
Finance
Journalism & M.C.
Landscape Arch.
Mgmt.
Marketing
Nursing
Occup. Therapy
Physical Therapy

FORDHAM UNIVERSITY

Contact Information
School Type: Private
Affiliation: Roman Catholic
Church (Society of Jesus)
Environment: Major City
Undergrad Enrollment: 4,474

Admissions
Applicants accepted: 70%
Acceptees attending: 34%
Average Verbal SAT: 583
Average Math SAT: 558
Average ACT: NR

General Information
441 East Fordham Road
New York, NY 10458

Admissions: 800-FORDHAM
Financial Aid: 718-817-3800
Web: www.fordham.edu

Program	*Rank*	*Score*
HUMANITIES		
Classics	22	4.11

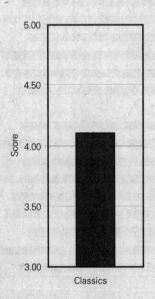

GEORGE WASHINGTON UNIVERSITY

Contact Information
School Type: Private
Affiliation: None
Environment: Major City
Undergrad Enrollment: 6,581

Admissions
Applicants accepted: 58%
Acceptees attending: 28%
Average Verbal SAT: 610
Average Math SAT: 600
Average ACT: 26

General Information
2121 I Street, NW
Washington, DC 20052

Admissions: 202-994-6040
Financial Aid: 202-994-6620
Web: www.gwu.edu

Program	Rank	Score
ENGINEERING		
Systems Engineering	8	4.60
PROFESSIONAL		
Accounting	35	4.14
Business Administration	37	4.21
Finance	35	4.26
Management	38	4.21
Marketing	36	4.21

Program	Rank	Score
SOCIAL SCIENCES		
American Studies	14	4.07
Latin American Studies	15	4.20

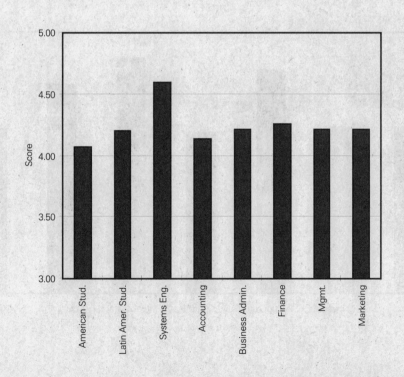

GEORGETOWN UNIVERSITY

Contact Information
School Type: Private
Affiliation: Roman Catholic
Church (Society of Jesus)
Environment: Major City
Undergrad Enrollment: 6,338

Admissions
Applicants accepted: 23%
Acceptees attending: 47%
Average Verbal SAT: 670
Average Math SAT: 660
Average ACT: 28

General Information
37th and O Streets, NW
Washington, DC 20057

Admissions: 202-687-3600
Financial Aid: 202-687-4547
Web: www.georgetown.edu

Program	Rank	Score
HUMANITIES		
Arabic	9	4.27
Chinese	14	4.27
Portuguese	5	4.71
Spanish	35	4.23

Program	Rank	Score
PROFESSIONAL		
Nursing	32	4.26
SOCIAL SCIENCES		
International Relations	4	4.79
Political Science	24	4.60

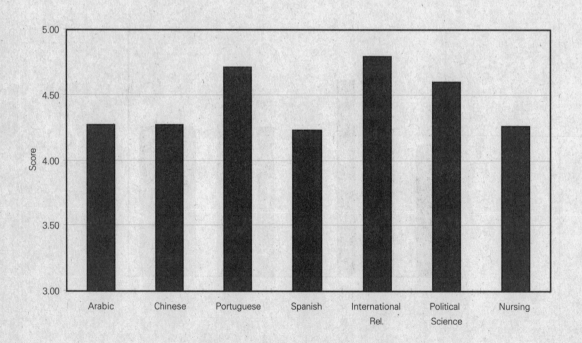

GEORGIA INSTITUTE OF TECHNOLOGY

Contact Information
School Type: Public
Affiliation: None
Environment: Major City
Undergrad Enrollment: 9,469

Admissions
Applicants accepted: 56%
Acceptees attending: 42%
Average Verbal SAT: 624
Average Math SAT: 674
Average ACT: NR

General Information
225 North Avenue, NW
Atlanta, GA 30332

Admissions: 404-894-4154
Financial Aid: 404-894-4160
Web: www.gatech.edu

Program	Rank	Score	Program	Rank	Score
ENGINEERING			**PROFESSIONAL**		
Aerospace Engineering	16	4.53	Architecture	9	4.27
Ceramic Engineering	7	4.57	Operations Research	9	4.58
Chemical Engineering	53	4.31	**SCIENCES**		
Civil Engineering	19	4.52	Chemistry	53	4.05
Computer Engineering	37	4.25	Computer Science	17	4.60
Electrical Engineering	29	4.65	Mathematics	20	4.61
Industrial Engineering	9	4.74	Physics	12	4.78
Materials Engineering/Materials Science And Engineering	23	4.47			
Mechanical Engineering	22	4.62			
Nuclear Engineering	14	4.58			

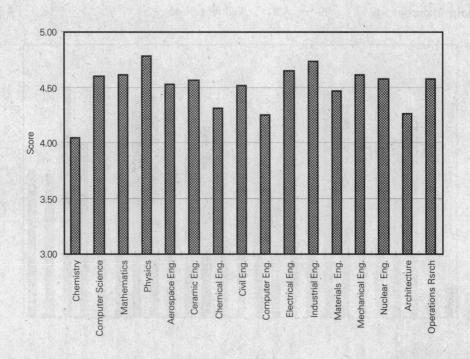

GEORGIA, UNIVERSITY OF

Contact Information
School Type: Public
Affiliation: None
Environment: Suburban
Undergrad Enrollment: 22,301

Admissions
Applicants accepted: 56%
Acceptees attending: 48%
Average Verbal SAT: 599
Average Math SAT: 590
Average ACT: NR

General Information
Athens, GA 30602

Admissions: 706-542-2112
Financial Aid: 706-542-6147
Web: www.uga.edu

Program	Rank	Score	Program	Rank	Score
ARTS			Entomology	24	4.32
Art	37	3.22	Genetics	11	4.55
			Nutrition	14	4.65
ENGINEERING			Wildlife Biology	18	4.55
Agricultural Engineering	43	4.08	Zoology	5	4.76
HUMANITIES			**SOCIAL SCIENCES**		
Art History	37	3.16	Geography	15	4.48
PROFESSIONAL			**TECHNICAL**		
Business Administration	44	4.07	Agriculture	23	4.37
Finance	44	4.02	Agronomy	25	4.39
Journalism and Mass			Animal Science	20	4.36
Communications	28	4.27	Food Sciences	15	4.40
Landscape Architecture	11	4.69	Food Services Management	12	4.45
Management	47	4.05	Forestry	11	4.64
Marketing	40	4.08	Home Economics	12	4.61
			Horticulture	17	4.62
SCIENCES			Wildlife Biology	18	4.55
Bacteriology/Microbiology	29	4.31			
Botany	14	4.55			

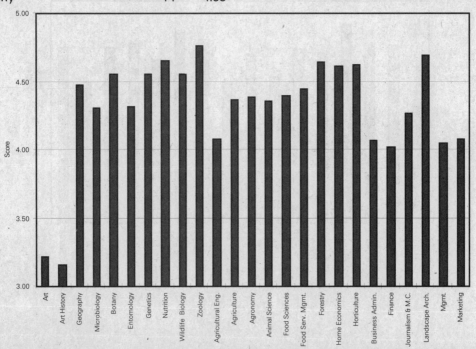

HARVARD AND RADCLIFFE COLLEGES

This is the college I want to go to ←

Contact Information
School Type: Private
Affiliation: None
Environment: City
Undergrad Enrollment: 7,098

Admissions
Applicants accepted: 11%
Acceptees attending: 78%
Average Verbal SAT: 745
Average Math SAT: 740
Average ACT: 32

General Information
Byerly Hall, 8 Garden Street
Cambridge, MA 02138

Admissions: 617-495-1551
Financial Aid: 617-495-1581
Web: www.fas.harvard.edu

Program	Rank	Score	Program	Rank	Score
ARTS			**SCIENCES**		
Art	2	4.89	Applied Mathematics	1	4.87
Music	9	4.79	Astronomy	3	4.82
			Astrophysics	6	4.61
ENGINEERING			Biochemistry	1	4.92
Engineering Science	1	4.85	Biology	4	4.88
			Chemistry	3	4.93
HUMANITIES			Ecology/Environmental Studies	1	4.89
Arabic	4	4.69	Environmental Sciences	1	4.89
Art History	2	4.91	Geology/Geoscience	6	4.82
Chinese	1	4.87	Geophysics/Geoscience	12	4.70
Classics	1	4.90	Mathematics	3	4.88
Comparative Literature	2	4.78	Molecular Biology	9	4.71
English	3	4.90	Physics	2	4.91
French	19	4.46			
German	10	4.69	**SOCIAL SCIENCES**		
Greek	1	4.87	American Studies	15	3.87
Hebrew	7	4.79	Anthropology	9	4.79
Information Science	8	4.59	Asian/Oriental Studies	1	4.82
Italian	12	4.42	East Asian Studies	1	4.86
Japanese	1	4.84	Economics	5	4.87
Latin	11	4.49	History	4	4.90
Linguistics	18	4.61	International Relations	6	4.75
Philosophy	3	4.87	Near/Middle Eastern Studies	2	4.80
Portuguese	1	4.86	Political Science	2	4.91
Religious Studies	19	4.48	Psychology	7	4.59
Russian	6	4.79	Russian/Slavic Studies	4	4.78
Scandinavian Languages	4	4.79	Sociology	5	4.72
Slavic Languages	5	4.73	South Asian Studies	1	4.86
Spanish	2	4.89	Southeast Asian Studies	1	4.87
PROFESSIONAL					
Environmental Design	2	4.89			
Sociology	5	4.72			

HARVARD AND RADCLIFFE COLLEGES (CONTINUED)

ILLINOIS, URBANA-CHAMPAIGN, UNIVERSITY OF

Contact Information
School Type: Public
Affiliation: None
Environment: City
Undergrad Enrollment: 26,738

Admissions
Applicants accepted: 70%
Acceptees attending: 49%
Average Verbal SAT: 608
Average Math SAT: 640
Average ACT: 27

General Information
506 South Wright Street
Urbana, IL 61801

Admissions: 217-333-0302
Financial Aid: 217-333-0100
Web: www.uiuc.edu

Program	Rank	Score	Program	Rank	Score
ARTS			Speech Pathology/Audiology	10	4.74
Drama/Theatre	24	3.68	Urban and Regional Planning	4	4.76
Music	7	4.82			
			SCIENCES		
ENGINEERING			Astronomy	13	4.38
Aerospace Engineering	5	4.80	Bacteriology/Microbiology	6	4.83
Agricultural Engineering	10	4.80	Biochemistry	10	4.70
Ceramic Engineering	2	4.88	Biology	31	4.32
Chemical Engineering	11	4.75	Biophysics	5	4.77
Civil Engineering	3	4.89	Botany	8	4.73
Computer Engineering	3	4.87	Chemistry	7	4.88
Electrical Engineering	4	4.86	Computer Science	5	4.85
Engineering Mechanics	1	4.82	Ecology/Environmental Studies	4	4.79
Engineering/General	1	4.85	Entomology	3	4.87
Industrial Engineering	21	4.55	Genetics	5	4.79
Mechanical Engineering	11	4.76	Geology/Geoscience	28	4.41
Metallurgical Engineering	1	4.91	Mathematics	15	4.68
Nuclear Engineering	7	4.72	Nutrition	8	4.76
			Physics	9	4.81
HUMANITIES			Statistics	9	4.74
Classics	15	4.41			
Comparative Literature	7	4.68	**SOCIAL SCIENCES**		
English	24	4.51	Anthropology	14	4.68
French	12	4.68	Asian/Oriental Studies	10	4.45
German	11	4.68	Economics	29	4.50
Greek	15	4.36	Geography	6	4.71
Italian	10	4.48	History	21	4.56
Linguistics	8	4.76	Medieval Studies	6	4.70
Portuguese	4	4.75	Political Science	32	4.50
Russian	16	4.50	Psychology	8	4.57
Spanish	12	4.69	Social Work/Social Welfare	16	4.58
Speech/Rhetoric	5	4.79	Sociology	19	4.50
PROFESSIONAL			**TECHNICAL**		
Accounting	8	4.79	Agricultural Business	4	4.73
Architecture	7	4.38	Agricultural Economics	6	4.77
Business Administration	7	4.76	Agriculture	5	4.82
Finance	7	4.82	Agronomy	6	4.81
Hotel, Restaurant, Institutional			Animal Science	6	4.80
Management	6	4.70	Dairy Sciences	7	4.67
Journalism and Mass			Dietetics	9	4.67
Communications	5	4.77	Food Sciences	8	4.68
Landscape Architecture	5	4.80	Food Services Management	7	4.62
Management	8	4.80	Forestry	28	4.17
Marketing	6	4.79	Home Economics	5	4.75
Social Work/Social Welfare	16	4.58	Horticulture	5	4.83
			Ornamental Horticulture	5	4.74
			Parks Management	5	4.70

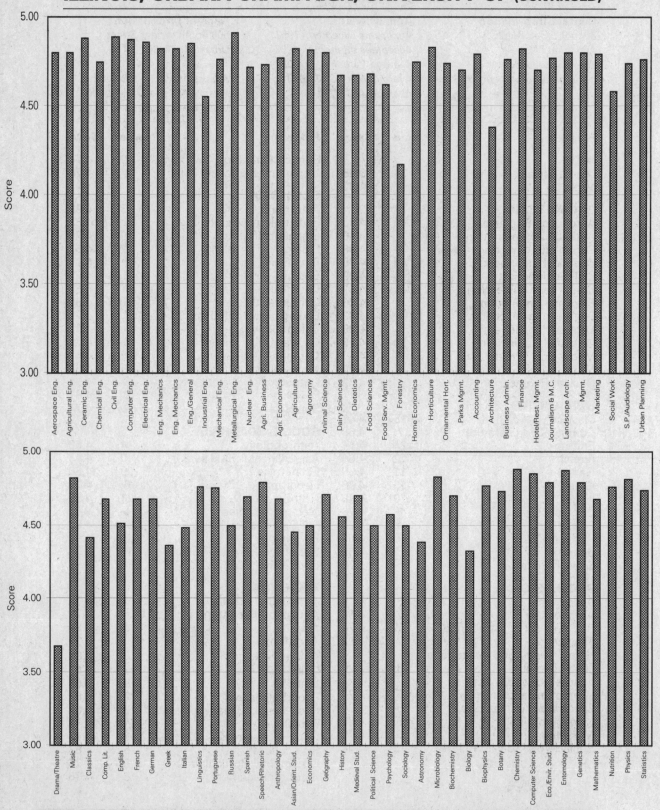

INDIANA UNIVERSITY-BLOOMINGTON

Contact Information
School Type: Public
Affiliation: None
Environment: City
Undergrad Enrollment: 27,480

Admissions
Applicants accepted: NR
Acceptees attending: 44%
Average Verbal SAT: 466
Average Math SAT: 530
Average ACT: 24

General Information
300 North Jordan Avenue
Bloomington, IN 47405

Admissions: 812-855-0661
Financial Aid: 812-855-0321
Web: www.indiana.edu/iub

Program	Rank	Score	Program	Rank	Score
ARTS			Journalism and Mass		
Art	18	4.21	Communications	12	4.62
Drama/Theatre	6	4.80	Management	3	4.88
Music	15	4.69	Marketing	2	4.88
			Social Work/Social Welfare	36	4.22
HUMANITIES			Speech Pathology/Audiology	6	4.82
Art History	18	4.20			
Chinese	13	4.32	**SCIENCES**		
Classics	19	4.18	Astronomy	18	4.25
Comparative Literature	12	4.52	Astrophysics	4	4.72
English	13	4.73	Bacteriology/Microbiology	19	4.68
French	6	4.85	Biology	20	4.55
German	4	4.84	Botany	12	4.61
Greek	7	4.61	Chemistry	20	4.59
Hebrew	11	4.68	Computer Science	34	3.86
Italian	5	4.61	Ecology/Environmental Studies	8	4.69
Japanese	14	4.32	Geology/Geoscience	24	4.49
Latin	2	4.86	Mathematics	24	4.55
Linguistics	12	4.69	Nutrition	25	4.46
Philosophy	18	4.53			
Portuguese	10	4.54	**SOCIAL SCIENCES**		
Religious Studies	1	4.84	Anthropology	26	4.45
Russian	7	4.76	East Asian Studies	8	4.64
Slavic Languages	3	4.80	History	12	4.73
Spanish	11	4.72	Near/Middle Eastern Studies	8	4.68
Speech/Rhetoric	4	4.82	Political Science	16	4.71
			Psychology	13	4.51
PROFESSIONAL			Radio/Television Studies	9	4.70
Accounting	2	4.90	Russian/Slavic Studies	12	4.60
Business Administration	2	4.89	Social Work/Social Welfare	36	4.22
Finance	2	4.91	Sociology	11	4.65

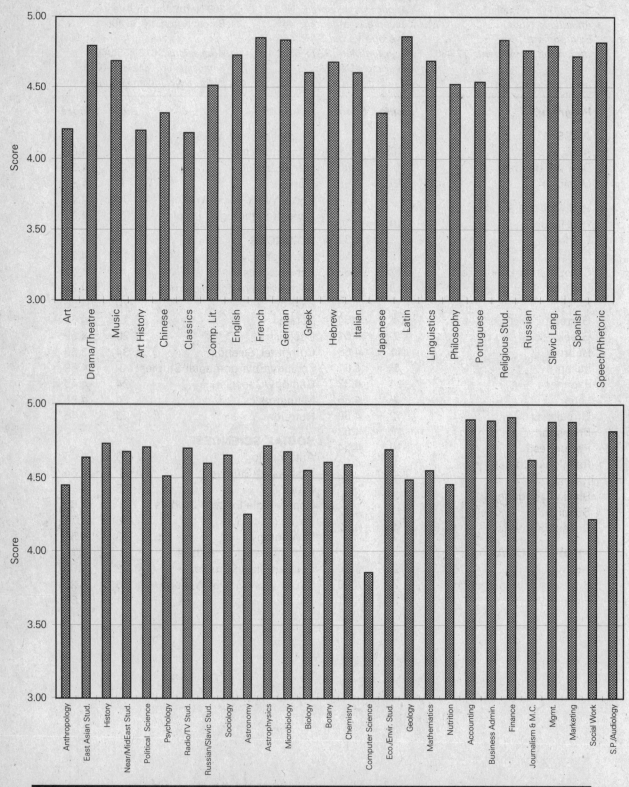

IOWA STATE UNIVERSITY

Contact Information
School Type: Public
Affiliation: None
Environment: City
Undergrad Enrollment: 18,235

Admissions
Applicants accepted: 90%
Acceptees attending: 44%
Average Verbal SAT: 542
Average Math SAT: 573
Average ACT: 24

General Information
100 Alumni Hall
Office of Admissions
Ames, IA 50011
Admissions: 515-294-5836
Financial Aid: 515-294-2223
Web: www.iastate.edu

Program	Rank	Score	Program	Rank	Score
ENGINEERING			Earth Science	6	4.64
Aerospace Engineering	11	4.65	Entomology	11	4.63
Agricultural Engineering	3	4.86	Fish/Game Management	11	4.64
Ceramic Engineering	5	4.74	Meteorology	3	4.83
Chemical Engineering	39	4.53	Nutrition	2	4.86
Civil Engineering	27	4.42	Statistics	6	4.79
Computer Engineering	22	4.59	Zoology	12	4.58
Electrical Engineering	65	4.25			
Engineering Science	4	4.70	**SOCIAL SCIENCES**		
Industrial Engineering	18	4.59	Child Psychology	9	4.28
Mechanical Engineering	25	4.58	Economics	38	4.24
Metallurgical Engineering	13	4.77			
			TECHNICAL		
PROFESSIONAL			Agricultural Business	6	4.66
Hotel, Restaurant, Institutional			Agriculture	3	4.88
Management	9	4.53	Agronomy	3	4.86
Journalism and Mass			Animal Science	4	4.85
Communications	26	4.32	Dairy Sciences	5	4.72
Landscape Architecture	9	4.74	Dietetics	6	4.76
Urban and Regional Planning	6	4.72	Farm/Ranch Management	8	4.55
			Fish/Game Management	11	4.64
SCIENCES			Food Sciences	3	4.87
Bacteriology/Microbiology	33	4.18	Food Services Management	5	4.67
Biochemistry	29	4.15	Forestry	14	4.59
Biology	47	3.58	Home Economics	6	4.73
Biophysics	12	4.46	Horticulture	3	4.88
Botany	18	4.40	Ornamental Horticulture	2	4.83
Chemistry	19	4.61			
Computer Science	38	3.75			

IOWA STATE UNIVERSITY (CONTINUED)

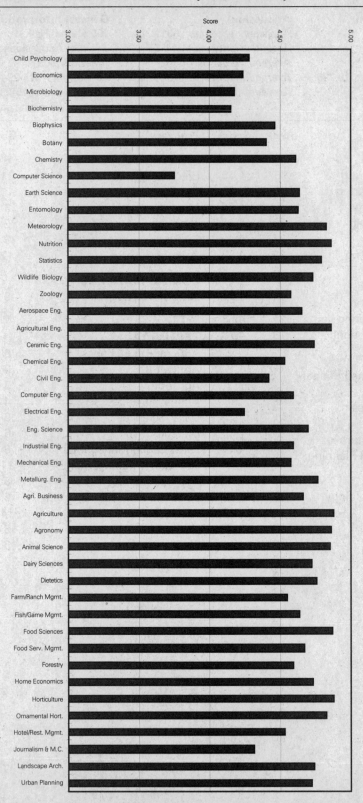

Score

| | 3.00 | 3.50 | 4.00 | 4.50 | 5.00 |

Child Psychology
Economics
Microbiology
Biochemistry
Biophysics
Botany
Chemistry
Computer Science
Earth Science
Entomology
Meteorology
Nutrition
Statistics
Wildlife Biology
Zoology
Aerospace Eng.
Agricultural Eng.
Ceramic Eng.
Chemical Eng.
Civil Eng.
Computer Eng.
Electrical Eng.
Eng. Science
Industrial Eng.
Mechanical Eng.
Metallurg. Eng.
Agri. Business
Agriculture
Agronomy
Animal Science
Dairy Sciences
Dietetics
Farm/Ranch Mgmt.
Fish/Game Mgmt.
Food Sciences
Food Serv. Mgmt.
Forestry
Home Economics
Horticulture
Ornamental Hort.
Hotel/Rest. Mgmt.
Journalism & M.C.
Landscape Arch.
Urban Planning

IOWA, UNIVERSITY OF

Contact Information
School Type: Public
Affiliation: None
Environment: City
Undergrad Enrollment: 18,586

Admissions
Applicants accepted: 86%
Acceptees attending: 42%
Average Verbal SAT: 570
Average Math SAT: 580
Average ACT: 24

General Information
107 Calvin Hall
Iowa City, IA 52242

Admissions: 319-335-3847
Financial Aid: 319-335-1450
Web: www.uiowa.edu

Program	Rank	Score
ARTS		
Art	29	3.53
Ceramic Art/Design	5	4.69
Drama/Theatre	8	4.70
Music	20	4.55
ENGINEERING		
Bioengineering/Biomedical Engineering	14	4.20
Chemical Engineering	70	4.04
Civil Engineering	28	4.40
Electrical Engineering	82	4.02
Industrial Engineering	17	4.62
Mechanical Engineering	37	4.39
HUMANITIES		
Art History	28	3.50
Comparative Literature	20	4.25
English	20	4.61
French	28	4.22
Linguistics	28	4.28
Religious Studies	11	4.65
Speech/Rhetoric	2	4.88

Program	Rank	Score
PROFESSIONAL		
Accounting	40	4.05
Business Administration	32	4.31
Finance	40	4.14
Journalism and Mass Communications	18	4.47
Management	43	4.12
Marketing	32	4.29
Nursing	21	4.40
Speech Pathology/Audiology	1	4.91
SCIENCES		
Bacteriology/Microbiology	18	4.69
Biochemistry	18	4.43
Biology	40	3.35
Chemistry	52	4.06
Computer Science	42	3.58
Statistics	12	4.68
SOCIAL SCIENCES		
American Studies	5	4.58
Child Psychology	6	4.40
Communication	6	4.67
Economics	40	4.17
Geography	11	4.58
History	25	4.52
Labor and Industrial Relations	8	4.56
Political Science	35	4.45

Score

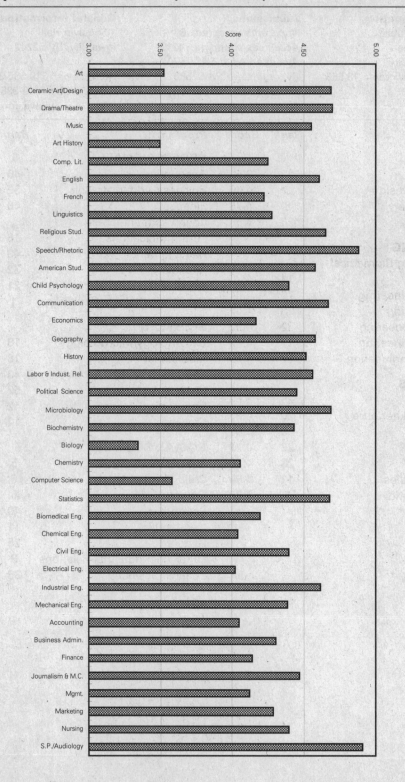

JOHNS HOPKINS UNIVERSITY

Contact Information
School Type: Private
Affiliation: None
Environment: Major City
Undergrad Enrollment: 3,623

Admissions
Applicants accepted: 40%
Acceptees attending: 30%
Average Verbal SAT: 660
Average Math SAT: 690
Average ACT: 31

General Information
3400 North Charles Street
Baltimore, MD 21218

Admissions: 410-516-8171
Financial Aid: 410-516-8028
Web: www.jhu.edu/~admis/

Program	Rank	Score	Program	Rank	Score
ARTS			**SCIENCES**		
Art	13	4.39	Applied Mathematics	14	4.43
			Biology	23	4.52
ENGINEERING			Biophysics	1	4.88
Bioengineering/Biomedical			Chemistry	41	4.28
Engineering	1	4.90	Earth Science	1	4.86
Electrical Engineering	42	4.53	Environmental Sciences	10	4.58
Engineering Mechanics	4	4.69	Geology/Geoscience	21	4.55
Materials Engineering/Materials			Mathematics	31	4.46
Science And Engineering	9	4.76	Physics	26	4.59
Mechanical Engineering	42	4.32			
			SOCIAL SCIENCES		
HUMANITIES			Behavioral Sciences	2	4.82
Arabic	7	4.40	Economics	16	4.72
Art History	10	4.63	History	9	4.80
Classics	17	4.29	International Relations	3	4.83
Comparative Literature	19	4.27	Near/Middle Eastern Studies	9	4.66
English	9	4.79	Political Science	18	4.68
French	24	4.32	Psychology	27	4.35
German	13	4.64			
Italian	4	4.66			
Philosophy	21	4.44			

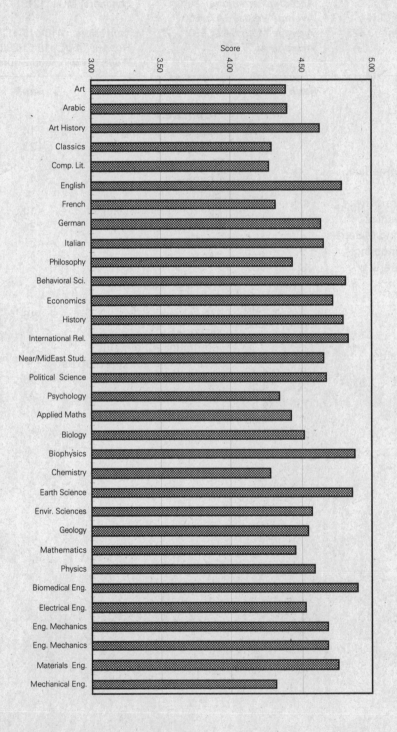

KANSAS STATE UNIVERSITY

Contact Information
School Type: Public
Affiliation: None
Environment: City
Undergrad Enrollment: 16,935

Admissions
Applicants accepted: 69%
Acceptees attending: 70%
Average Verbal SAT: NR
Average Math SAT: NR
Average ACT: 23

General Information
Anderson Hall Room 1
Manhattan, KS 66506

Admissions: 913-532-6250
Financial Aid: 913-532-6420
Web: www.ksu.edu

Program	Rank	Score
ENGINEERING		
Agricultural Engineering	20	4.54
Architectural Engineering	6	4.48
Industrial Engineering	22	4.53
Manufacturing Engineering	5	4.24
Nuclear Engineering	15	4.56
PROFESSIONAL		
Architecture	23	3.52
Hotel, Restaurant, Institutional Management	14	4.41
Journalism and Mass Communications	16	4.50
Landscape Architecture	3	4.82

Program	Rank	Score
SCIENCES		
Bacteriology/Microbiology	34	4.16
Computer Science	55	3.20
Fish/Game Management	13	4.62
TECHNICAL		
Agriculture	12	4.55
Agronomy	11	4.69
Animal Science	9	4.70
Dairy Sciences	3	4.82
Dietetics	7	4.71
Farm/Ranch Management	3	4.74
Fish/Game Management	13	4.62
Food Sciences	5	4.82
Food Services Management	4	4.73
Horticulture	10	4.73
Natural Resource Management	9	4.46
Parks Management	8	4.59

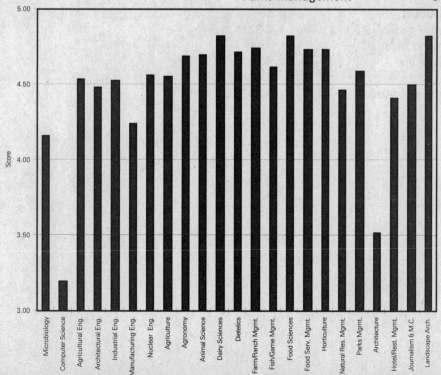

KANSAS, UNIVERSITY OF

Contact Information
School Type: Public
Affiliation: None
Environment: City
Undergrad Enrollment: 16,659

Admissions
Applicants accepted: 62%
Acceptees attending: 73%
Average Verbal SAT: NR
Average Math SAT: NR
Average ACT: 24

General Information
Office Of Admissions
126 Strong Hall
Lawrence, KS 66045
Admissions: 785 864-3911
Financial Aid: 785 864-4700
Web: www.ukans.edu

Program	Rank	Score	Program	Rank	Score
ARTS			**SCIENCES**		
Art	27	3.55	Astronomy	17	4.28
Ceramic Art/Design	6	4.64	Atmospheric Sciences	4	4.72
Drama/Theatre	44	3.07	Bacteriology/Microbiology	35	4.11
			Biology	44	3.20
ENGINEERING			Cell Biology	18	4.18
Aerospace Engineering	8	4.73	Computer Science	48	3.36
Architectural Engineering	3	4.64	Entomology	7	4.73
Civil Engineering	35	4.25	Genetics	12	4.52
Electrical Engineering	75	4.10	Geology/Geoscience	40	4.20
Engineering Physics	11	4.53	Geophysics/Geoscience	19	4.57
Petroleum Engineering	11	4.66	Meteorology	5	4.75
HUMANITIES			**SOCIAL SCIENCES**		
Art History	27	3.51	American Studies	9	4.39
German	27	4.44	Anthropology	49	4.04
Linguistics	20	4.52	Geography	13	4.51
Spanish	10	4.73	History	42	4.20
PROFESSIONAL					
Architecture	15	3.82			
Journalism and Mass Communications	14	4.55			
Nursing	20	4.42			
Speech Pathology/Audiology	7	4.80			

Score

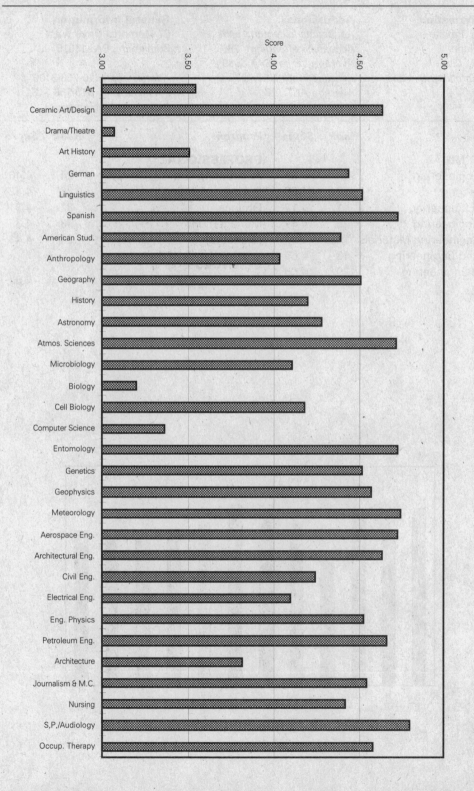

LEHIGH UNIVERSITY

Contact Information
School Type: Private
Affiliation: None
Environment: City
Undergrad Enrollment: 4,232

Admissions
Applicants accepted: 54%
Acceptees attending: 28%
Average Verbal SAT: 589
Average Math SAT: 625
Average ACT: 28

General Information
27 Memorial Drive West
Bethlehem, PA 18015

Admissions: 610-758-3100
Financial Aid: 610-758-3181
Web: www.lehigh.edu

Program	Rank	Score	Program	Rank	Score
ENGINEERING			**PROFESSIONAL**		
Chemical Engineering	49	4.39	Accounting	24	4.46
Civil Engineering	17	4.56	Business Administration	26	4.42
Computer Engineering	41	4.12	Finance	32	4.31
Industrial Engineering	25	4.47	Management	33	4.33
Materials Engineering/Materials			Marketing	24	4.41
Science And Engineering	13	4.65	**SCIENCES**		
Mechanical Engineering	20	4.65	Geophysics/Geoscience	16	4.62

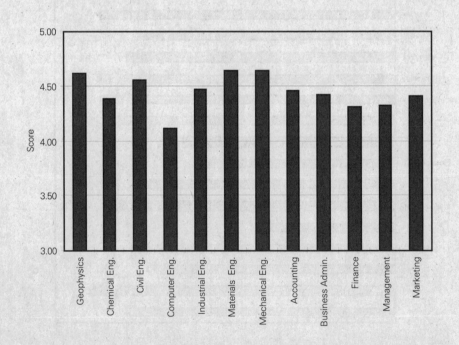

LOUISIANA TECH UNIVERSITY

Contact Information
School Type: Public
Affiliation: None
Environment: Rural
Undergrad Enrollment: 7,882

Admissions
Applicants accepted: 98%
Acceptees attending: 60%
Average Verbal SAT: NR
Average Math SAT: NR
Average ACT: 22

General Information
Box 3178 Tech Station
Ruston, LA 71272

Admissions: 318-257-3036
Financial Aid: 318-257-2641
Web: www.LaTech.edu

Program	Rank	Score
ENGINEERING		
Bioengineering/Biomedical Engineering	12	4.28
Petroleum Engineering	17	4.56

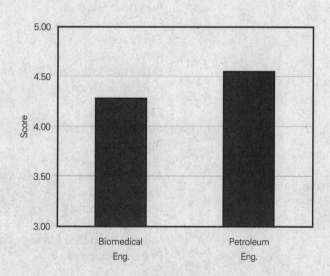

MARYLAND-COLLEGE PARK, UNIVERSITY OF

Contact Information
School Type: Public
Affiliation: None
Environment: Suburban
Undergrad Enrollment: 24,529

Admissions
Applicants accepted: 61%
Acceptees attending: 35%
Average Verbal SAT: 590
Average Math SAT: 605
Average ACT: NR

General Information
College Park, MD 20742

Admissions: 800-422-5867
Financial Aid: 301-314-9000
Web: www.umcp.umd.edu

Program	Rank	Score	Program	Rank	Score
ARTS			**SCIENCES**		
Art	22	3.79	Astronomy	8	4.53
			Bacteriology/Microbiology	25	4.48
ENGINEERING			Computer Science	11	4.70
Aerospace Engineering	7	4.76	Entomology	19	4.44
Agricultural Engineering	19	4.59	Mathematics	25	4.54
Chemical Engineering	66	4.10	Physics	19	4.69
Civil Engineering	42	4.17	Zoology	19	4.40
Electrical Engineering	31	4.64			
Engineering/General	3	4.78	**SOCIAL SCIENCES**		
Mechanical Engineering	34	4.44	American Studies	6	4.54
Nuclear Engineering	13	4.60	Economics	26	4.56
			Geography	26	4.25
HUMANITIES			History	33	4.42
Art History	22	3.74	Labor and Industrial Relations	10	4.47
Information Science	10	4.52	Political Science	34	4.47
Spanish	30	4.35			
			TECHNICAL		
PROFESSIONAL			Agricultural Economics	3	4.85
Accounting	31	4.27	Agriculture	17	4.47
Business Administration	34	4.26	Agronomy	18	4.52
Finance	31	4.33	Animal Science	18	4.43
Hotel, Restaurant, Institutional			Dairy Sciences	6	4.68
Management	10	4.52	Home Economics	9	4.66
Journalism and Mass			Horticulture	15	4.65
Communications	31	4.18	Natural Resource Management	15	4.29
Management	35	4.30	Poultry Sciences	7	4.74
Marketing	31	4.30			
Speech Pathology/Audiology	27	4.38			

MARYLAND-COLLEGE PARK, UNIVERSITY OF (CONTINUED)

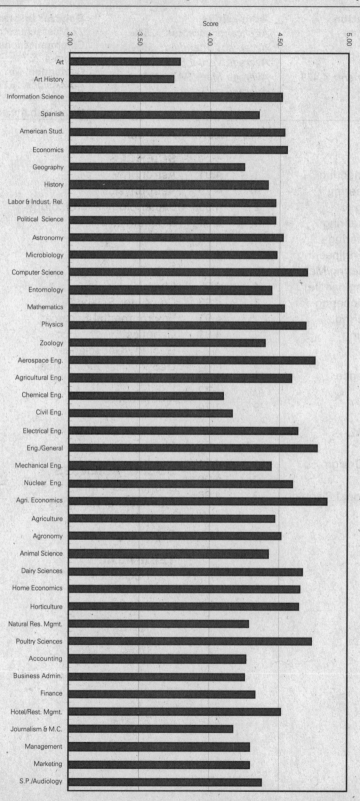

Score

MASSACHUSETTS INSTITUTE OF TECHNOLOGY

Contact Information
School Type: Private
Affiliation: None
Environment: City
Undergrad Enrollment: 4,429

Admissions
Applicants accepted: 25%
Acceptees attending: 55%
Average Verbal SAT: 700
Average Math SAT: 755
Average ACT: 31

General Information
77 Massachusetts Avenue
Communications Office
Room 4-237
Cambridge, MA 02139
Admissions: 617-258-5515
Financial Aid: 617-253-4971
Web: web.mit.edu

Program	Rank	Score	Program	Rank	Score
ENGINEERING			**SCIENCES**		
Aerospace Engineering	1	4.91	Astronomy	6	4.62
Chemical Engineering	10	4.79	Astrophysics	1	4.85
Civil Engineering	2	4.90	Bacteriology/Microbiology	1	4.92
Computer Engineering	1	4.91	Biochemistry	2	4.91
Electrical Engineering	1	4.92	Biology	2	4.91
Environmental Engineering	2	4.83	Biophysics	7	4.71
Materials Engineering/Materials			Cell Biology	1	4.91
Science And Engineering	4	4.85	Chemistry	4	4.92
Mechanical Engineering	1	4.93	Computer Science	1	4.92
Nuclear Engineering	1	4.91	Environmental Sciences	2	4.88
Ocean Engineering	1	4.91	Genetics	3	4.88
			Geology/Geoscience	2	4.91
HUMANITIES			Geophysics/Geoscience	2	4.90
Information Science	1	4.86	Marine Biology	1	4.80
Linguistics	10	4.72	Mathematics	4	4.86
Philosophy	9	4.70	Meteorology	2	4.87
			Molecular Biology	1	4.90
PROFESSIONAL			Physics	5	4.88
Architecture	2	4.76			
Environmental Design	1	4.91	**SOCIAL SCIENCES**		
Management	2	4.90	Economics	1	4.92
Urban and Regional Planning	3	4.80	International Relations	9	4.64
			Political Science	6	4.86
			Psychology	17	4.46
			TECHNICAL		
			Food Sciences	4	4.86

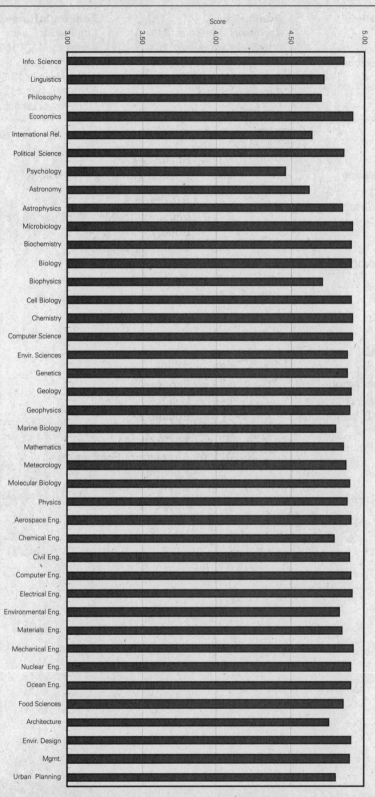

Score

MASSACHUSETTS-AMHERST, UNIVERSITY OF

Contact Information
School Type: Public
Affiliation: None
Environment: Suburban
Undergrad Enrollment: 19,467

Admissions
Applicants accepted: 74%
Acceptees attending: 30%
Average Verbal SAT: 556
Average Math SAT: 560
Average ACT: NR

General Information
Admissions Center
Amherst, MA 01003

Admissions: 413-545-0222
Financial Aid: 413-545-0801
Web: www.umass.edu

Program	Rank	Score	Program	Rank	Score
ENGINEERING			Sociology	24	4.45
Chemical Engineering	37	4.55	Speech Pathology/Audiology	25	4.43
Civil Engineering	29	4.38			
Electrical Engineering	60	4.32	**SCIENCES**		
Industrial Engineering	36	4.28	Bacteriology/Microbiology	22	4.58
			Botany	23	4.30
HUMANITIES			Computer Science	32	4.05
Comparative Literature	25	4.15	Entomology	20	4.43
English	40	4.15	Geology/Geoscience	34	4.31
German	16	4.60	Mathematics	49	4.19
Linguistics	29	4.26			
Philosophy	19	4.50	**SOCIAL SCIENCES**		
			American Studies	17	3.76
PROFESSIONAL			Anthropology	19	4.59
Accounting	27	4.37	Communication	17	4.16
Business Administration	30	4.34	Economics	41	4.15
Finance	27	4.40	Political Science	38	4.40
Hotel, Restaurant, Institutional			Sociology	24	4.45
Management	4	4.78			
Landscape Architecture	22	4.46	**TECHNICAL**		
Management	32	4.34	Agricultural Economics	11	4.62
Marketing	28	4.36	Agriculture	28	4.32
			Animal Science	26	4.12
			Home Economics	22	4.39

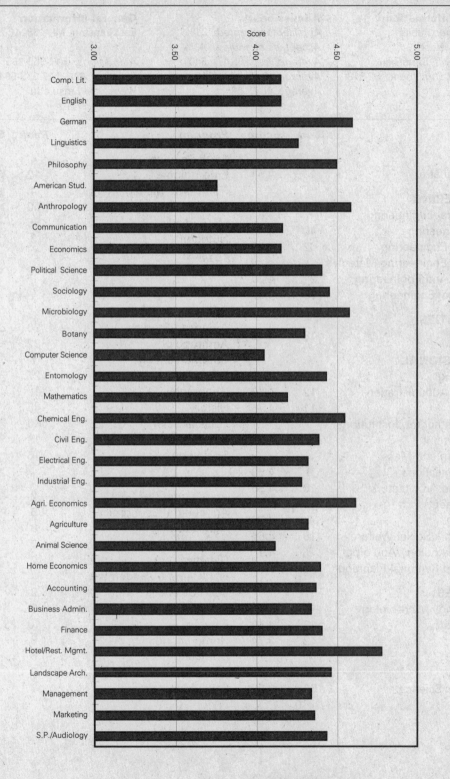

MICHIGAN STATE UNIVERSITY

Contact Information
School Type: Public
Affiliation: None
Environment: Suburban
Undergrad Enrollment: 32,318

Admissions
Applicants accepted: 81%
Acceptees attending: 41%
Average Verbal SAT: 540
Average Math SAT: 550
Average ACT: 23

General Information
East Lansing, MI 48824

Admissions: 517-355-1855
Financial Aid: 517-353-5940
Web: www.msu.edu

Program	Rank	Score
ARTS		
Drama/Theatre	13	4.51
ENGINEERING		
Agricultural Engineering	6	4.84
Civil Engineering	40	4.19
Electrical Engineering	62	4.28
Materials Engineering/Materials Science And Engineering	21	4.50
Mechanical Engineering	39	4.37
HUMANITIES		
Russian	18	4.46
PROFESSIONAL		
Accounting	12	4.68
Business Administration	12	4.66
Finance	11	4.75
Hotel, Restaurant, Institutional Management	3	4.83
Journalism and Mass Communications	9	4.68
Landscape Architecture	18	4.56
Management	11	4.74
Marketing	7	4.76
Social Work/Social Welfare	18	4.54
Speech Pathology/Audiology	8	4.78
Urban and Regional Planning	7	4.71
SCIENCES		
Bacteriology/Microbiology	15	4.72
Biochemistry	19	4.40
Biology	42	3.74
Botany	7	4.76
Chemistry	46	4.18
Computer Science	50	3.32

Program	Rank	Score
Earth Science	4	4.73
Entomology	12	4.60
Fish/Game Management	4	4.77
Geology/Geoscience	50	4.05
Mathematics	55	4.13
Nutrition	3	4.84
Physics	27	4.58
Statistics	22	4.50
Zoology	7	4.71
SOCIAL SCIENCES		
American Studies	20	3.64
Anthropology	32	4.32
Communication	7	4.65
Economics	27	4.54
Geography	19	4.41
History	46	4.10
Political Science	40	4.36
Social Work/Social Welfare	18	4.54
Sociology	16	4.57
TECHNICAL		
Agricultural Business	2	4.80
Agricultural Economics	5	4.80
Agriculture	6	4.79
Agronomy	7	4.79
Dietetics	2	4.89
Fish/Game Management	4	4.77
Food Sciences	2	4.88
Food Services Management	3	4.79
Forestry	10	4.66
Home Economics	8	4.68
Horticulture	6	4.81
Natural Resource Management	3	4.74
Parks Management	1	4.85

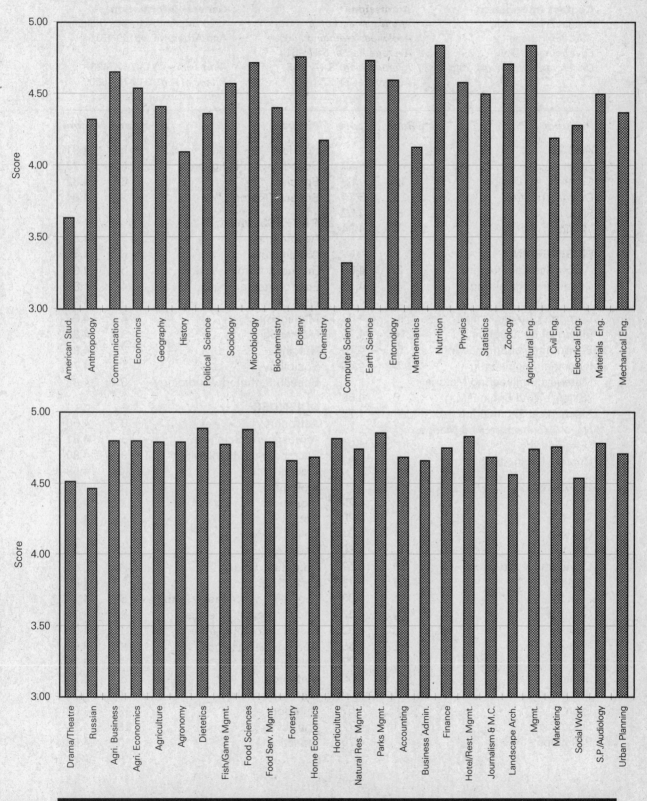

MICHIGAN-ANN ARBOR, UNIVERSITY OF

Contact Information
School Type: Public
Affiliation: None
Environment: City
Undergrad Enrollment: 23,515

Admissions
Applicants accepted: 68%
Acceptees attending: 40%
Average Verbal SAT: 610
Average Math SAT: 645
Average ACT: 27

General Information
1220 Student Activities Building
Ann Arbor, MI 48109-1316

Admissions: 313-764-7433
Financial Aid: 313-763-6600
Web: www.umich.edu

Program	Rank	Score	Program	Rank	Score
ARTS			Russian	5	4.81
Art	9	4.50	Scandinavian Languages	6	4.73
Ceramic Art/Design	13	4.39	Spanish	6	4.82
Drama/Theatre	23	3.74	Speech/Rhetoric	3	4.84
Film	8	4.52			
Music	6	4.84	**PROFESSIONAL**		
			Accounting	3	4.87
ENGINEERING			Architecture	6	4.49
Aerospace Engineering	2	4.89	Business Administration	3	4.87
Chemical Engineering	33	4.58	Environmental Design	4	4.83
Civil Engineering	9	4.74	Finance	3	4.88
Computer Engineering	4	4.83	Management	4	4.86
Electrical Engineering	14	4.75	Marketing	3	4.85
Environmental Engineering	5	4.75	Nursing	2	4.89
Industrial Engineering	2	4.88	Sociology	1	4.79
Materials Engineering/Materials Science And Engineering	18	4.55	Speech Pathology/Audiology	5	4.83
Mechanical Engineering	9	4.79	**SCIENCES**		
Naval Architecture And Marine Engineering	1	4.90	Astronomy	9	4.50
			Atmospheric Sciences	3	4.81
Nuclear Engineering	2	4.87	Bacteriology/Microbiology	9	4.80
			Biochemistry	12	4.58
HUMANITIES			Biology	16	4.66
Arabic	2	4.79	Biophysics	2	4.87
Art History	9	4.70	Botany	5	4.81
Chinese	9	4.54	Cell Biology	11	4.52
Classics	5	4.80	Chemistry	30	4.46
Comparative Literature	10	4.57	Computer Science	41	3.62
English	14	4.71	Earth Science	2	4.83
French	7	4.83	Ecology/Environmental Studies	5	4.78
German	14	4.63	Environmental Sciences	6	4.74
Greek	16	4.32	Fish/Game Management	19	4.55
Hebrew	12	4.65	Geology/Geoscience	20	4.57
Information Science	3	4.77	Mathematics	11	4.75
Italian	7	4.55	Meteorology	6	4.71
Japanese	7	4.54	Molecular Biology	8	4.72
Latin	7	4.67	Nutrition	13	4.67
Linguistics	11	4.71	Physics	18	4.71
Philosophy	7	4.76	Statistics	16	4.60

SOCIAL SCIENCES

American Studies	3	4.65
Anthropology	1	4.92
Asian/Oriental Studies	7	4.59
Child Psychology	5	4.44
Communication	4	4.77
East Asian Studies	10	4.56
Economics	15	4.73
Geography	7	4.70
History	6	4.86
Labor and Industrial Relations	5	4.71
Medieval Studies	7	4.68
Near/Middle Eastern Studies	7	4.70
Political Science	4	4.89
Psychology	4	4.63
Radio/Television Studies	8	4.71
Russian/Slavic Studies	5	4.75
Sociology	1	4.79
Southeast Asian Studies	5	4.79

TECHNICAL

Fish/Game Management	19	4.55
Forestry	21	4.41
Natural Resource Management	10	4.41

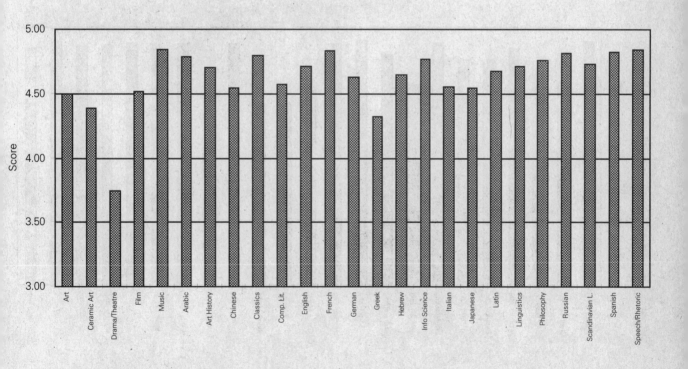

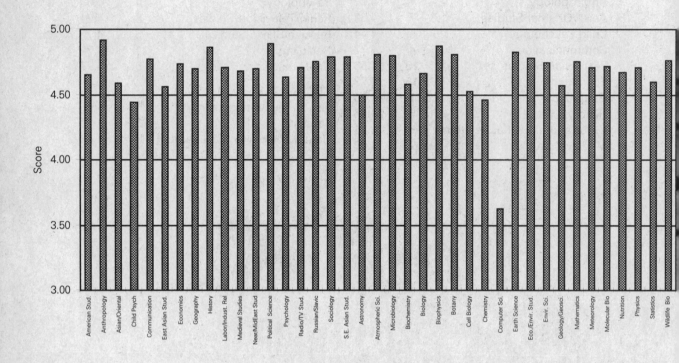

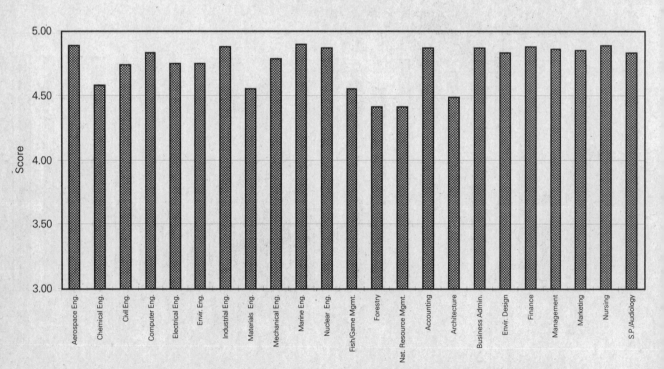

MINNESOTA, UNIVERSITY OF

Contact Information
School Type: Public
Affiliation: None
Environment: Major City
Undergrad Enrollment: 19,689

Admissions
Applicants accepted: 55%
Acceptees attending: 56%
Average Verbal SAT: 575
Average Math SAT: 602
Average ACT: 24

General Information
231 Pillsbury Drive, SE,
240 Williamson Hall
Minneapolis, MN 55455
Admissions: 612-625-2008
Financial Aid: 612-624-1665
Web: www.umn.edu/tc

Program	Rank	Score
ARTS		
Art	24	3.69
Drama/Theatre	11	4.60
ENGINEERING		
Aerospace Engineering	4	4.82
Agricultural Engineering	14	4.75
Chemical Engineering	1	4.91
Civil Engineering	26	4.44
Electrical Engineering	34	4.60
Geological Engineering	8	4.79
Materials Engineering/Materials Science And Engineering	3	4.87
Mechanical Engineering	4	4.89
HUMANITIES		
Art History	25	3.60
English	33	4.31
German	20	4.55
Greek	10	4.52
Hebrew	13	4.63
Italian	20	4.24
Latin	4	4.80
Linguistics	25	4.37
Philosophy	20	4.47
Scandinavian Languages	1	4.88
Spanish	18	4.57
PROFESSIONAL		
Accounting	15	4.62
Architecture	13	4.07
Business Administration	15	4.62
Environmental Design	14	4.52
Finance	28	4.39
Journalism and Mass Communications	4	4.79
Landscape Architecture	7	4.77
Management	16	4.65
Marketing	13	4.61
Nursing	12	4.61
Occupational Therapy	5	4.81
Physical Therapy	3	4.86
Sociology	15	4.59
Speech Pathology/Audiology	3	4.87
SCIENCES		
Astronomy	23	4.18
Astrophysics	5	4.66

Program	Rank	Score
Bacteriology/Microbiology	13	4.75
Biology	38	3.88
Botany	13	4.59
Cell Biology	13	4.38
Chemistry	22	4.57
Computer Science	21	4.50
Earth Science	11	4.42
Entomology	8	4.72
Environmental Sciences	12	4.52
Fish/Game Management	7	4.69
Genetics	9	4.62
Geology/Geoscience	25	4.48
Geophysics/Geoscience	10	4.73
Mathematics	17	4.65
Nutrition	11	4.71
Physics	23	4.63
Statistics	8	4.76
SOCIAL SCIENCES		
American Studies	7	4.46
Anthropology	46	4.07
Child Psychology	8	4.30
Communication	14	4.33
Economics	7	4.84
Geography	1	4.90
History	24	4.53
Near/Middle Eastern Studies	16	4.53
Political Science	9	4.82
Psychology	5	4.62
Sociology	15	4.59
South Asian Studies	7	4.72
TECHNICAL		
Agricultural Business	5	4.69
Agricultural Economics	1	4.91
Agriculture	9	4.66
Agronomy	9	4.75
Animal Science	7	4.76
Fish/Game Management	7	4.69
Food Sciences	10	4.61
Forestry	1	4.88
Home Economics	2	4.83
Horticulture	8	4.77
Natural Resource Management	7	4.57
Parks Management	12	4.48

MISSOURI-COLUMBIA, UNIVERSITY OF

Contact Information
School Type: Public
Affiliation: None
Environment: City
Undergrad Enrollment: 15,651

Admissions
Applicants accepted: 90%
Acceptees attending: 49%
Average Verbal SAT: NR
Average Math SAT: NR
Average ACT: 25

General Information
305 Jesse Hall
Columbia, MO 65211

Admissions: 573-882-2456
Financial Aid: 573-882-7506
Web: www.missouri.edu

Program	Rank	Score
ARTS		
Art	38	3.19
ENGINEERING		
Agricultural Engineering	16	4.69
Civil Engineering	46	4.12
Computer Engineering	29	4.48
Industrial Engineering	24	4.50
HUMANITIES		
Art History	38	3.15
Speech/Rhetoric	8	4.72
PROFESSIONAL		
Accounting	37	4.12
Business Administration	41	4.12
Finance	34	4.27
Journalism and Mass Communications	1	4.87
Management	42	4.15
Nursing	35	4.21
Occupational Therapy	14	4.65
Physical Therapy	16	4.57
Speech Pathology/Audiology	23	4.49

Program	Rank	Score
SCIENCES		
Atmospheric Sciences	8	4.55
Bacteriology/Microbiology	31	4.24
Biology	48	3.11
Nutrition	12	4.69
SOCIAL SCIENCES		
Anthropology	50	4.03
History	35	4.38
TECHNICAL		
Agricultural Economics	15	4.43
Agriculture	11	4.58
Agronomy	10	4.72
Animal Science	12	4.60
Dairy Sciences	8	4.63
Dietetics	14	4.40
Food Sciences	17	4.32
Forestry	5	4.71
Horticulture	11	4.72
Parks Management	14	4.45

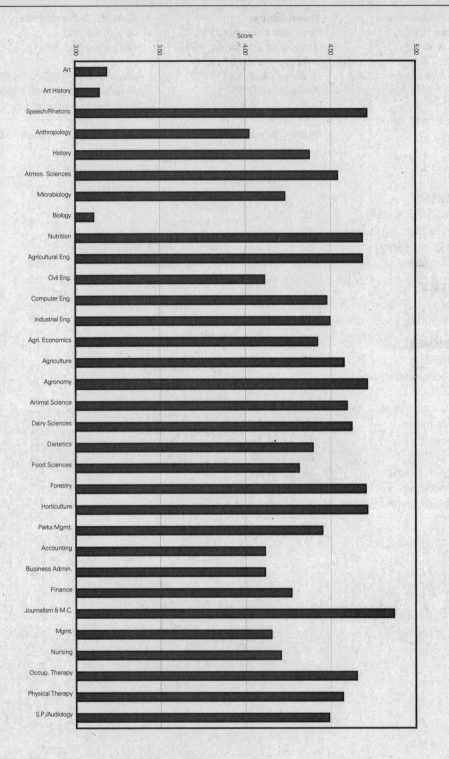

Score

| | 3.00 | 3.50 | 4.00 | 4.50 | 5.00 |

Art
Art History
Speech/Rhetoric
Anthropology
History
Atmos. Sciences
Microbiology
Biology
Nutrition
Agricultural Eng.
Civil Eng.
Computer Eng.
Industrial Eng.
Agri. Economics
Agriculture
Agronomy
Animal Science
Dairy Sciences
Dietetics
Food Sciences
Forestry
Horticulture
Parks Mgmt.
Accounting
Business Admin.
Finance
Journalism & M.C.
Mgmt.
Nursing
Occup. Therapy
Physical Therapy
S.P./Audiology

NEBRASKA-LINCOLN, UNIVERSITY OF

Contact Information
School Type: Public
Affiliation: None
Environment: City
Undergrad Enrollment: 18,954

Admissions
Applicants accepted: 83%
Acceptees attending: 60%
Average Verbal SAT: 557
Average Math SAT: 566
Average ACT: 23

General Information
14th and R Streets
Lincoln, NE 68588

Admissions: 800-742-8800
Financial Aid: 402-472-2030
Web: www.unl.edu

Program	Rank	Score	Program	Rank	Score
ENGINEERING			**TECHNICAL**		
Agricultural Engineering	42	4.10	Agricultural Economics	18	4.32
			Agriculture	19	4.44
PROFESSIONAL			Agronomy	17	4.53
Business Administration	45	4.03	Animal Science	17	4.46
Finance	43	4.03	Dairy Sciences	9	4.62
Management	46	4.07	Home Economics	15	4.53
Marketing	41	4.06	Horticulture	21	4.53
SCIENCES					
Botany	24	4.26			
Entomology	26	4.23			
SOCIAL SCIENCES					
Geography	22	4.34			

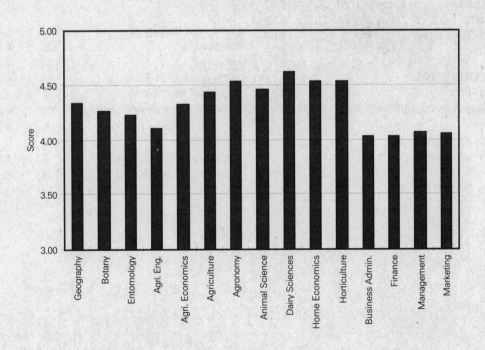

NEW YORK UNIVERSITY

Contact Information
School Type: Private
Affiliation: None
Environment: Major City
Undergrad Enrollment: 14,177

Admissions
Applicants accepted: 44%
Acceptees attending: 37%
Average Verbal SAT: 645
Average Math SAT: 640
Average ACT: 28

General Information
22 Washington Square North
New York, NY 10011

Admissions: 212-998-4500
Financial Aid: 212-998-4444
Web: www.nyu.edu

Program	Rank	Score	Program	Rank	Score
ARTS			Marketing	5	4.81
Art	1	4.90	Nursing	1	4.90
Drama/Theatre	10	4.62	Occupational Therapy	1	4.91
Film	3	4.81	Physical Therapy	1	4.91
Music	16	4.65	Social Work/Social Welfare	11	4.66
			Sociology	20	4.49
HUMANITIES			Speech Pathology/Audiology	11	4.72
Arabic	6	4.50			
Art History	1	4.92	**SCIENCES**		
Comparative Literature	18	4.32	Biochemistry	24	4.25
English	22	4.57	Biology	39	3.36
French	4	4.88	Computer Science	20	4.52
Greek	14	4.38	Mathematics	7	4.82
Hebrew	5	4.82			
Italian	2	4.80	**SOCIAL SCIENCES**		
Linguistics	15	4.64	American Studies	18	3.72
Portuguese	2	4.82	Anthropology	39	4.18
Russian	13	4.58	Behavioral Sciences	6	4.67
Slavic Languages	9	4.64	Child Psychology	4	4.47
Spanish	19	4.55	Economics	22	4.63
			History	30	4.46
PROFESSIONAL			Latin American Studies	14	4.26
Accounting	6	4.82	Medieval Studies	3	4.77
Business Administration	6	4.81	Near/Middle Eastern Studies	10	4.64
Finance	5	4.85	Political Science	39	4.38
Journalism and Mass			Psychology	30	4.30
Communications	11	4.63	Radio/Television Studies	3	4.82
Management	7	4.81	Russian/Slavic Studies	11	4.62
			Social Work/Social Welfare	11	4.66

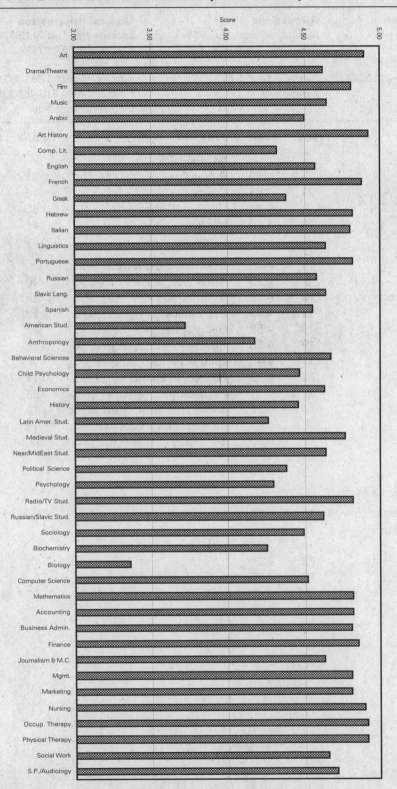

NORTH CAROLINA-CHAPEL HILL, UNIVERSITY OF

Contact Information
School Type: Public
Affiliation: None
Environment: Suburban
Undergrad Enrollment: 15,363

Admissions
Applicants accepted: 37%
Acceptees attending: 60%
Average Verbal SAT: 610
Average Math SAT: 611
Average ACT: NR

General Information
Jackson Hall UADM CB2200
Chapel Hill, NC 27599

Admissions: 919-966-3621
Financial Aid: 919-962-8396
Web: www.unc.edu

Program	Rank	Score	Program	Rank	Score
ARTS			**SCIENCES**		
Art	15	4.30	Biology	21	4.54
Drama/Theatre	21	3.83	Chemistry	16	4.69
Film	7	4.61	Geology/Geoscience	35	4.30
Music	12	4.76	Mathematics	41	4.31
			Statistics	21	4.52
HUMANITIES					
Art History	15	4.40	**SOCIAL SCIENCES**		
Classics	6	4.75	American Studies	10	4.32
Comparative Literature	16	4.39	Anthropology	29	4.37
English	19	4.63	Economics	28	4.52
French	16	4.59	Geography	23	4.31
German	19	4.56	History	15	4.67
Greek	11	4.49	Latin American Studies	4	4.71
Italian	21	4.23	Political Science	14	4.74
Latin	6	4.71	Psychology	23	4.39
Philosophy	16	4.57	Radio/Television Studies	10	4.66
Portuguese	7	4.63	Russian/Slavic Studies	15	4.53
Religious Studies	3	4.80	Sociology	3	4.76
Russian	14	4.55			
Spanish	23	4.48			
PROFESSIONAL					
Business Administration	10	4.72			
Journalism and Mass Communications	6	4.76			
Management	23	4.51			
Nursing	17	4.50			
Physical Therapy	2	4.88			
Sociology	3	4.76			

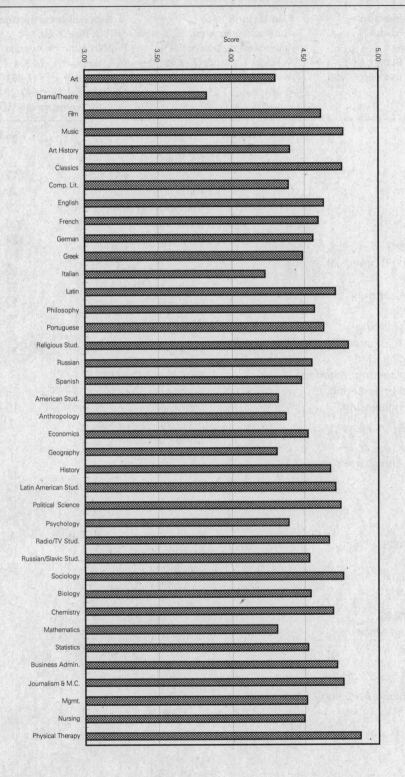

NORTHWESTERN UNIVERSITY

Contact Information
School Type: Private
Affiliation: None
Environment: Suburban
Undergrad Enrollment: 7,609

Admissions
Applicants accepted: 32%
Acceptees attending: 39%
Average Verbal SAT: 665
Average Math SAT: 679
Average ACT: 29

General Information
P.O. Box 3060,
1801 Hinman Avenue
Evanston, IL 60204
Admissions: 847-491-7271
Financial Aid: 847-491-7400
Web: www.acns.nwu.edu

Program	Rank	Score	Program	Rank	Score
ARTS			**SCIENCES**		
Art	23	3.72	Applied Mathematics	12	4.52
Drama/Theatre	1	4.91	Astronomy	19	4.23
Film	4	4.77	Bacteriology/Microbiology	27	4.38
Music	21	4.53	Biochemistry	16	4.49
			Biology	24	4.50
ENGINEERING			Cell Biology	10	4.59
Bioengineering/Biomedical			Chemistry	12	4.77
Engineering	5	4.78	Computer Science	27	4.22
Chemical Engineering	20	4.68	Geology/Geoscience	22	4.53
Civil Engineering	7	4.78	Mathematics	28	4.50
Electrical Engineering	35	4.58	Molecular Biology	6	4.75
Environmental Engineering	3	4.81	Physics	31	4.54
Industrial Engineering	6	4.78			
Materials Engineering/Materials			**SOCIAL SCIENCES**		
Science And Engineering	2	4.90	American Studies	25	3.22
Mechanical Engineering	13	4.74	Anthropology	10	4.77
			Behavioral Sciences	7	4.60
HUMANITIES			Child Psychology	2	4.55
Art History	23	3.69	Communication	1	4.86
Comparative Literature	14	4.42	Economics	11	4.79
English	16	4.68	History	17	4.62
French	26	4.28	Political Science	13	4.75
German	30	4.36	Psychology	25	4.37
Italian	13	4.40	Radio/Television Studies	4	4.80
Religious Studies	13	4.61	Russian/Slavic Studies	10	4.65
Russian	19	4.45	Sociology	25	4.43
Slavic Languages	11	4.60			
Speech/Rhetoric	1	4.90			
PROFESSIONAL					
Journalism and Mass					
Communications	2	4.84			
Nursing	5	4.85			
Sociology	25	4.43			
Speech Pathology/Audiology	2	4.90			

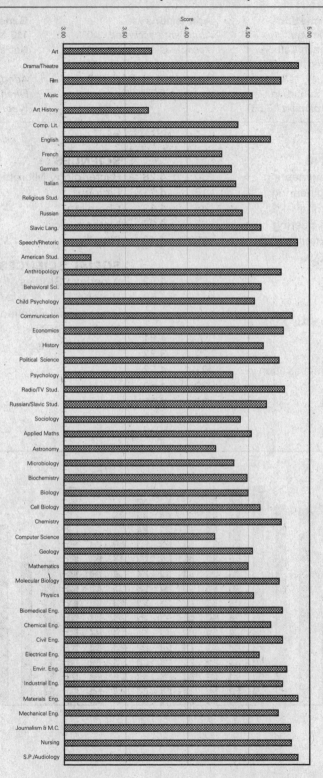

Score

	3.00	3.50	4.00	4.50	5.00

Art
Drama/Theatre
Film
Music
Art History
Comp. Lit.
English
French
German
Italian
Religious Stud.
Russian
Slavic Lang.
Speech/Rhetoric
American Stud.
Anthropology
Behavioral Sci.
Child Psychology
Communication
Economics
History
Political Science
Psychology
Radio/TV Stud.
Russian/Slavic Stud.
Sociology
Applied Maths
Astronomy
Microbiology
Biochemistry
Biology
Cell Biology
Chemistry
Computer Science
Geology
Mathematics
Molecular Biology
Physics
Biomedical Eng.
Chemical Eng.
Civil Eng.
Electrical Eng.
Envir. Eng.
Industrial Eng.
Materials Eng.
Mechanical Eng.
Journalism & M.C.
Nursing
S.P./Audiology

NOTRE DAME, UNIVERSITY OF

Contact Information
School Type: Private
Affiliation: Roman Catholic
Church (Congregation of Holy
Cross)
Environment: Suburban
Undergrad Enrollment: 7,857

Admissions
Applicants accepted: 40%
Acceptees attending: 51%
Average Verbal SAT: 641
Average Math SAT: 662
Average ACT: 29

General Information
113 Main Building
Notre Dame, IN 46556

Admissions: 219-631-7505
Financial Aid: 219-631-6436
Web: www.nd.edu

Program	Rank	Score	Program	Rank	Score
ENGINEERING			**SCIENCES**		
Aerospace Engineering	30	4.28	Bacteriology/Microbiology	20	4.67
Chemical Engineering	16	4.71	Biology	27	4.42
Civil Engineering	45	4.13	Chemistry	23	4.56
Electrical Engineering	63	4.27	Mathematics	19	4.62
Mechanical Engineering	35	4.42	Physics	28	4.57
HUMANITIES			**SOCIAL SCIENCES**		
English	23	4.53	American Studies	19	3.66
Philosophy	14	4.60	History	22	4.55
			International Relations	12	4.58
PROFESSIONAL			Medieval Studies	5	4.72
Accounting	7	4.81	Political Science	19	4.67
Architecture	29	3.32			
Business Administration	21	4.53			
Finance	20	4.60			
Management	22	4.52			
Marketing	22	4.48			

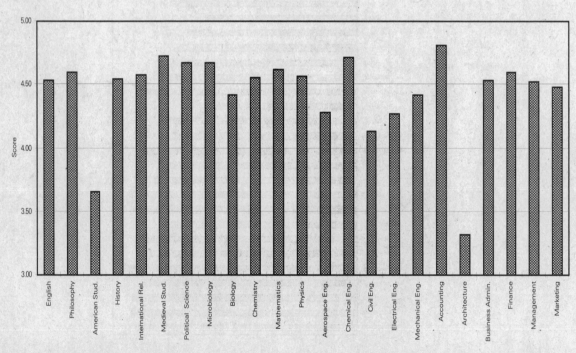

OHIO STATE UNIVERSITY-COLUMBUS

Contact Information
School Type: Public
Affiliation: None
Environment: Major City
Undergrad Enrollment: 35,486

Admissions
Applicants accepted: 85%
Acceptees attending: 42%
Average Verbal SAT: 560
Average Math SAT: 565
Average ACT: 24

General Information
Third Floor Lincoln Tower,
1800 Cannon Drive
Columbus, OH 43210
Admissions: 614-292-3980
Financial Aid: 614-292-0300
Web: www.acs.ohio-state.edu

Program	Rank	Score	Program	Rank	Score
ARTS			**SCIENCES**		
Art	32	3.39	Astronomy	21	4.21
Ceramic Art/Design	3	4.80	Bacteriology/Microbiology	37	4.06
Drama/Theatre	26	3.64	Biology	38	3.38
Music	24	4.46	Botany	19	4.38
			Chemistry	17	4.66
ENGINEERING			Computer Science	24	4.39
Aerospace Engineering	6	4.78	Earth Science	7	4.59
Agricultural Engineering	11	4.77	Entomology	10	4.66
Ceramic Engineering	3	4.82	Fish/Game Management	17	4.56
Chemical Engineering	52	4.33	Genetics	6	4.73
Civil Engineering	24	4.46	Geology/Geoscience	39	4.24
Electrical Engineering	32	4.63	Mathematics	33	4.43
Environmental Engineering	6	4.73	Nutrition	7	4.78
Industrial Engineering	11	4.70	Statistics	24	4.47
Materials Engineering/Materials			Zoology	9	4.66
Science And Engineering	26	4.44			
Mechanical Engineering	26	4.57	**SOCIAL SCIENCES**		
Metallurgical Engineering	2	4.87	Child Psychology	12	4.20
			Communication	13	4.37
HUMANITIES			Economics	37	4.27
Art History	32	3.36	Geography	5	4.75
German	18	4.58	History	34	4.40
Hebrew	15	4.59	Political Science	21	4.65
Information Science	5	4.70	Russian/Slavic Studies	16	4.48
Japanese	12	4.38	South Asian Studies	8	4.69
Linguistics	16	4.63	Southeast Asian Studies	9	4.68
Slavic Languages	14	4.53			
			TECHNICAL		
PROFESSIONAL			Agricultural Economics	12	4.57
Accounting	21	4.50	Agriculture	10	4.62
Architecture	25	3.40	Agronomy	5	4.82
Business Administration	23	4.48	Animal Science	11	4.62
Finance	21	4.57	Dairy Sciences	10	4.58
Hotel, Restaurant, Institutional			Dietetics	11	4.55
Management	15	4.36	Fish/Game Management	17	4.56
Journalism and Mass			Food Sciences	14	4.47
Communications	8	4.71	Home Economics	1	4.87
Landscape Architecture	6	4.78	Horticulture	9	4.75
Management	25	4.47	Natural Resource Management	8	4.52
Marketing	21	4.49	Parks Management	6	4.66
Nursing	16	4.53	Poultry Sciences	5	4.79
Occupational Therapy	11	4.70			
Physical Therapy	9	4.71			

OHIO STATE UNIVERSITY-COLUMBUS (CONTINUED)

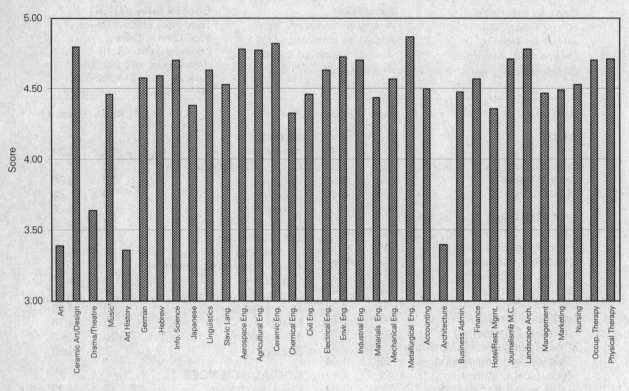

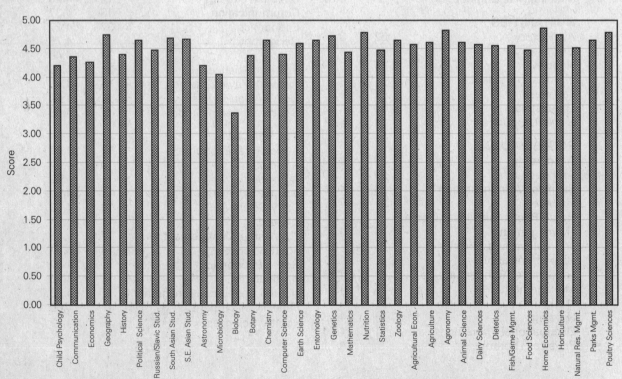

OREGON, UNIVERSITY OF

Contact Information
School Type: Public
Affiliation: None
Environment: City
Undergrad Enrollment: 13,874

Admissions
Applicants accepted: 90%
Acceptees attending: 34%
Average Verbal SAT: 550
Average Math SAT: 550
Average ACT: NR

General Information
1217 University of Oregon
Eugene, OR 97403

Admissions: 541-346-3201
Financial Aid: 541-346-3211
Web: www.uoregon.edu

Program	Rank	Score	Program	Rank	Score
ARTS			Marketing	29	4.33
Art	41	3.09	Speech Pathology/Audiology	22	4.51
			Urban and Regional Planning	13	4.56
HUMANITIES					
Art History	36	3.19	**SCIENCES**		
			Biochemistry	25	4.23
PROFESSIONAL			Biology	34	4.25
Accounting	34	4.16	Chemistry	44	4.23
Architecture	24	3.42	Geology/Geosciences	36	4.28
Business Administration	27	4.40	Mathematics	50	4.18
Finance	30	4.36			
Journalism and Mass			**SOCIAL SCIENCES**		
Communications	25	4.34	Anthropology	44	4.09
Landscape Architecture	28	4.36	Geography	29	4.16
Management	27	4.40	Political Science	33	4.48
			Psychology	20	4.42

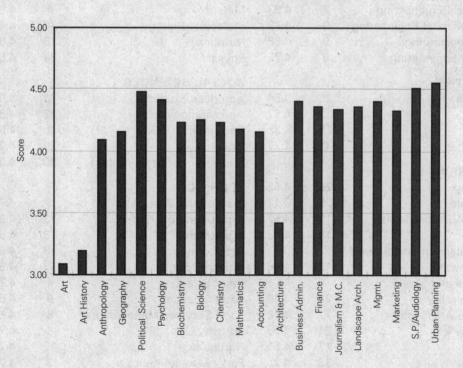

PENNSYLVANIA STATE UNIVERSITY-UNIVERSITY PARK

Contact Information
School Type: Public
Affiliation: None
Environment: City
Undergrad Enrollment: 31,009

Admissions
Applicants accepted: 49%
Acceptees attending: 37%
Average Verbal SAT: 593
Average Math SAT: 617
Average ACT: NR

General Information
University Park Campus
University Park, PA 16802

Admissions: 814-865-5471
Financial Aid: 814-865-6301
Web: www.psu.edu

Program	Rank	Score	Program	Rank	Score
ARTS			Operations Research	4	4.76
Art	26	3.59	Social Work/Social Welfare	30	4.33
Drama/Theatre	12	4.58	**SCIENCES**		
ENGINEERING			Astronomy	22	4.20
Aerospace Engineering	17	4.52	Bacteriology/Microbiology	24	4.50
Agricultural Engineering	18	4.61	Biochemistry	31	4.13
Architectural Engineering	2	4.73	Biology	41	3.32
Ceramic Engineering	10	4.28	Botany	11	4.63
Chemical Engineering	45	4.47	Cell Biology	15	4.30
Civil Engineering	38	4.21	Chemistry	24	4.53
Computer Engineering	42	4.11	Computer Science	35	3.85
Electrical Engineering	57	4.36	Earth Science	8	4.57
Engineering Science	6	4.63	Entomology	21	4.41
Industrial Engineering	23	4.52	Geology/Geoscience	12	4.70
Mechanical Engineering	27	4.55	Mathematics	35	4.40
Metallurgical Engineering	7	4.83	Meteorology	4	4.80
Mining & Mineral Engineering	9	4.79	Molecular Biology	20	4.45
Nuclear Engineering	9	4.68	Nutrition	16	4.63
Petroleum Engineering	8	4.75	Physics	34	4.51
HUMANITIES			**SOCIAL SCIENCES**		
Art History	26	3.54	American Studies	33	3.02
German	22	4.52	Anthropology	22	4.51
Spanish	28	4.38	Geography	3	4.86
Speech/Rhetoric	6	4.77	Psychology	29	4.32
			Social Work/Social Welfare	30	4.33
PROFESSIONAL					
Accounting	20	4.52	**TECHNICAL**		
Architecture	35	3.11	Agricultural Business	3	4.77
Business Administration	19	4.57	Agricultural Economics	13	4.50
Finance	18	4.63	Agriculture	13	4.52
Hotel, Restaurant, Institutional			Agronomy	13	4.66
Management	12	4.46	Animal Science	13	4.58
Journalism and Mass			Dairy Sciences	4	4.76
Communications	21	4.40	Food Sciences	9	4.63
Landscape Architecture	17	4.58	Food Services Management	8	4.60
Management	21	4.55	Forestry	3	4.75
Marketing	17	4.55	Horticulture	12	4.71
Nursing	33	4.25	Parks Management	3	4.78
			Poultry Sciences	9	4.72

PENNSYLVANIA STATE UNIVERSITY-UNIVERSITY PARK
(CONTINUED)

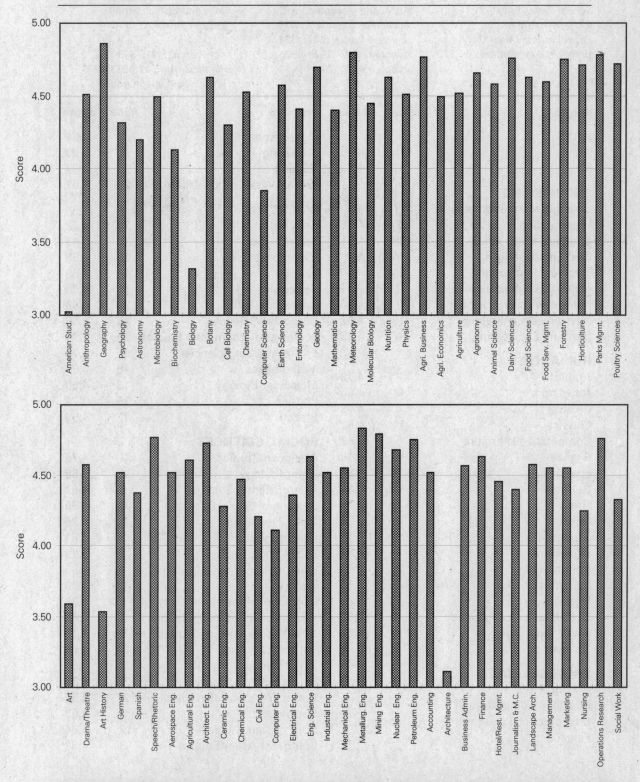

PENNSYLVANIA, UNIVERSITY OF

Contact Information
School Type: Private
Affiliation: None
Environment: Major City
Undergrad Enrollment: 14,520

Admissions
Applicants accepted: NR
Acceptees attending: 47%
Average Verbal SAT: 594
Average Math SAT: 680
Average ACT: 29

General Information
34th and Spruce Street
Philadelphia, PA 19104

Admissions: 215-898-7507
Financial Aid: 215-898-1988
Web: www.upenn.edu

Program	Rank	Score	Program	Rank	Score
ARTS			Management	1	4.91
Art	10	4.48	Marketing	1	4.90
Music	17	4.63	Nursing	3	4.87
			Social Work/Social Welfare	20	4.52
ENGINEERING					
Bioengineering/Biomedical			**SCIENCES**		
Engineering	2	4.88	Astronomy	20	4.22
Chemical Engineering	29	4.61	Astrophysics	8	4.45
Civil Engineering	44	4.15	Biochemistry	13	4.55
Electrical Engineering	54	4.40	Biology	18	4.62
Materials Engineering/Materials			Biophysics	8	4.68
Science And Engineering	7	4.80	Chemistry	28	4.48
Mechanical Engineering	18	4.67	Computer Science	18	4.58
Systems Engineering	4	4.75	Ecology/Environmental Studies	6	4.76
			Environmental Sciences	7	4.70
HUMANITIES			Mathematics	18	4.63
Arabic	3	4.73	Molecular Biology	13	4.60
Art History	11	4.60	Physics	15	4.74
Chinese	4	4.73	Statistics	17	4.59
Classics	11	4.59			
Comparative Literature	6	4.69	**SOCIAL SCIENCES**		
English	10	4.78	American Studies	2	4.76
French	8	4.80	Anthropology	4	4.88
German	15	4.62	Asian/Oriental Studies	6	4.62
Greek	5	4.72	Behavioral Sciences	5	4.70
Hebrew	1	4.91	Child Psychology	10	4.26
Japanese	3	4.73	Communication	3	4.81
Linguistics	4	4.85	East Asian Studies	3	4.79
Portuguese	8	4.61	Economics	8	4.83
Religious Studies	15	4.56	History	13	4.70
Russian	4	4.83	International Relations	5	4.78
Scandinavian Languages	8	4.66	Labor and Industrial Relations	2	4.85
Slavic Languages	10	4.63	Near/Middle Eastern Studies	5	4.75
Spanish	1	4.91	Political Science	22	4.63
			Psychology	3	4.64
PROFESSIONAL			Russian/Slavic Studies	9	4.67
Accounting	1	4.92	Social Work/Social Welfare	20	4.52
Business Administration	1	4.91	Sociology	12	4.63
Environmental Design	6	4.74	South Asian Studies	2	4.84
Finance	1	4.92	Southeast Asian Studies	3	4.83

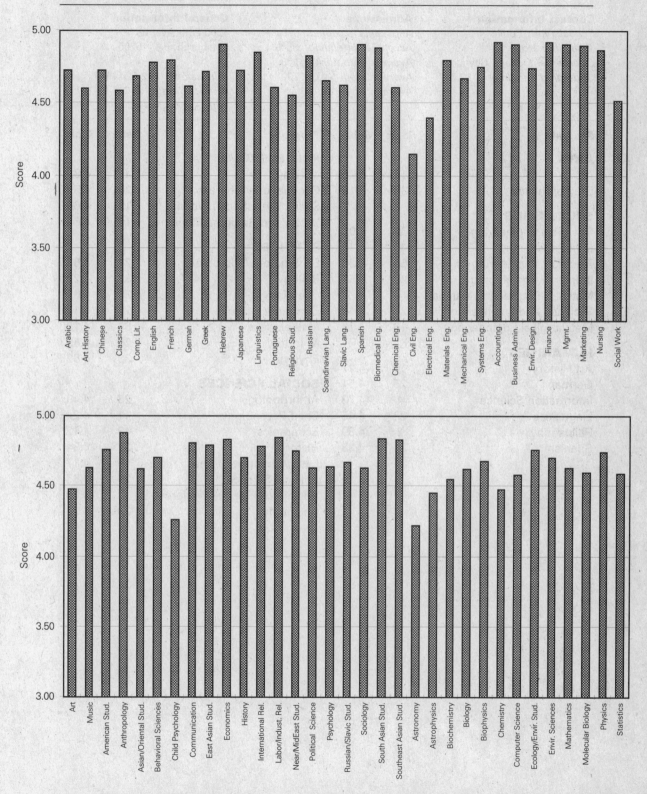

PITTSBURGH, UNIVERSITY OF

Contact Information
School Type: Public
Affiliation: None
Environment: Major City
Undergrad Enrollment: 12,757

Admissions
Applicants accepted: 67%
Acceptees attending: 35%
Average Verbal SAT: 573
Average Math SAT: 570
Average ACT: 25

General Information
4200 Fifth Avenue
Pittsburgh, PA 15260

Admissions: 412-624-PITT
Financial Aid: 412-624-PITT
Web: www.pitt.edu

Program	Rank	Score
ARTS		
Art	17	4.25
Drama/Theatre	38	3.18
ENGINEERING		
Chemical Engineering	69	4.05
Civil Engineering	48	4.10
Electrical Engineering	64	4.26
Industrial Engineering	20	4.57
Materials Engineering/Materials		
Science And Engineering	27	4.40
Metallurgical Engineering	16	4.73
HUMANITIES		
Art History	17	4.27
German	23	4.51
Information Science	4	4.73
Linguistics	23	4.45
Philosophy	2	4.89
Spanish	31	4.33

Program	Rank	Score
PROFESSIONAL		
Nursing	6	4.83
Occupational Therapy	20	4.55
Social Work/Social Welfare	13	4.60
Urban and Regional Planning	10	4.64
SCIENCES		
Bacteriology/Microbiology	21	4.63
Biology	32	4.29
Chemistry	35	4.39
Computer Science	29	4.14
Mathematics	56	4.12
Nutrition	20	4.55
Physics	33	4.52
SOCIAL SCIENCES		
Anthropology	23	4.49
Child Psychology	11	4.24
Economics	43	4.12
History	37	4.34
Latin American Studies	16	4.17
Political Science	27	4.55
Social Work/Social Welfare	13	4.60
Sociology	29	4.27

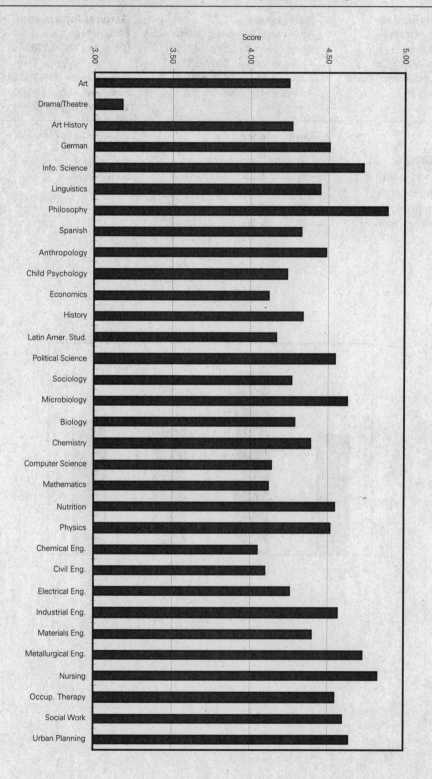

POLYTECHNIC UNIVERSITY

Contact Information
School Type: Private
Affiliation: None
Environment: Major City
Undergrad Enrollment: 1,588

Admissions
Applicants accepted: 81%
Acceptees attending: 48%
Average Verbal SAT: 530
Average Math SAT: 620
Average ACT: NR

General Information
6 Metrotech Center
Brooklyn, NY 11201

Admissions: 718-260-3600
Financial Aid: 718-260-3300
Web: www.poly.edu

Program	Rank	Score
ENGINEERING		
Aerospace Engineering	41	4.13
Electrical Engineering	16	4.73
Industrial Engineering	41	4.20
Mechanical Engineering	45	4.26

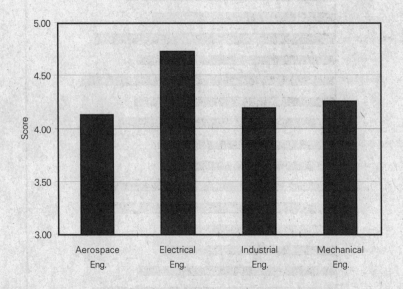

POMONA COLLEGE

Contact Information
School Type: Private
Affiliation: None
Environment: Suburban
Undergrad Enrollment: 1,428

Admissions
Applicants accepted: 34%
Acceptees attending: 27%
Average Verbal SAT: 702
Average Math SAT: 703
Average ACT: 31

General Information
333 North College Way
Claremont, CA 91711

Admissions: 909-621-8134
Financial Aid: 909-621-8205
Web: www.pomona.edu

Program	*Rank*	*Score*	*Program*	*Rank*	*Score*
HUMANITIES			**SOCIAL SCIENCES**		
English	36	4.23	Political Science	46	4.26

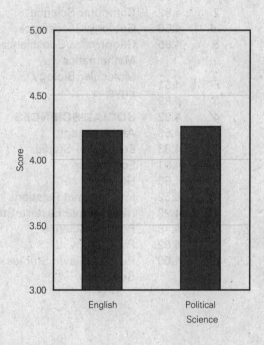

PRINCETON UNIVERSITY

Contact Information
School Type: Private
Affiliation: None
Environment: Suburban
Undergrad Enrollment: 4,601

Admissions
Applicants accepted: 13%
Acceptees attending: 67%
Average Verbal SAT: 725
Average Math SAT: 725
Average ACT: NR

General Information
Box 430
Princeton, NJ 08544

Admissions: 609-258-3060
Financial Aid: 609-258-3330
Web: www.princeton.edu

Program	Rank	Score	Program	Rank	Score
ARTS			**PROFESSIONAL**		
Art	3	4.83	Architecture	4	4.58
Music	3	4.90	Sociology	19	4.53
ENGINEERING			**SCIENCES**		
Aerospace Engineering	3	4.84	Astrophysics	3	4.79
Chemical Engineering	12	4.74	Biochemistry	17	4.46
Civil Engineering	12	4.66	Biology	25	4.45
Electrical Engineering	13	4.76	Chemistry	13	4.75
Engineering Physics	2	4.82	Computer Science	12	4.69
Geological Engineering	16	4.56	Geology/Geoscience	3	4.89
Mechanical Engineering	5	4.86	Geophysics/Geoscience	8	4.76
			Mathematics	1	4.92
HUMANITIES			Molecular Biology	10	4.68
Arabic	5	4.61	Physics	4	4.89
Art History	3	4.89			
Classics	4	4.82	**SOCIAL SCIENCES**		
Comparative Literature	8	4.63	Anthropology	40	4.16
English	7	4.83	East Asian Studies	9	4.61
French	2	4.91	Economics	4	4.89
German	3	4.86	History	3	4.91
Hebrew	18	4.52	International Relations	2	4.85
Philosophy	1	4.90	Near/Middle Eastern Studies	3	4.79
Religious Studies	4	4.78	Political Science	11	4.78
Slavic Languages	2	4.82	Psychology	18	4.45
Spanish	16	4.60	Russian/Slavic Studies	3	4.81
			Sociology	19	4.53

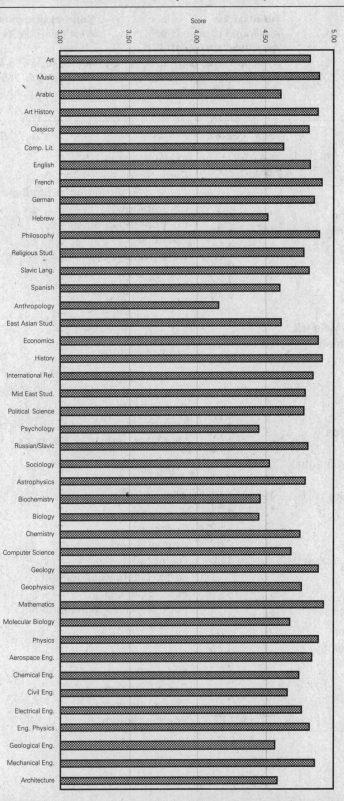

PURDUE UNIVERSITY-WEST LAFAYETTE

Contact Information
School Type: Public
Affiliation: None
Environment: City
Undergrad Enrollment: 26,401

Admissions
Applicants accepted: 90%
Acceptees attending: 43%
Average Verbal SAT: 528
Average Math SAT: 556
Average ACT: 24

General Information
West Lafayette, IN 47907

Admissions: 765-494-4600
Financial Aid: 765-494-5050
Web: www.purdue.edu

Program	Rank	Score
ARTS		
Ceramic Art/Design	9	4.50
ENGINEERING		
Aerospace Engineering	9	4.71
Agricultural Engineering	15	4.71
Chemical Engineering	15	4.72
Civil Engineering	8	4.77
Computer Engineering	6	4.77
Electrical Engineering	11	4.79
Industrial Engineering	4	4.81
Materials Engineering/Materials Science And Engineering	29	4.36
Mechanical Engineering	6	4.85
Nuclear Engineering	12	4.61
PROFESSIONAL		
Accounting	9	4.76
Business Administration	9	4.73
Finance	9	4.79
Hotel, Restaurant, Institutional Management	7	4.67
Landscape Architecture	19	4.53
Management	13	4.71
Marketing	8	4.72
Operations Research	8	4.61
Speech Pathology/Audiology	4	4.86
SCIENCES		
Applied Mathematics	10	4.61
Astrophysics	7	4.53
Atmospheric Sciences	6	4.64
Bacteriology/Microbiology	14	4.73
Biochemistry	22	4.33
Biology	19	4.59
Biophysics	6	4.73
Botany	16	4.48
Cell Biology	8	4.67

Program	Rank	Score
Chemistry	15	4.71
Earth Science	9	4.52
Ecology/Environmental Studies	13	4.49
Entomology	9	4.69
Environmental Sciences	11	4.53
Genetics	7	4.69
Geophysics/Geoscience	14	4.65
Mathematics	22	4.58
Meteorology	7	4.67
Molecular Biology	14	4.58
Nutrition	6	4.80
Statistics	5	4.81
Wildlife Biology	3	4.82
SOCIAL SCIENCES		
American Studies	30	3.08
Communication	15	4.25
Economics	33	4.40
Labor and Industrial Relations	7	4.61
TECHNICAL		
Agricultural Business	8	4.56
Agricultural Economics	10	4.67
Agriculture	4	4.85
Agronomy	4	4.84
Animal Science	5	4.82
Dietetics	4	4.82
Farm/Ranch Management	9	4.52
Food Sciences	7	4.72
Food Services Management	6	4.66
Forestry	9	4.67
Home Economics	4	4.79
Horticulture	4	4.85
Natural Resource Management	5	4.65
Parks Management	15	4.43
Poultry Sciences	12	4.66
Wildlife Biology	3	4.82

PURDUE UNIVERSITY-WEST LAFAYETTE (CONTINUED)

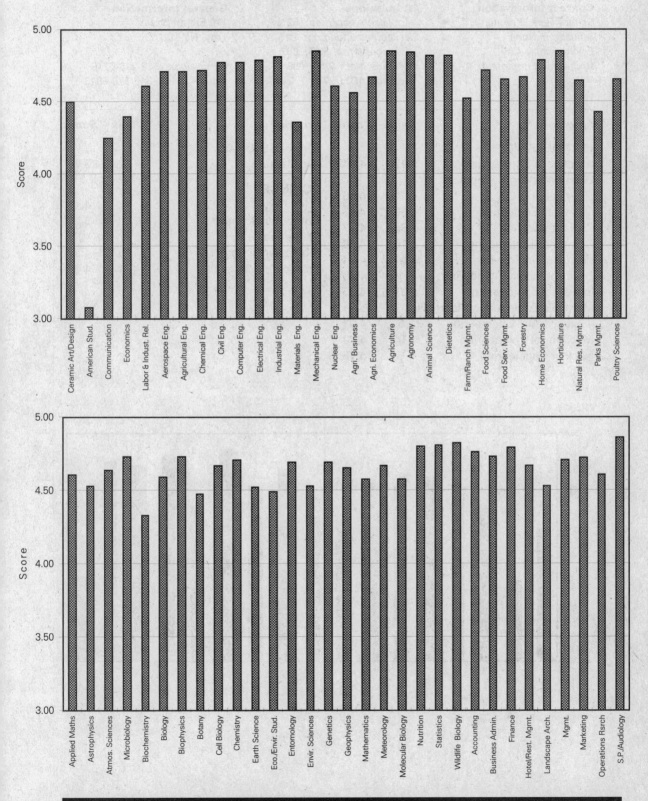

RENSSELAER POLYTECHNIC INSTITUTE

Contact Information
School Type: Private
Affiliation: None
Environment: City
Undergrad Enrollment: 4,137

Admissions
Applicants accepted: 82%
Acceptees attending: 24%
Average Verbal SAT: 607
Average Math SAT: 658
Average ACT: 27

General Information
110 Eighth Street
Troy, NY 12180

Admissions: 518-276-6216
Financial Aid: 518-276-6813
Web: www.rpi.edu

Program	Rank	Score
ENGINEERING		
Aerospace Engineering	12	4.64
Bioengineering/Biomedical Engineering	9	4.56
Chemical Engineering	56	4.23
Civil Engineering	34	4.27
Computer Engineering	15	4.68
Electrical Engineering	41	4.54
Environmental Engineering	1	4.86
Industrial Engineering	31	4.35
Materials Engineering/Materials Science And Engineering	6	4.81
Mechanical Engineering	14	4.72
Nuclear Engineering	6	4.75

Program	Rank	Score
PROFESSIONAL		
Architecture	17	3.74
SCIENCES		
Chemistry	47	4.16
Computer Science	39	3.70
Mathematics	37	4.37
Molecular Biology	15	4.57
Physics	24	4.61

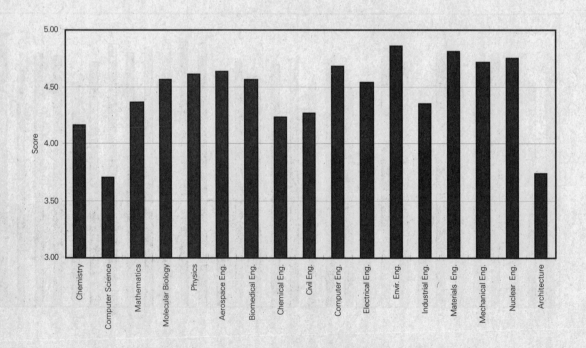

RICE UNIVERSITY

Contact Information
School Type: Private
Affiliation: None
Environment: Major City
Undergrad Enrollment: 2,633

Admissions
Applicants accepted: NR
Acceptees attending: 43%
Average Verbal SAT: NR
Average Math SAT: NR
Average ACT: NR

General Information
Office of Admissions
P.O. Box 1892
Houston, TX 77251
Admissions: 713-527-4036
Financial Aid: 713-527-4958
Web: www.rice.edu

Program	Rank	Score
ENGINEERING		
Chemical Engineering	34	4.57
Civil Engineering	33	4.29
Electrical Engineering	43	4.52
Materials Engineering/Materials Science And Engineering	5	4.83
Mechanical Engineering	32	4.47
HUMANITIES		
French	22	4.36
German	21	4.53
Linguistics	21	4.50

Program	Rank	Score
PROFESSIONAL		
Architecture	8	4.32
SCIENCES		
Biochemistry	20	4.38
Biology	46	3.61
Chemistry	29	4.47
Computer Science	25	4.33
Ecology/Environmental Studies	9	4.65
Geology/Geoscience	45	4.12
Mathematics	26	4.52
Statistics	18	4.57
SOCIAL SCIENCES		
History	38	4.33

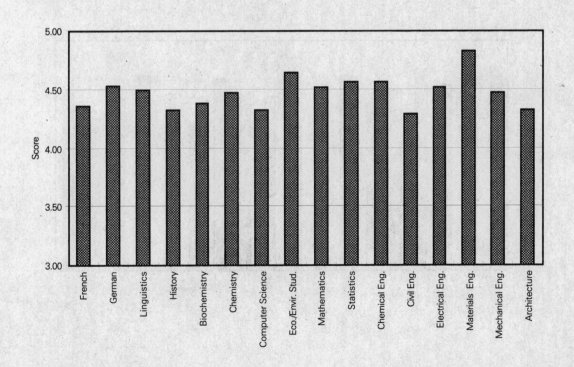

ROCHESTER, UNIVERSITY OF

Contact Information
School Type: Private
Affiliation: None
Environment: Suburban
Undergrad Enrollment: 4,727

Admissions
Applicants accepted: 52%
Acceptees attending: 18%
Average Verbal SAT: 640
Average Math SAT: 650
Average ACT: 28

General Information
Wilson Boulevard
Rochester, NY 14627

Admissions: 716-275-3221
Financial Aid: 716-275-3226
Web: www.rochester.edu

Program	Rank	Score	Program	Rank	Score
ARTS			**SCIENCES**		
Music	11	4.77	Bacteriology/Microbiology	17	4.70
			Biology	36	4.11
ENGINEERING			Cell Biology	16	4.26
Chemical Engineering	42	4.50	Chemistry	26	4.51
Mechanical Engineering	41	4.33	Computer Science	19	4.55
			Genetics	8	4.66
HUMANITIES			Mathematics	43	4.28
English	29	4.40	Physics	32	4.53
Linguistics	17	4.62	Statistics	11	4.70
PROFESSIONAL			**SOCIAL SCIENCES**		
Nursing	15	4.55	Economics	12	4.76
			History	20	4.57
			Political Science	28	4.54

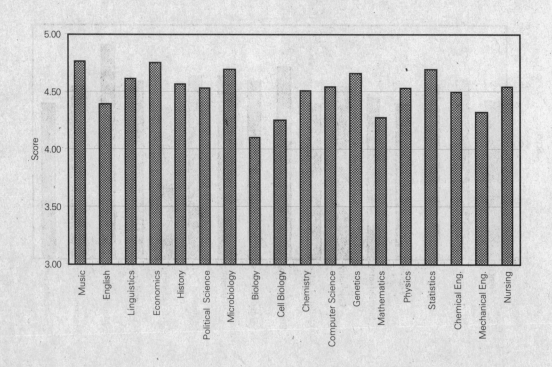

RUTGERS UNIVERSITY, NEW BRUNSWICK

Contact Information
School Type: NR
Affiliation: None
Environment: NR
Undergrad Enrollment:

Admissions
Applicants accepted: NR
Acceptees attending: NR
Average Verbal SAT: NR
Average Math SAT: NR
Average ACT: NR

General Information
P.O. Box 2101
New Brunswick, NJ 08903-2101
Admissions: 732-932-info
Web: www.rutgers.edu

Program	Rank	Score	Program	Rank	Score
ARTS			Biology	45	3.16
Art	25	3.64	Botany	27	4.17
Music	23	4.49	Computer Science	33	3.90
			Entomology	25	4.28
ENGINEERING			Genetics	10	4.58
Agricultural Engineering	28	4.36	Mathematics	23	4.57
Ceramic Engineering	9	4.33	Statistics	14	4.63
Mechanical Engineering	44	4.28			
			SOCIAL SCIENCES		
HUMANITIES			Anthropology	25	4.46
Art History	24	3.64	Economics	46	4.06
English	18	4.64	Geography	21	4.35
			History	27	4.50
PROFESSIONAL			Political Science	29	4.53
Urban and Regional Planning	2	4.81			
			TECHNICAL		
SCIENCES			Agriculture	14	4.51
Bacteriology/Microbiology	11	4.78	Agronomy	14	4.62
Biochemistry	26	4.20			

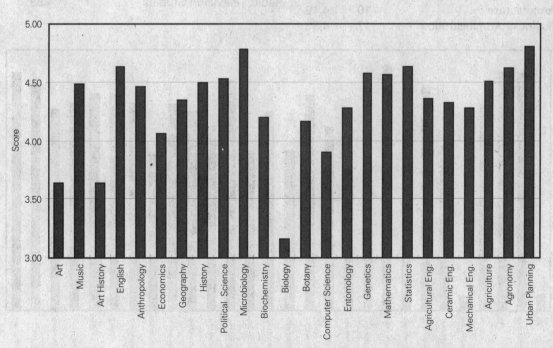

SOUTHERN CALIFORNIA, UNIVERSITY OF

Contact Information
School Type: Private
Affiliation: None
Environment: Major City
Undergrad Enrollment: 13,716

Admissions
Applicants accepted: 72%
Acceptees attending: 31%
Average Verbal SAT: 579
Average Math SAT: 608
Average ACT: 25

General Information
University Park
Los Angeles, CA 90089

Admissions: 213-740-1111
Financial Aid: 213-740-1111
Web: www.usc.edu

Program	Rank	Score
ARTS		
Art	39	3.12
Drama/Theatre	5	4.83
Film	2	4.83
Music	19	4.58
ENGINEERING		
Aerospace Engineering	18	4.52
Civil Engineering	37	4.22
Electrical Engineering	12	4.77
Industrial Engineering	27	4.42
Mechanical Engineering	28	4.53
HUMANITIES		
Art History	40	3.11
Spanish	34	4.26
PROFESSIONAL		
Accounting	18	4.58
Architecture	10	4.19
Business Administration	17	4.59

Program	Rank	Score
Finance	16	4.65
Journalism and Mass Communications	10	4.66
Management	19	4.59
Marketing	18	4.54
Occupational Therapy	10	4.72
Urban and Regional Planning	1	4.83
SCIENCES		
Astronomy	25	4.15
Biochemistry	32	4.10
Chemistry	34	4.41
Computer Science	14	4.65
Mathematics	47	4.22
SOCIAL SCIENCES		
Communication	5	4.71
Economics	34	4.38
Radio/Television Studies	1	4.89

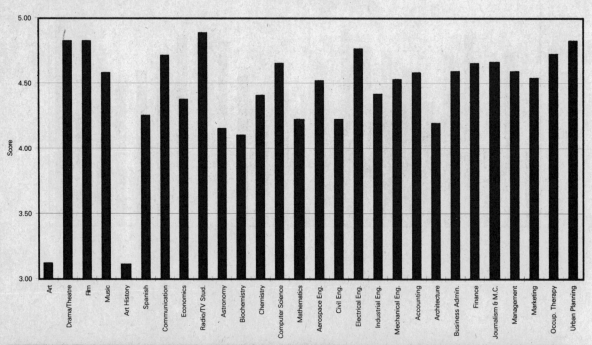

STANFORD UNIVERSITY

Contact Information
School Type: Private
Affiliation: None
Environment: Suburban
Undergrad Enrollment: 6,550

Admissions
Applicants accepted: 16%
Acceptees attending: 61%
Average Verbal SAT: 703
Average Math SAT: 709
Average ACT: 32

General Information
Stanford, CA 94305

Admissions: 415-723-2091
Financial Aid: 415-723-3058
Web: www.stanford.edu

Program	Rank	Score	Program	Rank	Score
ARTS			**PROFESSIONAL**		
Art	7	4.59	Sociology	6	4.71
Drama/Theatre	7	4.75	**SCIENCES**		
Music	13	4.71	Bacteriology/Microbiology	10	4.79
ENGINEERING			Biology	10	4.76
Chemical Engineering	6	4.82	Chemistry	6	4.90
Civil Engineering	4	4.85	Earth Science	12	4.41
Electrical Engineering	2	4.91	Geology/Geoscience	5	4.85
Industrial Engineering	1	4.90	Geophysics/Geoscience	4	4.83
Mechanical Engineering	2	4.92	Mathematics	6	4.84
Petroleum Engineering	6	4.81	Physics	7	4.85
HUMANITIES			Statistics	2	4.90
Art History	7	4.78	**SOCIAL SCIENCES**		
Chinese	7	4.65	American Studies	23	3.31
Classics	13	4.53	Anthropology	6	4.85
Comparative Literature	9	4.61	Asian/Oriental Studies	12	4.37
English	5	4.86	Communication	2	4.84
French	10	4.74	East Asian Studies	6	4.70
German	7	4.77	Economics	3	4.90
Japanese	11	4.40	History	5	4.88
Linguistics	9	4.74	International Relations	10	4.62
Philosophy	6	4.78	Latin American Studies	5	4.66
Portuguese	3	4.80	Political Science	7	4.84
Religious Studies	16	4.53	Psychology	1	4.66
Russian	9	4.70	Sociology	6	4.71
Spanish	9	4.75			

Score

Art	
Drama/Theatre	
Music	
Art History	
Chinese	
Classics	
Comp. Lit.	
English	
French	
German	
Japanese	
Linguistics	
Philosophy	
Portuguese	
Religious Stud.	
Russian	
Spanish	
American Stud.	
Anthropology	
Asian/Orient Stud.	
Communication	
East Asian Stud.	
Economics	
History	
International Rel.	
Latin Amer. Stud.	
Political Science	
Psychology	
Sociology	
Microbiology	
Biology	
Chemistry	
Earth Science	
Geology	
Geophysics	
Mathematics	
Physics	
Statistics	
Chemical Eng.	
Civil Eng.	
Electrical Eng.	
Industrial Eng.	
Mechanical Eng.	
Petroleum Eng.	

STATE UNIVERSITY OF NEW YORK AT BINGHAMTON

Contact Information
School Type: Public
Affiliation: None
Environment: Suburban
Undergrad Enrollment: 9,349

Admissions
Applicants accepted: 42%
Acceptees attending: 28%
Average Verbal SAT: 595
Average Math SAT: 619
Average ACT: NR

General Information
P.O. Box 6000
Binghamton, NY 13902

Admissions: 607-777-2171
Financial Aid: 607-777-2428
Web: www.binghamton.edu

Program	*Rank*	*Score*
SCIENCES		
Geophysics/Geoscience	22	4.51
SOCIAL SCIENCES		
Anthropology	33	4.30

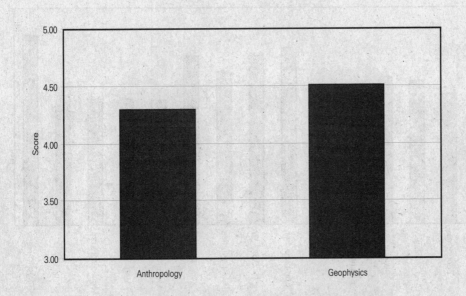

STATE UNIVERSITY OF NEW YORK AT STONY BROOK

Contact Information
School Type: Public
Affiliation: None
Environment: Suburban
Undergrad Enrollment: 11,267

Admissions
Applicants accepted: 58%
Acceptees attending: 24%
Average Verbal SAT: 520
Average Math SAT: 560
Average ACT: NR

General Information
Stony Brook, NY 11794

Admissions: 516-632-6868
Financial Aid: 516-632-6840
Web: www.sunysb.edu

Program	Rank	Score	Program	Rank	Score
ENGINEERING			**SCIENCES**		
Electrical Engineering	72	4.15	Biochemistry	27	4.19
Engineering Science	11	4.16	Biology	35	4.19
Mechanical Engineering	52	4.16	Computer Science	15	4.63
			Geology/Geoscience	19	4.58
HUMANITIES			Mathematics	34	4.41
English	28	4.43	Physics	29	4.56
PROFESSIONAL			**SOCIAL SCIENCES**		
Nursing	29	4.32	Economics	39	4.20
Physical Therapy	7	4.75	History	39	4.32
			Psychology	26	4.36

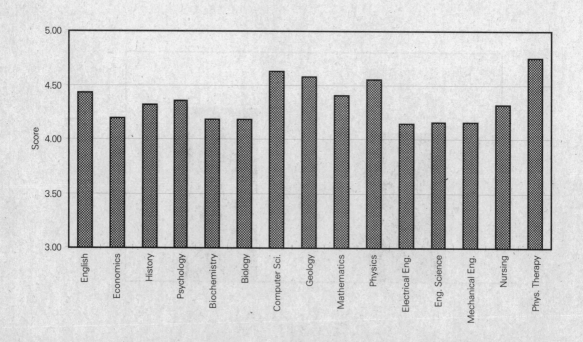

STATE UNIVERSITY OF NEW YORK AT BUFFALO

Contact Information
School Type: Public
Affiliation: None
Environment: City
Undergrad Enrollment: 9,421

Admissions
Applicants accepted: 60%
Acceptees attending: 31%
Average Verbal SAT: 485
Average Math SAT: 480
Average ACT: NR

General Information
1300 Elmwood Avenue
Buffalo, NY 14222

Admissions: 716-878-4017
Financial Aid: 716-878-4902
Web: www.snybuf.edu

Program	Rank	Score	Program	Rank	Score
ENGINEERING			Sociology	29	4.35
Aerospace Engineering	25	4.38	Speech Pathology/Audiology	18	4.59
Chemical Engineering	44	4.48			
Civil Engineering	47	4.11	**SCIENCES**		
Electrical Engineering	79	4.05	Biology	39	3.85
Industrial Engineering	28	4.40	Biophysics	13	4.40
Mechanical Engineering	50	4.19	Cell Biology	19	4.16
			Computer Science	28	4.18
HUMANITIES			Mathematics	45	4.25
French	29	4.19	Molecular Biology	16	4.53
Spanish	25	4.43	Statistics	23	4.49
PROFESSIONAL			**SOCIAL SCIENCES**		
Accounting	36	4.13	American Studies	24	3.27
Business Administration	24	4.46	Anthropology	31	4.33
Management	40	4.18	Communication	16	4.20
Nursing	31	4.28	Geography	17	4.46
Occupational Therapy	6	4.79	History	45	4.14
Physical Therapy	6	4.77	Political Science	37	4.42
			Sociology	29	4.35

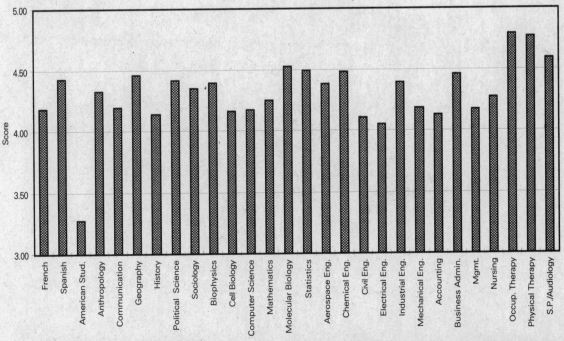

SWARTHMORE COLLEGE

Contact Information
School Type: Private
Affiliation: None
Environment: Suburban
Undergrad Enrollment: 1,435

Admissions
Applicants accepted: 30%
Acceptees attending: 34%
Average Verbal SAT: 689
Average Math SAT: 673
Average ACT: NR

General Information
500 College Avenue
Swarthmore, PA 19081

Admissions: 610-328-8300
Financial Aid: 610-328-8358
Web: www.swarthmore.edu

Program	Rank	Score
HUMANITIES		
English	38	4.19

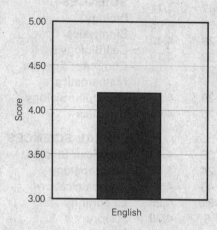

TEXAS A&M UNIVERSITY AT COLLEGE STATION

Contact Information
School Type: Public
Affiliation: None
Environment: City
Undergrad Enrollment: 31,914

Admissions
Applicants accepted: 69%
Acceptees attending: 58%
Average Verbal SAT: 630
Average Math SAT: 660
Average ACT: 28

General Information
College Station, TX 77553

Admissions: 409-845-3741
Web: www.tamu.edu

Program	Rank	Score	Program	Rank	Score
ENGINEERING			Genetics	13	4.49
Aerospace Engineering	15	4.57	Geology/Geoscience	37	4.26
Agricultural Engineering	1	4.90	Geophysics/Geoscience	18	4.59
Chemical Engineering	32	4.37	Marine Biology	2	4.75
Civil Engineering	21	4.49	Marine Sciences	3	4.65
Electrical Engineering	46	4.21	Meteorology	10	4.56
Environmental Design	7	4.71	Nutrition	26	4.43
Industrial Engineering	10	4.66	Zoology	18	4.43
Nuclear Engineering	17	4.52			
Ocean Engineering	3	4.85	**SOCIAL SCIENCES**		
Petroleum Engineering	1	4.91	Economics	30	4.48
Bioengineering	8	4.57	**TECHNICAL**		
			Agricultural Economics	9	4.71
PROFESSIONAL			Agriculture	2	4.91
Accounting	22	4.49	Agronomy	2	4.88
Architecture	22	3.53	Animal Science	3	4.86
Business Administration	20	4.55	Dairy Sciences	11	4.55
Finance	19	4.62	Entomology	16	4.51
Landscape Architecture	2	4.89	Forestry	16	4.53
Management	24	4.50	Horticulture	2	4.90
Marketing	19	4.52	Ornamental Horticulture	3	4.80
			Parks Management	9	4.54
SCIENCES			Poultry Sciences	13	4.63
Chemistry	33	4.43			
Computer Science	53	3.24			

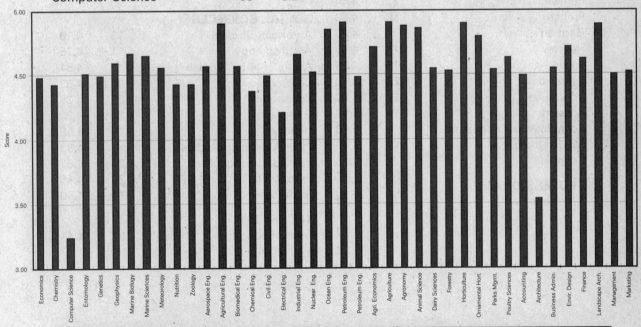

TEXAS-AUSTIN, UNIVERSITY OF

Contact Information
School Type: Public
Affiliation: None
Environment: City
Undergrad Enrollment: 35,789

Admissions
Applicants accepted: 61%
Acceptees attending: 61%
Average Verbal SAT: 601
Average Math SAT: 620
Average ACT: 25

General Information
Office of Admissions
Main Building Room 7
Austin, TX 78712
Admissions: 512-475-7399
Financial Aid: 512-475-6282
Web: www.utexas.edu

Program	Rank	Score	Program	Rank	Score
ARTS			Architecture	11	4.14
Art	28	3.54	Business Administration	13	4.65
Ceramic Art/Design	8	4.56	Finance	6	4.84
Drama/Theatre	45	3.04	Journalism and Mass		
Film	9	4.51	Communications	15	4.53
Music	22	4.52	Management	14	4.70
			Sociology	14	4.60
ENGINEERING					
Aerospace Engineering	19	4.51	**SCIENCES**		
Architectural Engineering	1	4.81	Astronomy	14	4.35
Chemical Engineering	26	4.63	Bacteriology/Microbiology	16	4.71
Civil Engineering	5	4.82	Biochemistry	28	4.17
Computer Engineering	43	4.10	Biology	40	3.81
Electrical Engineering	20	4.70	Botany	3	4.86
Mechanical Engineering	15	4.71	Chemistry	18	4.63
Petroleum Engineering	2	4.89	Computer Science	9	4.75
			Geology/Geoscience	13	4.69
HUMANITIES			Mathematics	29	4.48
Art History	29	3.48	Molecular Biology	18	4.50
Classics	8	4.69	Physics	21	4.67
Comparative Literature	22	4.23	Zoology	3	4.82
English	27	4.44			
French	18	4.50	**SOCIAL SCIENCES**		
German	6	4.80	American Studies	13	4.10
Hebrew	9	4.73	Anthropology	11	4.75
Italian	19	4.25	Asian/Oriental Studies	9	4.51
Linguistics	22	4.48	Communication	8	4.63
Portuguese	12	4.50	Economics	35	4.35
Russian	15	4.53	Geography	24	4.30
Scandinavian Languages	7	4.70	History	19	4.58
Slavic Languages	16	4.48	Latin American Studies	1	4.83
Spanish	3	4.86	Political Science	25	4.57
			Psychology	22	4.40
PROFESSIONAL			Sociology	14	4.60
Accounting	5	4.84			
			TECHNICAL		
			Home Economics	21	4.41

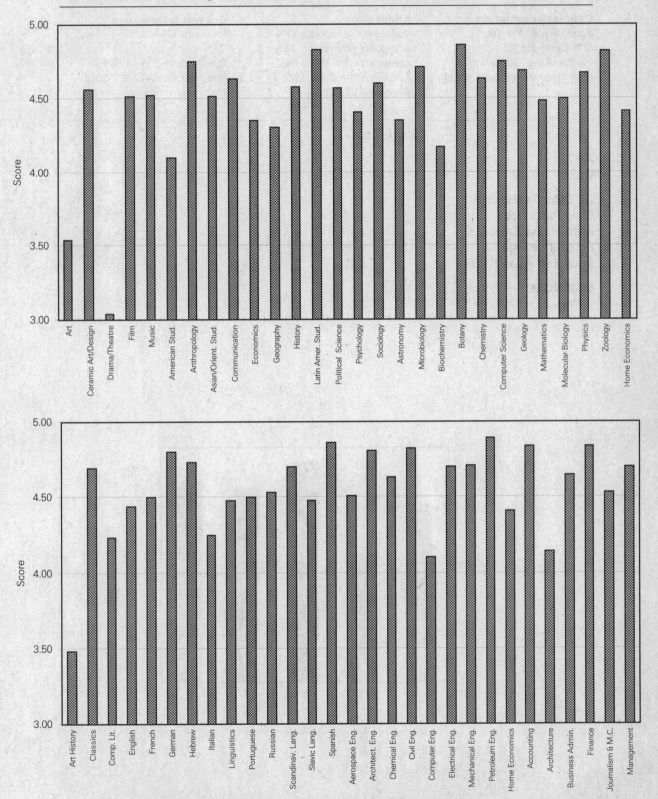

TUFTS UNIVERSITY

Contact Information
School Type: Private
Affiliation: None
Environment: Suburban
Undergrad Enrollment: 4,539

Admissions
Applicants accepted: 32%
Acceptees attending: 33%
Average Verbal SAT: 645
Average Math SAT: 665
Average ACT: 28

General Information
Medford, MA 02155

Admissions: 617-627-3170
Financial Aid: 617-627-3528
Web: www.tufts.edu

Program	*Rank*	*Score*
ARTS		
Drama/Theatre	14	4.46
SOCIAL SCIENCES		
Child Psychology	15	4.09
International Relations	1	4.88
Political Science	20	4.66
Southeast Asian Studies	8	4.72
SCIENCES		
Biology	37	3.90

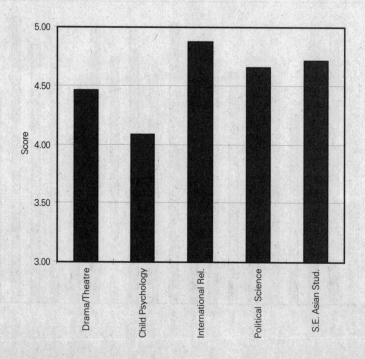

TULANE UNIVERSITY

Contact Information
School Type: Private
Affiliation: None
Environment: Major City
Undergrad Enrollment: 6,402

Admissions
Applicants accepted: 78%
Acceptees attending: 22%
Average Verbal SAT: 635
Average Math SAT: 622
Average ACT: NR

General Information
6823 St. Charles Avenue
New Orleans, LA 70118-5680
Admissions: 504-865-5731
Financial Aid: 504-865-5723
Web: www.tulane.edu

Program	Rank	Score	Program	Rank	Score
ARTS			**PROFESSIONAL**		
Drama/Theatre	22	3.78	Architecture	37	3.06
ENGINEERING			**SCIENCES**		
Bioengineering/Biomedical			Biology	46	3.15
Engineering	6	4.70	Mathematics	46	4.23
HUMANITIES			**SOCIAL SCIENCES**		
French	25	4.29	American Studies	26	3.18
Portuguese	11	4.52	Anthropology	38	4.19
			Latin American Studies	2	4.80
			Political Science	50	4.18

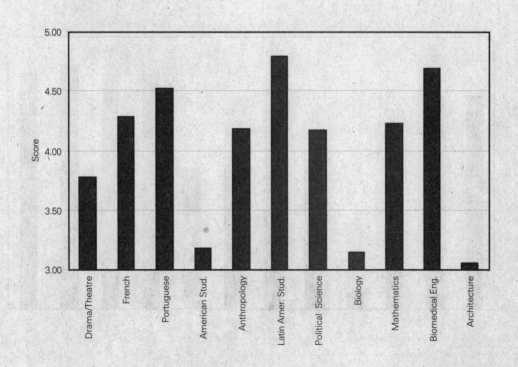

UNITED STATES AIR FORCE ACADEMY

Contact Information
School Type: Public
Affiliation: None
Environment: Suburban
Undergrad Enrollment: 4,083

Admissions
Applicants accepted: 18%
Acceptees attending: 73%
Average Verbal SAT: 626
Average Math SAT: 649
Average ACT: NR

General Information
2304 Cadet Drive, Suite 200
Colorado Springs, CO 80840-5025
Admissions: 719-333-2520
Web: www.usafa.af.mil

Program	Rank	Score	Program	Rank	Score
ENGINEERING			**SCIENCES**		
Aerospace Engineering	21	4.46	Biology	47	3.12
Civil Engineering	55	4.02	Mathematics	58	4.09
Electrical Engineering	81	4.03			
Engineering Mechanics	3	4.72	**SOCIAL SCIENCES**		
Engineering Science	3	4.79	Behavioral Sciences	8	4.57
			International Relations	13	4.57
PROFESSIONAL			Political Science	43	4.32
Operations Research	5	4.73			

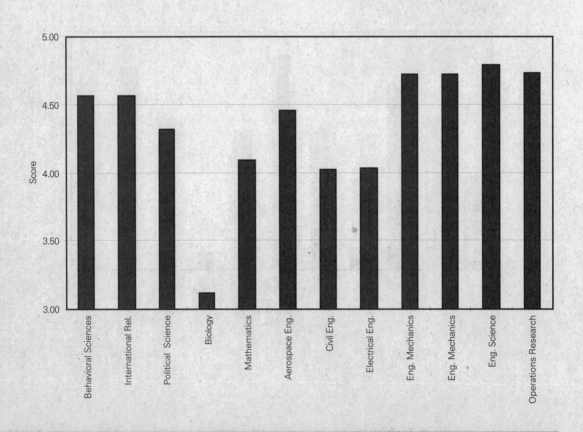

UNITED STATES MILITARY ACADEMY

Contact Information
School Type: Public
Affiliation: None
Environment: Rural
Undergrad Enrollment: 4,016

Admissions
Applicants accepted: 12%
Acceptees attending: 76%
Average Verbal SAT: 623
Average Math SAT: 643
Average ACT: 28

General Information
600 Thayer Road
West Point, NY 10996

Admissions: 914-938-4041
Financial Aid: 914-938-3516
Web: www.usma.edu

Program	Rank	Score	Program	Rank	Score
PROFESSIONAL			**SOCIAL SCIENCES**		
Operations Research	6	4.70	Behavioral Sciences	9	4.53
			International Relations	14	4.55
SCIENCES			Near/Middle Eastern Studies	17	4.51
Computer Science	46	3.39	Political Science	44	4.30

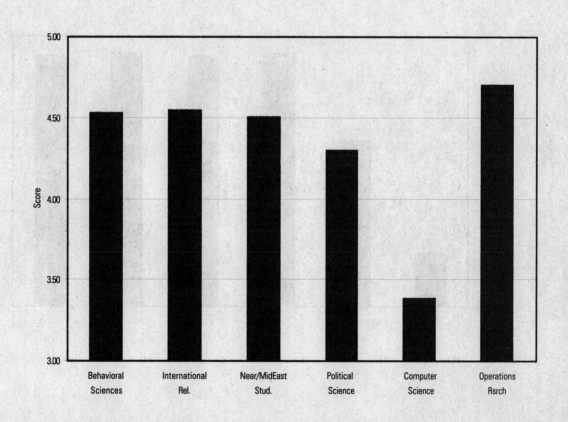

UNITED STATES NAVAL ACADEMY

Contact Information
School Type: Public
Affiliation: None
Environment: City
Undergrad Enrollment: 4,040

Admissions
Applicants accepted: 14%
Acceptees attending: 80%
Average Verbal SAT: 627
Average Math SAT: 653
Average ACT: NR

General Information
117 Decatur Road
Annapolis, MD 21402

Admissions: 410-267-4361
Financial Aid: 410-293-3306
Web: www.nadn.navy.mil

Program	Rank	Score	Program	Rank	Score
ENGINEERING			**SCIENCES**		
Aerospace Engineering	34	4.23	Computer Science	45	3.40
Naval Architecture	3	4.85			
MarineEngineering	2	4.87			
Ocean Engineering	2	4.87			
Systems Engineering	1	4.85			

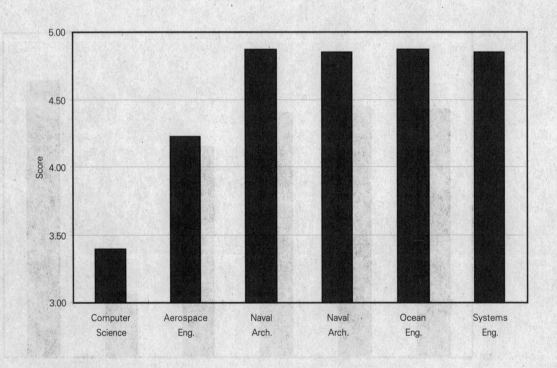

VANDERBILT UNIVERSITY

Contact Information
School Type: Private
Affiliation: None
Environment: Major City
Undergrad Enrollment: 5,807

Admissions
Applicants accepted: 60%
Acceptees attending: 30%
Average Verbal SAT: 637
Average Math SAT: 652
Average ACT: 28

General Information
2305 West End Avenue
Nashville, TN 37203-1727

Admissions: 615-322-2561
Financial Aid: 615-322-3591
Web: www.vanderbilt.edu

Program	Rank	Score	Program	Rank	Score
ENGINEERING			**SCIENCES**		
Civil Engineering	41	4.18	Biology	33	4.28
Mechanical Engineering	58	4.09	Chemistry	50	4.10
			Computer Science	56	3.18
HUMANITIES			Molecular Biology	21	4.43
Classics	23	4.10			
English	35	4.26	**SOCIAL SCIENCES**		
Religious Studies	12	4.63	Economics	36	4.31
Spanish	36	4.23	History	31	4.45
			Latin American Studies	8	4.52
			Political Science	31	4.51

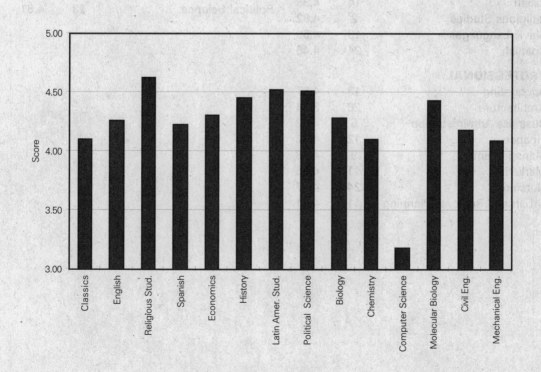

VIRGINIA, UNIVERSITY OF

Contact Information
School Type: Public
Affiliation: None
Environment: Suburban
Undergrad Enrollment: 12,211

Admissions
Applicants accepted: 33%
Acceptees attending: 50%
Average Verbal SAT: 643
Average Math SAT: 653
Average ACT: NR

General Information
Office of Admission
P.O. Box 9017
Charlottesville, VA 22906
Admissions: 804-982-3200
Financial Aid: 804-982-6000
Web: www.virginia.edu

Program	Rank	Score
ARTS		
Art	20	3.87
ENGINEERING		
Aerospace Engineering	13	4.62
Chemical Engineering	59	4.19
Mechanical Engineering	38	4.38
Nuclear Engineering	5	4.79
Systems Engineering	6	4.68
HUMANITIES		
Art History	20	3.85
English	21	4.59
French	11	4.71
German	9	4.71
Italian	14	4.38
Religious Studies	2	4.82
Slavic Languages	13	4.55
Spanish	24	4.46
PROFESSIONAL		
Accounting	13	4.67
Architecture	28	3.34
Business Administration	5	4.82
Finance	12	4.72
Management	9	4.78
Marketing	11	4.66
Nursing	24	4.37
Urban and Regional Planning	11	4.61

Program	Rank	Score
SCIENCES		
Applied Mathematics	15	4.37
Astronomy	15	4.32
Astrophysics	9	4.40
Biology	29	4.36
Chemistry	48	4.15
Computer Science	40	3.66
Environmental Sciences	8	4.65
Mathematics	36	4.38
SOCIAL SCIENCES		
Anthropology	30	4.35
Economics	23	4.60
History	18	4.61
International Relations	11	4.60
Political Science	23	4.61

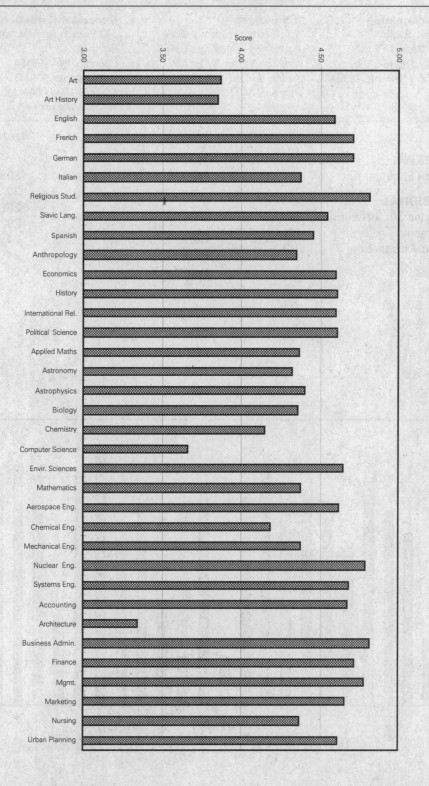

Score

WASHINGTON STATE UNIVERSITY

Contact Information
School Type: Public
Affiliation: None
Environment: Rural
Undergrad Enrollment: 16,686

Admissions
Applicants accepted: 89%
Acceptees attending: 39%
Average Verbal SAT: NR
Average Math SAT: NR
Average ACT: NR

General Information
342 French Administration
Building
Pullman, WA 99164
Admissions: 509-335-5586
Financial Aid: 509-335-9711
Web: www.wsu.edu

Program	Rank	Score
ENGINEERING		
Agricultural Engineering	31	4.30
PROFESSIONAL		
Hotel, Restaurant, Institutional Management	21	4.18
Landscape Architecture	23	4.43
SCIENCES		
Botany	28	4.13
Computer Science	57	3.14
Wildlife Biology	20	4.53
Zoology	10	4.64

Program	Rank	Score
TECHNICAL		
Agricultural Economics	20	4.20
Agriculture	26	4.34
Agronomy	26	4.38
Animal Science	29	4.08
Home Economics	24	4.35
Horticulture	24	4.48
Wildlife Biology	20	4.53

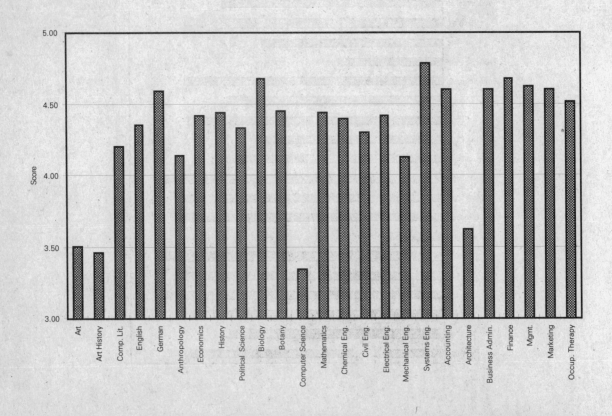

WASHINGTON, UNIVERSITY OF

Contact Information
School Type: Public
Affiliation: None
Environment: Major City
Undergrad Enrollment: 24,592

Admissions
Applicants accepted: NR.
Acceptees attending: 48%
Average Verbal SAT: NR
Average Math SAT: NR
Average ACT: NR

General Information
1400 NE Campus Parkway
Seattle, WA 98195

Admissions: 206-543-9686
Financial Aid: 206-543-6101
Web: www.washington.edu

Program	Rank	Score
ARTS		
Art	33	3.35
Drama/Theatre	4	4.85
Music	26	4.42
ENGINEERING		
Aerospace Engineering	14	4.60
Ceramic Engineering	8	4.48
Chemical Engineering	35	4.56
Civil Engineering	11	4.67
Electrical Engineering	67	4.22
Mechanical Engineering	30	4.50
HUMANITIES		
Art History	33	3.30
Chinese	11	4.46
Comparative Literature	15	4.41
English	25	4.48
French	27	4.25
German	25	4.47
Hebrew	20	4.48
Italian	22	4.21
Japanese	8	4.51
Linguistics	14	4.66
Russian	8	4.73
Scandinavian Languages	2	4.85
Slavic Languages	6	4.70
Spanish	27	4.40
PROFESSIONAL		
Accounting	11	4.70
Architecture	19	3.65
Business Administration	11	4.67
Finance	10	4.77
Journalism and Mass Communications	13	4.59

Program	Rank	Score
Landscape Architecture	15	4.61
Management	12	4.73
Marketing	9	4.71
Nursing	4	4.86
Occupational Therapy	13	4.66
Physical Therapy	5	4.80
Social Work/Social Welfare	12	4.63
Speech Pathology/Audiology	21	4.53
SCIENCES		
Astronomy	16	4.29
Bacteriology/Microbiology	4	4.86
Biology	11	4.72
Botany	15	4.50
Chemistry	31	4.45
Computer Science	13	4.67
Geology/Geoscience	23	4.51
Mathematics	21	4.60
Molecular Biology	19	4.48
Physics	17	4.72
Zoology	2	4.86
SOCIAL SCIENCES		
Anthropology	18	4.60
Asian/Oriental Studies	5	4.66
Communication	12	4.39
Economics	25	4.57
Geography	8	4.65
History	23	4.54
Near/Middle Eastern Studies	11	4.62
Political Science	26	4.56
Psychology	19	4.44
Russian/Slavic Studies	18	4.46
Social Work/Social Welfare	12	4.63
Sociology	8	4.69
South Asian Studies	3	4.81
TECHNICAL		
Forestry	7	4.69

WASHINGTON, UNIVERSITY OF (CONTINUED)

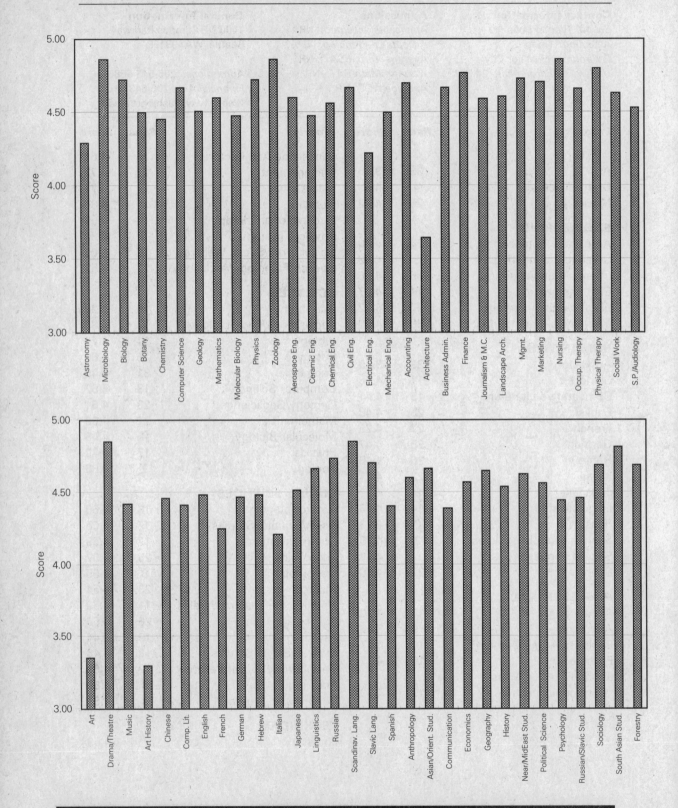

WAYNE STATE UNIVERSITY

Contact Information
School Type: Public
Affiliation: None
Environment: Major City
Undergrad Enrollment: 19,248

Admissions
Applicants accepted: 81%
Acceptees attending: 51%
Average Verbal SAT: NR
Average Math SAT: NR
Average ACT: 21

General Information
656 West Kirby
Detroit, MI 48202

Admissions: 313-577-3577
Financial Aid: 313-577-3378
Web: www.wayne.edu

Program	Rank	Score
ARTS		
Drama/Theatre	46	3.03
HUMANITIES		
Speech/Rhetoric	9	4.69
PROFESSIONAL		
Nursing	7	4.78
Occupational Therapy	3	4.85
Physical Therapy	17	4.53
Social Work/Social Welfare	7	4.71
Speech Pathology/Audiology	12	4.70

Program	Rank	Score
SCIENCES		
Bacteriology/Microbiology	26	4.43
Nutrition	24	4.47
SOCIAL SCIENCES		
Child Psychology	1	4.59
Communication	19	4.10
Labor and Industrial Relations	9	4.52
Social Work/Social Welfare	7	4.71
Sociology	13	4.62

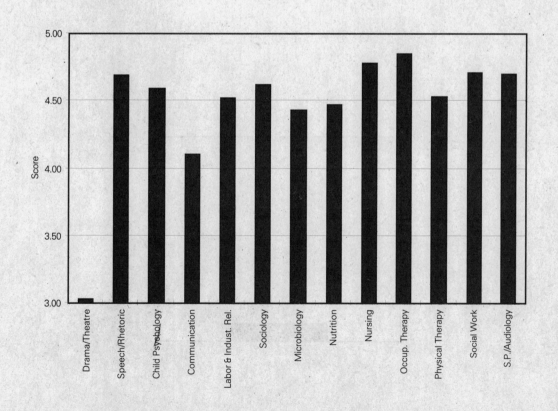

WILLIAMS COLLEGE

Contact Information
School Type: Private
Affiliation: None
Environment: Rural
Undergrad Enrollment: 1,992

Admissions
Applicants accepted: 24%
Acceptees attending: 44%
Average Verbal SAT: 710
Average Math SAT: 705
Average ACT: 30

General Information
P.O. Box 487
Williamstown, MA 01267

Admissions: 413-597-2211
Financial Aid: 413-597-4181
Web: www.williams.edu

Program	Rank	Score
SOCIAL SCIENCES		
American Studies	27	3.17

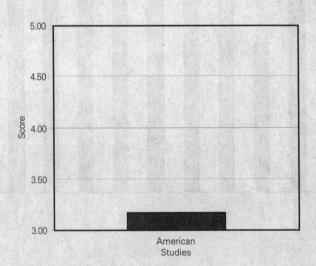

WISCONSIN-MADISON, UNIVERSITY OF

Contact Information
School Type: Public
Affiliation: None
Environment: City
Undergrad Enrollment: 26,910

Admissions
Applicants accepted: 69%
Acceptees attending: 44%
Average Verbal SAT: 610
Average Math SAT: 620
Average ACT: 26

General Information
140 Peterson Office Building 750
University Avenue
Madison, WI 53706
Admissions: 608-262-3961
Financial Aid: 608-262-3060
Web: www.wisc.edu

Program	Rank	Score	Program	Rank	Score
ARTS			Landscape Architecture	8	4.76
Art	31	3.42	Management	10	4.76
Drama/Theatre	16	4.30	Marketing	10	4.68
			Nursing	10	4.68
ENGINEERING			Occupational Therapy	12	4.68
Agricultural Engineering	9	4.82	Physical Therapy	4	4.83
Chemical Engineering	2	4.90	Social Work/Social Welfare	8	4.70
Civil Engineering	13	4.64			
Electrical Engineering	46	4.49	**SCIENCES**		
Engineering Mechanics	2	4.74	Applied Mathematics	5	4.76
Industrial Engineering	15	4.64	Astronomy	5	4.66
Mechanical Engineering	12	4.75	Bacteriology/Microbiology	8	4.81
Metallurgical Engineering	12	4.78	Biochemistry	4	4.85
Nuclear Engineering	4	4.80	Biology	5	4.87
			Botany	4	4.82
HUMANITIES			Cell Biology	3	4.83
Art History	31	3.41	Chemistry	10	4.80
Chinese	8	4.55	Computer Science	10	4.73
Comparative Literature	24	4.18	Earth Science	3	4.79
English	17	4.65	Ecology/Environmental Studies	7	4.72
French	13	4.67	Entomology	5	4.81
German	2	4.88	Genetics	4	4.82
Greek	8	4.59	Geology/Geoscience	14	4.68
Hebrew	2	4.90	Geophysics/Geoscience	15	4.63
Italian	8	4.53	Mathematics	9	4.78
Japanese	9	4.48	Molecular Biology	3	4.84
Linguistics	13	4.68	Nutrition	15	4.64
Philosophy	17	4.55	Physics	16	4.73
Portuguese	9	4.59	Statistics	4	4.83
Russian	10	4.68	Zoology	1	4.88
Scandinavian Languages	5	4.76			
Slavic Languages	7	4.68	**SOCIAL SCIENCES**		
Spanish	7	4.80	Anthropology	20	4.56
			Asian/Oriental Studies	13	4.33
PROFESSIONAL			Child Psychology	13	4.16
Accounting	10	4.73	Communication	11	4.43
Business Administration	8	4.74	Economics	9	4.82
Finance	8	4.80	Geography	2	4.89
Journalism and Mass			History	10	4.77
Communications	7	4.73	International Relations	8	4.69

Program	Rank	Score
Political Science	8	4.83
Psychology	16	4.47
Social Work/Social Welfare	8	4.70
Sociology	1	4.81
Southeast Asian Studies	7	4.74

TECHNICAL

Program	Rank	Score
Agricultural Business	9	4.50
Agricultural Economics	2	4.88
Agriculture	8	4.70
Agronomy	8	4.76
Animal Science	8	4.73
Dairy Sciences	1	4.91
Dietetics	10	4.61
Farm/Ranch Management	6	4.61
Food Sciences	18	4.30
Forestry	6	4.70
Home Economics	3	4.81
Horticulture	7	4.79
Natural Resource Management	11	4.40
Poultry Sciences	3	4.83

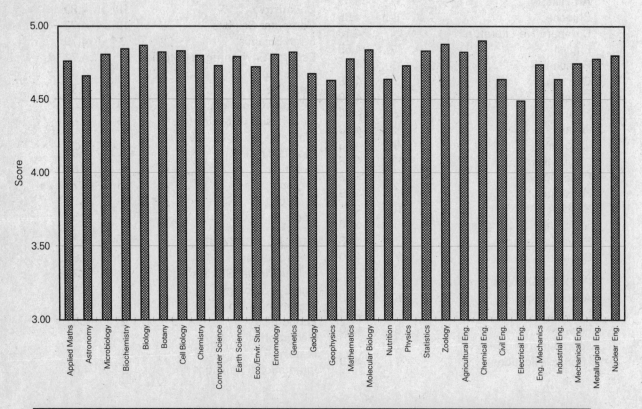

WISCONSIN-MADISON, UNIVERSITY OF (CONTINUED)

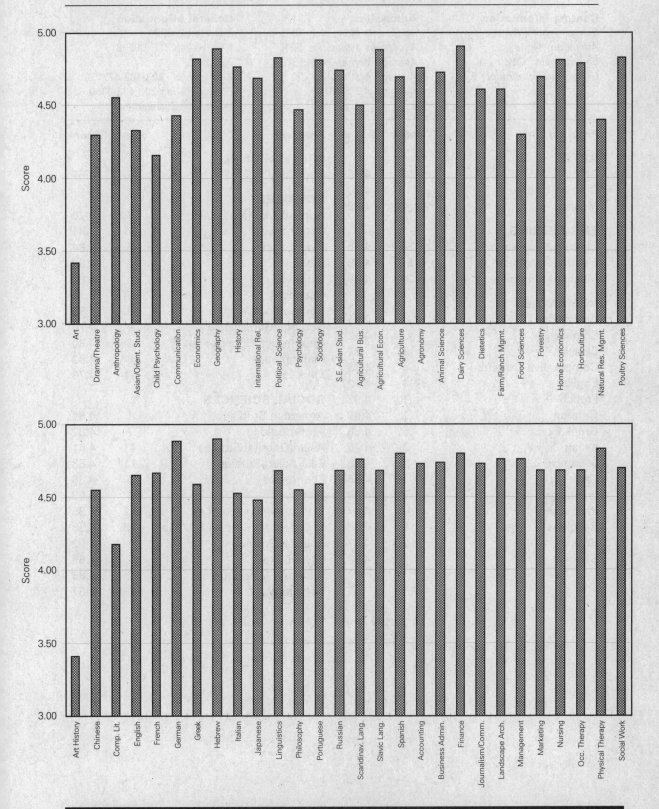

YALE UNIVERSITY

Contact Information
School Type: Private
Affiliation: None
Environment: City
Undergrad Enrollment: 5,401

Admissions
Applicants accepted: 18%
Acceptees attending: 59%
Average Verbal SAT: 730
Average Math SAT: 720
Average ACT: NR

General Information
P.O. Box 208234
New Haven, CT 06520

Admissions: 203-432-4771
Financial Aid: 203-432-0360
Web: www.yale.edu

Program	Rank	Score
ARTS		
Art	4	4.76
Drama/Theatre	18	4.20
Music	4	4.89
ENGINEERING		
Chemical Engineering	55	4.25
Electrical Engineering	55	4.38
Mechanical Engineering	31	4.48
HUMANITIES		
Art History	4	4.86
Chinese	12	4.42
Classics	3	4.87
Comparative Literature	4	4.73
English	1	4.92
French	1	4.92
German	1	4.90
Greek	6	4.66
Italian	3	4.75
Japanese	13	4.35
Latin	9	4.56
Linguistics	7	4.79
Philosophy	11	4.67
Religious Studies	5	4.76
Russian	2	4.87
Spanish	5	4.83

Program	Rank	Score
PROFESSIONAL		
Sociology	10	4.67
SCIENCES		
Applied Mathematics	7	4.70
Astronomy	11	4.41
Biochemistry	5	4.84
Biology	3	4.89
Biophysics	4	4.82
Chemistry	14	4.74
Computer Science	7	4.80
Geology/Geoscience	9	4.76
Geophysics/Geoscience	6	4.80
Mathematics	8	4.80
Physics	11	4.79
SOCIAL SCIENCES		
American Studies	1	4.81
Anthropology	7	4.82
Asian/Oriental Studies	11	4.41
East Asian Studies	11	4.53
Economics	6	4.85
History	1	4.93
Latin American Studies	12	4.36
Near/Middle Eastern Studies	13	4.58
Political Science	1	4.92
Psychology	2	4.65
Russian/Slavic Studies	2	4.83
Sociology	10	4.67

YALE UNIVERSITY (CONTINUED)

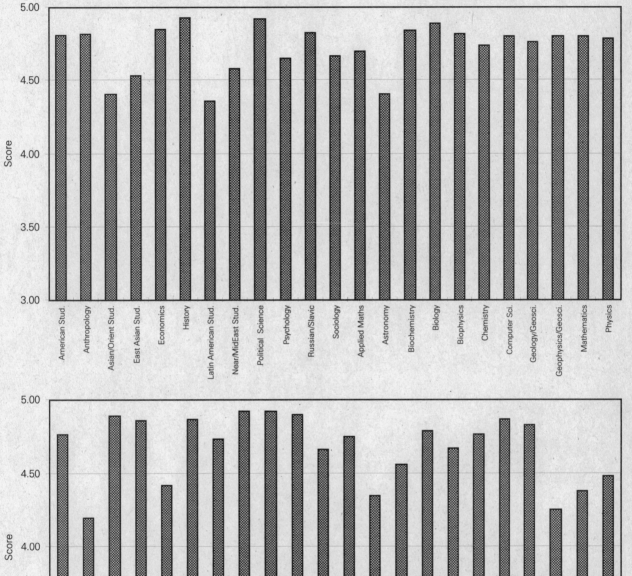

Part II

RATING OF AMERICAN UNDERGRADUATE INSTITUTIONS

INSTITUTION	Score	INSTITUTION	Score

ALABAMA

Alabama A&M University 3.07
Alabama State University 2.81
Alabama, University of 3.97
Alabama-Birmingham, University of 3.92
Alabama-Huntsville, University of 3.60
Auburn University 3.96
Auburn University-Montgomery 3.48
Birmingham-Southern College 3.38
Huntingdon College 3.04
Jacksonville State University 2.96
Judson College 2.69
Livingston University 3.02
Miles College 2.86
Mobile, University of 3.10
Montevallo, University of 3.40
North Alabama, University of 3.58
Oakwood College 2.64
Samford University 3.41
South Alabama, University of 3.70
Spring Hill College 3.44
Stillman College 2.29
Talladega College 2.25
Troy State University 3.46
Troy State University at Dothan 3.09
Troy State University at Montgomery 3.15
Tuskegee University 3.31

ALASKA

Alaska Pacific University 2.87
Alaska-Anchorage, University of 3.50
Alaska-Fairbanks, University of 3.45
Alaska-Southeast, University of 3.06

ARIZONA

Arizona State University 4.03
Arizona State University West 3.60
Arizona, University of 4.08
Grand Canyon University 3.03
Northern Arizona University 3.57
Prescott College 2.99

ARKANSAS

Arkansas State University 3.10
Arkansas Tech University 3.08
Arkansas, University of 3.97

Arkansas-Little Rock, University of 3.54
Arkansas-Monticello, University of 3.15
Arkansas-Pine Bluff, University of 3.20
Central Arkansas, University of 3.19
Harding University 3.03
Henderson State University 3.06
Hendrix College 3.04
John Brown University 2.70
Lyon College 2.99
Ouachita Baptist University 3.15
Ozarks, University of the 2.91
Philander Smith College 2.42
Southern Arkansas University-Magnolia . 3.02

CALIFORNIA

Azusa Pacific University 3.03
Biola University 3.02
California Baptist College 2.67
California Institute of Technology 4.84
California Lutheran University 3.05
California Polytechnic State University-
San Luis Obispo 3.69
California State Polytechnic University,
Pomona 3.55
California State University-Bakersfield 3.53
California State University-Chico 3.54
California State University-
Dominguez Hills 3.62
California State University-Fresno 3.63
California State University-Fullerton 3.61
California State University-Hayward 3.58
California State University-Long Beach ... 3.56
California State University-Los Angeles .. 3.59
California State University-Northridge 3.60
California State University-Sacramento ... 3.64
California State University-
San Bernardino 3.65
California State University-San Marcos ... 3.27
California State University-Stanislaus 3.29
California-Berkeley, University of 4.89
California-Davis, University of 4.57
California-Irvine, University of 4.60
California-Los Angeles, University of 4.86
California-Riverside, University of 4.33
California-San Diego, University of 4.71
California-Santa Barbara, University of 4.45

Strong = 4.41–4.99   Good = 4.01–4.40   Acceptable Plus = 3.51–3.99   Adequate = 3.01–3.50   Marginal = 2.01–2.99

INSTITUTION	Score	INSTITUTION	Score
California-Santa Cruz, University of	4.11	Fort Lewis College	3.22
Chapman University	3.05	Mesa State College	3.02
Claremont McKenna College	4.00	Metropolitan State College of Denver	3.12
Dominican College of San Rafael	3.06	Northern Colorado, University of	3.30
Golden Gate University	3.09	Regis University	3.06
Harvey Mudd College	3.89	Southern Colorado, University of	3.26
Holy Names College	2.90	United States Air Force Academy	4.43
Humboldt State University	3.57	Western State College of Colorado	3.12
LaVerne, University of	3.13		

CONNECTICUT

INSTITUTION	Score
Loma Linda University	3.61
Loyola Marymount University	3.52
Mills College	3.16
Mount Saint Mary's College)	3.04
Notre Dame, College of	3.01
Occidental College	3.50
Pacific, University of the	3.81
Pepperdine University	3.26
Pitzer College	3.40
Point Loma Nazarene College	2.73
Pomona College	4.01
Redlands, University of	3.40
Saint Mary's College	3.49
San Diego State University	3.66
San Diego, University of	3.12
San Francisco State University	3.67
San Francisco, University of	3.47
San Jose State University	3.68
Santa Clara University	3.64
Scripps College	3.27
Sonoma State University	3.30
Southern California College	2.81
Southern California, University of	3.95
Stanford University	4.91
United States International University	3.11
Westmont College	2.86
Whittier College	3.00

CONNECTICUT

Albertus Magnus College	2.88
Bridgeport, University of	3.48
Central Connecticut State University	3.14
Connecticut at Avery Point, University of	3.02
Connecticut at Hartford, University of	3.05
Connecticut at Stamford, University of	3.13
Connecticut at Waterbury, University of	3.01
Connecticut College	3.11
Connecticut, University of	3.94
Eastern Connecticut State University	3.12
Fairfield University	3.04
Hartford, University of	2.75
New Haven, University of	3.21
Quinnipiac College	3.20
Sacred Heart University	3.03
Saint Joseph College	2.96
Southern Connecticut State University	3.16
Trinity College	3.62
United States Coast Guard Academy	3.41
Wesleyan University	3.63
Western Connecticut State University	3.33
Yale University	4.92

DELAWARE

Delaware State University	2.83
Delaware, University of	3.95

COLORADO

Adams State College	3.15
Colorado College	3.18
Colorado School of Mines	4.20
Colorado State University	3.58
Colorado-Boulder, University of	3.99
Colorado-Colorado Springs, Univ. of	3.30
Colorado-Denver , University of	3.54
Denver, University of	3.90

DISTRICT OF COLUMBIA

American University	3.87
Catholic University of America, The	3.97
District of Columbia, University of the	3.04
Gallaudet University	3.14
George Washington University	3.96
Georgetown University	4.15
Howard University	3.78
Mount Vernon College	2.88

Strong = 4.41–4.99   Good = 4.01–4.40   Acceptable Plus = 3.51–3.99   Adequate = 3.01–3.50   Marginal = 2.01–2.99

INSTITUTION	Score	INSTITUTION	Score
Trinity College	3.02	Georgia Southwestern University	2.88
		Georgia State University	3.35
FLORIDA		Georgia, University of	3.97
Barry University	3.03	Kennesaw State College	2.86
Bethune-Cookman College	2.67	LaGrange College	2.92
Central Florida, University of	3.36	Mercer University	3.15
Eckerd College	3.22	Morehouse College	3.04
Edward Waters College	2.86	Morris Brown College	2.73
Flagler College	2.73	North Georgia College	2.83
Florida A&M University	3.19	Oglethorpe University	3.14
Florida Atlantic University	3.26	Paine College	2.57
Florida Institute of Technology	3.14	Piedmont College	2.58
Florida International University	3.21	Savannah State University	2.79
Florida Memorial College	2.70	Shorter College	2.98
Florida Southern College	2.93	Spelman College	2.62
Florida State University	3.91	Valdosta State University	3.06
Florida, University of	3.98	Wesleyan College	2.87
Jacksonville University	3.26	West Georgia College	2.99
Miami, University of	3.76		
New College of the University		**GUAM**	
of South Florida	3.12	Guam, University of	2.87
North Florida, University of	3.20		
Nova Southeastern University	3.15	**HAWAII**	
Palm Beach Atlantic College	2.85	Brigham Young University-	
Rollins College	3.20	Hawaii Campus	2.70
Saint Leo College	2.87	Chaminade University of Honolulu	2.78
Saint Thomas University	2.95	Hawaii at Hilo, University of	3.02
South Florida, University of	3.37	Hawaii Pacific University	2.66
Stetson University	3.17	Hawaii-Manoa, University of	3.84
Tampa, University of	3.18	Hawaii-West Oahu, University of	3.01
West Florida, University of	3.16		
		IDAHO	
GEORGIA		Albertson College	3.10
Agnes Scott College	3.08	Boise State University	3.18
Albany State College	3.01	Idaho State University	3.21
Armstrong State College	3.02	Idaho, University of	3.90
Augusta College	2.93	Lewis-Clark State College	3.02
Berry College	2.90	Northwest Nazarene College	2.95
Brenau University	3.00		
Clark Atlanta University	2.96	**ILLINOIS**	
Columbus College	2.89	Augustana College	3.11
Emory University	4.36	Aurora University	3.05
Fort Valley State College	2.82	Barat College	3.06
Georgia College	2.85	Blackburn College	2.94
Georgia Institute of Technology	4.54	Bradley University	3.39
Georgia Southern University	3.09	Chicago State University	3.16

Strong = 4.41–4.99   Good = 4.01–4.40   Acceptable Plus = 3.51–3.99   Adequate = 3.01–3.50   Marginal = 2.01–2.99

INSTITUTION	Score
Chicago, University of	4.88
Concordia University	2.93
DePaul University	3.68
Dominican University	3.03
Eastern Illinois University	3.67
Elmhurst College	3.01
Eureka College	2.96
Greenville College	2.88
Illinois College	2.76
Illinois Institute of Technology	3.30
Illinois State University	3.45
Illinois Wesleyan University	3.07
Illinois,Urbana-Champaign, University of	4.75
Illinois-Chicago, University of	3.82
Judson College	2.66
Knox College	3.10
Lake Forest College	3.09
Lewis University	2.90
Loyola University of Chicago	3.84
MacMurray College	2.79
McKendree College	2.73
Millikin University	2.92
Monmouth College	3.04
Mundelein College	3.00
North Central College	2.93
Northeastern Illinois University	3.14
Northern Illinois University	3.40
Northwestern University	4.82
Olivet Nazarene University	2.85
Principia College	2.83
Quincy University	2.90
Rockford College	3.12
Roosevelt University	3.16
Saint Francis, College of	2.84
Saint Xavier University	2.70
Southern Illinois University-Carbondale	3.80
Southern Illinois University-Edwardsville	3.30
Western Illinois University	3.38
Wheaton College	3.13

INDIANA

Anderson University	3.08
Ball State University	3.46
Bethel College	3.05
Butler University	3.39

INSTITUTION	Score
Calumet College of Saint Joseph	2.88
DePauw University	3.49
Earlham College	3.42
Evansville, University of	3.22
Franklin College	3.09
Goshen College	3.04
Grace College and Seminary	2.86
Hanover College	3.06
Indiana Institute of Technology	2.95
Indiana State University	3.20
Indiana University East	3.07
Indiana University Northwest	3.11
Indiana University Southeast	3.16
Indiana University-Bloomington	4.69
Indiana University-Kokomo	3.03
Indiana University-Purdue University Fort Wayne	3.47
Indiana University-Purdue University Indianapolis	3.51
Indiana University-South Bend	3.28
Indianapolis, University of	3.17
Manchester College	3.10
Marian College	2.92
Notre Dame, University of	4.80
Oakland City University	2.68
Purdue University North Central	3.13
Purdue University-Calumet	3.30
Purdue University-West Lafayette	4.52
Rose-Hulman Institute of Technology	3.35
Saint Francis College	2.77
Saint Joseph's College	3.14
Saint Mary's College	3.21
Saint Mary-of-the-Woods College	3.02
Taylor University	2.96
Tri-State University	3.15
Valparaiso University	3.46
Wabash College	3.29

IOWA

Briar Cliff College	3.04
Buena Vista College	3.05
Central College	2.89
Clarke College	3.06
Coe College	3.03
Cornell College	3.17
Dordt College	2.90

Strong = 4.41–4.99   Good = 4.01–4.40   Acceptable Plus = 3.51–3.99   Adequate = 3.01–3.50   Marginal = 2.01–2.99

INSTITUTION	Score	INSTITUTION	Score
Drake University	3.42	Bellarmine College	2.98
Dubuque, University of	3.20	Berea College	3.05
Graceland College	2.96	Brescia College	2.79
Grand View College	2.83	Campbellsville University	2.94
Grinnell College	3.30	Centre College	3.06
Iowa State University	4.30	Cumberland College	2.88
Iowa, University of	4.55	Eastern Kentucky University	3.22
Loras College	3.09	Georgetown College	2.97
Luther College	3.10	Kentucky State University	3.09
Morningside College	3.06	Kentucky Wesleyan College	2.74
Mount Mercy College	2.78	Kentucky, University of	3.90
Northern Iowa, University of	3.28	Louisville, University of	3.62
Northwestern College	2.85	Morehead State University	3.16
Saint Ambrose University	3.12	Murray State University	3.17
Simpson College	3.14	Northern Kentucky University	3.13
Teikyo Marycrest University	2.80	Pikeville College	2.70
Upper Iowa University	3.00	Spalding University	2.95
Wartburg College	2.93	Thomas More College	2.92
Westmar University	2.86	Transylvania University	2.98
William Penn College	2.91	Western Kentucky University	3.44

KANSAS

Baker University	3.10	**LOUISIANA**	
Benedictine College	2.90	Centenary College of Louisiana	3.15
Bethany College	2.91	Dillard University	3.01
Bethel College	2.80	Grambling State University	2.96
Emporia State University	3.25	Louisiana College	2.97
Fort Hays State University	3.15	Louisiana State University and	
Friends University	3.10	A&M College	3.98
Kansas Newman College	2.73	Louisiana State University-Shreveport	3.31
Kansas State University	3.93	Louisiana Tech University	3.23
Kansas Wesleyan University	3.04	Loyola University New Orleans	3.27
Kansas, University of	4.34	McNeese State University	3.16
McPherson College	3.02	New Orleans, University of	3.31
Mid America Nazarine College	2.88	Nicholls State University	3.20
Ottawa University	3.06	Northeast Louisiana University	3.17
Pittsburg State University	3.08	Northwestern State University	
Saint Mary College	2.66	of Louisiana	3.13
Southwestern College	2.84	Our Lady of Holy Cross College	2.75
Sterling College	2.98	Southeastern Louisiana University	3.11
Tabor College	3.07	Southern University and Agricultural	
Washburn University	3.32	and Mechanical College	3.05
Wichita State University	3.29	Southern University of New Orleans	2.70
		Southwestern Louisiana, University of	3.22
		Tulane University	4.50
KENTUCKY		Xavier University of Louisiana	3.02
Asbury College	2.80		

Strong = 4.41–4.99   Good = 4.01–4.40   Acceptable Plus = 3.51–3.99   Adequate = 3.01–3.50   Marginal = 2.01–2.99

INSTITUTION	Score	INSTITUTION	Score
MAINE		Boston College	3.88
Bates College	3.28	Boston University	4.03
Bowdoin College	3.30	Bradford College	2.75
Colby College	3.15	Brandeis University	4.44
Maine, University of	3.90	Bridgewater State College	3.23
Maine-Augusta, University of	2.80	Clark University	3.85
Maine-Farmington, University of	3.16	Curry College	2.77
Maine-Fort Kent, University of	3.14	Eastern Nazarene College	2.78
Maine-Machias, University of	3.13	Elms College	2.81
Maine-Presque Isle, University of	3.19	Emerson College	2.86
New England, University of	3.04	Emmanuel College	2.85
Saint Joseph's College	2.80	Fitchburg State College	3.17
Southern Maine, University of	3.06	Framingham State College	3.18
		Gordon College	2.79
MARYLAND		Harvard and Radcliffe Colleges	4.94
Baltimore, University of	3.12	Holy Cross, College of the	3.68
Bowie State University	2.80	Massachusetts Institute of Technology	4.85
Columbia Union College	2.63	Massachusetts-Amherst, University of	3.91
Coppin State College	2.85	Massachusetts-Boston, University of	3.26
Frostburg State University	3.13	Massachusetts-Dartmouth,	
Goucher College	3.10	University of	3.18
Hood College	2.97	Massachusetts-Lowell, University of	3.39
Johns Hopkins University	4.77	Merrimack College	3.02
Loyola College	3.11	Mount Holyoke College	3.89
Maryland-Baltimore County,		North Adams State College	3.04
University of	3.14	Northeastern University	3.44
Maryland-College Park, University of	4.01	Pine Manor College	2.71
Maryland-Eastern Shore, University of	3.03	Regis College	2.90
Maryland-University College,		Salem State College	3.11
University of	3.20	Simmons College	3.20
Morgan State University	2.90	Simon's Rock College of Bard	2.80
Mount Saint Mary's College	2.93	Smith College	3.90
Notre Dame of Maryland, College of	3.01	Springfield College	3.12
Saint John's College	3.15	Stonehill College	3.00
Salisbury State University	3.18	Suffolk University	3.40
Towson State University	3.17	Tufts University	4.65
United States Naval Academy	4.36	Wellesley College	3.60
Washington College	3.02	Western New England College	3.06
Western Maryland College	3.09	Westfield State College	3.07
		Wheaton College	3.03
MASSACHUSETTS		Williams College	3.91
Amerian International College	3.15	Worcester Polytechnic Institute	3.41
Amherst College	4.14	Worcester State College	3.28
Anna Maria College	2.87		
Assumption College	2.85	**MICHIGAN**	
Atlantic Union College	2.82	Adrian College	2.90

Strong = 4.41–4.99   Good = 4.01–4.40   Acceptable Plus = 3.51–3.99   Adequate = 3.01–3.50   Marginal = 2.01–2.99

INSTITUTION	Score	INSTITUTION	Score

INSTITUTION	Score
Albion College	2.91
Alma College	3.01
Andrews University	2.82
Aquinas College	2.76
Calvin College	3.03
Central Michigan University	3.27
Detroit Mercy, University of	3.80
Eastern Michigan University	3.26
Ferris State University	3.35
GMI Engineering and Management Institute	3.41
Grand Valley State University	3.05
Hillsdale College	2.94
Hope College	2.77
Kalamazoo College	3.10
Lake Superior State University	3.07
Lawrence Technological University	3.15
Madonna University	2.75
Marygrove College	2.70
Michigan State University	4.53
Michigan Technological University	3.56
Michigan-Ann Arbor, University of	4.93
Michigan-Dearborn, University of	3.66
Michigan-Flint, University of	3.60
Northern Michigan University	3.13
Oakland University	3.80
Olivet College	2.96
Saginaw Valley State University	3.04
Saint Mary's College (MI)	2.69
Siena Heights College	2.99
Spring Arbor College	2.95
Wayne State University	4.11
Western Michigan University	3.54

MINNESOTA

Institution	Score
Augsburg College	2.95
Bemidji State University	3.11
Bethel College	2.80
Carleton College	3.33
Concordia College	2.72
Concordia College (Moorhead)	2.77
Concordia College (Saint Paul)	2.74
Gustavus Adolphus College	3.10
Hamline University	3.28
Macalester College	3.31
Mankato State University	3.14
Minnesota, University of	4.74
Minnesota-Crookston, University of	3.07
Minnesota-Duluth, University of	3.66
Minnesota-Morris, University of	3.59
Moorhead State University	3.16
Northwestern College	2.69
Saint Benedict, College of	2.90
Saint Catherine, The College of	3.04
Saint Cloud State University	3.17
Saint John's University	3.18
Saint Mary's College of Minnesota	2.88
Saint Scholastica, College of	2.90
Saint Thomas, University of	3.22
Southwest State University	3.08
St. Olaf College	3.03
Winona State University	3.29

MISSISSIPPI

Institution	Score
Alcorn State University	2.85
Belhaven College	2.80
Delta State University	2.84
Jackson State University	2.94
Millsaps College	3.09
Mississippi College	2.96
Mississippi State University	3.66
Mississippi University for Women	3.01
Mississippi Valley State University	2.86
Mississippi, University of	3.78
Rust College	2.60
Southern Mississippi, University of	3.31
Tougaloo College	2.58
William Carey College	2.98

MISSOURI

Institution	Score
Avila College	2.81
Central Methodist College	2.72
Central Missouri State University	3.06
Columbia College	2.73
Culver-Stockton College	2.95
Drury College	2.94
Evangel College	2.83
Fontbonne College	2.86
Lincoln University	2.75
Lindenwood College	2.92
Maryville University of Saint Louis	2.75
Missouri Baptist College	2.78

Strong = 4.41–4.99   Good = 4.01–4.40   Acceptable Plus = 3.51–3.99   Adequate = 3.01–3.50   Marginal = 2.01–2.99

INSTITUTION	Score	INSTITUTION	Score

Missouri Southern State College 3.05
Missouri Valley College 2.79
Missouri Western State College 3.07
Missouri-Columbia, University of 4.38
Missouri-Kansas City, University of 3.70
Missouri-Rolla, University of 3.30
Missouri-Saint Louis, University of 3.60
Northeast Missouri State University 3.10
Northwest Missouri State University 3.21
Ozarks, College of the 2.91
Park College 2.85
Rockhurst College 3.04
Saint Louis University 3.88
Southeast Missouri State University 3.15
Southwest Baptist University 2.84
Southwest Missouri State University 3.23
Stephens College 3.16
Washington University in Saint Louis 4.67
Webster University 3.06
Westminster College 2.96
William Jewell College 2.82
William Woods University 2.81

MONTANA
Carroll College 3.01
Eastern Montana College 3.05
Great Falls, University of 3.02
Montana State University-Bozeman 3.50
Montana Tech of the University
  of Montana 3.38
Montana, University of 3.65
Northern Montana College 3.03
Rocky Mountain College 3.00
Western Montana College 2.97

NEBRASKA
Bellevue University 2.83
Chadron State College 3.08
Concordia College 2.75
Concordia College 2.87
Creighton University 3.76
Dana College 2.87
Doane College 2.85
Hastings College 3.04
Midland Lutheran College 2.80
Nebraska Wesleyan University 3.02

Nebraska-Kearney, University of 3.14
Nebraska-Lincoln, University of 3.95
Nebraska-Omaha, University of 3.43
Peru State College 3.05
Saint Mary, College of 2.75
Union College 2.88
Wayne State College 3.06

NEVADA
Nevada-Las Vegas, University of 3.20
Nevada-Reno, University of 3.40

NEW HAMPSHIRE
Colby-Sawyer College 2.87
Dartmouth College 4.76
Franklin Pierce College 3.03
Keene State College 3.18
New England College 3.04
New Hampshire, University of 3.80
New Haven, University of 3.10
Notre Dame College 2.85
Plymouth State College 3.20
Rivier College 2.96
Saint Anselm College 3.07

NEW JERSEY
Bloomfield College 2.86
Caldwell College 2.91
Centenary College 2.82
Drew University 3.31
Fairleigh Dickinson University 3.27
Fairleigh Dickinson University,
  Florham Madison Campus 3.34
Felician College 2.81
Georgian Court College 2.88
Jersey City State College 3.16
Kean College of New Jersey 3.20
Monmouth University 3.12
Montclair State University 3.14
New Jersey Institute of Technology 3.18
New Jersey, The College of 3.25
Princeton University 4.95
Ramapo College of New Jersey 3.04
Rider University 3.05
Rowan College of New Jersey 3.22
Rutgers University, New Brunswick 4.48

Strong = 4.41–4.99   Good = 4.01–4.40   Acceptable Plus = 3.51–3.99   Adequate = 3.01–3.50   Marginal = 2.01–2.99

INSTITUTION	Score	INSTITUTION	Score

Rutgers University-Camden
College of Arts & Sciences 3.23
Rutgers University-Newark College
of Arts & Sciences 3.24
Saint Elizabeth, College of 2.76
Saint Peter's College 3.06
Seton Hall University 3.15
Stevens Institute of Technology 3.80
Thomas Edison State College 3.11
William Paterson College of
New Jersey 3.17

NEW MEXICO

Eastern New Mexico University 3.13
New Mexico Highlands University 3.02
New Mexico Institute of
Mining & Technology 3.30
New Mexico State University 3.44
New Mexico, University of 3.78
Saint John's College 3.01
Santa Fe, College of 2.95
Southwest, College of the 2.76
Western New Mexico University 3.15

NEW YORK

Adelphi University 3.10
Alfred University 3.52
Bard College 3.11
Barnard College 3.57
Canisius College 3.08
City University of New York-
Baruch College 3.40
City University of New York-
Brooklyn College 3.41
City University of New York-
City College 3.42
City University of New York-
College of Staten Island 3.09
City University of New York-
Hunter College 3.38
City University of New York-
John Jay College of Criminal Justice ...3.47
City University of New York-
Lehman College 3.39
City University of New York-
Medgar Evers College 3.03

City University of New York-
Queens College 3.44
City University of New York-
York College 3.12
Clarkson University 3.60
Colgate University 4.11
Columbia University 4.83
Concordia College 2.74
Cooper Union 3.70
Cornell University 4.90
D'Youville College 2.71
Daemen College 2.79
Dominican College of Blauvelt 2.75
Dowling College 2.81
Elmira College 2.86
Eugene Lang College 3.07
Fordham University 4.02
Hamilton College 3.45
Hartwick College 3.09
Hobart and William Smith Colleges 3.23
Hofstra University 3.50
Houghton College 2.93
Iona College 2.87
Ithaca College 3.04
Keuka College 2.63
LeMoyne College 2.94
Long Island University-Brooklyn 3.18
Long Island University-C.W. Post 3.27
Long Island University-Southampton 2.88
Manhattan College 3.19
Manhattanville College 3.03
Marist College 2.80
Marymount College 2.94
Marymount Manhattan College 2.76
Medaille College 2.69
Mercy College 2.86
Molloy College 2.68
Mount Saint Mary College 2.66
Mount Saint Vincent, College of 2.91
Nazareth College of Rochester 2.92
New Rochelle, College of 2.90
New York Institute of Technology 3.00
New York University 4.58
Niagara University 3.09
Nyack College 2.78
Pace University 3.06

Strong = 4.41–4.99   Good = 4.01–4.40   Acceptable Plus = 3.51–3.99   Adequate = 3.01–3.50   Marginal = 2.01–2.99

INSTITUTION	Score	INSTITUTION	Score
Pace University	3.01	State University of New York College at Potsdam	3.27
Polytechnic University	3.91	State University of New York College at Brockport	3.26
Polytechnic University, Farmdale	3.22	State University of New York College at Purchase	2.97
Pratt Institute	3.79	State University of New York Maritime College	3.31
Rensselaer Polytechnic Institute	4.38	SUNY College of Environmental Science and Forestry	3.90
Roberts Wesleyan College	2.77		
Rochester Institute of Technology	3.12	Syracuse University	3.82
Rochester, University of	4.56	Touro College	3.26
Russell Sage College	3.17	Union College	3.69
Saint Bonaventure University	2.90	United States Merchant Marine Academy	3.15
Saint Francis College	2.62	United States Military Academy	4.02
Saint John Fisher College	2.94	Utica College of Syracuse University	3.16
Saint John's University	3.20	Vassar College	3.56
Saint Joseph's College (Brooklyn)	2.97	Wagner College	2.84
Saint Joseph's College, (Suffolk)	2.93	Webb Institute	3.56
Saint Lawrence University	3.51	Wells College	3.54
Saint Rose, The College of	2.87	William Smith College	3.05
Saint Thomas Aquinas College	2.64	Yeshiva University	3.92
Sarah Lawrence College	3.52		
Siena College	2.65	**NORTH CAROLINA**	
Skidmore College	3.60	Appalachian State University	3.08
State University of New York at Albany	4.01	Atlantic Christian College	2.71
State University of New York at Binghamton	4.03	Barber Scotia College	2.78
		Belmont Abbey College	2.85
State University of New York at Buffalo	4.66	Bennett College	2.81
		Campbell University	3.14
State University of New York at Stony Brook	4.46	Catawba College	3.06
State University of New York College at New Paltz	3.37	Davidson College	3.33
		Duke University	4.79
State University of New York College at Oswego	3.36	East Carolina University	3.20
State University of New York College at Cortland	3.35	Elizabeth City State College	2.82
		Elon College	3.04
State University of New York College at Oneonta	3.34	Fayetteville State University	2.74
State University of New York College at Geneseo	3.33	Gardner-Webb College	2.87
		Greensboro College	2.83
State University of New York College at Fredonia	3.30	Guilford College	2.97
		High Point University	2.86
State University of New York College at Plattsburg	3.29	Johnson C. Smith University	2.67
State University of New York College at Old Westbury	3.28	Lenoir-Rhyne College	2.99
		Livingstone College/Hood Theological Seminary	2.61

Strong = 4.41–4.99   Good = 4.01–4.40   Acceptable Plus = 3.51–3.99   Adequate = 3.01–3.50   Marginal = 2.01–2.99

INSTITUTION	Score	INSTITUTION	Score
Mars Hill College	3.00	Bowling Green State University	3.45
Meredith College	2.90	Capital University	3.19
Methodist College	2.84	Case Western Reserve University	4.39
Nort Carolina Wesleyan College	2.76	Cedarville College	2.88
North Carolina A&T State University	3.12	Central State University	2.97
North Carolina Central University	3.11	Cincinnati, University of	3.58
North Carolina State University	3.72	Cleveland State University	3.20
North Carolina-Asheville, University of	3.19	Dayton, University of	3.22
		Defiance College	2.95
North Carolina-Chapel Hill, University of	4.68	Denison University	3.13
		Findlay, University of	2.94
North Carolina-Charlotte, University of	3.61	Franciscan University of Steubenville	2.84
		Franklin University	2.91
North Carolina-Greensboro, University of	3.51	Heidelberg College	2.96
		Hiram College	2.90
North Carolina-Wilmington, University of	3.50	John Carroll University	3.08
		Kent State University	3.27
Pembroke State University	3.07	Kenyon College	3.33
Pfeiffer College	2.86	Lake Erie College	2.87
Queens College	2.96	Malone College	2.86
Saint Andrews Presbyterian College	2.88	Marietta College	3.05
Saint Augustine's College	2.60	Miami University	3.47
Salem College	2.75	Mount Saint Joseph, College of	3.02
Shaw University	2.64	Mount Union College	2.81
Wake Forest University	3.84	Mount Vernon Nazarene College	2.78
Warren Wilson College	2.72	Muskingum College	2.92
Western Carolina University	3.24	Notre Dame College of Ohio	2.85
Wingate College	2.70	Oberlin College	3.67
Winston-Salem State University	2.73	Ohio Dominican College	2.82
		Ohio Northern University	3.21
NORTH DAKOTA		Ohio State University, Lima	3.14
Dickinson State University	3.06	Ohio State University, Mansfield	3.15
Jamestown College	2.94	Ohio State University, Marion	3.16
Mary, University of	2.76	Ohio State University, Newark	3.17
Mayville State University	3.03	Ohio State University-Columbus	4.62
Minot State University	3.10	Ohio University	3.60
North Dakota State University	3.50	Ohio University, Chillecothe	2.93
North Dakota, University of	3.61	Ohio University, Eastern	2.99
Valley City State University	3.05	Ohio University, Lancaster	3.01
		Ohio University, Southern	3.03
OHIO		Ohio University, Zanesville	3.11
Akron, University of	3.28	Ohio Wesleyan University	3.29
Antioch College	3.30	Otterbein College	2.98
Ashland University	2.97	Rio Grande, University of	2.74
Baldwin-Wallace College	3.04	Toledo, University of	3.23
Bluffton College	2.89	Urbana University	2.65

Strong = 4.41–4.99   Good = 4.01–4.40   Acceptable Plus = 3.51–3.99   Adequate = 3.01–3.50   Marginal = 2.01–2.99

INSTITUTION	Score	INSTITUTION	Score

INSTITUTION	Score
Ursuline College	2.75
Walsh University	3.18
Wilberforce University	2.79
Wilmington College	2.66
Wittenberg University	3.00
Wooster, College of	3.09
Wright State University	3.35
Xavier University	3.06
Youngstown State University	3.07

OKLAHOMA

Bartlesville Wesleyan College	2.67
Cameron University	2.69
East Central University	2.98
Langston University	2.65
Northeastern State University	3.06
Northwestern Oklahoma State University	3.11
Oklahoma Baptist University	3.01
Oklahoma Christian University of Science and Arts	3.02
Oklahoma City University	3.16
Oklahoma Panhandle State University	3.03
Oklahoma State University	3.59
Oklahoma, University of	3.81
Oral Roberts University	3.04
Phillips University	3.22
Science & Arts of Oklahoma, University of	2.96
Southwestern Oklahoma State University	3.12
Tulsa, University of	3.63

OREGON

Blue Mountain College	2.62
Eastern Oregon State College	3.06
George Fox University	2.74
Lewis & Clark College	3.14
Linfield College	3.08
Marylhurst College	2.90
Oregon State University	3.90
Oregon, University of	3.91
Pacific University	3.12
Portland State University	3.34
Portland, University of	3.15
Reed College	3.32

INSTITUTION	Score
Southern Oregon State College	3.07
Warner Pacific College	3.02
Western Oregon State College	3.04
Willamette University	2.80

PENNSYLVANIA

Albright College	3.06
Allegheny College	3.05
Allentown College of Saint Francis de Sales	2.66
Alvernia College	2.65
Beaver College	2.73
Bloomsburg University of Pennsylvania	3.24
Bryn Mawr College	4.02
Bucknell University	3.30
Cabrini College	2.56
California University of Pennsylvania	3.29
Carlow College	2.79
Carnegie Mellon University	4.72
Cedar Crest College	2.82
Chatham College	2.98
Chestnut Hill College	2.93
Cheyney University of Pennsylvania	3.27
College Misericordia	2.75
Delaware Valley College	2.89
Dickinson College	3.18
Drexel University	3.65
Duquesne University	3.32
East Stroudsburg University of Pennsylvania	3.28
Eastern College	2.72
Edinboro University of Pennsylvania	3.26
Elizabethtown College	2.47
Franklin & Marshall College	3.04
Gannon University	2.96
Geneva College	2.80
Gettysburg College	2.99
Grove City College	2.84
Gwynedd-Mercy College	2.81
Haverford College	3.90
Holy Family College	2.62
Immaculata College	2.69
Indiana University of Pennsylvania	3.20
Juniata College	2.94
King's College	2.61
Kutztown University of Pennsylvania	3.10

Strong = 4.41–4.99   Good = 4.01–4.40   Acceptable Plus = 3.51–3.99   Adequate = 3.01–3.50   Marginal = 2.01–2.99

INSTITUTION	Score
Lafayette College	3.49
LaRoche College	2.60
LaSalle University	3.09
Lebanon Valley College	2.85
Lehigh University	3.94
Lincoln University	2.59
Lock Haven University of Pennsylvania	3.25
Lycoming College	2.49
Mansfield University of Pennsylvania	3.13
Marywood College	2.46
Mercyhurst College	2.53
Messiah College	2.52
Millersville University of Pennsylvania	3.14
Moravian College	2.86
Muhlenberg College	3.00
Neumann College	2.57
Pennsylvania State University-Behrend College	2.97
Pennsylvania State University-University Park	4.59
Pennsylvania, University of	4.81
Philadelphia College of Pharmacy and Science	3.12
Philadelphia College of Textiles and Science	3.26
Pittsburgh at Bradford, University of	3.17
Pittsburgh, University of	4.36
Pittsburgh-Greensburg, University of	3.08
Pittsburgh-Johnstown, University of	3.19
Point Park College	2.58
Rosemont College	2.90
Saint Francis College	2.54
Saint Joseph's University	2.85
Saint Vincent College	2.55
Scranton, University of	3.02
Seton Hill College	2.77
Shippensburg University of Pennsylvania	3.11
Slippery Rock University of Pennsylvania	3.03
Spring Garden College	2.48
Susquehanna University	3.15
Swarthmore College	3.91
Temple University	3.66
Thiel College	2.70
Ursinus College	3.07

INSTITUTION	Score
Villa Maria College	2.53
Villanova University	3.46
Washington & Jefferson College	3.23
West Chester University of Pennsylvania	3.21
Westminster College	2.69
Widener University	3.16
Wilkes University	2.88
Wilson College	2.87
York College of Pennsylvania	3.05

RHODE ISLAND

Brown University	4.78
Providence College	3.08
Rhode Island College	3.15
Rhode Island, University of	3.67
Roger Williams University	3.06
Salve Regina University	3.03

SOUTH CAROLINA

Benedict College	2.50
Central Wesleyan College	2.414
Charleston, College of	3.02
Citadel, The	3.30
Claflin College	2.40
Clemson University	3.46
Coker College	2.37
Columbia College	2.86
Converse College	2.88
Erskine College	2.93
Francis Marion University	3.01
Furman University	3.17
Lander University	2.67
Limestone College	2.42
Newberry College	2.84
Presbyterian College	3.05
South Carolina at Coastal Carolina College, University of	3.04
South Carolina State University	2.70
South Carolina-Aiken, University of	3.09
South Carolina-Columbia, University of	3.68
South Carolina-Spartanburg, University of	3.07
Voorhees College	2.54
Winthrop University	2.97

Strong = 4.41–4.99   Good = 4.01–4.40   Acceptable Plus = 3.51–3.99   Adequate = 3.01–3.50   Marginal = 2.01–2.99

INSTITUTION	Score
Wofford College	3.08

SOUTH DAKOTA

INSTITUTION	Score
Augustana College	3.15
Black Hills State University	3.02
Dakota State University	2.91
Dakota Wesleyan University	2.81
Huron University	2.74
Mount Marty College	2.72
Northern State University	3.03
Sioux Falls College	2.87
South Dakota School of Mines & Technology	3.79
South Dakota State University	3.27
South Dakota, University of	3.76

TENNESSEE

INSTITUTION	Score
Austin Peay State University	2.86
Belmont University	2.71
Bethel College	2.75
Carson-Newman College	2.85
Christian Brothers University	3.00
East Tennessee State University	3.07
Fisk University	3.02
Freed-Hardeman University	2.73
King College	2.70
Knoxville College	2.69
Lambuth University	2.68
Lane College	2.61
LeMoyne-Owen College	2.60
Lincoln Memorial University	2.77
Lipscomb University	3.03
Maryville College	2.64
Memphis, The University of	3.61
Middle Tennessee State University	3.13
Milligan College	2.76
Rhodes College	3.23
South, University of the	3.07
Southern College of Seventh-Day Adventists	2.85
Tennessee at Chattanooga, University of	3.17
Tennessee at Martin, University of	3.10
Tennessee State University	3.04
Tennessee Technological University	3.06
Tennessee Wesleyan College	2.59

INSTITUTION	Score
Tennessee-Knoxville, University of	3.88
Trevecca Nazarene College	2.60
Tusculum College	2.61
Union University	2.66
Vanderbilt University	4.64

TEXAS

INSTITUTION	Score
Abilene Christian University	3.05
Angelo State University	3.02
Baylor University	2.69
Central Texas, University of	2.98
Dallas Baptist University	2.61
Dallas, University of	3.09
East Texas Baptist University	2.72
East Texas State University	3.07
East Texas State University at Texarkana	2.94
Hardin-Simmons University	3.21
Houston Baptist University	2.85
Houston, University of	3.68
Houston-Clear Lake, University of	3.15
Houston-Downtown, University of	3.08
Houston-Victoria Campus, University of	3.01
Howard Payne University	2.82
Huston-Tillotson College	2.58
Incarnate Word College	2.56
Jarvis Christian College	2.54
Lamar University	3.06
Lee College	2.67
LeTourneau University	2.79
Lubbock Christian University	2.42
Mary Hardin-Baylor, University of	2.67
McMurry University	2.75
Midwestern State University	2.96
North Texas, University of	3.24
Our Lady of the Lake University	2.63
Paul Quinn College	2.58
Prairie View A&M University	2.97
Rice University	4.73
Saint Edward's University	2.83
Saint Mary's University	3.10
Saint Thomas, University of	2.65
Sam Houston State University	3.13
Southern Methodist University	3.79
Southwest Texas State University	3.09

Strong = 4.41–4.99   Good = 4.01–4.40   Acceptable Plus = 3.51–3.99   Adequate = 3.01–3.50   Marginal = 2.01–2.99

INSTITUTION	Score	INSTITUTION	Score
Southwestern Adventist College	2.40	Lyndon State College	2.90
Southwestern University	2.68	Marlboro College	2.70
Stephen F. Austin State University	3.19	Middlebury College	3.15
Sul Ross State University	3.11	Norwich University	3.19
Tarleton State University	3.17	Saint Michael's College	2.96
Texas at Brownsville, University of	2.90	Southern Vermont College	2.63
Texas at Tyler, University of	3.18	Trinity College of Vermont	2.72
Texas A&M International University	2.84	Vermont, University of	3.61
Texas A&M University	3.00		

VIRGINIA

INSTITUTION	Score
Texas A&M University at Galveston	3.12
Texas A&M University, Corpus Christi	3.16
Texas A&M University-College Station	3.99
Texas Christian University	3.63
Texas College	2.42
Texas Lutheran College	2.59
Texas Southern University	3.20
Texas Tech University	3.58
Texas Wesleyan University	2.64
Texas Woman's University	3.23
Texas-Arlington, University of	3.26
Texas-Austin, University of	4.14
Texas-Dallas , University of	3.31
Texas-El Paso, University of	3.27
Texas-Pan American, University of	2.91
Texas-Permian Basin, University of	2.91
Texas-San Antonio, University of	3.30
Trinity University	2.88
Wayland Baptist University	2.74
West Texas A&M University	3.14
Wiley College	2.48

VIRGINIA

INSTITUTION	Score
Averett College	2.63
Bluefield College	2.53
Bridgewater College	2.52
Christopher Newport University	2.84
Clinch Valley College of the University of Virginia	3.06
Eastern Mennonite University	2.92
Emory and Henry College	3.03
Ferrum College	2.54
George Mason University	3.22
Hampden-Sydney College	3.11
Hampton University	2.76
Hollins College	2.93
James Madison University	3.32
Liberty University	2.90
Longwood College	2.86
Lynchburg College	2.88
Mary Baldwin College	2.64
Mary Washington College	2.90
Marymount University	2.77
Norfolk State University	2.72
Old Dominion University	3.36
Radford University	3.09
Randolph-Macon College	3.05
Randolph-Macon Woman's College	3.03
Richmond, University of	3.12
Roanoke College	2.96
Saint Paul's College	2.48
Shenandoah University	2.57
Sweet Briar College	3.07
Virginia Commonwealth University	3.39
Virginia Intermont College	2.61
Virginia Military Institute	3.21
Virginia State University	2.50
Virginia Tech	3.68
Virginia Union University	2.49

UTAH

INSTITUTION	Score
Brigham Young University	3.62
Southern Utah University	3.07
Utah State University	3.60
Utah, University of	3.80
Weber State University	3.09
Westminster College of Salt Lake City	3.01

VERMONT

INSTITUTION	Score
Bennington College	3.09
Castleton State College	3.04
Goddard College	2.60
Green Mountain College	2.51
Johnson State College	2.87

Strong = 4.41–4.99   Good = 4.01–4.40   Acceptable Plus = 3.51–3.99   Adequate = 3.01–3.50   Marginal = 2.01–2.99

INSTITUTION	Score	INSTITUTION	Score

WISCONSIN

Virginia Wesleyan College 2.58
Virginia, University of 4.61
Washington and Lee University 3.77
William and Mary, The College of 3.89

VIRGIN ISLANDS
Virgin Islands, University of the 2.71

WASHINGTON
Central Washington University 3.12
Eastern Washington University 3.16
Evergreen State College, The 3.06
Gonzaga University 3.51
Pacific Lutheran University 3.10
Puget Sound, University of 3.14
Saint Martin's College 3.05
Seattle Pacific University 3.09
Seattle University 3.62
Walla Walla College 2.97
Washington State University 3.80
Washington, University of 4.70
Western Washington University 3.17
Whitman College 3.29
Whitworth College 2.86

WEST VIRGINIA
Alderson-Broaddus College 2.73
Bethany College 2.76
Bluefield State College 2.68
Charleston, University of 2.81
Concord College 2.67
Davis & Elkins College 3.11
Fairmont State College 2.75
Glenville State College 2.74
Marshall University 3.20
Salem-Teikyo University 2.79
Shepherd College 2.77
West Liberty State College 2.80
West Virginia State College 2.62
West Virginia University 3.62
West Virginia Wesleyan College 2.70
Wheeling Jesuit University 2.94

WISCONSIN
Alverno College 3.03
Beloit College 3.06
Cardinal Stritch College 2.74
Carroll College 2.77
Carthage College 2.78
Concordia University 2.73
Edgewood College 2.72
Lakeland College 2.71
Lawrence University 3.77
Marian College of Fond Du Lac 2.70
Marquette University 3.89
Mount Mary College 2.68
Mount Senario College 2.66
Northland College 2.65
Ripon College 3.08
Saint Norbert College 3.04
Silver Lake College 2.62
Viterbo College 2.69
Wisconsin-Eau Claire, University of 3.31
Wisconsin-Green Bay, University of 3.29
Wisconsin-LaCrosse, University of 3.27
Wisconsin-Madison, University of 4.87
Wisconsin-Milwaukee, University of 3.79
Wisconsin-Oshkosh , University of 3.26
Wisconsin-Parkside, University of 3.25
Wisconsin-Platteville, University of 3.23
Wisconsin-River Falls, University of 3.21
Wisconsin-Stevens Point, University of ... 3.28
Wisconsin-Stout, University of 3.30
Wisconsin-Superior, University of 3.19
Wisconsin-Whitewater, University of 3.17

WYOMING
Wyoming, University of 3.69

Strong = 4.41–4.99   Good = 4.01–4.40   Acceptable Plus = 3.51–3.99   Adequate = 3.01–3.50   Marginal = 2.01–2.99

Part III
RATING OF UNDERGRADUATE PROGRAMS

Accounting	Ecology/Environmental Studies
Aerospace Engineering	Economics
Agricultural Business	Electrical Engineering
Agricultural Economics	Engineering Mechanics
Agricultural Engineering	Engineering Physics
Agriculture	Engineering Science
Agronomy	Engineering/General
American Studies	English
Animal Science	Entomology
Anthropology	Environmental Design
Applied Mathematics	Environmental Engineering
Arabic	Environmental Sciences
Architectural Engineering	Farm/Ranch Management
Architecture	Film
Art	Finance
Art History	Fish/Game Management
Asian/Oriental Studies	Food Sciences
Astronomy	Food Services Management
Astrophysics	Forestry
Atmospheric Sciences	French
Bacteriology/Microbiology	Genetics
Behavioral Sciences	Geography
Biochemistry	Geological Engineering
Bioengineering/Biomedical Engineering	Geology/Geoscience
Biology	Geophysics/Geoscience
Biophysics	German
Botany	Greek
Business Administration	Hebrew
Cell Biology	History
Ceramic Art/Design	Home Economics
Ceramic Engineering	Horticulture
Chemical Engineering	Hotel, Restaurant, Institutional Management
Chemistry	Industrial Engineering
Child Psychology	Information Science
Chinese	International Relations
Civil Engineering	Italian
Classics	Japanese
Communication	Journalism and Mass Communications
Comparative Literature	Labor and Industrial Relations
Computer Engineering	Landscape Architecture
Computer Science	Latin
Dairy Sciences	Latin American Studies
Dietetics	Linguistics
Drama/Theatre	Management
Earth Science	Manufacturing Engineering
East Asian Studies	Marine Biology

Marine Sciences
Marketing
Materials Engineering/Materials Science
And Engineering
Mathematics
Mechanical Engineering
Medieval Studies
Metallurgical Engineering
Meteorology
Mining and Mineral Engineering
Molecular Biology
Music
Natural Resource Management
Naval Architecture And Marine Engineering
Near/Middle Eastern Studies
Nuclear Engineering
Nursing
Nutrition
Occupational Therapy
Ocean Engineering
Operations Research
Ornamental Horticulture
Parks Management
Petroleum Engineering
Philosophy
Physical Therapy
Physics
Political Science
Portuguese
Poultry Sciences
Psychology
Radio/Television Studies
Religious Studies
Russian
Russian/Slavic Studies
Scandinavian Languages
Slavic Languages
Social Work/Social Welfare
Sociology
South Asian Studies
Southeast Asian Studies
Spanish
Speech Pathology/Audiology
Speech/Rhetoric
Statistics
Systems Engineering
Urban and Regional Planning
Wildlife Biology
Zoology

ACCOUNTING
LEADING INSTITUTIONS—RATING OF UNDERGRADUATE PROGRAMS

INSTITUTION	RANK	SCORE
Pennsylvania, University of	1	4.92
Indiana University-Bloomington	2	4.90
Michigan-Ann Arbor, University of	3	4.87
California-Berkeley, University of	4	4.86
Texas-Austin, University of	5	4.84
New York University	6	4.82
Notre Dame, University of	7	4.81
Illinois,Urbana-Champaign, University of	8	4.79
Purdue University-West Lafayette	9	4.76
Wisconsin-Madison, University of	10	4.73
Washington, University of	11	4.70
Michigan State University	12	4.68
Virginia, University of	13	4.67
City University of New York-Baruch College	14	4.64
Minnesota, University of	15	4.62
Washington University in Saint Louis	16	4.60
Case Western Reserve University	17	4.59
Southern California, University of	18	4.58
Houston, University of	19	4.55
Pennsylvania State University-University Park	20	4.52
Ohio State University-Columbus	21	4.50
Texas A&M University-College Station	22	4.49
Utah, University of	23	4.47
Lehigh University	24	4.46
Florida, University of	25	4.40
Southern Methodist University	26	4.39
Massachusetts-Amherst, University of	27	4.37
Arizona, University of	28	4.34
Louisiana State University-Baton Rouge	29	4.32
Temple University	30	4.28
Maryland-College Park, University of	31	4.27
Georgia State University	32	4.23
South Carolina-Columbia, University of,	33	4.20
Oregon, University of	34	4.16
George Washington University	35	4.14
State University of New York College at Buffalo	36	4.13
Missouri-Columbia, University of	37	4.12
Colorado-Boulder, University of	38	4.08
Arizona State University	39	4.06
Iowa, University of	40	4.05
Emory University	41	4.02

AEROSPACE ENGINEERING
LEADING INSTITUTIONS—RATING OF UNDERGRADUATE PROGRAMS

INSTITUTION	RANK	SCORE
Massachusetts Institute of Technology[4]	1	4.91
Michigan-Ann Arbor, University of[5]	2	4.89
Princeton University[5]	3	4.84
Minnesota, University of[7]	4	4.82
Illinois,Urbana-Champaign, University of[2]	5	4.80
Ohio State University-Columbus[2]	6	4.78
Maryland-College Park, University of[5]	7	4.76
Kansas, University of[5]	8	4.73
Purdue University-West Lafayette[2]	9	4.71
Arizona, University of[5]	10	4.68
Iowa State University[5]	11	4.65
Rensselaer Polytechnic Institute[1]	12	4.64
Virginia, University of[5]	13	4.62
Washington, University of[3]	14	4.60
Texas A&M University-College Station[5]	15	4.57
Georgia Institute of Technology[5]	16	4.53
Pennsylvania State University-University Park[5]	17	4.52
Southern California, University of[5]	18	4.52
Texas-Austin, University of[5]	19	4.51
Colorado-Boulder, University of[8]	20	4.50
United States Air Force Academy[1,9]	21	4.46
Missouri-Rolla, University of[5]	22	4.44
Cincinnati, University of[5]	23	4.42
Oklahoma, University of[5]	24	4.40
State University of New York College at Buffalo[5]	25	4.38
Florida, University of[5]	26	4.37
Tennessee-Knoxville, University of[5]	27	4.33
Syracuse University[5]	28	4.32
Virginia Tech[5]	29	4.30
Notre Dame, University of[5]	30	4.28
California-Los Angeles, University of[5]	31	4.26
North Carolina State University[5]	32	4.24
United States Naval Academy[5]	33	4.23
Alabama-Birmingham, University of[5]	34	4.22
Auburn University[5]	35	4.21
West Virginia University[5]	36	4.19
Wichita State University[1]	37	4.17
California-Davis, University of[3]	38	4.15
Boston University[5]	39	4.14
Polytechnic University[5]	40	4.13
Parks College of Saint Louis University[5]	41	4.12
Mississippi State University[5]	42	4.11
Oklahoma State University[6]	43	4.08

Explanatory Note: Actual titles by the institution to identify their curricula
[1]Aeronautical Engineering
[2]Aeronautical and Astronautical Engineering
[3]Aeronautical Science and Engineering
[4]Aeronautics and Astronautics
[5]Aerospace Engineering
[6]Aerospace Option in Mechanical Engineering
[7]Aerospace Engineering and Mechanics
[8]Aerospace Engineering Sciences
[9]Astronautical Engineering

AGRICULTURAL BUSINESS

Leading Institutions—Rating of Undergraduate Programs

INSTITUTION	RANK	SCORE
Cornell University	1	4.83
Michigan State University	2	4.80
Pennsylvania State University-University Park	3	4.77
Illinois,Urbana-Champaign, University of	4	4.73
Minnesota, University of	5	4.69
Iowa State University	6	4.66
Colorado State University	7	4.60
Purdue University-West Lafayette	8	4.56
Wisconsin-Madison, University of	9	4.50
California-Davis, University of	10	4.45

AGRICULTURAL ECONOMICS
LEADING INSTITUTIONS—RATING OF UNDERGRADUATE PROGRAMS

INSTITUTION	RANK	SCORE
Minnesota, University of	1	4.91
Wisconsin-Madison, University of	2	4.88
Maryland-College Park, University of	3	4.85
Cornell University	4	4.83
Michigan State University	5	4.80
Illinois,Urbana-Champaign, University of	6	4.77
Virginia Tech	7	4.75
California-Davis, University of	8	4.73
Texas A&M University-College Station	9	4.71
Purdue University-West Lafayette	10	4.67
Massachusetts-Amherst, University of	11	4.62
Ohio State University-Columbus	12	4.57
Pennsylvania State University-University Park	13	4.50
Colorado State University	14	4.46
Missouri-Columbia, University of	15	4.43
Oklahoma State University	16	4.40
Connecticut, University of	17	4.35
Nebraska-Lincoln, University of	18	4.32
Hawaii-Manoa, University of	19	4.27
Washington State University	20	4.20
West Virginia University	21	4.19

AGRICULTURAL ENGINEERING
Leading Institutions—Rating of Undergraduate Programs

INSTITUTION	RANK	SCORE
Cornell University [1]	1	4.91
Texas A&M University-College Station	2	4.90
Iowa State University	3	4.86
Michigan State University	4	4.84
Wisconsin-Madison, University of	5	4.82
Illinois,Urbana-Champaign, University of	6	4.80
Ohio State University-Columbus	7	4.77
Minnesota, University of	8	4.75
Purdue University-West Lafayette	9	4.71
Missouri-Columbia, University of	10	4.69
California-Davis, University of	11	4.65
Pennsylvania State University-University Park	12	4.61
Maryland-College Park, University of	13	4.59
Kansas State University [6]	14	4.54
Oklahoma State University	15	4.50
Tennessee-Knoxville, University of	16	4.44
Louisiana State University-Baton Rouge [4]	17	4.42
Utah State University [4]	18	4.40
Colorado State University	19	4.38
Auburn University	20	4.37
Rutgers University, New Brunswick [3]	21	4.36
Clemson University	22	4.34
Florida, University of	23	4.32
Kentucky, University of	24	4.28
Virginia Tech [5]	25	4.27
Arizona, University of [2]	26	4.25
Texas Tech University	27	4.23
Idaho, University of	28	4.21
Arkansas, University of [4]	29	4.18
South Dakota State University	30	4.16
North Carolina State University [4]	31	4.15
Maine, University of [3]	32	4.14
North Dakota State University	33	4.12
Nebraska-Lincoln, University of	34	4.10
Georgia, University of	35	4.08
New Mexico State University	36	4.06
California Polytechnic State University-San Luis Obispo	37	4.04

Explanatory Note: Actual titles used by the institution to identify their curricula
[1] Agricultural and Biological Engineering
[2] Agricultural and Biosystems Engineering
[3] Bio-Resource Engineering
[4] Biological and Agricultural Engineering
[5] Biological Engineering
[6] Biosystems Engineering

AGRICULTURE

Leading Institutions—Rating of Undergraduate Programs

INSTITUTION	RANK	SCORE
Cornell University	1	4.93
Texas A&M University-College Station	2	4.91
Iowa State University	3	4.88
Purdue University-West Lafayette	4	4.85
Illinois,Urbana-Champaign, University of	5	4.82
Michigan State University	6	4.79
California-Davis, University of	7	4.74
Wisconsin-Madison, University of	8	4.70
Minnesota, University of	9	4.66
Ohio State University-Columbus	10	4.62
Missouri-Columbia, University of	11	4.58
Kansas State University	12	4.55
Pennsylvania State University-University Park	13	4.52
Rutgers University, New Brunswick	14	4.51
Colorado State University	15	4.50
Louisiana State University-Baton Rouge	16	4.48
Maryland-College Park, University of	17	4.47
North Carolina State University	18	4.45
Nebraska-Lincoln, University of	19	4.44
Oklahoma State University	20	4.42
Oregon State University	21	4.41
Tennessee-Knoxville, University of	22	4.39
Georgia, University of	23	4.37
Auburn University	24	4.36
Utah State University	25	4.35
Washington State University	26	4.34
Maine, University of	27	4.33
Massachusetts-Amherst, University of	28	4.32
New Hampshire, University of	29	4.31
North Dakota State University	30	4.30
Montana State University-Bozeman	31	4.29
Vermont, University of	32	4.28
Wyoming, University of	33	4.27
Florida, University of	34	4.25
Clemson University	35	4.23
Arkansas, University of	36	4.21
Kentucky, University of	37	4.20
South Dakota State University	38	4.18
West Virginia University	39	4.16
Arizona, University of	40	4.15
Idaho, University of	41	4.13
Mississippi State University	42	4.12
Virginia Tech	43	4.09
Texas Tech University	44	4.06
New Mexico State University	45	4.05
Connecticut, University of	46	4.03

AGRONOMY
LEADING INSTITUTIONS—RATING OF UNDERGRADUATE PROGRAMS

INSTITUTION	RANK	SCORE
Cornell University	1	4.90
Texas A&M University-College Station	2	4.88
Iowa State University	3	4.86
Purdue University-West Lafayette	4	4.84
Ohio State University-Columbus	5	4.82
Illinois,Urbana-Champaign, University of	6	4.81
Michigan State University	7	4.79
Wisconsin-Madison, University of	8	4.76
Minnesota, University of	9	4.75
Missouri-Columbia, University of	10	4.72
Kansas State University	11	4.69
California-Davis, University of	12	4.67
Pennsylvania State University-University Park	13	4.66
Rutgers University, New Brunswick	14	4.62
Louisiana State University-Baton Rouge	15	4.60
Colorado State University	16	4.57
Nebraska-Lincoln, University of	17	4.53
Maryland-College Park, University of	18	4.52
Oklahoma State University	19	4.51
North Carolina State University	20	4.49
Oregon State University	21	4.48
Tennessee-Knoxville, University of	22	4.46
Utah State University	23	4.43
Auburn University	24	4.40
Georgia, University of	25	4.39
Washington State University	26	4.38
Florida, University of	27	4.37
Maine, University of	28	4.35
New Hampshire, University of	29	4.33
Arizona, University of	30	4.30
Kentucky, University of	31	4.26
Vermont, University of	32	4.23
Mississippi State University	33	4.20
North Dakota State University	34	4.18
Idaho, University of	35	4.17
Wyoming, University of	36	4.16
South Dakota State University	37	4.15
Arkansas, University of	38	4.12
Virginia Tech	39	4.10
Clemson University	40	4.09
New Mexico State University	41	4.08
Montana State University-Bozeman	42	4.06
West Virginia University	43	4.05
Connecticut, University of	44	4.04
Texas Tech University	45	4.02

AMERICAN STUDIES

LEADING INSTITUTIONS—RATING OF UNDERGRADUATE PROGRAMS

INSTITUTION	RANK	SCORE
Yale University	1	4.81
Pennsylvania, University of	2	4.76
Michigan-Ann Arbor, University of	3	4.65
Case Western Reserve University	4	4.60
Iowa, University of	5	4.58
Maryland-College Park, University of	6	4.54
Minnesota, University of	7	4.46
Brown University	8	4.44
Kansas, University of	9	4.39
North Carolina-Chapel Hill, University of	10	4.32
Cornell University	11	4.26
Brandeis University	12	4.15
Texas-Austin, University of	13	4.10
George Washington University	14	4.07
Harvard and Radcliffe Colleges	15	3.87
Chicago, University of	16	3.80
Massachusetts-Amherst, University of	17	3.76
New York University	18	3.72
Notre Dame, University of	19	3.66
Michigan State University	20	3.64
New Mexico, University of	21	3.43
Saint Louis University	22	3.39
Stanford University	23	3.31
State University of New York College at Buffalo	24	3.27
Northwestern University	25	3.22
Tulane University	26	3.18
Williams College	27	3.17
Miami, University of	28	3.13
Hawaii-Manoa, University of	29	3.10
Purdue University-West Lafayette	30	3.08
Florida State University	31	3.05
Smith College	32	3.04
Pennsylvania State University-University Park	33	3.02

ANIMAL SCIENCE
Leading Institutions—Rating of Undergraduate Programs

INSTITUTION	RANK	SCORE
Cornell University	1	4.91
California-Davis, University of	2	4.89
Texas A&M University-College Station	3	4.86
Iowa State University	4	4.85
Purdue University-West Lafayette	5	4.82
Illinois,Urbana-Champaign, University of	6	4.80
Minnesota, University of	7	4.76
Wisconsin-Madison, University of	8	4.73
Kansas State University	9	4.70
Colorado State University	10	4.66
Ohio State University-Columbus	11	4.62
Missouri-Columbia, University of	12	4.60
Pennsylvania State University-University Park	13	4.58
Louisiana State University-Baton Rouge	14	4.55
Florida, University of	15	4.50
Wyoming, University of	16	4.47
Nebraska-Lincoln, University of	17	4.46
Maryland-College Park, University of	18	4.43
Oklahoma State University	19	4.41
Georgia, University of	20	4.36
Clemson University	21	4.30
Oregon State University	22	4.26
North Carolina State University	23	4.22
Delaware, University of	24	4.19
Virginia Tech	25	4.16
Massachusetts-Amherst, University of	26	4.12
Connecticut, University of	27	4.10
West Virginia University	28	4.09
Washington State University	29	4.08
Utah State University	30	4.07
North Dakota State University	31	4.06
Texas Tech University	32	4.05
Hawaii-Manoa, University of	33	4.04
Tennessee-Knoxville, University of	34	4.03
Mississippi State University	35	4.02

ANTHROPOLOGY
LEADING INSTITUTIONS—RATING OF UNDERGRADUATE PROGRAMS

INSTITUTION	RANK	SCORE
Michigan-Ann Arbor, University of	1	4.92
Chicago, University of	2	4.91
California-Berkeley, University of	3	4.90
Pennsylvania, University of	4	4.88
Arizona, University of	5	4.86
Stanford University	6	4.85
Yale University	7	4.82
California-Los Angeles, University of	8	4.80
Harvard and Radcliffe Colleges	9	4.79
Northwestern University	10	4.77
Texas-Austin, University of	11	4.75
New Mexico, University of	12	4.72
Cornell University	13	4.70
Illinois,Urbana-Champaign, University of	14	4.68
Columbia University	15	4.67
California-Santa Barbara, University of	16	4.64
California-San Diego, University of	17	4.62
Washington, University of	18	4.60
Massachusetts-Amherst, University of	19	4.59
Wisconsin-Madison, University of	20	4.56
Florida, University of	21	4.52
Pennsylvania State University-University Park	22	4.51
Pittsburgh, University of	23	4.49
Duke University	24	4.48
Rutgers University, New Brunswick	25	4.46
Indiana University-Bloomington	26	4.45
Hawaii-Manoa, University of	27	4.42
California-Irvine, University of	28	4.40
North Carolina-Chapel Hill, University of	29	4.37
Virginia, University of	30	4.35
State University of New York College at Buffalo	31	4.33
Michigan State University	32	4.32
State University of New York at Binghamton	33	4.30
Arizona State University	34	4.27
Brandeis University	35	4.26
California-Davis, University of	36	4.23
Colorado-Boulder, University of	37	4.20
Tulane University	38	4.19
New York University	39	4.18
Princeton University	40	4.16
Washington University in Saint Louis	41	4.14
Connecticut, University of	42	4.12
Bryn Mawr College	43	4.10

Anthropology—*continued*

INSTITUTION	RANK	SCORE
Oregon, University of	44	4.09
California-Riverside, University of	45	4.08
Minnesota, University of	46	4.07
Brown University	47	4.06
Southern Methodist University	48	4.05
Kansas, University of	49	4.04
Missouri-Columbia, University of	50	4.03

APPLIED MATHEMATICS

Leading Institutions—Rating of Undergraduate Programs

INSTITUTION	RANK	SCORE
Harvard and Radcliffe Colleges	1	4.87
Chicago, University of	2	4.85
California-Berkeley, University of	3	4.83
Brown University	4	4.80
Wisconsin-Madison, University of	5	4.76
Columbia University	6	4.74
Yale University	7	4.70
California-Los Angeles, University of	8	4.66
California Institute of Technology	9	4.63
Purdue University-West Lafayette	10	4.61
California-San Diego, University of	11	4.55
Northwestern University	12	4.52
Carnegie Mellon University	13	4.48
Johns Hopkins University	14	4.43
Virginia, University of	15	4.37
Colorado-Boulder, University of	16	4.32

ARABIC
LEADING INSTITUTIONS—RATING OF UNDERGRADUATE PROGRAMS

INSTITUTION	RANK	SCORE
Chicago, University of	1	4.84
Michigan-Ann Arbor, University of	2	4.79
Pennsylvania, University of	3	4.73
Harvard and Radcliffe Colleges	4	4.69
Princeton University	5	4.61
New York University	6	4.50
Johns Hopkins University	7	4.40
Columbia University	8	4.33
Georgetown University	9	4.27

ARCHITECTURAL ENGINEERING
Leading Institutions—Rating of Undergraduate Programs

INSTITUTION	RANK	SCORE
Texas-Austin, University of	1	4.81
Pennsylvania State University-University Park	2	4.73
Kansas, University of	3	4.64
Colorado-Boulder, University of	4	4.61
Miami, University of	5	4.54
Kansas State University	6	4.48
California Polytechnic State University-San Luis Obispo	7	4.40
Oklahoma State University	8	4.32

ARCHITECTURE
LEADING INSTITUTIONS—RATING OF UNDERGRADUATE PROGRAMS

INSTITUTION	RANK	SCORE
California-Berkeley, University of	1	4.89
Massachusetts Institute of Technology	2	4.76
Carnegie Mellon University	3	4.62
Princeton University	4	4.58
Cornell University	5	4.53
Michigan-Ann Arbor, University of	6	4.49
Illinois,Urbana-Champaign, University of	7	4.38
Rice University	8	4.32
Georgia Institute of Technology	9	4.27
Southern California, University of	10	4.19
Texas-Austin, University of	11	4.14
Pratt Institute	12	4.10
Minnesota, University of	13	4.07
Cincinnati, University of	14	3.86
Kansas, University of	15	3.82
Oklahoma, University of	16	3.77
Rensselaer Polytechnic Institute	17	3.74
Arizona, University of	18	3.70
Washington, University of	19	3.65
Washington University in Saint Louis	20	3.62
Virginia Tech	21	3.58
Texas A&M University-College Station	22	3.53
Kansas State University	23	3.52
Oregon, University of	24	3.42
Ohio State University-Columbus	25	3.40
Cooper Union	26	3.38
Houston, University of	27	3.36
Virginia, University of	28	3.34
Notre Dame, University of	29	3.32
Miami, University of	30	3.26
Hawaii-Manoa, University of	31	3.23
Florida, University of	32	3.22
Louisiana State University-Baton Rouge	33	3.17
City University of New York-City College	34	3.12
Pennsylvania State University-University Park	35	3.11
Syracuse University	36	3.08
Tulane University	37	3.06
Wisconsin-Milwaukee, University of	38	3.04
North Carolina State University	39	3.03

ART

LEADING INSTITUTIONS—RATING OF UNDERGRADUATE PROGRAMS

INSTITUTION	RANK	SCORE
New York University	1	4.90
Harvard and Radcliffe Colleges	2	4.89
Princeton University	3	4.83
Yale University	4	4.76
California-Berkeley, University of	5	4.67
Columbia University	6	4.60
Stanford University	7	4.59
Bryn Mawr College	8	4.54
Michigan-Ann Arbor, University of	9	4.50
Pennsylvania, University of	10	4.48
Chicago, University of	11	4.46
Cornell University	12	4.41
Johns Hopkins University	13	4.39
Brown University	14	4.35
North Carolina-Chapel Hill, University of	15	4.30
California-Los Angeles, University of	16	4.27
Pittsburgh, University of	17	4.25
Indiana University-Bloomington	18	4.21
Delaware, University of	19	3.89
Virginia, University of	20	3.87
Boston University	21	3.80
Maryland-College Park, University of	22	3.79
Northwestern University	23	3.72
Minnesota, University of	24	3.69
Rutgers University, New Brunswick	25	3.64
Pennsylvania State University-University Park	26	3.59
Kansas, University of	27	3.55
Texas-Austin, University of	28	3.54
Iowa, University of	29	3.53
Washington University in Saint Louis	30	3.51
Wisconsin-Madison, University of	31	3.42
Ohio State University-Columbus	32	3.39
Washington, University of	33	3.35
Case Western Reserve University	34	3.30
New Mexico, University of	35	3.29
Arizona, University of	36	3.28
Georgia, University of	37	3.22
Missouri-Columbia, University of	38	3.19
Southern California, University of	39	3.12
Florida State University	40	3.10
Oregon, University of	41	3.09
Ohio University	42	3.07

ART HISTORY
LEADING INSTITUTIONS—RATING OF UNDERGRADUATE PROGRAMS

INSTITUTION	RANK	SCORE
New York University	1	4.92
Harvard and Radcliffe Colleges	2	4.91
Princeton University	3	4.89
Yale University	4	4.86
Columbia University	5	4.83
California-Berkeley, University of	6	4.80
Stanford University	7	4.78
Bryn Mawr College	8	4.75
Michigan-Ann Arbor, University of	9	4.70
Johns Hopkins University	10	4.63
Pennsylvania, University of	11	4.60
California-Los Angeles, University of	12	4.59
Chicago, University of	13	4.55
Brown University	14	4.46
North Carolina-Chapel Hill, University of	15	4.40
Cornell University	16	4.33
Pittsburgh, University of	17	4.27
Indiana University-Bloomington	18	4.20
Delaware, University of	19	4.14
Virginia, University of	20	3.85
Boston University	21	3.80
Maryland-College Park, University of	22	3.74
Northwestern University	23	3.69
Rutgers University, New Brunswick	24	3.64
Minnesota, University of	25	3.60
Pennsylvania State University-University Park	26	3.54
Kansas, University of	27	3.51
Iowa, University of	28	3.50
Texas-Austin, University of	29	3.48
Washington University in Saint Louis	30	3.46
Wisconsin-Madison, University of	31	3.41
Ohio State University-Columbus	32	3.36
Washington, University of	33	3.30
Case Western Reserve University	34	3.27
New Mexico, University of	35	3.20
Oregon, University of	36	3.19
Georgia, University of	37	3.16
Missouri-Columbia, University of	38	3.15
Florida State University	39	3.13
Southern California, University of	40	3.11
Ohio University	41	3.05

ASIAN/ORIENTAL STUDIES
LEADING INSTITUTIONS—RATING OF UNDERGRADUATE PROGRAMS

INSTITUTION	RANK	SCORE
Harvard and Radcliffe Colleges	1	4.82
California-Berkeley, University of	2	4.78
Chicago, University of	3	4.73
Cornell University	4	4.70
Washington, University of	5	4.66
Pennsylvania, University of	6	4.62
Michigan-Ann Arbor, University of	7	4.59
Hawaii-Manoa, University of	8	4.56
Texas-Austin, University of	9	4.51
Illinois,Urbana-Champaign, University of	10	4.45
Yale University	11	4.41
Stanford University	12	4.37
Wisconsin-Madison, University of	13	4.33

ASTRONOMY
LEADING INSTITUTIONS—RATING OF UNDERGRADUATE PROGRAMS

INSTITUTION	RANK	SCORE
California Institute of Technology	1	4.92
California-Berkeley, University of	2	4.86
Harvard and Radcliffe Colleges	3	4.82
Cornell University	4	4.75
Wisconsin-Madison, University of	5	4.66
Massachusetts Institute of Technology	6	4.62
Arizona, University of	7	4.59
Maryland-College Park, University of	8	4.53
Michigan-Ann Arbor, University of	9	4.50
California-Los Angeles, University of	10	4.46
Yale University	11	4.41
Case Western Reserve University	12	4.40
Illinois,Urbana-Champaign, University of	13	4.38
Texas-Austin, University of	14	4.35
Virginia, University of	15	4.32
Washington, University of	16	4.29
Kansas, University of	17	4.28
Indiana University-Bloomington	18	4.25
Northwestern University	19	4.23
Pennsylvania, University of	20	4.22
Ohio State University-Columbus	21	4.21
Pennsylvania State University-University Park	22	4.20
Minnesota, University of	23	4.18
Oklahoma, University of	24	4.16
Southern California, University of	25	4.15

ASTROPHYSICS
LEADING INSTITUTIONS—RATING OF UNDERGRADUATE PROGRAMS

INSTITUTION	RANK	SCORE
Massachusetts Institute of Technology	1	4.85
California Institute of Technology	2	4.81
Princeton University	3	4.79
Indiana University-Bloomington	4	4.72
Minnesota, University of	5	4.66
Harvard and Radcliffe Colleges	6	4.61
Purdue University-West Lafayette	7	4.53
Pennsylvania, University of	8	4.45
Virginia, University of	9	4.40
Oklahoma, University of	10	4.34

ATMOSPHERIC SCIENCES
LEADING INSTITUTIONS—RATING OF UNDERGRADUATE PROGRAMS

INSTITUTION	RANK	SCORE
Cornell University	1	4.90
Arizona, University of	2	4.85
Michigan-Ann Arbor, University of	3	4.81
Kansas, University of	4	4.72
California-Davis, University of	5	4.69
Purdue University-West Lafayette	6	4.64
California-Los Angeles, University of	7	4.59
Missouri-Columbia, University of	8	4.55

BACTERIOLOGY/MICROBIOLOGY
LEADING INSTITUTIONS—RATING OF UNDERGRADUATE PROGRAMS

INSTITUTION	RANK	SCORE
Massachusetts Institute of Technology	1	4.92
California-San Diego, University of	2	4.90
California-Berkeley, University of	3	4.88
Washington, University of	4	4.86
California-Los Angeles, University of	5	4.84
Illinois,Urbana-Champaign, University of	6	4.83
California-Davis, University of	7	4.82
Wisconsin-Madison, University of	8	4.81
Michigan-Ann Arbor, University of	9	4.80
Stanford University	10	4.79
Rutgers University, New Brunswick	11	4.78
Cornell University	12	4.77
Minnesota, University of	13	4.75
Purdue University-West Lafayette	14	4.73
Michigan State University	15	4.72
Texas-Austin, University of	16	4.71
Rochester, University of	17	4.70
Iowa, University of	18	4.69
Indiana University-Bloomington	19	4.68
Notre Dame, University of	20	4.67
Pittsburgh, University of	21	4.63
Massachusetts-Amherst, University of	22	4.58
Oregon State University	23	4.55
Pennsylvania State University-University Park	24	4.50
Maryland-College Park, University of	25	4.48
Wayne State University	26	4.43
Northwestern University	27	4.38
Connecticut, University of	28	4.35
Georgia, University of	29	4.31
North Carolina State University	30	4.26
Missouri-Columbia, University of	31	4.24
Tennessee-Knoxville, University of	32	4.21
Iowa State University	33	4.18
Kansas State University	34	4.16
Kansas, University of	35	4.11
Colorado State University	36	4.08
Ohio State University-Columbus	37	4.06

BEHAVIORAL SCIENCES
LEADING INSTITUTIONS—RATING OF UNDERGRADUATE PROGRAMS

INSTITUTION	RANK	SCORE
Cornell University	1	4.86
Johns Hopkins University	2	4.82
Carnegie Mellon University	3	4.79
Chicago, University of	4	4.74
Pennsylvania, University of	5	4.70
New York University	6	4.67
Northwestern University	7	4.60
United States Air Force Academy	8	4.57
United States Military Academy	9	4.53

BIOCHEMISTRY
Leading Institutions—Rating of Undergraduate Programs

INSTITUTION	RANK	SCORE
Harvard and Radcliffe Colleges	1	4.92
Massachusetts Institute of Technology	2	4.91
California-Berkeley, University of	3	4.90
Wisconsin-Madison, University of	4	4.85
Yale University	5	4.84
California-Los Angeles, University of	6	4.81
Cornell University	7	4.79
California-San Diego, University of	8	4.75
Chicago, University of	9	4.71
Illinois,Urbana-Champaign, University of	10	4.70
Columbia University	11	4.63
Michigan-Ann Arbor, University of	12	4.58
Pennsylvania, University of	13	4.55
California-Davis, University of	14	4.53
Brandeis University	15	4.50
Northwestern University	16	4.49
Princeton University	17	4.46
Iowa, University of	18	4.43
Michigan State University	19	4.40
Rice University	20	4.38
Case Western Reserve University	21	4.34
Purdue University-West Lafayette	22	4.33
Oregon State University	23	4.28
New York University	24	4.25
Oregon, University of	25	4.23
Rutgers University, New Brunswick	26	4.20
State University of New York at Stony Brook	27	4.19
Texas-Austin, University of	28	4.17
Iowa State University	29	4.15
California-Riverside, University of	30	4.14
Pennsylvania State University-University Park	31	4.13
Southern California, University of	32	4.10

BIOENGINEERING/BIOMEDICAL ENGINEERING

LEADING INSTITUTIONS—RATING OF UNDERGRADUATE PROGRAMS

INSTITUTION	RANK	SCORE
Johns Hopkins University[2]	1	4.90
Pennsylvania, University of[1]	2	4.88
Brown University[2]	3	4.87
Duke University[2]	4	4.84
Northwestern University[2]	5	4.78
Tulane University[2]	6	4.70
Case Western Reserve University[2]	7	4.62
Texas A&M University-College Station[1]	8	4.57
Rensselaer Polytechnic Institute[2]	9	4.56
Marquette University[2]	10	4.46
California-San Diego, University of	11	4.44
Louisiana Tech University[2]	12	4.28
Boston University[2]	13	4.25
Iowa, University of	14	4.20
Arizona State University	15	4.16
Illinois-Chicago, University of[1]	16	4.02

Explanatory Note: Actual titles used by the institution to identify their curricula
[1]Bioengineering
[2]Biomedical Engineering

BIOLOGY
Leading Institutions—Rating of Undergraduate Programs

INSTITUTION	RANK	SCORE
California Institute of Technology	1	4.92
Massachusetts Institute of Technology	2	4.91
Yale University	3	4.89
Harvard and Radcliffe Colleges	4	4.88
Wisconsin-Madison, University of	5	4.87
California-San Diego, University of	6	4.86
California-Berkeley, University of	7	4.84
Colorado-Boulder, University of	8	4.82
Columbia University	9	4.80
Stanford University	10	4.76
Washington, University of	11	4.72
Chicago, University of	12	4.70
Duke University	13	4.69
Washington University in Saint Louis	14	4.68
California-Los Angeles, University of	15	4.67
Michigan-Ann Arbor, University of	16	4.66
Cornell University	17	4.64
Pennsylvania, University of	18	4.62
Purdue University-West Lafayette	19	4.59
Indiana University-Bloomington	20	4.55
North Carolina-Chapel Hill, University of	21	4.54
Utah, University of	22	4.53
Johns Hopkins University	23	4.52
Northwestern University	24	4.50
Princeton University	25	4.45
California-Irvine, University of	26	4.43
Notre Dame, University of	27	4.42
California-Santa Barbara, University of	28	4.38
Virginia, University of	29	4.36
Brown University	30	4.35
Illinois,Urbana-Champaign, University of	31	4.32
Pittsburgh, University of	32	4.29
Vanderbilt University	33	4.28
Oregon, University of	34	4.25
State University of New York at Stony Brook	35	4.19
Rochester, University of	36	4.11
Tufts University	37	3.90
Minnesota, University of	38	3.88
State University of New York College at Buffalo	39	3.85
Texas-Austin, University of	40	3.81
Florida State University	41	3.77
Michigan State University	42	3.74
Southern California, University of	43	3.71
Connecticut, University of	44	3.67
California, Riverside, University of	45	3.63

Biology—*continued*

INSTITUTION	RANK	SCORE
Rice University	46	3.61
Iowa State University	47	3.58
State University of New York at Albany	48	3.55
Case Western Reserve University	49	3.53
Boston University	50	3.40
Ohio State University-Columbus	51	3.38
New York University	52	3.36
Iowa, University of	53	3.35
Pennsylvania State University-University Park	54	3.32
Emory University	55	3.27
Brandeis University	56	3.25
Kansas, University of	57	3.20
Rutgers University, New Brunswick	58	3.16
Tulane University	59	3.15
United States Air Force Academy	60	3.12
Missouri-Columbia, University of	61	3.11

BIOPHYSICS
LEADING INSTITUTIONS—RATING OF UNDERGRADUATE PROGRAMS

INSTITUTION	RANK	SCORE
Johns Hopkins University	1	4.88
Michigan-Ann Arbor, University of	2	4.87
California-San Diego, University of	3	4.85
Yale University	4	4.82
Illinois,Urbana-Champaign, University of	5	4.77
Purdue University-West Lafayette	6	4.73
Massachusetts Institute of Technology	7	4.71
Pennsylvania, University of	8	4.68
Cornell University	9	4.61
Carnegie Mellon University	10	4.56
Brown University	11	4.51
Iowa State University	12	4.46
State University of New York College at Buffalo	13	4.40

BOTANY
LEADING INSTITUTIONS—RATING OF UNDERGRADUATE PROGRAMS

INSTITUTION	RANK	SCORE
California-Davis, University of	1	4.90
Cornell University	2	4.89
Texas-Austin, University of	3	4.86
Wisconsin-Madison, University of	4	4.82
Michigan-Ann Arbor, University of	5	4.81
Duke University	6	4.78
Michigan State University	7	4.76
Illinois,Urbana-Champaign, University of	8	4.73
California-Riverside, University of	9	4.70
North Carolina State University	10	4.66
Pennsylvania State University-University Park	11	4.63
Indiana University-Bloomington	12	4.61
Minnesota, University of	13	4.59
Georgia, University of	14	4.55
Washington, University of	15	4.50
Purdue University-West Lafayette	16	4.48
Washington University in Saint Louis	17	4.45
Iowa State University	18	4.40
Ohio State University-Columbus	19	4.38
Kentucky, University of	20	4.36
Oregon State University	21	4.34
Florida, University of	22	4.32
Massachusetts-Amherst, University of	23	4.30
Nebraska-Lincoln, University of	24	4.26
SUNY College of Environmental Science and Forestry	25	4.25
Oklahoma, University of	26	4.20
Rutgers University, New Brunswick	27	4.17
Washington State University	28	4.13
Colorado State University	29	4.12
Hawaii-Manoa, University of	30	4.10
Tennessee-Knoxville, University of	31	4.08

BUSINESS ADMINISTRATION

LEADING INSTITUTIONS—RATING OF UNDERGRADUATE PROGRAMS

INSTITUTION	RANK	SCORE
Pennsylvania, University of	1	4.91
Indiana University-Bloomington	2	4.89
Michigan-Ann Arbor, University of	3	4.87
California-Berkeley, University of	4	4.85
Virginia, University of	5	4.82
New York University	6	4.81
Illinois,Urbana-Champaign, University of	7	4.76
Wisconsin-Madison, University of	8	4.74
Purdue University-West Lafayette	9	4.73
North Carolina-Chapel Hill, University of	10	4.72
Washington, University of	11	4.67
Michigan State University	12	4.66
Texas-Austin, University of	13	4.65
City University of New York-Baruch College	14	4.64
Minnesota, University of	15	4.62
Washington University in Saint Louis	16	4.60
Southern California, University of	17	4.59
Houston, University of	18	4.58
Pennsylvania State University-University Park	19	4.57
Texas A&M University-College Station	20	4.55
Notre Dame, University of	21	4.53
Southern Methodist University	22	4.51
Ohio State University-Columbus	23	4.48
State University of New York College at Buffalo	24	4.46
Utah, University of	25	4.43
Lehigh University	26	4.42
Oregon, University of	27	4.40
Florida, University of	28	4.39
Louisiana State University-Baton Rouge	29	4.36
Massachusetts-Amherst, University of	30	4.34
Arizona, University of	31	4.33
Iowa, University of	32	4.31
Arizona State University	33	4.28
Maryland-College Park, University of	34	4.26
Georgia State University	35	4.25
Temple University	36	4.23
George Washington University	37	4.21
Syracuse University	38	4.20
Colorado-Boulder, University of	39	4.16
Emory University	40	4.14
Missouri-Columbia, University of	41	4.12
South Carolina-Columbia , University of,	42	4.11
Denver, University of	43	4.08
Georgia, University of	44	4.07
Nebraska-Lincoln, University of	45	4.03

CELL BIOLOGY
LEADING INSTITUTIONS—RATING OF UNDERGRADUATE PROGRAMS

INSTITUTION	RANK	SCORE
Massachusetts Institute of Technology	1	4.91
California Institute of Technology	2	4.90
Wisconsin-Madison, University of	3	4.83
California-San Diego, University of	4	4.81
Chicago, University of	5	4.77
California-Berkeley, University of	6	4.74
Colorado-Boulder, University of	7	4.71
Purdue University-West Lafayette	8	4.67
Brown University	9	4.62
Northwestern University	10	4.59
Michigan-Ann Arbor, University of	11	4.52
Carnegie Mellon University	12	4.49
Minnesota, University of	13	4.38
Cornell University	14	4.37
Pennsylvania State University-University Park	15	4.30
Rochester, University of	16	4.26
Arizona, University of	17	4.24
Kansas, University of	18	4.18
State University of New York College at Buffalo	19	4.16

CERAMIC ART/DESIGN
LEADING INSTITUTIONS—RATING OF UNDERGRADUATE PROGRAMS

INSTITUTION	RANK	SCORE
Alfred University	1	4.86
Carnegie Mellon University	2	4.83
Ohio State University-Columbus	3	4.80
Pratt Institute	4	4.72
Iowa, University of	5	4.69
Kansas, University of	6	4.64
Oklahoma, University of	7	4.60
Texas-Austin, University of	8	4.56
Purdue University-West Lafayette	9	4.50
Louisiana State University-Baton Rouge	10	4.49
Florida, University of	11	4.46
Houston, University of	12	4.42
Michigan-Ann Arbor, University of	13	4.39
Miami, University of	14	4.35

CERAMIC ENGINEERING
LEADING INSTITUTIONS—RATING OF UNDERGRADUATE PROGRAMS

INSTITUTION	RANK	SCORE
State University of New York College of Technology at Alfred [1,2,4]	1	4.90
Illinois,Urbana-Champaign, University of [1]	2	4.88
Ohio State University-Columbus [1]	3	4.82
Iowa State University [1]	4	4.74
Missouri-Rolla, University of [1]	5	4.68
Georgia Institute of Technology [1]	6	4.57
Washington, University of [1]	7	4.48
Rutgers University, New Brunswick [1]	8	4.33
Pennsylvania State University-University Park [3]	9	4.28
Clemson University [1]	10	4.24

Explanatory Note: Actual titles used by the institution to identify their curricula
[1] Ceramic Engineering
[2] Ceramic Engineering Science
[3] Ceramic Science and Engineering
[4] Glass Engineering Science

CHEMICAL ENGINEERING

LEADING INSTITUTIONS—RATING OF UNDERGRADUATE PROGRAMS

INSTITUTION	RANK	SCORE
Minnesota, University of	1	4.91
Wisconsin-Madison, University of	2	4.90
California-Berkeley, University of	3	4.88
California Institute of Technology	4	4.85
Stanford University	5	4.82
Delaware, University of	6	4.80
Massachusetts Institute of Technology	7	4.79
Illinois,Urbana-Champaign, University of	8	4.75
Princeton University	9	4.74
Houston, University of	10	4.73
Purdue University-West Lafayette	11	4.72
Notre Dame, University of	12	4.71
Northwestern University	13	4.68
Cornell University	14	4.65
Texas-Austin, University of	15	4.63
Stevens Institute of Technology	16	4.62
Pennsylvania, University of	17	4.61
Carnegie Mellon University	18	4.60
Michigan-Ann Arbor, University of	19	4.58
Rice University	20	4.57
Washington, University of	21	4.56
Massachusetts-Amherst, University of	22	4.55
Iowa State University	23	4.53
Florida, University of	24	4.51
Rochester, University of	25	4.50
State University of New York College at Buffalo	26	4.48
Pennsylvania State University-University Park	27	4.47
Case Western Reserve University	28	4.44
Colorado-Boulder, University of	29	4.43
Washington University in Saint Louis	30	4.40
Lehigh University	31	4.39
Texas A&M University-College Station	32	4.37
City University of New York-City College	33	4.35
Ohio State University-Columbus	34	4.33
Georgia Institute of Technology	35	4.31
North Carolina State University	36	4.29
Yale University	37	4.25
Rensselaer Polytechnic Institute	38	4.23
Virginia Tech	39	4.21
Tennessee-Knoxville, University of	40	4.20
Virginia, University of	41	4.19
Columbia University	42	4.18
Arizona, University of	43	4.17

Chemical Engineering—*continued*

INSTITUTION	RANK	SCORE
Syracuse University	44	4.16
Utah, University of	45	4.15
California-Los Angeles, University of	46	4.13
Oklahoma, University of	47	4.11
Maryland-College Park, University of	48	4.10
Oregon State University	49	4.09
Louisiana State University-Baton Rouge	50	4.06
Pittsburgh, University of	51	4.05
Iowa, University of	52	4.04
Clarkson University	53	4.02

CHEMISTRY

LEADING INSTITUTIONS—RATING OF UNDERGRADUATE PROGRAMS

INSTITUTION	RANK	SCORE
California Institute of Technology	1	4.95
California-Berkeley, University of	2	4.94
Harvard and Radcliffe Colleges	3	4.93
Massachusetts Institute of Technology	4	4.92
Columbia University	5	4.91
Stanford University	6	4.90
Illinois,Urbana-Champaign, University of	7	4.88
Chicago, University of	8	4.85
California-Los Angeles, University of	9	4.82
Wisconsin-Madison, University of	10	4.80
Cornell University	11	4.78
Northwestern University	12	4.77
Princeton University	13	4.75
Yale University	14	4.74
Purdue University-West Lafayette	15	4.71
North Carolina-Chapel Hill, University of	16	4.69
Ohio State University-Columbus	17	4.66
Texas-Austin, University of	18	4.63
Iowa State University	19	4.61
Indiana University-Bloomington	20	4.59
California-San Diego, University of	21	4.58
Minnesota, University of	22	4.57
Notre Dame, University of	23	4.56
Pennsylvania State University-University Park	24	4.53
Brown University	25	4.52
Rochester, University of	26	4.51
Carnegie Mellon University	27	4.50
Pennsylvania, University of	28	4.48
Rice University	29	4.47
Michigan-Ann Arbor, University of	30	4.46
Washington, University of	31	4.45
Colorado-Boulder, University of	32	4.44
Texas A&M University-College Station	33	4.43
Southern California, University of	34	4.41
Pittsburgh, University of	35	4.39
Florida, University of	36	4.37
California-Riverside, University of	37	4.35
Dartmouth College	38	4.34
California-Santa Barbara, University of	39	4.32
California-Irvine, University of	40	4.30
Johns Hopkins University	41	4.28
California-Davis, University of	42	4.27
Utah, University of	43	4.25

Chemistry—*continued*

INSTITUTION	RANK	SCORE
Oregon, University of	44	4.23
Duke University	45	4.20
Michigan State University	46	4.18
Rensselaer Polytechnic Institute	47	4.16
Virginia, University of	48	4.15
Florida State University	49	4.14
Vanderbilt University	50	4.10
Case Western Reserve University	51	4.09
Iowa, University of	52	4.06
Georgia Institute of Technology	53	4.05

CHILD PSYCHOLOGY

LEADING INSTITUTIONS—RATING OF UNDERGRADUATE PROGRAMS

INSTITUTION	RANK	SCORE
Wayne State University	1	4.59
Northwestern University	2	4.55
Cornell University	3	4.52
New York University	4	4.47
Michigan-Ann Arbor, University of	5	4.44
Iowa, University of	6	4.40
Carnegie Mellon University	7	4.37
Minnesota, University of	8	4.30
Iowa State University	9	4.28
Pennsylvania, University of	10	4.26
Pittsburgh, University of	11	4.24
Ohio State University-Columbus	12	4.20
Wisconsin-Madison, University of	13	4.16
Syracuse University	14	4.14
Tufts University	15	4.09
Florida State University	16	4.05
Utah, University of	17	4.04

CHINESE

LEADING INSTITUTIONS—RATING OF UNDERGRADUATE PROGRAMS

INSTITUTION	RANK	SCORE
Harvard and Radcliffe Colleges	1	4.87
Cornell University	2	4.85
Chicago, University of	3	4.82
Pennsylvania, University of	4	4.73
California-Berkeley, University of	5	4.68
Columbia University	6	4.67
Stanford University	7	4.65
Wisconsin-Madison, University of	8	4.55
Michigan-Ann Arbor, University of	9	4.54
Hawaii-Manoa, University of	10	4.48
Washington, University of	11	4.46
Yale University	12	4.42
Indiana University-Bloomington	13	4.32
Georgetown University	14	4.27

CIVIL ENGINEERING

LEADING INSTITUTIONS—RATING OF UNDERGRADUATE PROGRAMS

INSTITUTION	RANK	SCORE
California-Berkeley, University of	1	4.92
Massachusetts Institute of Technology	2	4.90
Illinois,Urbana-Champaign, University of	3	4.89
Stanford University	4	4.85
Texas-Austin, University of	5	4.82
Cornell University	6	4.80
Northwestern University	7	4.78
Purdue University-West Lafayette	8	4.77
Michigan-Ann Arbor, University of	9	4.74
Colorado State University	10	4.72
Washington, University of	11	4.67
Princeton University	12	4.66
Wisconsin-Madison, University of	13	4.64
Stevens Institute of Technology	14	4.62
Columbia University	15	4.60
Brown University	16	4.59
Lehigh University	17	4.56
California-Los Angeles, University of	18	4.55
Georgia Institute of Technology	19	4.52
Carnegie Mellon University	20	4.50
Texas A&M University-College Station	21	4.49
California-Davis, University of	22	4.48
Colorado-Boulder, University of	23	4.47
Ohio State University-Columbus	24	4.46
North Carolina State University	25	4.45
Minnesota, University of	26	4.44
Iowa State University	27	4.42
Iowa, University of	28	4.40
Massachusetts-Amherst, University of	29	4.38
Virginia Tech	30	4.35
Florida, University of	31	4.32
Washington University in Saint Louis	32	4.30
Rice University	33	4.29
Rensselaer Polytechnic Institute	34	4.27
Kansas, University of	35	4.25
Duke University	36	4.23
Southern California, University of	37	4.22
Pennsylvania State University-University Park	38	4.21
Oregon State University	39	4.20
Michigan State University	40	4.19
Vanderbilt University [1]	41	4.18
Maryland-College Park, University of	42	4.17
Missouri-Rolla, University of	43	4.16

Civil Engineering—*continued*

INSTITUTION	RANK	SCORE
Pennsylvania, University of[2]	44	4.15
Notre Dame, University of	45	4.13
Missouri-Columbia, University of	46	4.12
State University of New York College at Buffalo	47	4.11
Pittsburgh, University of	48	4.10
Oklahoma, University of	49	4.09
Utah State University	50	4.08
Tennessee-Knoxville, University of	51	4.07
Oklahoma State University	52	4.06
Arizona, University of	53	4.04
City University of New York-City College	54	4.03
United States Air Force Academy	55	4.02

Explanatory Note: Actual titles used by the institution to identify their curricula
[1]Civil and Environmental Engineering
[2]Civil Engineering Systems

CLASSICS

LEADING INSTITUTIONS—RATING OF UNDERGRADUATE PROGRAMS

INSTITUTION	RANK	SCORE
Harvard and Radcliffe Colleges	1	4.90
California-Berkeley, University of	2	4.89
Yale University	3	4.87
Princeton University	4	4.82
Michigan-Ann Arbor, University of	5	4.80
North Carolina-Chapel Hill, University of	6	4.75
Bryn Mawr College	7	4.71
Texas-Austin, University of	8	4.69
Brown University	9	4.64
Columbia University	10	4.62
Pennsylvania, University of	11	4.59
Cornell University	12	4.57
Stanford University	13	4.53
Chicago, University of	14	4.47
Illinois,Urbana-Champaign, University of	15	4.41
Duke University	16	4.33
Johns Hopkins University	17	4.29
California-Los Angeles, University of	18	4.23
Indiana University-Bloomington	19	4.18
Boston University	20	4.16
Catholic University of America, The	21	4.14
Fordham University	22	4.11
Vanderbilt University	23	4.10

COMMUNICATION

LEADING INSTITUTIONS—RATING OF UNDERGRADUATE PROGRAMS

INSTITUTION	RANK	SCORE
Northwestern University	1	4.86
Stanford University	2	4.84
Pennsylvania, University of	3	4.81
Michigan-Ann Arbor, University of	4	4.77
Southern California, University of	5	4.71
Iowa, University of	6	4.67
Michigan State University	7	4.65
Texas-Austin, University of	8	4.63
Syracuse University	9	4.60
Florida State University	10	4.54
Wisconsin-Madison, University of	11	4.43
Washington, University of	12	4.39
Ohio State University-Columbus	13	4.37
Minnesota, University of	14	4.33
Purdue University-West Lafayette	15	4.25
State University of New York College at Buffalo	16	4.20
Massachusetts-Amherst, University of	17	4.16
Ohio University	18	4.11
Wayne State University	19	4.10

COMPARATIVE LITERATURE
LEADING INSTITUTIONS—RATING OF UNDERGRADUATE PROGRAMS

INSTITUTION	RANK	SCORE
California-Berkeley, University of	1	4.81
Harvard and Radcliffe Colleges	2	4.78
Columbia University	3	4.76
Yale University	4	4.73
Chicago, University of	5	4.71
Pennsylvania, University of	6	4.69
Illinois,Urbana-Champaign, University of	7	4.68
Princeton University	8	4.63
Stanford University	9	4.61
Michigan-Ann Arbor, University of	10	4.57
Cornell University	11	4.54
Indiana University-Bloomington	12	4.52
Brown University	13	4.47
Northwestern University	14	4.42
Washington, University of	15	4.41
North Carolina-Chapel Hill, University of	16	4.39
California-Irvine, University of	17	4.35
New York University	18	4.32
Johns Hopkins University	19	4.27
Iowa, University of	20	4.25
Brandeis University	21	4.24
Texas-Austin, University of	22	4.23
Washington University in Saint Louis	23	4.20
Wisconsin-Madison, University of	24	4.18
Massachusetts-Amherst, University of	25	4.15
Duke University	26	4.13
Denver, University of	27	4.12
California-Santa Barbara, University of	28	4.08

COMPUTER ENGINEERING
Leading Institutions—Rating of Undergraduate Programs

INSTITUTION	RANK	SCORE
Massachusetts Institute of Technology[5]	1	4.91
California-Berkeley, University of[4]	2	4.90
Illinois,Urbana-Champaign, University of[1]	3	4.87
Michigan-Ann Arbor, University of[1]	4	4.83
Purdue University-West Lafayette[2]	5	4.77
Case Western Reserve University[1]	6	4.74
Rensselaer Polytechnic Institute[4]	7	4.68
Carnegie Mellon University[1]	8	4.60
Iowa State University[1]	9	4.59
Florida, University of[1]	10	4.54
Missouri-Columbia, University of[1]	11	4.48
Arizona State University[6]	12	4.46
Stevens Institute of Technology[1]	13	4.41
Syracuse University[1]	14	4.35
California-Los Angeles, University of[5]	15	4.31
Georgia Institute of Technology[1]	16	4.25
Arizona, University of[1]	17	4.21
Cincinnati, University of[1]	18	4.17
Boston University[1]	19	4.13
Lehigh University[1]	20	4.12
Pennsylvania State University-University Park[1]	21	4.11
Texas-Austin, University of[1]	22	4.10

Explanatory Note: Actual titles used by the institution to identify their curricula
[1]Computer Engineering
[2]Computer and Electrical Engineering
[3]Computer and Systems Engineering
[4]Computer Science
[5]Computer Science and Engineering
[6]Computer Systems Engineering

COMPUTER SCIENCE
LEADING INSTITUTIONS—RATING OF UNDERGRADUATE PROGRAMS

INSTITUTION	RANK	SCORE
Massachusetts Institute of Technology	1	4.92
Carnegie Mellon University	2	4.91
California-Berkeley, University of	3	4.89
Cornell University	4	4.87
Illinois,Urbana-Champaign, University of	5	4.85
California-Los Angeles, University of	6	4.82
Yale University	7	4.80
California Institute of Technology	8	4.79
Texas-Austin, University of	9	4.75
Wisconsin-Madison, University of	10	4.73
Maryland-College Park, University of	11	4.70
Princeton University	12	4.69
Washington, University of	13	4.67
Southern California, University of	14	4.65
State University of New York at Stony Brook	15	4.63
Brown University	16	4.61
Georgia Institute of Technology	17	4.60
Pennsylvania, University of	18	4.58
Rochester, University of	19	4.55
New York University	20	4.52
Minnesota, University of	21	4.50
Utah, University of	22	4.48
Columbia University	23	4.42
Ohio State University-Columbus	24	4.39
Rice University	25	4.33
Duke University	26	4.28
Northwestern University	27	4.22
State University of New York College at Buffalo	28	4.18
Pittsburgh, University of	29	4.14
California-Irvine, University of	30	4.11
California-San Diego, University of	31	4.08
Massachusetts-Amherst, University of	32	4.05
Rutgers University, New Brunswick	33	3.90
Indiana University-Bloomington	34	3.86
Pennsylvania State University-University Park	35	3.85
California-Santa Barbara, University of	36	3.81
Syracuse University	37	3.80
Iowa State University	38	3.75
Rensselaer Polytechnic Institute	39	3.70
Virginia, University of	40	3.66
Michigan-Ann Arbor, University of	41	3.62
Iowa, University of	42	3.58
Connecticut, University of	43	3.54

Computer Science—*continued*

INSTITUTION	RANK	SCORE
Southern Methodist University	44	3.53
United States Naval Academy	45	3.40
United States Military Academy	46	3.39
Houston, University of	47	3.38
Kansas, University of	48	3.36
Washington University in Saint Louis	49	3.34
Michigan State University	50	3.32
Stevens Institute of Technology	51	3.28
Case Western Reserve University	52	3.26
Texas A&M University-College Station	53	3.24
Oklahoma, University of	54	3.22
Kansas State University	55	3.20
Vanderbilt University	56	3.18
Washington State University	57	3.14

DAIRY SCIENCES

LEADING INSTITUTIONS—RATING OF UNDERGRADUATE PROGRAMS

INSTITUTION	RANK	SCORE
Wisconsin-Madison, University of	1	4.91
Cornell University	2	4.90
Kansas State University	3	4.82
Pennsylvania State University-University Park	4	4.76
Iowa State University	5	4.72
Maryland-College Park, University of	6	4.68
Illinois,Urbana-Champaign, University of	7	4.67
Missouri-Columbia, University of	8	4.63
Nebraska-Lincoln, University of	9	4.62
Ohio State University-Columbus	10	4.58
Texas A&M University-College Station	11	4.55

DIETETICS
LEADING INSTITUTIONS—RATING OF UNDERGRADUATE PROGRAMS

INSTITUTION	RANK	SCORE
Cornell University	1	4.90
Michigan State University	2	4.89
California-Davis, University of	3	4.85
Purdue University-West Lafayette	4	4.82
Colorado State University	5	4.80
Iowa State University	6	4.76
Kansas State University	7	4.71
California-Berkeley, University of	8	4.69
Illinois,Urbana-Champaign, University of	9	4.67
Wisconsin-Madison, University of	10	4.61
Ohio State University-Columbus	11	4.55
Alabama, University of	12	4.50
Florida State University	13	4.46
Missouri-Columbia, University of	14	4.40
Oklahoma State University	15	4.35

DRAMA/THEATRE

Leading Institutions—Rating of Undergraduate Programs

INSTITUTION	RANK	SCORE
Northwestern University	1	4.91
California-Los Angeles, University of	2	4.90
Cornell University	3	4.88
Washington, University of	4	4.85
Southern California, University of	5	4.83
Indiana University-Bloomington	6	4.80
Stanford University	7	4.75
Iowa, University of	8	4.70
Carnegie Mellon University	9	4.66
New York University	10	4.62
Minnesota, University of	11	4.60
Pennsylvania State University-University Park	12	4.58
Michigan State University	13	4.51
Tufts University	14	4.46
California-Berkeley, University of	15	4.39
Wisconsin-Madison, University of	16	4.30
Catholic University of America, The	17	4.25
Yale University [1]	18	4.20
Florida State University	19	4.18
Baylor University	20	3.90
North Carolina-Chapel Hill, University of	21	3.83
Tulane University	22	3.78
Michigan-Ann Arbor, University of	23	3.74
Illinois,Urbana-Champaign, University of	24	3.68
California-Santa Barbara, University of	25	3.66
Ohio State University-Columbus	26	3.64
Boston University	27	3.60
Brandeis University	28	3.55
Case Western Reserve University	29	3.53
Southern Methodist University	30	3.51
Syracuse University	31	3.40
San Francisco State University	32	3.38
Bowling Green State University	33	3.37
Arizona, University of	34	3.30
Florida, University of	35	3.23
Ohio University	36	3.22
Temple University	37	3.21
Pittsburgh, University of	38	3.18
Miami, University of	39	3.16
Arizona State University	40	3.13
City University of New York-City College	41	3.11
Dartmouth College	42	3.09
Occidental College	43	3.08
Kansas, University of	44	3.07
Texas-Austin, University of	45	3.04
Wayne State University	46	3.03

Explanatory Note: Actual title used by the institution to identify their curricula
[1] Theatre Studies

EARTH SCIENCE
LEADING INSTITUTIONS—RATING OF UNDERGRADUATE PROGRAMS

INSTITUTION	RANK	SCORE
Johns Hopkins University	1	4.86
Michigan-Ann Arbor, University of	2	4.83
Wisconsin-Madison, University of	3	4.79
Michigan State University	4	4.73
Dartmouth College	5	4.70
Iowa State University	6	4.64
Ohio State University-Columbus	7	4.59
Pennsylvania State University-University Park	8	4.57
Purdue University-West Lafayette	9	4.52
Arizona, University of	10	4.49
Minnesota, University of	11	4.42
Stanford University	12	4.41

EAST ASIAN STUDIES
LEADING INSTITUTIONS—RATING OF UNDERGRADUATE PROGRAMS

INSTITUTION	RANK	SCORE
Harvard and Radcliffe Colleges	1	4.86
California-Berkeley, University of	2	4.83
Pennsylvania, University of	3	4.79
Columbia University	4	4.77
Chicago, University of	5	4.73
Stanford University	6	4.70
Cornell University	7	4.68
Indiana University-Bloomington	8	4.64
Princeton University	9	4.61
Michigan-Ann Arbor, University of	10	4.56
Yale University	11	4.53

ECOLOGY/ENVIRONMENTAL STUDIES
LEADING INSTITUTIONS—RATING OF UNDERGRADUATE PROGRAMS

INSTITUTION	RANK	SCORE
Harvard and Radcliffe Colleges	1	4.89
Cornell University	2	4.87
California-Berkeley, University of	3	4.84
Illinois,Urbana-Champaign, University of	4	4.79
Michigan-Ann Arbor, University of	5	4.78
Pennsylvania, University of	6	4.76
Wisconsin-Madison, University of	7	4.72
Indiana University-Bloomington	8	4.69
Rice University	9	4.65
Colorado-Boulder, University of	10	4.60
Arizona, University of	11	4.57
SUNY College of Environmental Science and Forestry	12	4.52
Purdue University-West Lafayette	13	4.49

ECONOMICS
LEADING INSTITUTIONS—RATING OF UNDERGRADUATE PROGRAMS

INSTITUTION	RANK	SCORE
Massachusetts Institute of Technology	1	4.92
Chicago, University of	2	4.91
Stanford University	3	4.90
Princeton University	4	4.89
Harvard and Radcliffe Colleges	5	4.87
Yale University	6	4.85
Minnesota, University of	7	4.84
Pennsylvania, University of	8	4.83
Wisconsin-Madison, University of	9	4.82
California-Berkeley, University of	10	4.81
Northwestern University	11	4.79
Rochester, University of	12	4.76
Columbia University	13	4.75
California-Los Angeles, University of	14	4.74
Michigan-Ann Arbor, University of	15	4.73
Johns Hopkins University	16	4.72
Carnegie Mellon University	17	4.71
Brown University	18	4.69
California-San Diego, University of	19	4.67
Duke University	20	4.66
Cornell University	21	4.65
New York University	22	4.63
Virginia, University of	23	4.60
California-Davis, University of	24	4.58
Washington, University of	25	4.57
Maryland-College Park, University of	26	4.56
Michigan State University	27	4.54
North Carolina-Chapel Hill, University of	28	4.52
Illinois,Urbana-Champaign, University of	29	4.50
Texas A&M University-College Station	30	4.48
Boston University	31	4.44
Washington University in Saint Louis	32	4.42
Purdue University-West Lafayette	33	4.40
Southern California, University of	34	4.38
Texas-Austin, University of	35	4.35
Vanderbilt University	36	4.31
Ohio State University-Columbus	37	4.27
Iowa State University	38	4.24
State University of New York at Stony Brook	39	4.20
Iowa, University of	40	4.17
Massachusetts-Amherst, University of	41	4.15
California-Santa Barbara, University of	42	4.13
Pittsburgh, University of	43	4.12
Virginia Tech	44	4.10
Claremont McKenna College	45	4.08
Rutgers University, New Brunswick	46	4.06

ELECTRICAL ENGINEERING
LEADING INSTITUTIONS—RATING OF UNDERGRADUATE PROGRAMS

INSTITUTION	RANK	SCORE
Massachusetts Institute of Technology[3]	1	4.92
Stanford University	2	4.91
California-Berkeley, University of[2]	3	4.88
Illinois,Urbana-Champaign, University of	4	4.86
California-Los Angeles, University of	5	4.82
Cornell University	6	4.81
Purdue University-West Lafayette	7	4.79
Southern California, University of	8	4.77
Princeton University	9	4.76
Michigan-Ann Arbor, University of	10	4.75
Carnegie Mellon University	11	4.74
Polytechnic University	12	4.73
Texas-Austin, University of	13	4.70
Columbia University	14	4.66
Georgia Institute of Technology	15	4.65
Maryland-College Park, University of	16	4.64
Ohio State University-Columbus	17	4.63
Stevens Institute of Technology	18	4.62
Minnesota, University of	19	4.60
Northwestern University	20	4.58
California-Santa Barbara, University of	21	4.57
Florida, University of	22	4.56
Rensselaer Polytechnic Institute[1]	23	4.54
Johns Hopkins University	24	4.53
Rice University	25	4.52
Brown University	26	4.50
Wisconsin-Madison, University of	27	4.49
Arizona, University of	28	4.46
California-San Diego, University of	29	4.45
Colorado-Boulder, University of[2]	30	4.43
Washington University in Saint Louis	31	4.42
Pennsylvania, University of	32	4.40
Yale University	33	4.38
Virginia Tech	34	4.37
Pennsylvania State University-University Park	35	4.36
Case Western Reserve University	36	4.35
Missouri-Rolla, University of	37	4.34
Massachusetts-Amherst, University of	38	4.32
Syracuse University	39	4.30
Michigan State University	40	4.28
Notre Dame, University of	41	4.27
Pittsburgh, University of	42	4.26
Iowa State University	43	4.25

Electrical Engineering—*continued*

INSTITUTION	RANK	SCORE
North Carolina State University	44	4.24
Washington, University of	45	4.22
Texas A&M University-College Station	46	4.21
Southern Methodist University	47	4.20
California-Davis, University of	48	4.18
Duke University	49	4.17
State University of New York at Stony Brook	50	4.15
Tennessee-Knoxville, University of	51	4.13
Arizona State University	52	4.11
Kansas, University of	53	4.10
Hawaii-Manoa, University of	54	4.08
Texas Tech University	55	4.07
Colorado State University	56	4.06
State University of New York College at Buffalo	57	4.05
Utah, University of	58	4.04
United States Air Force Academy	59	4.03
Iowa, University of	60	4.02
City University of New York-City College	61	4.01
Connecticut, University of	62	4.00

Explanatory Note: Actual titles used by the institution to identify their curricula
[1]Electric Power Engineering
[2]Electrical and Computer Engineering
[3]Electrical Science and Engineering

ENGINEERING MECHANICS
LEADING INSTITUTIONS—RATING OF UNDERGRADUATE PROGRAMS

INSTITUTION	RANK	SCORE
Illinois,Urbana-Champaign, University of	1	4.82
Wisconsin-Madison, University of	2	4.74
United States Air Force Academy	3	4.72
Johns Hopkins University	4	4.69
Virginia Tech [1]	5	4.64
Cincinnati, University of	6	4.61

Explanatory Note: Actual titles used by the institution to identify their curricula
[1]Engineering Science and Mechanics

ENGINEERING PHYSICS
Leading Institutions—Rating of Undergraduate Programs

INSTITUTION	RANK	SCORE
Princeton University	1	4.82
Cornell University	2	4.77
Kansas, University of	3	4.53
Oklahoma, University of	4	4.49
Colorado School of Mines	5	4.44
Texas Tech University	6	4.33
Stevens Institute of Technology	7	4.27
Tulsa, University of	8	4.23

ENGINEERING SCIENCE
LEADING INSTITUTIONS—RATING OF UNDERGRADUATE PROGRAMS

INSTITUTION	RANK	SCORE
Harvard and Radcliffe Colleges	1	4.85
United States Air Force Academy	2	4.79
Iowa State University	3	4.70
Florida, University of	4	4.68
Pennsylvania State University-University Park	5	4.63
Colorado State University	6	4.61
Case Western Reserve University [1]	7	4.58
Tennessee-Knoxville, University of	8	4.53
Montana Tech of the University of Montana	9	4.49
State University of New York at Stony Brook	10	4.16

Explanatory Note: Actual titles used by the institution to identify their curricula
[1]Fluid and Thermal Engineering Science

ENGINEERING/GENERAL

LEADING INSTITUTIONS—RATING OF UNDERGRADUATE PROGRAMS

INSTITUTION	RANK	SCORE
Illinois,Urbana-Champaign, University of	1	4.85
Oklahoma, University of	2	4.80
Maryland-College Park, University of	3	4.78
Carnegie Mellon University	4	4.76
Colorado School of Mines	5	4.75
Harvey Mudd College	6	4.72
Stevens Institute of Technology	7	4.70
Dartmouth College	8	4.66
Oklahoma State University	9	4.62
Michigan Technological University	10	4.58

ENGLISH
LEADING INSTITUTIONS—RATING OF UNDERGRADUATE PROGRAMS

INSTITUTION	RANK	SCORE
Yale University	1	4.92
California-Berkeley, University of	2	4.91
Harvard and Radcliffe Colleges	3	4.90
Chicago, University of	4	4.87
Stanford University	5	4.86
Cornell University	6	4.84
Princeton University	7	4.83
Columbia University	8	4.81
Johns Hopkins University	9	4.79
Pennsylvania, University of	10	4.78
California-Los Angeles, University of	11	4.76
Brown University	12	4.74
Indiana University-Bloomington	13	4.73
Michigan-Ann Arbor, University of	14	4.71
California-Irvine, University of	15	4.69
Northwestern University	16	4.68
Wisconsin-Madison, University of	17	4.65
Rutgers University, New Brunswick	18	4.64
North Carolina-Chapel Hill, University of	19	4.63
Iowa, University of	20	4.61
Virginia, University of	21	4.59
New York University	22	4.57
Notre Dame, University of	23	4.53
Illinois,Urbana-Champaign, University of	24	4.51
Washington, University of	25	4.48
Duke University	26	4.45
Texas-Austin, University of	27	4.44
State University of New York at Stony Brook	28	4.43
Rochester, University of	29	4.40
Emory University	30	4.38
Washington University in Saint Louis	31	4.35
Dartmouth College	32	4.32
Minnesota, University of	33	4.31
California-San Diego, University of	34	4.28
Vanderbilt University	35	4.26
Pomona College	36	4.23
Brandeis University	37	4.20
Swarthmore College	38	4.19
Haverford College	39	4.17
Massachusetts-Amherst, University of	40	4.15
California-Santa Barbara, University of	41	4.12

ENTOMOLOGY

LEADING INSTITUTIONS—RATING OF UNDERGRADUATE PROGRAMS

INSTITUTION	RANK	SCORE
California-Berkeley, University of	1	4.91
Cornell University	2	4.90
Illinois,Urbana-Champaign, University of	3	4.87
California-Davis, University of	4	4.82
Wisconsin-Madison, University of	5	4.81
California-Riverside, University of	6	4.76
Kansas, University of	7	4.73
Minnesota, University of	8	4.72
Purdue University-West Lafayette	9	4.69
Ohio State University-Columbus	10	4.66
Iowa State University	11	4.63
Michigan State University	12	4.60
Oregon State University	13	4.58
Louisiana State University-Baton Rouge	14	4.55
North Carolina State University	15	4.53
Texas A&M University-College Station	16	4.51
Florida, University of	17	4.49
Arizona, University of	18	4.47
Maryland-College Park, University of	19	4.44
Massachusetts-Amherst, University of	20	4.43
Pennsylvania State University-University Park	21	4.41
Colorado State University	22	4.39
Auburn University	23	4.36
Georgia, University of	24	4.32
Rutgers University, New Brunswick	25	4.28
Nebraska-Lincoln, University of	26	4.23

ENVIRONMENTAL DESIGN
LEADING INSTITUTIONS—RATING OF UNDERGRADUATE PROGRAMS

INSTITUTION	RANK	SCORE
Massachusetts Institute of Technology	1	4.91
Harvard and Radcliffe Colleges	2	4.89
Cornell University	3	4.85
Michigan-Ann Arbor, University of	4	4.83
California-Davis, University of	5	4.78
Pennsylvania, University of	6	4.74
Texas A&M University-College Station	7	4.71
Colorado-Boulder, University of	8	4.67
North Carolina State University	9	4.64
New Mexico, University of	10	4.60
Oklahoma, University of	11	4.58
Houston, University of	12	4.55
SUNY College of Environmental Science and Forestry	13	4.53
Minnesota, University of	14	4.52

ENVIRONMENTAL ENGINEERING

LEADING INSTITUTIONS—RATING OF UNDERGRADUATE PROGRAMS

INSTITUTION	RANK	SCORE
Rensselaer Polytechnic Institute	1	4.86
Massachusetts Institute of Technology[2]	2	4.83
Northwestern University	3	4.81
Florida, University of	4	4.80
Michigan-Ann Arbor, University of[1]	5	4.75
Ohio State University-Columbus[3]	6	4.73
Michigan Technological University	7	4.72
Montana Tech of the University of Montana	8	4.69
Oklahoma State University[1]	9	4.66
California Polytechnic State University-San Luis Obispo	10	4.62
Syracuse University	11	4.58

Explanatory Note: Actual title used by the institution to identify their curricula
[1]Civil and Environmental Engineering
[2]Environmental Engineering Science
[3]Environmental Engineering option in Civil Engineering

ENVIRONMENTAL SCIENCES
Leading Institutions—Rating of Undergraduate Programs

INSTITUTION	RANK	SCORE
Harvard and Radcliffe Colleges	1	4.89
Massachusetts Institute of Technology	2	4.88
Cornell University	3	4.85
California-Berkeley, University of	4	4.82
California-Davis, University of	5	4.79
Michigan-Ann Arbor, University of	6	4.74
Pennsylvania, University of	7	4.70
Virginia, University of	8	4.65
SUNY College of Environmental Science and Forestry	9	4.62
Johns Hopkins University	10	4.58
Purdue University-West Lafayette	11	4.53
Minnesota, University of	12	4.52

FARM/RANCH MANAGEMENT
Leading Institutions—Rating of Undergraduate Programs

INSTITUTION	RANK	SCORE
Cornell University	1	4.85
Colorado State University	2	4.80
Kansas State University	3	4.74
Texas Tech University	4	4.71
California-Davis, University of	5	4.65
Wisconsin-Madison, University of	6	4.61
Arizona, University of	7	4.59
Iowa State University	8	4.55
Purdue University-West Lafayette	9	4.52

FILM
Leading Institutions—Rating of Undergraduate Programs

INSTITUTION	RANK	SCORE
California-Los Angeles, University of	1	4.86
Southern California, University of	2	4.83
New York University	3	4.81
Northwestern University	4	4.77
Syracuse University	5	4.73
California-Berkeley, University of	6	4.65
Michigan-Ann Arbor, University of	7	4.52
Texas-Austin, University of	8	4.51
Florida State University	9	4.49

FINANCE
LEADING INSTITUTIONS—RATING OF UNDERGRADUATE PROGRAMS

INSTITUTION	RANK	SCORE
Pennsylvania, University of	1	4.92
Indiana University-Bloomington	2	4.91
Michigan-Ann Arbor, University of	3	4.88
California-Berkeley, University of	4	4.86
New York University	5	4.85
Texas-Austin, University of	6	4.84
Illinois,Urbana-Champaign, University of	7	4.82
Wisconsin-Madison, University of	8	4.80
Purdue University-West Lafayette	9	4.79
Washington, University of	10	4.77
Michigan State University	11	4.75
Virginia, University of	12	4.72
City University of New York-Baruch College	13	4.70
Washington University in Saint Louis	14	4.68
Case Western Reserve University	15	4.66
Southern California, University of	16	4.65
Houston, University of	17	4.64
Pennsylvania State University-University Park	18	4.63
Texas A&M University-College Station	19	4.62
Notre Dame, University of	20	4.60
Ohio State University-Columbus	21	4.57
Florida, University of	22	4.54
Arizona, University of	23	4.47
Utah, University of	24	4.45
Emory University	25	4.44
Louisiana State University-Baton Rouge	26	4.42
Massachusetts-Amherst, University of	27	4.40
Minnesota, University of	28	4.39
Southern Methodist University	29	4.38
Oregon, University of	30	4.36
Maryland-College Park, University of	31	4.33
Lehigh University	32	4.31
Arizona State University	33	4.28
Missouri-Columbia, University of	34	4.27
George Washington University	35	4.26
Syracuse University	36	4.25
Georgia State University	37	4.24
Colorado-Boulder, University of	38	4.20
Temple University	39	4.15
Iowa, University of	40	4.14
Denver, University of	41	4.12
South Carolina-Columbia , University of,	42	4.09
Nebraska-Lincoln, University of	43	4.03
Georgia, University of	44	4.02

FISH/GAME MANAGEMENT

LEADING INSTITUTIONS—RATING OF UNDERGRADUATE PROGRAMS

INSTITUTION	RANK	SCORE
California-Davis, University of	1	4.83
Colorado State University	2	4.82
Michigan State University	3	4.77
Texas A&M University at Galveston	4	4.73
Minnesota, University of	5	4.69
Iowa State University	6	4.64
Kansas State University	7	4.62
Ohio State University-Columbus	8	4.56
Michigan-Ann Arbor, University of	9	4.55
Auburn University	10	4.48
Wyoming, University of	11	4.46
Montana State University-Bozeman	12	4.42

FOOD SCIENCES

LEADING INSTITUTIONS—RATING OF UNDERGRADUATE PROGRAMS

INSTITUTION	RANK	SCORE
Cornell University	1	4.91
Michigan State University	2	4.88
Iowa State University	3	4.87
Massachusetts Institute of Technology	4	4.86
Kansas State University	5	4.82
California-Davis, University of	6	4.76
Purdue University-West Lafayette	7	4.72
Illinois,Urbana-Champaign, University of	8	4.68
Pennsylvania State University-University Park	9	4.63
Minnesota, University of	10	4.61
Oregon State University	11	4.59
Tennessee-Knoxville, University of	12	4.55
Alabama, University of	13	4.51
Ohio State University-Columbus	14	4.47
Georgia, University of	15	4.40
Oklahoma State University	16	4.34
Missouri-Columbia, University of	17	4.32
Wisconsin-Madison, University of	18	4.30

FOOD SERVICES MANAGEMENT
LEADING INSTITUTIONS—RATING OF UNDERGRADUATE PROGRAMS

INSTITUTION	RANK	SCORE
Cornell University	1	4.86
Nevada-Las Vegas, University of	2	4.85
Michigan State University	3	4.79
Kansas State University	4	4.73
Iowa State University	5	4.67
Purdue University-West Lafayette	6	4.66
Illinois,Urbana-Champaign, University of	7	4.62
Pennsylvania State University-University Park	8	4.60
California-Davis, University of	9	4.57
Oregon State University	10	4.55
Alabama, University of	11	4.51
Georgia, University of	12	4.45

FORESTRY
LEADING INSTITUTIONS—RATING OF UNDERGRADUATE PROGRAMS

INSTITUTION	RANK	SCORE
Minnesota, University of	1	4.88
SUNY College of Environmental Science and Forestry	2	4.87
Pennsylvania State University-University Park	3	4.75
North Carolina State University	4	4.72
Missouri-Columbia, University of	5	4.71
Wisconsin-Madison, University of	6	4.70
Washington, University of	7	4.69
Oregon State University	8	4.68
Purdue University-West Lafayette	9	4.67
Michigan State University	10	4.66
Georgia, University of	11	4.64
Virginia Tech	12	4.61
Colorado State University	13	4.60
Iowa State University	14	4.59
Auburn University	15	4.55
Texas A&M University-College Station	16	4.53
Utah State University	17	4.50
California-Berkeley, University of	18	4.47
Montana, University of	19	4.46
Idaho, University of	20	4.43
Michigan-Ann Arbor, University of	21	4.41
Maine, University of	22	4.35
Florida, University of	23	4.33
Clemson University	24	4.26
Louisiana State University-Baton Rouge	25	4.22
Tennessee-Knoxville, University of	26	4.20
West Virginia University	27	4.19
Illinois,Urbana-Champaign, University of	28	4.17
Kentucky, University of	29	4.14
Oklahoma State University	30	4.12

FRENCH

Leading Institutions—Rating of Undergraduate Programs

INSTITUTION	RANK	SCORE
Yale University	1	4.92
Princeton University	2	4.91
Columbia University	3	4.90
New York University	4	4.88
Cornell University	5	4.86
Indiana University-Bloomington	6	4.85
Michigan-Ann Arbor, University of	7	4.83
Pennsylvania, University of	8	4.80
California-Berkeley, University of	9	4.77
Stanford University	10	4.74
Virginia, University of	11	4.71
Illinois,Urbana-Champaign, University of	12	4.68
Wisconsin-Madison, University of	13	4.67
Duke University	14	4.64
Chicago, University of	15	4.62
North Carolina-Chapel Hill, University of	16	4.59
California-Irvine, University of	17	4.53
Texas-Austin, University of	18	4.50
Harvard and Radcliffe Colleges	19	4.46
Brown University	20	4.42
California-Santa Barbara, University of	21	4.40
Rice University	22	4.36
Bryn Mawr College	23	4.33
Johns Hopkins University	24	4.32
Tulane University	25	4.29
Northwestern University	26	4.28
Washington, University of	27	4.25
Iowa, University of	28	4.22
State University of New York College at Buffalo	29	4.19
California-Los Angeles, University of	30	4.17

GENETICS
LEADING INSTITUTIONS—RATING OF UNDERGRADUATE PROGRAMS

INSTITUTION	RANK	SCORE
California-Davis, University of	1	4.91
Cornell University	2	4.90
Massachusetts Institute of Technology	3	4.88
Wisconsin-Madison, University of	4	4.82
Illinois,Urbana-Champaign, University of	5	4.79
Ohio State University-Columbus	6	4.73
Purdue University-West Lafayette	7	4.69
Rochester, University of	8	4.66
Minnesota, University of	9	4.62
Rutgers University, New Brunswick	10	4.58
Georgia, University of	11	4.55
Kansas, University of	12	4.52
Texas A&M University-College Station	13	4.49

GEOGRAPHY
LEADING INSTITUTIONS—RATING OF UNDERGRADUATE PROGRAMS

INSTITUTION	RANK	SCORE
Minnesota, University of	1	4.90
Wisconsin-Madison, University of	2	4.89
Pennsylvania State University-University Park	3	4.86
California-Berkeley, University of	4	4.82
Ohio State University-Columbus	5	4.75
Illinois,Urbana-Champaign, University of	6	4.71
Michigan-Ann Arbor, University of	7	4.70
Washington, University of	8	4.65
California-Los Angeles, University of	9	4.62
Syracuse University	10	4.59
Iowa, University of	11	4.58
Colorado-Boulder, University of	12	4.53
Kansas, University of	13	4.51
Louisiana State University-Baton Rouge	14	4.50
Georgia, University of	15	4.48
Wisconsin-Milwaukee, University of	16	4.47
State University of New York College at Buffalo	17	4.46
Hawaii-Manoa, University of	18	4.44
Michigan State University	19	4.41
Arizona, University of	20	4.37
Rutgers University, New Brunswick	21	4.35
Nebraska-Lincoln, University of	22	4.34
North Carolina-Chapel Hill, University of	23	4.31
Texas-Austin, University of	24	4.30
Clark University	25	4.28
Maryland-College Park, University of	26	4.25
Florida, University of	27	4.23
Oklahoma, University of	28	4.20
Oregon, University of	29	4.16
Utah, University of	30	4.14

GEOLOGICAL ENGINEERING
LEADING INSTITUTIONS—RATING OF UNDERGRADUATE PROGRAMS

INSTITUTION	RANK	SCORE
Colorado School of Mines [1]	1	4.91
Missouri-Rolla, University of	2	4.87
Minnesota, University of	3	4.79
Arizona, University of	4	4.73
Utah, University of	5	4.68
South Dakota School of Mines & Technology	6	4.62
Princeton University	7	4.56
Michigan Technological University	8	4.51
Idaho, University of	9	4.47
Alaska-Fairbanks, University of	10	4.43
Montana Tech of the University of Montana [1]	11	4.42
Nevada-Reno, University of	12	4.36

Explanatory Note: Actual titles used by the institution to identify their curricula
[1] Geophysical Engineering
Note: Majors
Colorado School of Mines
   Geological Engineering
   Geophysical Engineering
Montana College of Mineral Science and Technology
   Geological Engineering
   Geophysical Engineering

GEOLOGY/GEOSCIENCE
LEADING INSTITUTIONS—RATING OF UNDERGRADUATE PROGRAMS

INSTITUTION	RANK	SCORE
California Institute of Technology	1	4.92
Massachusetts Institute of Technology	2	4.91
Princeton University	3	4.89
Columbia University	4	4.87
Stanford University	5	4.85
Harvard and Radcliffe Colleges	6	4.82
Chicago, University of	7	4.80
California-Los Angeles, University of	8	4.79
Yale University	9	4.76
California-Berkeley, University of	10	4.74
Cornell University	11	4.72
Pennsylvania State University-University Park	12	4.70
Texas-Austin, University of	13	4.69
Wisconsin-Madison, University of	14	4.68
Arizona, University of	15	4.66
California-Santa Barbara, University of	16	4.64
Brown University	17	4.62
Virginia Tech	18	4.61
State University of New York at Stony Brook	19	4.58
Michigan-Ann Arbor, University of	20	4.57
Johns Hopkins University	21	4.55
Northwestern University	22	4.53
Washington, University of	23	4.51
Indiana University-Bloomington	24	4.49
Minnesota, University of	25	4.48
California-Davis, University of	26	4.45
Colorado-Boulder, University of	27	4.42
Illinois, Urbana-Champaign, University of	28	4.41
Southern California, University of	29	4.39
Arizona State University	30	4.37
California-Santa Cruz, University of	31	4.36
Miami, University of	32	4.34
Utah, University of	33	4.32
Massachusetts-Amherst, University of	34	4.31
North Carolina-Chapel Hill, University of	35	4.30
Oregon, University of	36	4.28
Texas A&M University at College Station	37	4.26
State University of New York at Albany	38	4.25
Ohio State University- Columbus	39	4.24
Kansas, University of	40	4.20
South Carolina-Columbia, University of	41	4.19
Wyoming, University of	42	4.17
Cincinnati, University of	43	4.16
New Mexico, University of	44	4.14
Rice University	45	4.12
Iowa, University of	46	4.10

Louisiana State University-Baton Rouge	47	4.08
Oregon State University-Columbus	48	4.07
Hawaii-Manoa, University of	49	4.06
Michigan State University	50	4.05

GEOPHYSICS/GEOSCIENCE
LEADING INSTITUTIONS—RATING OF UNDERGRADUATE PROGRAMS

INSTITUTION	RANK	SCORE
California Institute of Technology	1	4.92
Massachusetts Institute of Technology	2	4.90
California-Berkeley, University of	3	4.89
Stanford University	4	4.83
California-Los Angeles, University of	5	4.82
Yale University	6	4.80
Chicago, University of	7	4.78
Princeton University	8	4.76
Brown University	9	4.75
Minnesota, University of	10	4.73
California-Santa Cruz, University of	11	4.71
Harvard and Radcliffe Colleges	12	4.70
Columbia University	13	4.68
Purdue University-West Lafayette	14	4.65
Wisconsin-Madison, University of	15	4.63
Lehigh University	16	4.62
Virginia Tech	17	4.61
Texas A&M University-College Station	18	4.59
Kansas, University of	19	4.57
Utah, University of	20	4.55
Hawaii-Manoa, University of	21	4.53
State University of New York at Binghamton	22	4.51
New Mexico Institute of Mining & Technology	23	4.49
Oklahoma, University of	24	4.48
Saint Louis University	25	4.46
Houston, University of	26	4.43
Missouri-Rolla, University of	27	4.42
Tulsa, University of	28	4.40

GERMAN

LEADING INSTITUTIONS—RATING OF UNDERGRADUATE PROGRAMS

INSTITUTION	RANK	SCORE
Yale University	1	4.90
Wisconsin-Madison, University of	2	4.88
Princeton University	3	4.86
Indiana University-Bloomington	4	4.84
California-Berkeley, University of	5	4.82
Texas-Austin, University of	6	4.80
Stanford University	7	4.77
Cornell University	8	4.73
Virginia, University of	9	4.71
Harvard and Radcliffe Colleges	10	4.69
Illinois,Urbana-Champaign, University of	11	4.68
California-Los Angeles, University of	12	4.67
Johns Hopkins University	13	4.64
Michigan-Ann Arbor, University of	14	4.63
Pennsylvania, University of	15	4.62
Massachusetts-Amherst, University of	16	4.60
Washington University in Saint Louis	17	4.59
Ohio State University-Columbus	18	4.58
North Carolina-Chapel Hill, University of	19	4.56
Minnesota, University of	20	4.55
Rice University	21	4.53
Pennsylvania State University-University Park	22	4.52
Pittsburgh, University of	23	4.51
California-Irvine, University of	24	4.49
Washington, University of	25	4.47
Brown University	26	4.45
Kansas, University of	27	4.44
California-Santa Barbara, University of	28	4.43
Duke University	29	4.39
Northwestern University	30	4.36

GREEK

LEADING INSTITUTIONS—RATING OF UNDERGRADUATE PROGRAMS

INSTITUTION	RANK	SCORE
Harvard and Radcliffe Colleges	1	4.87
California-Berkeley, University of	2	4.85
Brown University	3	4.80
Columbia University	4	4.77
Pennsylvania, University of	5	4.72
Yale University	6	4.66
Indiana University-Bloomington	7	4.61
Wisconsin-Madison, University of	8	4.59
Bryn Mawr College	9	4.56
Minnesota, University of	10	4.52
North Carolina-Chapel Hill, University of	11	4.49
Cornell University	12	4.42
Chicago, University of	13	4.40
New York University	14	4.38
Illinois,Urbana-Champaign, University of	15	4.36
Michigan-Ann Arbor, University of	16	4.32

HEBREW
LEADING INSTITUTIONS—RATING OF UNDERGRADUATE PROGRAMS

INSTITUTION	RANK	SCORE
Pennsylvania, University of	1	4.91
Wisconsin-Madison, University of	2	4.90
Columbia University	3	4.86
California-Berkeley, University of	4	4.85
New York University	5	4.82
Yeshiva University	6	4.81
Harvard and Radcliffe Colleges	7	4.79
Brandeis University	8	4.76
Texas-Austin, University of	9	4.73
Chicago, University of	10	4.70
Indiana University-Bloomington	11	4.68
Michigan-Ann Arbor, University of	12	4.65
Minnesota, University of	13	4.63
Temple University	14	4.62
Ohio State University-Columbus	15	4.59
California-Los Angeles, University of	16	4.55
Cornell University	17	4.53
Princeton University	18	4.52
Brown University	19	4.51
Washington, University of	20	4.48

HISTORY
LEADING INSTITUTIONS—RATING OF UNDERGRADUATE PROGRAMS

INSTITUTION	RANK	SCORE
Yale University	1	4.93
California-Berkeley, University of	2	4.92
Princeton University	3	4.91
Harvard and Radcliffe Colleges	4	4.90
Stanford University	5	4.88
Michigan-Ann Arbor, University of	6	4.86
Columbia University	7	4.84
Chicago, University of	8	4.81
Johns Hopkins University	9	4.80
Wisconsin-Madison, University of	10	4.77
Cornell University	11	4.75
Indiana University-Bloomington	12	4.73
Pennsylvania, University of	13	4.70
Brown University	14	4.68
North Carolina-Chapel Hill, University of	15	4.67
California-Los Angeles, University of	16	4.66
Northwestern University	17	4.62
Virginia, University of	18	4.61
Texas-Austin, University of	19	4.58
Rochester, University of	20	4.57
Illinois,Urbana-Champaign, University of	21	4.56
Notre Dame, University of	22	4.55
Washington, University of	23	4.54
Minnesota, University of	24	4.53
Iowa, University of	25	4.52
Duke University	26	4.51
Rutgers University, New Brunswick	27	4.50
California-Santa Barbara, University of	28	4.48
California-San Diego, University of	29	4.47
New York University	30	4.46
Vanderbilt University	31	4.45
Washington University in Saint Louis	32	4.44
Maryland-College Park, University of	33	4.42
Ohio State University-Columbus	34	4.40
Missouri-Columbia, University of	35	4.38
Emory University	36	4.35
Pittsburgh, University of	37	4.34
Rice University	38	4.33
State University of New York at Stony Brook	39	4.32
Dartmouth College	40	4.27
Brandeis University	41	4.23
Kansas, University of	42	4.20
Boston University	43	4.18
California-Davis, University of	44	4.15
State University of New York College at Buffalo	45	4.14
Michigan State University	46	4.10

HOME ECONOMICS

LEADING INSTITUTIONS—RATING OF UNDERGRADUATE PROGRAMS

INSTITUTION	RANK	SCORE
Ohio State University-Columbus	1	4.87
Minnesota, University of	2	4.83
Wisconsin-Madison, University of	3	4.81
Purdue University-West Lafayette	4	4.79
Illinois,Urbana-Champaign, University of	5	4.75
Iowa State University	6	4.73
Florida State University	7	4.71
Michigan State University	8	4.68
Maryland-College Park, University of	9	4.66
Colorado State University	10	4.65
Houston, University of	11	4.63
Georgia, University of	12	4.61
Texas Tech University	13	4.58
Auburn University	14	4.56
Nebraska-Lincoln, University of	15	4.53
Virginia Tech	16	4.52
Arizona State University	17	4.50
Oklahoma State University	18	4.48
Oregon State University	19	4.46
Alabama, University of	20	4.43
Texas-Austin, University of	21	4.41
Massachusetts-Amherst, University of	22	4.39
Texas Woman's University	23	4.37
Washington State University	24	4.35
Brigham Young University	25	4.33
Arkansas, University of	26	4.32
Idaho, University of	27	4.29
Ohio University	28	4.26
Arizona, University of	29	4.23
Hawaii-Manoa, University of	30	4.21

HORTICULTURE
Leading Institutions—Rating of Undergraduate Programs

INSTITUTION	RANK	SCORE
Cornell University	1	4.92
Texas A&M University-College Station	2	4.90
Iowa State University	3	4.88
Purdue University-West Lafayette	4	4.85
Illinois,Urbana-Champaign, University of	5	4.83
Michigan State University	6	4.81
Wisconsin-Madison, University of	7	4.79
Minnesota, University of	8	4.77
Ohio State University-Columbus	9	4.75
Kansas State University	10	4.73
Missouri-Columbia, University of	11	4.72
Pennsylvania State University-University Park	12	4.71
Colorado State University	13	4.69
Louisiana State University-Baton Rouge	14	4.67
Maryland-College Park, University of	15	4.65
Oklahoma State University	16	4.63
Georgia, University of	17	4.62
North Carolina State University	18	4.60
Oregon State University	19	4.58
Tennessee-Knoxville, University of	20	4.55
Nebraska-Lincoln, University of	21	4.53
Florida, University of	22	4.52
Auburn University	23	4.50
Washington State University	24	4.48
Vermont, University of	25	4.46
Kentucky, University of	26	4.44
Arizona, University of	27	4.42
Arkansas, University of	28	4.40
Mississippi State University	29	4.38
Virginia Tech	30	4.36
New Hampshire, University of	31	4.33
North Dakota State University	32	4.32
Montana State University-Bozeman	33	4.31
South Dakota State University	34	4.29
Texas Tech University	35	4.27
Connecticut, University of	36	4.26

HOTEL, RESTAURANT, INSTITUTIONAL MANAGEMENT

LEADING INSTITUTIONS—RATING OF UNDERGRADUATE PROGRAMS

INSTITUTION	RANK	SCORE
Cornell University	1	4.90
Nevada-Las Vegas, University of	2	4.87
Michigan State University	3	4.83
Massachusetts-Amherst, University of	4	4.78
Houston, University of	5	4.74
Illinois,Urbana-Champaign, University of	6	4.70
Purdue University-West Lafayette	7	4.67
Denver, University of	8	4.62
Iowa State University	9	4.53
Maryland-College Park, University of	10	4.52
Tennessee-Knoxville, University of	11	4.48
Pennsylvania State University-University Park	12	4.46
Florida State University	13	4.43
Kansas State University	14	4.41
Fairleigh Dickinson University	15	4.38
Ohio State University-Columbus	16	4.36
Drexel University	17	4.33
Golden Gate University	18	4.31
Syracuse University	19	4.27
South Carolina-Columbia , University of,	20	4.24
Virginia Tech	21	4.20
Washington State University	22	4.18
Florida International University	23	4.16

INDUSTRIAL ENGINEERING
LEADING INSTITUTIONS—RATING OF UNDERGRADUATE PROGRAMS

INSTITUTION	RANK	SCORE
Stanford University	1	4.90
Michigan-Ann Arbor, University of[2]	2	4.88
California-Berkeley, University of	3	4.85
Purdue University-West Lafayette	4	4.81
Northwestern University	5	4.78
Georgia Institute of Technology	6	4.74
Cornell University[6]	7	4.72
Ohio State University-Columbus[3]	8	4.70
Columbia University	9	4.68
Texas A&M University-College Station	10	4.66
Wisconsin-Madison, University of	11	4.64
Iowa, University of	12	4.62
Iowa State University	13	4.59
Pittsburgh, University of	14	4.57
Illinois,Urbana-Champaign, University of	15	4.55
Kansas State University	16	4.53
Pennsylvania State University-University Park	17	4.52
Missouri-Columbia, University of	18	4.50
Lehigh University	19	4.47
Oklahoma, University of	20	4.46
Southern California, University of[3]	21	4.42
State University of New York College at Buffalo	22	4.40
Virginia Tech[3]	23	4.37
Rensselaer Polytechnic Institute[1]	24	4.35
North Carolina State University	25	4.33
Auburn University	26	4.30
Massachusetts-Amherst, University of[5]	27	4.28
Cincinnati, University of	28	4.26
Louisiana State University-Baton Rouge	29	4.25
Florida, University of[3]	30	4.24
Texas Tech University	31	4.23
Polytechnic University	32	4.20
Oklahoma State University[4]	33	4.19
Arizona, University of	34	4.18

Explanatory Note: Actual titles used by the institution to identify their curricula
[1]Industrial and Management Engineering
[2]Industrial and Operations Engineering
[3]Industrial and Systems Engineering
[4]Industrial Engineering and Management
[5]Industrial Engineering and Operations Research
[6]Operations Research and Industrial Engineering

INFORMATION SCIENCE

Leading Institutions—Rating of Undergraduate Programs

INSTITUTION	RANK	SCORE
Massachusetts Institute of Technology	1	4.86
California-San Diego, University of	2	4.83
Michigan-Ann Arbor, University of	3	4.77
Pittsburgh, University of	4	4.73
Ohio State University-Columbus	5	4.70
Carnegie Mellon University	6	4.66
Alabama-Birmingham, University of	7	4.63
Harvard and Radcliffe Colleges	8	4.59
California-Irvine, University of	9	4.55
Maryland-College Park, University of	10	4.52

INTERNATIONAL RELATIONS
LEADING INSTITUTIONS—RATING OF UNDERGRADUATE PROGRAMS

INSTITUTION	RANK	SCORE
Tufts University	1	4.88
Princeton University	2	4.85
Johns Hopkins University	3	4.83
Georgetown University	4	4.79
Pennsylvania, University of	5	4.78
Harvard and Radcliffe Colleges	6	4.75
Cornell University	7	4.72
Wisconsin-Madison, University of	8	4.69
Massachusetts Institute of Technology	9	4.64
Stanford University	10	4.62
Virginia, University of	11	4.60
Notre Dame, University of	12	4.58
United States Air Force Academy	13	4.57
United States Military Academy	14	4.55
Claremont McKenna College	15	4.50

ITALIAN
LEADING INSTITUTIONS—RATING OF UNDERGRADUATE PROGRAMS

INSTITUTION	RANK	SCORE
Columbia University	1	4.82
New York University	2	4.80
Yale University	3	4.75
Johns Hopkins University	4	4.66
Indiana University-Bloomington	5	4.61
California-Berkeley, University of	6	4.58
Michigan-Ann Arbor, University of	7	4.55
Wisconsin-Madison, University of	8	4.53
Brown University	9	4.50
Illinois,Urbana-Champaign, University of	10	4.48
Catholic University of America, The	11	4.46
Harvard and Radcliffe Colleges	12	4.42
Northwestern University	13	4.40
Virginia, University of	14	4.38
Bryn Mawr College	15	4.35
California-Los Angeles, University of	16	4.33
Chicago, University of	17	4.30
California-Santa Cruz, University of	18	4.27
Texas-Austin, University of	19	4.25
Minnesota, University of	20	4.24
North Carolina-Chapel Hill, University of	21	4.23
Washington, University of	22	4.21

JAPANESE
LEADING INSTITUTIONS—RATING OF UNDERGRADUATE PROGRAMS

INSTITUTION	RANK	SCORE
Harvard and Radcliffe Colleges	1	4.84
Chicago, University of	2	4.80
Pennsylvania, University of	3	4.73
Columbia University	4	4.71
California-Berkeley, University of	5	4.64
Cornell University	6	4.62
Michigan-Ann Arbor, University of	7	4.54
Washington, University of	8	4.51
Wisconsin-Madison, University of	9	4.48
Hawaii-Manoa, University of	10	4.44
Stanford University	11	4.40
Ohio State University-Columbus	12	4.38
Yale University	13	4.35
Indiana University-Bloomington	14	4.32

JOURNALISM AND MASS COMMUNICATIONS

LEADING INSTITUTIONS—RATING OF UNDERGRADUATE PROGRAMS

INSTITUTION	RANK	SCORE
Missouri-Columbia, University of	1	4.87
Northwestern University	2	4.84
Syracuse University	3	4.82
Minnesota, University of	4	4.79
Illinois,Urbana-Champaign, University of	5	4.77
North Carolina-Chapel Hill, University of	6	4.76
Wisconsin-Madison, University of	7	4.73
Ohio State University-Columbus	8	4.71
Michigan State University	9	4.68
Southern California, University of	10	4.66
New York University	11	4.63
Indiana University-Bloomington	12	4.62
Washington, University of	13	4.59
Kansas, University of	14	4.55
Texas-Austin, University of	15	4.53
Kansas State University	16	4.50
Marquette University	17	4.48
Iowa, University of	18	4.47
Colorado-Boulder, University of	19	4.45
Ohio University	20	4.43
Pennsylvania State University-University Park	21	4.40
Florida, University of	22	4.38
Montana, University of	23	4.37
Arizona, University of	24	4.35
Oregon, University of	25	4.34
Iowa State University	26	4.32
Oklahoma, University of	27	4.30
Georgia, University of	28	4.27
Utah, University of	29	4.25
Arizona State University	30	4.20
Maryland-College Park, University of	31	4.18

LABOR AND INDUSTRIAL RELATIONS

LEADING INSTITUTIONS—RATING OF UNDERGRADUATE PROGRAMS

INSTITUTION	RANK	SCORE
Cornell University	1	4.91
Pennsylvania, University of	2	4.85
Carnegie Mellon University	3	4.82
Syracuse University	4	4.73
Michigan-Ann Arbor, University of	5	4.71
Temple University	6	4.67
Purdue University-West Lafayette	7	4.61
Iowa, University of	8	4.56
Wayne State University	9	4.52
Maryland-College Park, University of	10	4.47

LANDSCAPE ARCHITECTURE

LEADING INSTITUTIONS—RATING OF UNDERGRADUATE PROGRAMS

INSTITUTION	RANK	SCORE
Cornell University	1	4.90
Texas A&M University-College Station	2	4.89
Kansas State University	3	4.82
California-Davis, University of	4	4.81
Illinois,Urbana-Champaign, University of	5	4.80
Ohio State University-Columbus	6	4.78
Minnesota, University of	7	4.77
Wisconsin-Madison, University of	8	4.76
Iowa State University	9	4.74
Louisiana State University-Baton Rouge	10	4.72
Georgia, University of	11	4.69
Florida, University of	12	4.68
Virginia Tech	13	4.65
SUNY College of Environmental Science and Forestry	14	4.63
Washington, University of	15	4.61
Arizona, University of	16	4.60
Pennsylvania State University-University Park	17	4.58
Michigan State University	18	4.56
Purdue University-West Lafayette	19	4.53
Colorado State University	20	4.50
Utah State University	21	4.48
Massachusetts-Amherst, University of	22	4.46
Washington State University	23	4.43
City University of New York-City College	24	4.41
California Polytechnic State University-San Luis Obispo	25	4.39
Oklahoma State University	26	4.38
West Virginia University	27	4.37
Oregon, University of	28	4.36
Mississippi State University	29	4.33
Idaho, University of	30	4.32
Texas Tech University	31	4.31
Kentucky, University of	32	4.29
California State Polytechnic University, Pomona	33	4.27

LATIN

INSTITUTION	RANK	SCORE
Columbia University	1	4.89
Indiana University-Bloomington	2	4.86
Bryn Mawr College	3	4.83
Minnesota, University of	4	4.80
Catholic University of America, The	5	4.75
North Carolina-Chapel Hill, University of	6	4.71
Michigan-Ann Arbor, University of	7	4.67
California-Berkeley, University of	8	4.61
Yale University	9	4.56
Chicago, University of	10	4.51
Harvard and Radcliffe Colleges	11	4.49

LATIN AMERICAN STUDIES

LEADING INSTITUTIONS—RATING OF UNDERGRADUATE PROGRAMS

INSTITUTION	RANK	SCORE
Texas-Austin, University of	1	4.83
Tulane University	2	4.80
California-Berkeley, University of	3	4.74
North Carolina-Chapel Hill, University of	4	4.71
Stanford University	5	4.66
Columbia University	6	4.60
New Mexico, University of	7	4.55
Vanderbilt University	8	4.52
Miami, University of	9	4.49
California-Los Angeles, University of	10	4.44
Chicago, University of	11	4.38
Yale University	12	4.36
Arizona, University of	13	4.30
New York University	14	4.26
George Washington University	15	4.20
Pittsburgh, University of	16	4.17

LINGUISTICS
LEADING INSTITUTIONS—RATING OF UNDERGRADUATE PROGRAMS

INSTITUTION	RANK	SCORE
California-Los Angeles, University of	1	4.91
Chicago, University of	2	4.90
California-Berkeley, University of	3	4.88
Pennsylvania, University of	4	4.85
Cornell University	5	4.83
California-San Diego, University of	6	4.81
Yale University	7	4.79
Illinois,Urbana-Champaign, University of	8	4.76
Stanford University	9	4.74
Massachusetts Institute of Technology	10	4.72
Michigan-Ann Arbor, University of	11	4.71
Indiana University-Bloomington	12	4.69
Wisconsin-Madison, University of	13	4.68
Washington, University of	14	4.66
New York University	15	4.64
Ohio State University-Columbus	16	4.63
Rochester, University of	17	4.62
Harvard and Radcliffe Colleges	18	4.61
Hawaii-Manoa, University of	19	4.59
Kansas, University of	20	4.52
Rice University	21	4.50
Texas-Austin, University of	22	4.48
Pittsburgh, University of	23	4.45
Arizona, University of	24	4.41
Minnesota, University of	25	4.37
California-Irvine, University of	26	4.35
Florida, University of	27	4.32
Iowa, University of	28	4.28
Massachusetts-Amherst, University of	29	4.26
California-Santa Barbara, University of	30	4.22

MANAGEMENT

LEADING INSTITUTIONS—RATING OF UNDERGRADUATE PROGRAMS

INSTITUTION	RANK	SCORE
Pennsylvania, University of	1	4.91
Massachusetts Institute of Technology	2	4.90
Indiana University-Bloomington	3	4.88
Michigan-Ann Arbor, University of	4	4.86
California-Berkeley, University of	5	4.84
Carnegie Mellon University	6	4.82
New York University	7	4.81
Illinois,Urbana-Champaign, University of	8	4.80
Virginia, University of	9	4.78
Wisconsin-Madison, University of	10	4.76
Michigan State University	11	4.74
Washington, University of	12	4.73
Purdue University-West Lafayette	13	4.71
Texas-Austin, University of	14	4.70
City University of New York-Baruch College	15	4.66
Minnesota, University of	16	4.65
Washington University in Saint Louis	17	4.62
Case Western Reserve University	18	4.60
Southern California, University of	19	4.59
Houston, University of	20	4.57
Pennsylvania State University-University Park	21	4.55
Notre Dame, University of	22	4.52
North Carolina-Chapel Hill, University of	23	4.51
Texas A&M University-College Station	24	4.50
Ohio State University-Columbus	25	4.47
Florida, University of	26	4.44
Oregon, University of	27	4.40
Southern Methodist University	28	4.39
Utah, University of	29	4.38
Georgia State University	30	4.36
Louisiana State University-Baton Rouge	31	4.35
Massachusetts-Amherst, University of	32	4.34
Lehigh University	33	4.33
Arizona, University of	34	4.32
Maryland-College Park, University of	35	4.30
Arizona State University	36	4.28
South Carolina-Columbia , University of,	37	4.25
George Washington University	38	4.21
Emory University	39	4.20
State University of New York College at Buffalo	40	4.18
Colorado-Boulder, University of	41	4.16
Missouri-Columbia, University of	42	4.15
Iowa, University of	43	4.12
Syracuse University	44	4.10
Denver, University of	45	4.08
Nebraska-Lincoln, University of	46	4.07
Georgia, University of	47	4.05

MANUFACTURING ENGINEERING
LEADING INSTITUTIONS—RATING OF UNDERGRADUATE PROGRAMS

INSTITUTION	RANK	SCORE
California–Berkeley, University of	1	4.42
Boston University	2	4.38
Utah State University [1]	3	4.32
Oregon State University [2]	4	4.29
Kansas State University [3]	5	4.24
Miami, University of	6	4.20

Explanatory Note: Actual titles used by the institution to identify their curricula
[1] Manufacturing Engineering option in Mechanical Engineering
[2] Manufacturing Engineering option in Industrial Engineering
[3] Manufacturing Systems Engineering

MARINE BIOLOGY

Leading Institutions—Rating of Undergraduate Programs

INSTITUTION	RANK	SCORE
Massachusetts Institute of Technology	1	4.80
California-Santa Barbara, University of	2	4.75
Texas A&M University-College Station	3	4.67
Miami, University of	4	4.59
North Carolina-Wilmington, University of	5	4.51
Brown University	6	4.50
Florida Institute of Technology	7	4.48

MARINE SCIENCES

LEADING INSTITUTIONS—RATING OF UNDERGRADUATE PROGRAMS

INSTITUTION	RANK	SCORE
Cornell University	1	4.82
United States Coast Guard Academy	2	4.76
Texas A&M University-College Station	3	4.65
Miami, University of	4	4.60
South Carolina-Columbia , University of,	5	4.55
Long Island University-Southampton	6	4.52

MARKETING

Leading Institutions—Rating of Undergraduate Programs

INSTITUTION	RANK	SCORE
Pennsylvania, University of	1	4.90
Indiana University-Bloomington	2	4.88
Michigan-Ann Arbor, University of	3	4.85
California-Berkeley, University of	4	4.83
New York University	5	4.81
Illinois,Urbana-Champaign, University of	6	4.79
Michigan State University	7	4.76
Purdue University-West Lafayette	8	4.72
Washington, University of	9	4.71
Wisconsin-Madison, University of	10	4.68
Virginia, University of	11	4.66
City University of New York-Baruch College	12	4.63
Minnesota, University of	13	4.61
Washington University in Saint Louis	14	4.60
Case Western Reserve University	15	4.58
Houston, University of	16	4.57
Pennsylvania State University-University Park	17	4.55
Southern California, University of	18	4.54
Texas A&M University-College Station	19	4.52
Florida, University of	20	4.50
Ohio State University-Columbus	21	4.49
Notre Dame, University of	22	4.48
Southern Methodist University	23	4.45
Lehigh University	24	4.41
Utah, University of	25	4.40
Emory University	26	4.39
Louisiana State University-Baton Rouge	27	4.38
Massachusetts-Amherst, University of	28	4.36
Oregon, University of	29	4.33
Arizona, University of	30	4.32
Maryland-College Park, University of	31	4.30
Iowa, University of	32	4.29
Georgia State University	33	4.27
Arizona State University	34	4.25
Syracuse University	35	4.23
George Washington University	36	4.21
Colorado-Boulder, University of	37	4.16
Denver, University of	38	4.13
South Carolina-Columbia , University of,	39	4.11
Georgia, University of	40	4.08
Nebraska-Lincoln, University of	41	4.06

MATERIALS ENGINEERING/MATERIALS SCIENCE AND ENGINEERING

LEADING INSTITUTIONS—RATING OF UNDERGRADUATE PROGRAMS

INSTITUTION	RANK	SCORE
Cornell University [2]	1	4.91
Northwestern University [2]	2	4.90
Minnesota, University of [2]	3	4.87
Massachusetts Institute of Technology [2]	4	4.85
Rice University [2]	5	4.83
Rensselaer Polytechnic Institute [1]	6	4.81
Pennsylvania, University of [2]	7	4.80
Brown University [1]	8	4.77
Johns Hopkins University [2]	9	4.76
Case Western Reserve University [2]	10	4.74
North Carolina State University [2]	11	4.72
Florida, University of [2]	12	4.69
Lehigh University [2]	13	4.65
Virginia Tech [1]	14	4.62
California-Los Angeles, University of [1]	15	4.60
Columbia University [2]	16	4.58
Michigan-Ann Arbor, University of [2]	17	4.55
Utah, University of [2]	18	4.53
Michigan State University [2]	19	4.50
Georgia Institute of Technology [1]	20	4.47
Drexel University [1]	21	4.45
Ohio State University-Columbus [2]	22	4.44
Pittsburgh, University of [2]	23	4.40
California-Davis, University of [2]	24	4.38
Purdue University-West Lafayette [2]	25	4.36
Auburn University [1]	26	4.34
Cincinnati, University of [1]	27	4.30
Alabama-Birmingham, University of [1]	28	4.28
Arizona, University of [2]	29	4.25
Tennessee-Knoxville, University of [2]	30	4.23
New Mexico Institute of Mining & Technology [1]	31	4.22
Kentucky, University of [2]	32	4.19

Explanatory Note: Actual titles used by the institution to identify their curricula
[1]Materials Engineering
[2]Materials Science and Engineering

MATHEMATICS

LEADING INSTITUTIONS—RATING OF UNDERGRADUATE PROGRAMS

INSTITUTION	RANK	SCORE
Princeton University	1	4.92
California-Berkeley, University of	2	4.91
Harvard and Radcliffe Colleges	3	4.88
Massachusetts Institute of Technology	4	4.86
Chicago, University of	5	4.85
Stanford University	6	4.84
New York University	7	4.82
Yale University	8	4.80
Wisconsin-Madison, University of	9	4.78
Columbia University	10	4.76
Michigan-Ann Arbor, University of	11	4.75
Brown University	12	4.73
Cornell University	13	4.71
California-Los Angeles, University of	14	4.69
Illinois,Urbana-Champaign, University of	15	4.68
California Institute of Technology	16	4.66
Minnesota, University of	17	4.65
Pennsylvania, University of	18	4.63
Notre Dame, University of	19	4.62
Georgia Institute of Technology	20	4.61
Washington, University of	21	4.60
Purdue University-West Lafayette	22	4.58
Rutgers University, New Brunswick	23	4.57
Indiana University-Bloomington	24	4.55
Maryland-College Park, University of	25	4.54
Rice University	26	4.52
California-San Diego, University of	27	4.51
Northwestern University	28	4.50
Texas-Austin, University of	29	4.48
Carnegie Mellon University	30	4.47
Johns Hopkins University	31	4.46
Washington University in Saint Louis	32	4.44
Ohio State University-Columbus	33	4.43
State University of New York at Stony Brook	34	4.41
Pennsylvania State University-University Park	35	4.40
Virginia, University of	36	4.38
Rensselaer Polytechnic Institute	37	4.37
Illinois-Chicago, University of	38	4.36
Colorado-Boulder, University of	39	4.34
Kentucky, University of	40	4.32
North Carolina-Chapel Hill, University of	41	4.31
Dartmouth College	42	4.30
Rochester, University of	43	4.28

Mathematics—*continued*

INSTITUTION	RANK	SCORE
Utah, University of	44	4.26
State University of New York College at Buffalo	45	4.25
Tulane University	46	4.23
Southern California, University of	47	4.22
California-Santa Barbara, University of	48	4.20
Massachusetts-Amherst, University of	49	4.19
Oregon, University of	50	4.18
Duke University	51	4.17
Louisiana State University-Baton Rouge	52	4.16
Arizona, University of	53	4.15
Case Western Reserve University	54	4.14
Michigan State University	55	4.13
Pittsburgh, University of	56	4.12
Brandeis University	57	4.11
United States Air Force Academy	58	4.09

MECHANICAL ENGINEERING

LEADING INSTITUTIONS—RATING OF UNDERGRADUATE PROGRAMS

INSTITUTION	RANK	SCORE
Massachusetts Institute of Technology	1	4.93
Stanford University	2	4.92
California-Berkeley, University of	3	4.91
Minnesota, University of	4	4.89
Princeton University	5	4.86
Purdue University-West Lafayette	6	4.85
Brown University	7	4.83
Cornell University	8	4.81
Michigan-Ann Arbor, University of	9	4.79
California-Los Angeles, University of	10	4.77
Illinois,Urbana-Champaign, University of	11	4.76
Wisconsin-Madison, University of	12	4.75
Northwestern University	13	4.74
Rensselaer Polytechnic Institute	14	4.72
Texas-Austin, University of	15	4.71
Stevens Institute of Technology	16	4.70
Columbia University	17	4.68
Pennsylvania, University of[1]	18	4.67
Carnegie Mellon University	19	4.66
Lehigh University	20	4.65
Case Western Reserve University	21	4.63
Georgia Institute of Technology	22	4.62
California-Davis, University of	23	4.60
Virginia Tech	24	4.59
Iowa State University	25	4.58
Ohio State University-Columbus	26	4.57
Pennsylvania State University-University Park	27	4.55
Southern California, University of	28	4.53
North Carolina State University	29	4.52
Washington, University of	30	4.50
Yale University	31	4.48
Rice University	32	4.47
Houston, University of	33	4.45
Maryland-College Park, University of	34	4.44
Notre Dame, University of	35	4.42
Syracuse University	36	4.40
Iowa, University of	37	4.39
Virginia, University of	38	4.38
Michigan State University	39	4.37
Oklahoma State University	40	4.35
Rochester, University of	41	4.33
Johns Hopkins University	42	4.32
Florida, University of	43	4.30

Explanatory Note: Actual titles used by the institution to identify their curricula
[1]Mechanical Engineering and Applied Mechanics

Mechanical Engineering—*continued*

INSTITUTION	RANK	SCORE
Rutgers University, New Brunswick	44	4.28
Polytechnic University	45	4.26
Delaware, University of	46	4.25
Oregon State University	47	4.24
Drexel University	48	4.23
Cincinnati, University of	49	4.20
State University of New York College at Buffalo	50	4.19
Missouri-Rolla, University of	51	4.18
State University of New York at Stony Brook	52	4.16
Arizona, University of	53	4.15
Washington University in Saint Louis	54	4.13
Arizona State University	55	4.12
Colorado State University	56	4.11
Oklahoma, University of	57	4.10
Vanderbilt University	58	4.09

MEDIEVAL STUDIES
LEADING INSTITUTIONS—RATING OF UNDERGRADUATE PROGRAMS

INSTITUTION	RANK	SCORE
Columbia University	1	4.83
Cornell University	2	4.80
New York University	3	4.77
Chicago, University of	4	4.74
Notre Dame, University of	5	4.72
Illinois,Urbana-Champaign, University of	6	4.70
Michigan-Ann Arbor, University of	7	4.68
Washington University in Saint Louis	8	4.65
Duke University	9	4.63
Catholic University of America, The	10	4.60

METALLURGICAL ENGINEERING
LEADING INSTITUTIONS—RATING OF UNDERGRADUATE PROGRAMS

INSTITUTION	RANK	SCORE
Illinois, Urbana-Champaign, University of	1	4.91
Ohio State University-Columbus	2	4.87
Carnegie Mellon University[3]	3	4.85
Pennsylvania State University-University Park[4]	4	4.83
Colorado School of Mines	5	4.81
Wisconsin-Madison, University of	6	4.78
Iowa State University	7	4.77
Missouri-Rolla, University of	8	4.75
Pittsburgh, University of	9	4.73
Michigan Technological University[2]	10	4.68
Utah, University of	11	4.66
Stevens Institute of Technology[1]	12	4.62
South Dakota School of Mines & Technology	13	4.60
Montana Tech of the University of Montana	14	4.56
Texas-El Paso, University of	15	4.53
Idaho, University of	16	4.51
Alabama, University of	17	4.48
Illinois Institute of Technology	18	4.45

Explanatory Note: Actual titles used by the institution to identify their curricula
[1] Materials and Metallurgical Engineering
[2] Materials Science and Engineering Option in Metallurgical Engineering
[3] Material Science and Engineering
[4] Metals Science and Engineering

METEOROLOGY
LEADING INSTITUTIONS—RATING OF UNDERGRADUATE PROGRAMS

INSTITUTION	RANK	SCORE
Cornell University	1	4.89
Massachusetts Institute of Technology	2	4.87
Iowa State University	3	4.83
Pennsylvania State University-University Park	4	4.80
Kansas, University of	5	4.75
Michigan-Ann Arbor, University of	6	4.71
Purdue University-West Lafayette	7	4.67
North Carolina State University	8	4.64
Oklahoma, University of	9	4.58
Texas A&M University-College Station	10	4.56

MINING AND MINERAL ENGINEERING
LEADING INSTITUTIONS—RATING OF UNDERGRADUATE PROGRAMS

INSTITUTION	RANK	SCORE
Colorado School of Mines [1]	1	4.89
Arizona, University of [1]	2	4.87
Missouri-Rolla, University of [1]	3	4.84
Virginia Tech [3]	4	4.82
Pennsylvania State University-University Park [4]	5	4.79
Pennsylvania State University-University Park [5]		
Columbia University [1]	6	4.75
West Virginia University [1]	7	4.72
Utah, University of [1]	8	4.69
Idaho, University of [1]	9	4.66
South Dakota School of Mines & Technology [1]	10	4.63
Michigan Technological University [2]	11	4.60
Montana Tech of the University of Montana [1]	12	4.57
Alaska-Fairbanks, University of [1]	13	4.53
Nevada-Reno, University of	14	4.51
Kentucky, University of [1]	15	4.49
Alabama, University of	16	4.45
Southern Illinois University-Carbondale [1]	17	4.41

Explanatory Note: Actual titles used by the institution to identify their curricula
[1] Mining Engineering
[2] Mineral Processing Engineering
[3] Mining and Minerals Engineering
[4] Mining Engineering – Mineral Processing Option
[5] Mining Engineering – Mining Option

MOLECULAR BIOLOGY
LEADING INSTITUTIONS—RATING OF UNDERGRADUATE PROGRAMS

INSTITUTION	RANK	SCORE
Massachusetts Institute of Technology	1	4.90
California Institute of Technology	2	4.88
Wisconsin-Madison, University of	3	4.84
California-Berkeley, University of	4	4.82
Colorado-Boulder, University of	5	4.79
Northwestern University	6	4.75
California-San Diego, University of	7	4.73
Michigan-Ann Arbor, University of	8	4.72
Harvard and Radcliffe Colleges	9	4.71
Princeton University	10	4.68
Carnegie Mellon University	11	4.66
Cornell University	12	4.62
Pennsylvania, University of	13	4.60
Purdue University-West Lafayette	14	4.58
Rensselaer Polytechnic Institute	15	4.57
State University of New York College at Buffalo	16	4.53
Arizona, University of	17	4.52
Texas-Austin, University of	18	4.50
Washington, University of	19	4.48
Pennsylvania State University-University Park	20	4.45
Vanderbilt University	21	4.43
California-Santa Cruz, University of	22	4.42

MUSIC

Leading Institutions—Rating of Undergraduate Programs

INSTITUTION	RANK	SCORE
California-Berkeley, University of	1	4.92
Chicago, University of	2	4.91
Princeton University	3	4.90
Yale University	4	4.89
Cornell University	5	4.87
Michigan-Ann Arbor, University of	6	4.84
Illinois,Urbana-Champaign, University of	7	4.82
Columbia University	8	4.80
Harvard and Radcliffe Colleges	9	4.79
California-Los Angeles, University of	10	4.78
Rochester, University of	11	4.77
North Carolina-Chapel Hill, University of	12	4.76
Stanford University	13	4.71
Oberlin College	14	4.70
Indiana University-Bloomington	15	4.69
New York University	16	4.65
Pennsylvania, University of	17	4.63
Brandeis University	18	4.61
Southern California, University of	19	4.58
Iowa, University of	20	4.55
Northwestern University	21	4.53
Texas-Austin, University of	22	4.52
Rutgers University, New Brunswick	23	4.49
Ohio State University-Columbus	24	4.46
North Texas, University of	25	4.44
Washington, University of	26	4.42
California State University-Northridge	27	4.41
Florida State University	28	4.40
Boston University	29	4.36
Cincinnati, University of	30	4.33

NATURAL RESOURCE MANAGEMENT

LEADING INSTITUTIONS—RATING OF UNDERGRADUATE PROGRAMS

INSTITUTION	RANK	SCORE
Cornell University	1	4.84
Colorado State University	2	4.80
Michigan State University	3	4.74
Arizona, University of	4	4.72
Purdue University-West Lafayette	5	4.65
California-Davis, University of	6	4.61
Minnesota, University of	7	4.57
Ohio State University-Columbus	8	4.52
Kansas State University	9	4.46
Michigan-Ann Arbor, University of	10	4.41
Wisconsin-Madison, University of	11	4.40
Montana, University of	12	4.36
Maine, University of	13	4.33
Idaho, University of	14	4.31
Maryland-College Park, University of	15	4.29

NAVAL ARCHITECTURE AND MARINE ENGINEERING
Leading Institutions—Rating of Undergraduate Programs

INSTITUTION	RANK	SCORE
Michigan-Ann Arbor, University of[4]	1	4.90
United States Naval Academy[1]	2	4.87
United States Naval Academy[3]	3	4.85
State University of New York Maritime College[1]	4	4.83
State University of New York Maritime College[3]	5	4.82
United States Coast Guard Academy[4]	6	4.81
Webb Institute[4]	7	4.77
United States Merchant Marine Academy[2]	8	4.75

Explanatory Note: Actual titles used by the institution to identify their curricula
[1]Marine Engineering
[2]Marine Engineering Systems
[3]Naval Architecture
[4]Naval Architecture and Marine Engineering

NEAR/MIDDLE EASTERN STUDIES
LEADING INSTITUTIONS—RATING OF UNDERGRADUATE PROGRAMS

INSTITUTION	RANK	SCORE
Chicago, University of	1	4.82
Harvard and Radcliffe Colleges	2	4.80
Princeton University	3	4.79
Columbia University	4	4.77
Pennsylvania, University of	5	4.75
California-Berkeley, University of	6	4.72
Michigan-Ann Arbor, University of	7	4.70
Indiana University-Bloomington	8	4.68
Johns Hopkins University	9	4.66
New York University	10	4.64
Washington, University of	11	4.62
California-Los Angeles, University of	12	4.60
Yale University	13	4.58
Cornell University	14	4.56
Brown University	15	4.55
Minnesota, University of	16	4.53
United States Military Academy	17	4.51

NUCLEAR ENGINEERING
LEADING INSTITUTIONS—RATING OF UNDERGRADUATE PROGRAMS

INSTITUTION	RANK	SCORE
Massachusetts Institute of Technology	1	4.91
Michigan-Ann Arbor, University of	2	4.87
California-Berkeley, University of	3	4.83
Wisconsin-Madison, University of	4	4.80
Virginia, University of	5	4.79
Rensselaer Polytechnic Institute	6	4.75
Illinois,Urbana-Champaign, University of	7	4.72
Arizona, University of	8	4.70
Pennsylvania State University-University Park	9	4.68
Cincinnati, University of[1]	10	4.65
Florida, University of	11	4.63
Purdue University-West Lafayette	12	4.61
Maryland-College Park, University of	13	4.60
Georgia Institute of Technology	14	4.58
Kansas State University	15	4.56
Tennessee-Knoxville, University of	16	4.53
Texas A&M University-College Station	17	4.52
North Carolina State University	18	4.50
Missouri-Rolla, University of	19	4.48
California-Santa Barbara, University of	20	4.46
Oregon State University	21	4.43
New Mexico, University of	22	4.40

Explanatory Note: Actual title used by the institution to identify their curricula
[1]Nuclear and Power Engineering

NURSING
LEADING INSTITUTIONS—RATING OF UNDERGRADUATE PROGRAMS

INSTITUTION	RANK	SCORE
New York University	1	4.90
Michigan-Ann Arbor, University of	2	4.89
Pennsylvania, University of	3	4.87
Washington, University of	4	4.86
Northwestern University	5	4.85
Pittsburgh, University of	6	4.83
Wayne State University	7	4.78
Catholic University of America, The	8	4.75
California-San Francisco, University of	9	4.72
Wisconsin-Madison, University of	10	4.68
Maryland-Baltimore County, University of	11	4.66
Minnesota, University of	12	4.61
Columbia University	13	4.59
Saint Louis University	14	4.57
Rochester, University of	15	4.55
Ohio State University-Columbus	16	4.53
North Carolina-Chapel Hill, University of	17	4.50
Illinois-Chicago, University of	18	4.49
Alabama-Birmingham, University of	19	4.44
Kansas, University of	20	4.42
Iowa, University of	21	4.40
Emory University	22	4.39
Utah, University of	23	4.38
Virginia, University of	24	4.37
Arizona, University of	25	4.36
Tennessee-Knoxville, University of	26	4.35
Florida, University of	27	4.34
Loma Linda University	28	4.33
State University of New York at Stony Brook	29	4.32
Indiana University-Purdue Univ. Indianapolis	30	4.30
State University of New York College at Buffalo	31	4.28
Georgetown University	32	4.26
Pennsylvania State University-University Park	33	4.25
Loyola University of Chicago	34	4.23
Missouri-Columbia, University of	35	4.21
Texas Woman's University	36	4.19
Marquette University	37	4.18
Cincinnati, University of	38	4.17
South Carolina-Columbia , University of,	39	4.15

NUTRITION

LEADING INSTITUTIONS—RATING OF UNDERGRADUATE PROGRAMS

INSTITUTION	RANK	SCORE
Cornell University	1	4.89
Iowa State University	2	4.86
Michigan State University	3	4.84
California-Davis, University of	4	4.83
Colorado State University	5	4.81
Purdue University-West Lafayette	6	4.80
Ohio State University-Columbus	7	4.78
Illinois,Urbana-Champaign, University of	8	4.76
California-Berkeley, University of	9	4.75
Arizona, University of	10	4.73
Minnesota, University of	11	4.71
Missouri-Columbia, University of	12	4.69
Michigan-Ann Arbor, University of	13	4.67
Georgia, University of	14	4.65
Wisconsin-Madison, University of	15	4.64
Pennsylvania State University-University Park	16	4.63
Alabama, University of	17	4.61
Florida State University	18	4.60
Oklahoma State University	19	4.58
Pittsburgh, University of	20	4.55
Texas Health and Science Center-Houston, University of	21	4.53
Florida, University of	22	4.50
Texas Woman's University	23	4.48
Wayne State University	24	4.47
Indiana University-Bloomington	25	4.46
Texas A&M University-College Station	26	4.43
Oregon State University	27	4.41
Oklahoma Health Sciences Center, University of	28	4.38

OCCUPATIONAL THERAPY

LEADING INSTITUTIONS—RATING OF UNDERGRADUATE PROGRAMS

INSTITUTION	RANK	SCORE
New York University	1	4.91
Boston University	2	4.88
Wayne State University	3	4.85
Temple University	4	4.83
Minnesota, University of	5	4.81
State University of New York College at Buffalo	6	4.79
Colorado State University	7	4.78
Florida, University of	8	4.76
Oklahoma Health Sciences Center, University of	9	4.74
Southern California, University of	10	4.72
Ohio State University-Columbus	11	4.70
Wisconsin-Madison, University of	12	4.68
Washington, University of	13	4.66
Missouri-Columbia, University of	14	4.65
Texas-San Antonio, University of	15	4.63
Indiana University-Purdue Univ. Indianapolis	16	4.61
Louisiana State University-Baton Rouge	17	4.60
Kansas-Medical Center University of	18	4.58
State University of New York Health Science Center at Brooklyn	19	4.56
Pittsburgh, University of	20	4.55
Washington University in Saint Louis	21	4.52
Alabama-Birmingham, University of	22	4.50
Medical University of South Carolina	23	4.46
Medical College of Georgia	24	4.43
Texas Tech University	25	4.41
Illinois-Chicago, University of	26	4.40
Texas Medical Branch at Galveston, University of	27	4.38
Western Michigan University	28	4.37
Virginia Commonwealth University	29	4.35
Loma Linda University	30	4.34
Thomas Jefferson University	31	4.32
Syracuse University	32	4.29

OCEAN ENGINEERING
Leading Institutions—Rating of Undergraduate Programs

INSTITUTION	RANK	SCORE
Massachusetts Institute of Technology	1	4.91
United States Naval Academy	2	4.87
Texas A&M University-College Station	3	4.85
Florida Institute of Technology	4	4.82
Florida Atlantic University	5	4.79
Virginia Tech	6	4.75

OPERATIONS RESEARCH
LEADING INSTITUTIONS—RATING OF UNDERGRADUATE PROGRAMS

INSTITUTION	RANK	SCORE
Cornell University	1	4.87
Columbia University	2	4.83
Carnegie Mellon University	3	4.79
Pennsylvania State University-University Park	4	4.76
United States Air Force Academy	5	4.73
United States Military Academy	6	4.70
Case Western Reserve University	7	4.65
Purdue University-West Lafayette	8	4.61
Georgia Institute of Technology	9	4.58
Colorado-Boulder, University of	10	4.56

ORNAMENTAL HORTICULTURE

LEADING INSTITUTIONS—RATING OF UNDERGRADUATE PROGRAMS

INSTITUTION	RANK	SCORE
Cornell University	1	4.87
Iowa State University	2	4.83
Texas A&M University-College Station	3	4.80
North Carolina State University	4	4.77
Illinois,Urbana-Champaign, University of	5	4.74
Texas Tech University	6	4.72
Auburn University	7	4.69

PARKS MANAGEMENT
LEADING INSTITUTIONS—RATING OF UNDERGRADUATE PROGRAMS

INSTITUTION	RANK	SCORE
Michigan State University	1	4.85
Colorado State University	2	4.81
Pennsylvania State University-University Park	3	4.78
Texas Tech University	4	4.73
Illinois,Urbana-Champaign, University of	5	4.70
Ohio State University-Columbus	6	4.66
Oregon State University	7	4.61
Kansas State University	8	4.59
Texas A&M University-College Station	9	4.54
Clemson University	10	4.52
Maine, University of	11	4.50
Minnesota, University of	12	4.48
Arizona, University of	13	4.46
Missouri-Columbia, University of	14	4.45
Purdue University-West Lafayette	15	4.43
North Carolina State University	16	4.40
Montana, University of	17	4.38

PETROLEUM ENGINEERING
Leading Institutions—Rating of Undergraduate Programs

INSTITUTION	RANK	SCORE
Texas A&M University-College Station	1	4.91
Texas-Austin, University of	2	4.89
Tulsa, University of	3	4.86
Louisiana State University-Baton Rouge	4	4.83
Stanford University	5	4.81
Oklahoma, University of	6	4.78
Pennsylvania State University-University Park[2]	7	4.75
Colorado School of Mines	8	4.73
Texas Tech University	9	4.70
Kansas, University of	10	4.66
Missouri-Rolla, University of	11	4.65
New Mexico Institute of Mining & Technology	12	4.63
Wyoming, University of	13	4.61
Mississippi State University	14	4.59
Southwestern Louisiana, University of	15	4.57
Louisiana Tech University	16	4.56
Marietta College	17	4.52
Montana Tech of the University of Montana	18	4.50
Texas A&I University[1]	19	4.48
West Virginia University[2]	20	4.45
Alabama, University of	21	4.42
Alaska-Fairbanks, University of	22	4.40

Explanatory Note: Actual titles used by the institution to identify their curricula
[1]Natural Gas Engineering
[2]Petroleum and Natural Gas Engineering

PHILOSOPHY
LEADING INSTITUTIONS—RATING OF UNDERGRADUATE PROGRAMS

INSTITUTION	RANK	SCORE
Princeton University	1	4.90
Pittsburgh, University of	2	4.89
Harvard and Radcliffe Colleges	3	4.87
California-Berkeley, University of	4	4.83
Chicago, University of	5	4.80
Stanford University	6	4.78
Michigan-Ann Arbor, University of	7	4.76
California-Los Angeles, University of	8	4.73
Massachusetts Institute of Technology	9	4.70
Cornell University	10	4.68
Yale University	11	4.67
Brown University	12	4.65
Columbia University	13	4.62
Notre Dame, University of	14	4.60
Boston University	15	4.58
North Carolina-Chapel Hill, University of	16	4.57
Wisconsin-Madison, University of	17	4.55
Indiana University-Bloomington	18	4.53
Massachusetts-Amherst, University of	19	4.50
Minnesota, University of	20	4.47
Johns Hopkins University	21	4.44

PHYSICAL THERAPY

LEADING INSTITUTIONS—RATING OF UNDERGRADUATE PROGRAMS

INSTITUTION	RANK	SCORE
New York University	1	4.91
North Carolina-Chapel Hill, University of	2	4.88
Minnesota, University of	3	4.86
Wisconsin-Madison, University of	4	4.83
Washington, University of	5	4.80
State University of New York College at Buffalo	6	4.77
State University of New York at Stony Brook	7	4.75
Oklahoma Health Sciences Center, University of	8	4.73
Ohio State University-Columbus	9	4.71
Tennessee-Memphis, University of	10	4.69
Texas-Dallas , University of	11	4.66
State University of New York Health Science Center at Brooklyn	12	4.64
Illinois-Chicago, University of	13	4.61
Indiana University-Purdue Univ. Indianapolis	14	4.59
Texas-San Antonio, University of	15	4.58
Missouri-Columbia, University of	16	4.57
Wayne State University	17	4.53
Louisiana State University-Baton Rouge	18	4.50
Utah, University of	19	4.48
Medical College of Georgia	20	4.46
Florida, University of	21	4.40
Medical University of South Carolina	22	4.39
Medicine & Dentistry/Kean College of N.J./Seton Hall U., University of	23	4.38
Connecticut, University of	24	4.35

PHYSICS
LEADING INSTITUTIONS—RATING OF UNDERGRADUATE PROGRAMS

INSTITUTION	RANK	SCORE
California Institute of Technology	1	4.92
Harvard and Radcliffe Colleges	2	4.91
Cornell University	3	4.90
Princeton University	4	4.89
Massachusetts Institute of Technology	5	4.88
California-Berkeley, University of	6	4.87
Stanford University	7	4.85
Chicago, University of	8	4.83
Illinois,Urbana-Champaign, University of	9	4.81
Columbia University	10	4.80
Yale University	11	4.79
Georgia Institute of Technology	12	4.78
California-San Diego, University of	13	4.77
California-Los Angeles, University of	14	4.76
Pennsylvania, University of	15	4.74
Wisconsin-Madison, University of	16	4.73
Washington, University of	17	4.72
Michigan-Ann Arbor, University of	18	4.71
Maryland-College Park, University of	19	4.69
California-Santa Barbara, University of	20	4.68
Texas-Austin, University of	21	4.67
Carnegie Mellon University	22	4.64
Minnesota, University of	23	4.63
Rensselaer Polytechnic Institute	24	4.61
Brown University	25	4.60
Johns Hopkins University	26	4.59
Michigan State University	27	4.58
Notre Dame, University of	28	4.57
State University of New York at Stony Brook	29	4.56
Case Western Reserve University	30	4.55
Northwestern University	31	4.54
Rochester, University of	32	4.53
Pittsburgh, University of	33	4.52
Pennsylvania State University-University Park	34	4.51
Colorado-Boulder, University of	35	4.50

POLITICAL SCIENCE
LEADING INSTITUTIONS—RATING OF UNDERGRADUATE PROGRAMS

INSTITUTION	RANK	SCORE
Yale University	1	4.92
Harvard and Radcliffe Colleges	2	4.91
California-Berkeley, University of	3	4.90
Michigan-Ann Arbor, University of	4	4.89
Chicago, University of	5	4.87
Massachusetts Institute of Technology	6	4.86
Stanford University	7	4.84
Wisconsin-Madison, University of	8	4.83
Minnesota, University of	9	4.82
Cornell University	10	4.80
Princeton University	11	4.78
California-Los Angeles, University of	12	4.76
Northwestern University	13	4.75
North Carolina-Chapel Hill, University of	14	4.74
Columbia University	15	4.73
Indiana University-Bloomington	16	4.71
Duke University	17	4.70
Johns Hopkins University	18	4.68
Notre Dame, University of	19	4.67
Tufts University	20	4.66
Ohio State University-Columbus	21	4.65
Pennsylvania, University of	22	4.63
Virginia, University of	23	4.61
Georgetown University	24	4.60
Texas-Austin, University of	25	4.57
Washington, University of	26	4.56
Pittsburgh, University of	27	4.55
Rochester, University of	28	4.54
Rutgers University, New Brunswick	29	4.53
Brandeis University	30	4.52
Vanderbilt University	31	4.51
Illinois,Urbana-Champaign, University of	32	4.50
Oregon, University of	33	4.48
Maryland-College Park, University of	34	4.47
Iowa, University of	35	4.45
California-Santa Barbara, University of	36	4.44
State University of New York College at Buffalo	37	4.42
Massachusetts-Amherst, University of	38	4.40
New York University	39	4.38
Michigan State University	40	4.36
Syracuse University	41	4.34
Washington University in Saint Louis	42	4.33
United States Air Force Academy	43	4.32

Political Science—*continued*

INSTITUTION	RANK	SCORE
United States Military Academy	44	4.30
Dartmouth College	45	4.28
Pomona College	46	4.26
Emory University	47	4.25
California-Davis, University of	48	4.23
Boston University	49	4.21
Tulane University	50	4.18

PORTUGUESE
LEADING INSTITUTIONS—RATING OF UNDERGRADUATE PROGRAMS

INSTITUTION	RANK	SCORE
Harvard and Radcliffe Colleges	1	4.86
New York University	2	4.82
Stanford University	3	4.80
Illinois,Urbana-Champaign, University of	4	4.75
Georgetown University	5	4.71
New Mexico, University of	6	4.69
North Carolina-Chapel Hill, University of	7	4.63
Pennsylvania, University of	8	4.61
Wisconsin-Madison, University of	9	4.59
Indiana University-Bloomington	10	4.54
Tulane University	11	4.52
Texas-Austin, University of	12	4.50

POULTRY SCIENCES
LEADING INSTITUTIONS—RATING OF UNDERGRADUATE PROGRAMS

INSTITUTION	RANK	SCORE
Cornell University	1	4.89
California-Davis, University of	2	4.85
Wisconsin-Madison, University of	3	4.83
Virginia Tech	4	4.82
Ohio State University-Columbus	5	4.79
North Carolina State University	6	4.77
Maryland-College Park, University of	7	4.74
Florida, University of	8	4.73
Pennsylvania State University-University Park	9	4.72
Oregon State University	10	4.69
Auburn University	11	4.68
Purdue University-West Lafayette	12	4.66
Texas A&M University-College Station	13	4.63

PSYCHOLOGY

LEADING INSTITUTIONS—RATING OF UNDERGRADUATE PROGRAMS

INSTITUTION	RANK	SCORE
Stanford University	1	4.66
Yale University	2	4.65
Pennsylvania, University of	3	4.64
Michigan-Ann Arbor, University of	4	4.63
Minnesota, University of	5	4.62
California-Berkeley, University of	6	4.61
Harvard and Radcliffe Colleges	7	4.59
Illinois,Urbana-Champaign, University of	8	4.57
Chicago, University of	9	4.56
Columbia University	10	4.55
California-San Diego, University of	11	4.54
California-Los Angeles, University of	12	4.52
Indiana University-Bloomington	13	4.51
Colorado-Boulder, University of	14	4.49
Carnegie Mellon University	15	4.48
Wisconsin-Madison, University of	16	4.47
Massachusetts Institute of Technology	17	4.46
Princeton University	18	4.45
Washington, University of	19	4.44
Oregon, University of	20	4.42
Cornell University	21	4.41
Texas-Austin, University of	22	4.40
North Carolina-Chapel Hill, University of	23	4.39
Brown University	24	4.38
Northwestern University	25	4.37
State University of New York at Stony Brook	26	4.36
Johns Hopkins University	27	4.35
Duke University	28	4.34
Pennsylvania State University-University Park	29	4.32
New York University	30	4.30

RADIO/TELEVISION STUDIES
LEADING INSTITUTIONS—RATING OF UNDERGRADUATE PROGRAMS

INSTITUTION	RANK	SCORE
Southern California, University of	1	4.89
California-Los Angeles, University of	2	4.86
New York University	3	4.82
Northwestern University	4	4.80
Arizona State University	5	4.77
Florida State University	6	4.75
Syracuse University	7	4.73
Michigan-Ann Arbor, University of	8	4.71
Indiana University-Bloomington	9	4.70

RELIGIOUS STUDIES

LEADING INSTITUTIONS—RATING OF UNDERGRADUATE PROGRAMS

INSTITUTION	RANK	SCORE
Indiana University-Bloomington	1	4.84
Virginia, University of	2	4.82
North Carolina-Chapel Hill, University of	3	4.80
Princeton University	4	4.78
Yale University	5	4.76
Duke University	6	4.74
Southern Methodist University	7	4.72
Dartmouth College	8	4.70
California-Santa Barbara, University of	9	4.68
Syracuse University	10	4.67
Iowa, University of	11	4.65
Vanderbilt University	12	4.63
Northwestern University	13	4.61
Arizona State University	14	4.59
Pennsylvania, University of	15	4.56
Stanford University	16	4.53
Temple University	17	4.52
Colorado-Boulder, University of	18	4.50
Harvard and Radcliffe Colleges	19	4.48
Brown University	20	4.46
Oberlin College	21	4.43

RUSSIAN
LEADING INSTITUTIONS—RATING OF UNDERGRADUATE PROGRAMS

INSTITUTION	RANK	SCORE
Columbia University	1	4.89
Yale University	2	4.87
Chicago, University of	3	4.85
Pennsylvania, University of	4	4.83
Michigan-Ann Arbor, University of	5	4.81
Harvard and Radcliffe Colleges	6	4.79
Indiana University-Bloomington	7	4.76
Washington, University of	8	4.73
Stanford University	9	4.70
Wisconsin-Madison, University of	10	4.68
Brown University	11	4.64
Cornell University	12	4.60
New York University	13	4.58
North Carolina-Chapel Hill, University of	14	4.55
Texas-Austin, University of	15	4.53
Illinois,Urbana-Champaign, University of	16	4.50
California-Los Angeles, University of	17	4.48
Michigan State University	18	4.46
Northwestern University	19	4.45
Syracuse University	20	4.42

RUSSIAN/SLAVIC STUDIES
LEADING INSTITUTIONS—RATING OF UNDERGRADUATE PROGRAMS

INSTITUTION	RANK	SCORE
Chicago, University of	1	4.85
Yale University	2	4.83
Princeton University	3	4.81
Harvard and Radcliffe Colleges	4	4.78
Michigan-Ann Arbor, University of	5	4.75
Columbia University	6	4.73
California-Berkeley, University of	7	4.71
Cornell University	8	4.69
Pennsylvania, University of	9	4.67
Northwestern University	10	4.65
New York University	11	4.62
Indiana University-Bloomington	12	4.60
Brown University	13	4.58
Syracuse University	14	4.57
North Carolina-Chapel Hill, University of	15	4.53
Ohio State University-Columbus	16	4.48
Boston University	17	4.47
Washington, University of	18	4.46

SCANDINAVIAN LANGUAGES

LEADING INSTITUTIONS—RATING OF UNDERGRADUATE PROGRAMS

INSTITUTION	RANK	SCORE
Minnesota, University of	1	4.88
Washington, University of	2	4.85
California-Berkeley, University of	3	4.82
Harvard and Radcliffe Colleges	4	4.79
Wisconsin-Madison, University of	5	4.76
Michigan-Ann Arbor, University of	6	4.73
Texas-Austin, University of	7	4.70
Pennsylvania, University of	8	4.66

SLAVIC LANGUAGES
Leading Institutions—Rating of Undergraduate Programs

INSTITUTION	RANK	SCORE
Chicago, University of	1	4.85
Princeton University	2	4.82
Indiana University-Bloomington	3	4.80
California-Berkeley, University of	4	4.78
Harvard and Radcliffe Colleges	5	4.73
Washington, University of	6	4.70
Wisconsin-Madison, University of	7	4.68
Brown University	8	4.66
New York University	9	4.64
Pennsylvania, University of	10	4.63
Northwestern University	11	4.60
Syracuse University	12	4.58
Virginia, University of	13	4.55
Ohio State University-Columbus	14	4.53
Columbia University	15	4.50
Texas-Austin, University of	16	4.48
Duke University	17	4.44

SOCIAL WORK/SOCIAL WELFARE

LEADING INSTITUTIONS—RATING OF UNDERGRADUATE PROGRAMS

INSTITUTION	RANK	SCORE
Wayne State University	1	4.71
Wisconsin-Madison, University of	2	4.70
New York University	3	4.66
Washington, University of	4	4.63
Pittsburgh, University of	5	4.60
Illinois,Urbana-Champaign, University of	6	4.58
Michigan State University	7	4.54
Pennsylvania, University of	8	4.52
Temple University	9	4.49
Syracuse University	10	4.46
Loyola University of Chicago	11	4.41
Florida State University	12	4.38
Pennsylvania State University-University Park	13	4.33
Catholic University of America, The	14	4.28
California-Berkeley, University of	15	4.26
Illinois-Chicago, University of	16	4.25
Indiana University-Bloomington	17	4.22

SOCIOLOGY

LEADING INSTITUTIONS—RATING OF UNDERGRADUATE PROGRAMS

INSTITUTION	RANK	SCORE
Wisconsin-Madison, University of	1	4.81
Michigan-Ann Arbor, University of	2	4.79
Chicago, University of	3	4.78
North Carolina-Chapel Hill, University of	4	4.76
Columbia University	5	4.74
Harvard and Radcliffe Colleges	6	4.72
Stanford University	7	4.71
Washington, University of	8	4.69
California-Los Angeles, University of	9	4.68
Yale University	10	4.67
Indiana University-Bloomington	11	4.65
Pennsylvania, University of	12	4.63
Wayne State University	13	4.62
Texas-Austin, University of	14	4.60
Minnesota, University of	15	4.59
Michigan State University	16	4.57
Cornell University	17	4.55
Princeton University	18	4.53
Illinois, Urbana-Champaign, University of	19	4.50
New York University	20	4.49
Duke University	21	4.47
Massachusetts-Amherst, University of	22	4.45
Northwestern University	23	4.43
Catholic University of America, The	24	4.40
Arizona, University of	25	4.38
State University of New York College at Buffalo	26	4.35
Boston University	27	4.32
Brandeis University	28	4.30
Pittsburgh, University of	29	4.27
California-Berkeley, University of	30	4.26

SOUTH ASIAN STUDIES

LEADING INSTITUTIONS—RATING OF UNDERGRADUATE PROGRAMS

INSTITUTION	RANK	SCORE
Harvard and Radcliffe Colleges	1	4.86
Pennsylvania, University of	2	4.84
Washington, University of	3	4.81
California-Berkeley, University of	4	4.79
Chicago, University of	5	4.78
Brown University	6	4.74
Minnesota, University of	7	4.72
Ohio State University-Columbus	8	4.69
Syracuse University	9	4.66

SOUTHEAST ASIAN STUDIES
LEADING INSTITUTIONS—RATING OF UNDERGRADUATE PROGRAMS

INSTITUTION	RANK	SCORE
Harvard and Radcliffe Colleges	1	4.87
California-Berkeley, University of	2	4.85
Pennsylvania, University of	3	4.83
Chicago, University of	4	4.81
Michigan-Ann Arbor, University of	5	4.79
Cornell University	6	4.76
Wisconsin-Madison, University of	7	4.74
Tufts University	8	4.72
Ohio State University-Columbus	9	4.68

SPANISH
LEADING INSTITUTIONS—RATING OF UNDERGRADUATE PROGRAMS

INSTITUTION	RANK	SCORE
Pennsylvania, University of	1	4.91
Harvard and Radcliffe Colleges	2	4.89
Texas-Austin, University of	3	4.86
California-Berkeley, University of	4	4.84
Yale University	5	4.83
Michigan-Ann Arbor, University of	6	4.82
Wisconsin-Madison, University of	7	4.80
California-Los Angeles, University of	8	4.77
Stanford University	9	4.75
Kansas, University of	10	4.73
Indiana University-Bloomington	11	4.72
Illinois,Urbana-Champaign, University of	12	4.69
Cornell University	13	4.66
Brown University	14	4.63
California-San Diego, University of	15	4.62
Princeton University	16	4.60
Columbia University	17	4.58
Minnesota, University of	18	4.57
New York University	19	4.55
California-Irvine, University of	20	4.53
Arizona, University of	21	4.52
New Mexico, University of	22	4.50
North Carolina-Chapel Hill, University of	23	4.48
Virginia, University of	24	4.46
State University of New York College at Buffalo	25	4.43
California-Santa Barbara, University of	26	4.41
Washington, University of	27	4.40
Pennsylvania State University-University Park	28	4.38
Kentucky, University of	29	4.36
Maryland-College Park, University of	30	4.35
Pittsburgh, University of	31	4.33
Duke University	32	4.31
Arizona State University	33	4.29
Southern California, University of	34	4.26
Georgetown University	35	4.23
Vanderbilt University	36	4.23

SPEECH PATHOLOGY/AUDIOLOGY

Leading Institutions—Rating of Undergraduate Programs

INSTITUTION	RANK	SCORE
Iowa, University of	1	4.91
Northwestern University	2	4.90
Minnesota, University of	3	4.87
Purdue University-West Lafayette	4	4.86
Michigan-Ann Arbor, University of	5	4.83
Indiana University-Bloomington	6	4.82
Kansas, University of	7	4.80
Michigan State University	8	4.78
Boston University	9	4.76
Illinois,Urbana-Champaign, University of	10	4.74
New York University	11	4.72
Wayne State University	12	4.70
Colorado-Boulder, University of	13	4.68
Marquette University	14	4.67
Baylor University	15	4.66
Utah, University of	16	4.64
Syracuse University	17	4.61
State University of New York College at Buffalo	18	4.59
Louisiana State University-Baton Rouge	19	4.58
Arizona, University of	20	4.55
Washington, University of	21	4.53
Oregon, University of	22	4.51
Missouri-Columbia, University of	23	4.49
Florida State University	24	4.46
Massachusetts-Amherst, University of	25	4.43
Ohio University	26	4.41
Maryland-College Park, University of	27	4.38
Case Western Reserve University	28	4.36

SPEECH/RHETORIC

Leading Institutions—Rating of Undergraduate Programs

INSTITUTION	RANK	SCORE
Northwestern University	1	4.90
Iowa, University of	2	4.88
Michigan-Ann Arbor, University of	3	4.84
Indiana University-Bloomington	4	4.82
Illinois,Urbana-Champaign, University of	5	4.79
Pennsylvania State University-University Park	6	4.77
California-Berkeley, University of	7	4.74
Missouri-Columbia, University of	8	4.72
Wayne State University	9	4.69
Baylor University	10	4.66
Ohio University	11	4.63
Arizona, University of	12	4.60
Louisiana State University-Baton Rouge	13	4.59
Utah, University of	14	4.57

STATISTICS
Leading Institutions—Rating of Undergraduate Programs

INSTITUTION	RANK	SCORE
California-Berkeley, University of	1	4.91
Stanford University	2	4.90
Columbia University	3	4.84
Wisconsin-Madison, University of	4	4.83
Purdue University-West Lafayette	5	4.81
Iowa State University	6	4.79
Chicago, University of	7	4.78
Minnesota, University of	8	4.76
Illinois,Urbana-Champaign, University of	9	4.74
Virginia Tech	10	4.72
Rochester, University of	11	4.70
Iowa, University of	12	4.68
North Carolina State University	13	4.65
Rutgers University, New Brunswick	14	4.63
California-Santa Barbara, University of	15	4.62
Michigan-Ann Arbor, University of	16	4.60
Pennsylvania, University of	17	4.59
Rice University	18	4.57
California-Davis, University of	19	4.56
Florida State University	20	4.53
North Carolina-Chapel Hill, University of	21	4.52
Michigan State University	22	4.50
State University of New York College at Buffalo	23	4.49
Ohio State University-Columbus	24	4.47
Cornell University	25	4.45

SYSTEMS ENGINEERING

LEADING INSTITUTIONS—RATING OF UNDERGRADUATE PROGRAMS

INSTITUTION	RANK	SCORE
United States Naval Academy	1	4.85
Case Western Reserve University [3]	2	4.82
Washington University in Saint Louis [4]	3	4.78
Pennsylvania, University of [4]	4	4.75
Arizona, University of	5	4.71
Virginia, University of	6	4.68
California-San Diego, University of [3]	7	4.65
George Washington University [2]	8	4.60
Boston University	9	4.57
Oakland University	10	4.52
Texas A&M University at Galveston [1]	11	4.48
West Florida, University of [2]	12	4.40

Explanatory Note: Actual titles used by the institution to identify their curricula
[1] Maritime Systems Engineering
[2] Systems Analysis and Engineering
[3] Systems and Control Engineering
[4] Systems Science and Engineering

URBAN AND REGIONAL PLANNING

Leading Institutions—Rating of Undergraduate Programs

INSTITUTION	RANK	SCORE
Southern California, University of	1	4.83
Rutgers University, New Brunswick	2	4.81
Massachusetts Institute of Technology	3	4.80
Illinois,Urbana-Champaign, University of	4	4.76
Cornell University	5	4.74
Iowa State University	6	4.72
Michigan State University	7	4.71
Cincinnati, University of	8	4.68
Colorado-Boulder, University of	9	4.66
Pittsburgh, University of	10	4.64
Virginia, University of	11	4.61
Arizona State University	12	4.58
Oregon, University of	13	4.56

WILDLIFE BIOLOGY
LEADING INSTITUTIONS—RATING OF UNDERGRADUATE PROGRAMS

INSTITUTION	RANK	SCORE
Purdue University-West Lafayette	1	4.82
North Carolina State University	2	4.71
SUNY College of Environmental Science and Forestry	3	4.68
Montana, University of	4	4.66
North Dakota State University	5	4.65
South Dakota State University	6	4.63
New Hampshire, University of	7	4.61
Vermont, University of	8	4.59
New Mexico State University	9	4.57
Georgia, University of	10	4.55
Washington State University	11	4.53
Clemson University	12	4.50

ZOOLOGY
LEADING INSTITUTIONS—RATING OF UNDERGRADUATE PROGRAMS

INSTITUTION	RANK	SCORE
Wisconsin-Madison, University of	1	4.88
Washington, University of	2	4.86
Texas-Austin, University of	3	4.82
Cornell University	4	4.80
Georgia, University of	5	4.76
California-Davis, University of	6	4.73
Michigan State University	7	4.71
Florida, University of	8	4.69
Ohio State University-Columbus	9	4.66
Washington State University	10	4.64
Arizona State University	11	4.59
Iowa State University	12	4.58
Oregon State University	13	4.57
Colorado State University	14	4.54
North Carolina State University	15	4.52
Louisiana State University-Baton Rouge	16	4.49
SUNY College of Environmental Science and Forestry	17	4.47
Texas A&M University-College Station	18	4.43
Maryland-College Park, University of	19	4.40

Part IV
RATING OF
UNDERGRADUATE SCHOOLS
IN ENGINEERING IN THE U.S.

INSTITUTIONS (Listed in Alphabetical Order)	Rank	Score
AKRON, UNIVERSITY OF Akron, Ohio	129	3.47
ALABAMA, UNIVERSITY OF Tuscaloosa, Alabama	90	3.88
ALABAMA-BIRMINGHAM, UNIVERSITY OF Birmingham, Alabama	141	3.35
ALABAMA-HUNTSVILLE, UNIVERSITY OF Huntsville, Alabama	160	3.15
ALASKA-FAIRBANKS, UNIVERSITY OF Fairbanks, Alaska	155	3.20
ARIZONA STATE UNIVERSITY Tempe, Arizona	82	3.96
ARIZONA, UNIVERSITY OF Tucson, Arizona	37	4.46
ARKANSAS, UNIVERSITY OF Fayetteville, Arkansas	138	3.38
AUBURN UNIVERSITY Auburn University, Alabama	80	4.00
BOSTON UNIVERSITY Boston, Massachusetts	74	4.06
BRADLEY UNIVERSITY Peoria, Illinois	169	3.05
BRIDGEPORT, UNIVERSITY OF Bridgeport, Connecticut	225	2.25
BRIGHAM YOUNG UNIVERSITY Provo, Utah	139	3.37
BROWN UNIVERSITY Providence, Rhode Island	23	4.66
BUCKNELL UNIVERSITY Lewisburg, Pennsylvania	162	3.13
CALIFORNIA INSTITUTE OF TECHNOLOGY Pasadena, California	3	4.89
CALIFORNIA POLYTECHNIC STATE UNIVERSITY-SAN LUIS OBISPO San Luis Obispo, California	113	3.64
CALIFORNIA STATE POLYTECHNIC UNIVERSITY, POMONA Pomona, California	165	3.10

Very Strong = 4.51–4.99   Strong = 4.01–4.49   Good = 3.61–3.99   Acceptable Plus = 3.01–3.59   Adequate = 2.01–2.99

INSTITUTIONS (Listed in Alphabetical Order)	Rank	Score
CALIFORNIA STATE UNIVERSITY-CHICO Chico, California	207	2.50
CALIFORNIA STATE UNIVERSITY-FRESNO Fresno, California	161	3.14
CALIFORNIA STATE UNIVERSITY-FULLERTON Fullerton, California	158	3.17
CALIFORNIA STATE UNIVERSITY-LONG BEACH Long Beach, California	135	3.41
CALIFORNIA STATE UNIVERSITY-LOS ANGELES Los Angeles, California	153	3.22
CALIFORNIA STATE UNIVERSITY-NORTHRIDGE Northridge, California	137	3.39
CALIFORNIA STATE UNIVERSITY-SACRAMENTO Sacramento, California	202	2.62
CALIFORNIA-BERKELEY, UNIVERSITY OF Berkeley, California	2	4.90
CALIFORNIA-DAVIS, UNIVERSITY OF Davis, California	45	4.36
CALIFORNIA-IRVINE, UNIVERSITY OF Irvine, California	125	3.51
CALIFORNIA-LOS ANGELES, UNIVERSITY OF Los Angeles, California	29	4.58
CALIFORNIA-SAN DIEGO, UNIVERSITY OF La Jolla, California	73	4.07
CALIFORNIA-SANTA BARBARA, UNIVERSITY OF Santa Barbara, California	72	4.08
CARNEGIE MELLON UNIVERSITY Pittsburgh, Pennsylvania	12	4.78
CASE WESTERN RESERVE UNIVERSITY Cleveland, Ohio	25	4.62
CATHOLIC UNIVERSITY OF AMERICA, THE Washington, District of Columbia	121	3.55
CENTRAL FLORIDA, UNIVERSITY OF Orlando, Florida	152	3.23
CHRISTIAN BROTHERS UNIVERSITY Memphis, Tennessee	237	2.09

Very Strong = 4.51–4.99   Strong = 4.01–4.49   Good = 3.61–3.99   Acceptable Plus = 3.01–3.59   Adequate = 2.01–2.99

INSTITUTIONS (Listed in Alphabetical Order)	Rank	Score
CINCINNATI, UNIVERSITY OF Cincinnati, Ohio	60	4.20
CITADEL, THE Charleston, South Carolina	186	2.80
CITY UNIVERSITY OF NEW YORK-CITY COLLEGE New York, New York	70	4.10
CLARKSON UNIVERSITY Potsdam, New York	66	4.14
CLEMSON UNIVERSITY Clemson, South Carolina	104	3.73
CLEVELAND STATE UNIVERSITY Cleveland, Ohio	182	2.85
COLORADO SCHOOL OF MINES Golden, Colorado	14	4.76
COLORADO STATE UNIVERSITY Fort Collins, Colorado	62	4.18
COLORADO-BOULDER, UNIVERSITY OF Boulder, Colorado	50	4.31
COLORADO-DENVER , UNIVERSITY OF Denver, Colorado	174	2.95
COLUMBIA UNIVERSITY New York, New York	20	4.70
CONNECTICUT, UNIVERSITY OF Storrs, Connecticut	117	3.59
COOPER UNION New York, New York	130	3.46
CORNELL UNIVERSITY Ithaca, New York	5	4.85
DARTMOUTH COLLEGE Hanover, New Hampshire	65	4.15
DAYTON, UNIVERSITY OF Dayton, Ohio	150	3.25
DELAWARE, UNIVERSITY OF Newark, Delaware	69	4.11
DETROIT MERCY, UNIVERSITY OF Detroit, Michigan	147	3.29

Very Strong = 4.51–4.99   Strong = 4.01–4.49   Good = 3.61–3.99   Acceptable Plus = 3.01–3.59   Adequate = 2.01–2.99

INSTITUTIONS (Listed in Alphabetical Order)	Rank	Score
DISTRICT OF COLUMBIA, UNIVERSITY OF THE Washington, District of Columbia	238	2.01
DREXEL UNIVERSITY Philadelphia, Pennsylvania	85	3.92
DUKE UNIVERSITY Durham, North Carolina	44	4.37
EVANSVILLE, UNIVERSITY OF Evansville, Indiana	217	2.35
FLORIDA A&M UNIVERSITY / FLORIDA STATE UNIVERSITY (FAMU/FSU) Tallahassee, Florida	126	3.50
FLORIDA ATLANTIC UNIVERSITY Boca Raton, Florida	140	3.36
FLORIDA INSTITUTE OF TECHNOLOGY Melbourne, Florida	156	3.19
FLORIDA INTERNATIONAL UNIVERSITY Miami, Florida	214	2.41
FLORIDA, UNIVERSITY OF Gainesville, Florida	41	4.40
GANNON UNIVERSITY Erie, Pennsylvania	235	2.11
GEORGE MASON UNIVERSITY Fairfax, Virginia	233	2.13
GEORGE WASHINGTON UNIVERSITY Washington, District of Columbia	95	3.83
GEORGIA INSTITUTE OF TECHNOLOGY Atlanta, Georgia	18	4.72
GEORGIA, UNIVERSITY OF Athens, Georgia	36	4.10
GMI ENGINEERING AND MANAGEMENT INSTITUTE Flint, Michigan	171	3.04
GONZAGA UNIVERSITY Spokane, Washington	177	2.91
HARTFORD, UNIVERSITY OF West Hartford, Connecticut	213	2.42
HARVARD AND RADCLIFFE COLLEGES Cambridge, Massachusetts	6	4.84

(handwritten note: ← I'm going to go there someday!)

Very Strong = 4.51–4.99 Strong = 4.01–4.49 Good = 3.61–3.99 Acceptable Plus = 3.01–3.59 Adequate = 2.01–2.99

INSTITUTIONS (Listed in Alphabetical Order)	Rank	Score
HARVEY MUDD COLLEGE Claremont, California	46	4.35
HAWAII-MANOA, UNIVERSITY OF Honolulu, Hawaii	93	3.85
HOFSTRA UNIVERSITY Hempstead, New York	218	2.35
HOUSTON, UNIVERSITY OF Houston, Texas	56	4.24
HOWARD UNIVERSITY Washington, District of Columbia	203	2.56
IDAHO, UNIVERSITY OF Moscow, Idaho	97	3.81
ILLINOIS INSTITUTE OF TECHNOLOGY Chicago, Illinois	84	3.93
ILLINOIS,URBANA-CHAMPAIGN, UNIVERSITY OF Urbana, Illinois	7	4.83
ILLINOIS-CHICAGO, UNIVERSITY OF Chicago, Illinois	83	3.95
INDIANA UNIVERSITY-PURDUE UNIV. INDIANAPOLIS Indianapolis, Indiana	222	2.31
IOWA STATE UNIVERSITY Ames, Iowa	24	4.64
IOWA, UNIVERSITY OF Iowa City, Iowa	54	4.26
JOHNS HOPKINS UNIVERSITY Baltimore, Maryland	31	4.55
KANSAS STATE UNIVERSITY Manhattan, Kansas	71	4.09
KANSAS, UNIVERSITY OF Lawrence, Kansas	53	4.27
KENTUCKY, UNIVERSITY OF Lexington, Kentucky	96	3.82
LAFAYETTE COLLEGE Easton, Pennsylvania	131	3.45
LAMAR UNIVERSITY Beaumont, Texas	216	2.39

Very Strong = 4.51–4.99   Strong = 4.01–4.49   Good = 3.61–3.99   Acceptable Plus = 3.01–3.59   Adequate = 2.01–2.99

INSTITUTIONS (Listed in Alphabetical Order)

INSTITUTIONS (Listed in Alphabetical Order)	Rank	Score
LAWRENCE TECHNOLOGICAL UNIVERSITY Southfield, Michigan	114	3.62
LEHIGH UNIVERSITY Bethlehem, Pennsylvania	40	4.41
LOUISIANA STATE UNIVERSITY-BATON ROUGE Baton Rouge, Louisiana	78	4.02
LOUISIANA TECH UNIVERSITY Ruston, Louisiana	112	3.65
LOYOLA MARYMOUNT UNIVERSITY Los Angeles, California	224	2.26
MAINE, UNIVERSITY OF Orono, Maine	124	3.52
MANHATTAN COLLEGE Riverdale, New York	176	2.93
MARIETTA COLLEGE Marietta, Ohio	17	4.52
MARQUETTE UNIVERSITY Milwaukee, Wisconsin	100	3.78
MARYLAND-COLLEGE PARK, UNIVERSITY OF College Park, Maryland	35	4.48
MASSACHUSETTS INSTITUTE OF TECHNOLOGY Cambridge, Massachusetts	1	4.91
MASSACHUSETTS-AMHERST, UNIVERSITY OF Amherst, Massachusetts	55	4.25
MASSACHUSETTS-DARTMOUTH, UNIVERSITY OF North Dartmouth, Massachusetts	199	2.65
MASSACHUSETTS-LOWELL, UNIVERSITY OF Lowell, Massachusetts	132	3.44
MEMPHIS, THE UNIVERSITY OF Memphis, Tennessee	181	2.86
MERRIMACK COLLEGE North Andover, Massachusetts	236	2.10
MIAMI, UNIVERSITY OF Coral Gables, Florida	94	3.84
MICHIGAN STATE UNIVERSITY East Lansing, Michigan	49	4.32

Very Strong = 4.51–4.99   Strong = 4.01–4.49   Good = 3.61–3.99   Acceptable Plus = 3.01–3.59   Adequate = 2.01–2.99

INSTITUTIONS (Listed in Alphabetical Order)	Rank	Score
MICHIGAN TECHNOLOGICAL UNIVERSITY Houghton, Michigan	103	3.74
MICHIGAN-ANN ARBOR, UNIVERSITY OF Ann Arbor, Michigan	9	4.81
MICHIGAN-DEARBORN, UNIVERSITY OF Dearborn, Michigan	209	2.47
MILWAUKEE SCHOOL OF ENGINEERING Milwaukee, Wisconsin	191	2.74
MINNESOTA, UNIVERSITY OF Minneapolis, Minnesota	10	4.80
MISSISSIPPI STATE UNIVERSITY Mississippi State, Mississippi	107	3.70
MISSISSIPPI, UNIVERSITY OF University, Mississippi	159	3.16
MISSOURI-COLUMBIA, UNIVERSITY OF Columbia, Missouri	64	4.16
MISSOURI-ROLLA, UNIVERSITY OF Rolla, Missouri	43	4.38
MONTANA STATE UNIVERSITY-BOZEMAN Bozeman, Montana	146	3.30
MONTANA TECH OF THE UNIVERSITY OF MONTANA Butte, Montana	105	3.72
NEBRASKA-LINCOLN, UNIVERSITY OF Lincoln, Nebraska	120	3.56
NEVADA-LAS VEGAS, UNIVERSITY OF Las Vegas, Nevada	193	2.72
NEVADA-RENO, UNIVERSITY OF Reno, Nevada	102	3.75
NEW HAMPSHIRE, UNIVERSITY OF Durham, New Hampshire	178	2.90
NEW HAVEN, UNIVERSITY OF West Haven, Connecticut	201	2.63
NEW JERSEY INSTITUTE OF TECHNOLOGY Newark, New Jersey	115	3.62
NEW MEXICO INSTITUTE OF MINING & TECHNOLOGY Socorro, New Mexico	92	3.86

Very Strong = 4.51–4.99   Strong = 4.01–4.49   Good = 3.61–3.99   Acceptable Plus = 3.01–3.59   Adequate = 2.01–2.99

INSTITUTIONS (Listed in Alphabetical Order)	Rank	Score
NEW MEXICO STATE UNIVERSITY Las Cruces, New Mexico	119	3.57
NEW MEXICO, UNIVERSITY OF Albuquerque, New Mexico	98	3.80
NEW ORLEANS, UNIVERSITY OF New Orleans, Louisiana	230	2.19
NEW YORK INSTITUTE OF TECHNOLOGY Old Westbury, New York	196	2.68
NORTH CAROLINA A&T STATE UNIVERSITY Greensboro, North Carolina	183	2.84
NORTH CAROLINA STATE UNIVERSITY Raleigh, North Carolina	51	4.30
NORTH CAROLINA-CHARLOTTE, UNIVERSITY OF Charlotte, North Carolina	175	2.94
NORTH DAKOTA STATE UNIVERSITY Fargo, North Dakota	142	3.34
NORTH DAKOTA, UNIVERSITY OF Grand Forks, North Dakota	166	3.09
NORTHEASTERN UNIVERSITY Boston, Massachusetts	157	3.18
NORTHERN ARIZONA UNIVERSITY Flagstaff, Arizona	212	2.43
NORTHWESTERN UNIVERSITY Evanston, Illinois	13	4.77
NORWICH UNIVERSITY Northfield, Vermont	184	2.83
NOTRE DAME, UNIVERSITY OF Notre Dame, Indiana	32	4.53
OAKLAND UNIVERSITY Rochester, Michigan	123	3.53
OHIO NORTHERN UNIVERSITY Ada, Ohio	215	2.40
OHIO STATE UNIVERSITY-COLUMBUS Columbus, Ohio	17	4.73
OHIO UNIVERSITY Athens, Ohio	144	3.32

Very Strong = 4.51–4.99   Strong = 4.01–4.49   Good = 3.61–3.99   Acceptable Plus = 3.01–3.59   Adequate = 2.01–2.99

INSTITUTIONS (Listed in Alphabetical Order)	Rank	Score
OKLAHOMA STATE UNIVERSITY Stillwater, Oklahoma	76	4.04
OKLAHOMA, UNIVERSITY OF Norman, Oklahoma	58	4.22
OLD DOMINION UNIVERSITY Norfolk, Virginia	192	2.73
OREGON STATE UNIVERSITY Corvallis, Oregon	75	4.05
PACIFIC, UNIVERSITY OF THE Stockton, California	190	2.75
PARKS COLLEGE OF SAINT LOUIS UNIVERSITY Cahokia, Illinois	208	2.49
PENNSYLVANIA STATE UNIVERSITY-UNIVERSITY PARK University Park, Pennsylvania	26	4.61
PENNSYLVANIA, UNIVERSITY OF Philadelphia, Pennsylvania	19	4.71
PITTSBURGH, UNIVERSITY OF Pittsburgh, Pennsylvania	36	4.47
POLYTECHNIC UNIVERSITY Brooklyn, New York	61	4.19
PORTLAND STATE UNIVERSITY Portland, Oregon	206	2.52
PORTLAND, UNIVERSITY OF Portland, Oregon	223	2.30
PRAIRIE VIEW A&M UNIVERSITY Prairie View, Texas	227	2.22
PRINCETON UNIVERSITY Princeton, New Jersey	8	4.82
PUERTO RICO-MAYAGÜEZ CAMPUS, UNIVERSITY OF PUERTO RICO	221	2.32
PURDUE UNIVERSITY-CALUMET Hammond, Indiana	229	2.20
PURDUE UNIVERSITY-WEST LAFAYETTE West Lafayette, Indiana	15	4.75
RENSSELAER POLYTECHNIC INSTITUTE Troy, New York	22	4.68

Very Strong = 4.51–4.99   Strong = 4.01–4.49   Good = 3.61–3.99   Acceptable Plus = 3.01–3.59   Adequate = 2.01–2.99

INSTITUTIONS (Listed in Alphabetical Order)	Rank	Score
RHODE ISLAND, UNIVERSITY OF Kingston, Rhode Island	116	3.61
RICE UNIVERSITY Houston, Texas	21	4.69
ROCHESTER INSTITUTE OF TECHNOLOGY Rochester, New York	163	3.12
ROCHESTER, UNIVERSITY OF Rochester, New York	57	4.23
ROSE-HULMAN INSTITUTE OF TECHNOLOGY Terre Haute, Indiana	133	3.43
RUTGERS UNIVERSITY, NEW BRUNSWICK NEW BRUNSWICK, NEW JERSEY	86	3.92
SAINT MARTIN'S COLLEGE Lacey, Washington	232	2.14
SAINT MARY'S UNIVERSITY San Antonio, Texas	231	2.17
SAN DIEGO STATE UNIVERSITY San Diego, California	164	3.11
SAN FRANCISCO STATE UNIVERSITY San Francisco, California	185	2.81
SAN JOSE STATE UNIVERSITY San Jose, California	149	3.27
SANTA CLARA UNIVERSITY Santa Clara, California	118	3.58
SEATTLE UNIVERSITY Seattle, Washington	198	2.66
SOUTH ALABAMA, UNIVERSITY OF Mobile, Alabama	197	2.67
SOUTH CAROLINA-COLUMBIA , UNIVERSITY OF, Columbia, South Carolina	151	3.24
SOUTH DAKOTA SCHOOL OF MINES & TECHNOLOGY Rapid City, South Dakota	108	3.69
SOUTH DAKOTA STATE UNIVERSITY Brookings, South Dakota	143	3.33
SOUTH FLORIDA, UNIVERSITY OF Tampa, Florida	179	2.89

Very Strong = 4.51–4.99   Strong = 4.01–4.49   Good = 3.61–3.99   Acceptable Plus = 3.01–3.59   Adequate = 2.01–2.99

INSTITUTIONS (Listed in Alphabetical Order)	Rank	Score
SOUTHERN CALIFORNIA, UNIVERSITY OF Los Angeles, California	38	4.44
SOUTHERN ILLINOIS UNIVERSITY-CARBONDALE Carbondale, Illinois	134	3.42
SOUTHERN ILLINOIS UNIVERSITY-EDWARDSVILLE Edwardsville, Illinois	228	2.21
SOUTHERN METHODIST UNIVERSITY Dallas, Texas	110	3.67
SOUTHERN UNIVERSITY AND AGRICULTURAL AND MECHANICAL COLLEGE BATON ROUGE, LOUISIANA	226	2.24
SOUTHWESTERN LOUISIANA, UNIVERSITY OF Lafayette, Louisiana	168	3.07
STANFORD UNIVERSITY Stanford, California	4	4.88
STATE UNIVERSITY OF NEW YORK AT BINGHAMTON Binghamton, New York	205	2.54
STATE UNIVERSITY OF NEW YORK AT STONY BROOK Stony Brook, New York	106	3.71
STATE UNIVERSITY OF NEW YORK COLLEGE AT BUFFALO Buffalo, New York	52	4.28
STATE UNIVERSITY OF NEW YORK COLLEGE OF TECHNOLOGY AT ALFRED Alfred, New York	1	4.86
STATE UNIVERSITY OF NEW YORK MARITIME COLLEGE Bronx, New York	4	4.83
STEVENS INSTITUTE OF TECHNOLOGY Hoboken, New Jersey	30	4.57
SYRACUSE UNIVERSITY Syracuse, New York	59	4.20
TEMPLE UNIVERSITY Philadelphia, Pennsylvania	127	3.49
TENNESSEE STATE UNIVERSITY Nashville, Tennessee	200	2.64
TENNESSEE TECHNOLOGICAL UNIVERSITY Cookeville, Tennessee	194	2.71
TENNESSEE-KNOXVILLE, UNIVERSITY OF Knoxville, Tennessee	67	4.13

Very Strong = 4.51–4.99   Strong = 4.01–4.49   Good = 3.61–3.99   Acceptable Plus = 3.01–3.59   Adequate = 2.01–2.99

INSTITUTIONS (Listed in Alphabetical Order)	Rank	Score
TEXAS A&M UNIVERSITY AT GALVESTON Galveston, Texas	3	4.85
TEXAS A&M UNIVERSITY, CORPUS CHRISTI Corpus Christi, Texas	172	3.03
TEXAS A&M UNIVERSITY-COLLEGE STATION College Station, Texas	27	4.60
TEXAS TECH UNIVERSITY Lubbock, Texas	77	4.03
TEXAS-ARLINGTON, UNIVERSITY OF Arlington, Texas	148	3.28
TEXAS-AUSTIN, UNIVERSITY OF Austin, Texas	11	4.79
TEXAS-EL PASO, UNIVERSITY OF El Paso, Texas	136	3.40
TEXAS-SAN ANTONIO, UNIVERSITY OF San Antonio, Texas	189	2.76
TOLEDO, UNIVERSITY OF Toledo, Ohio	154	3.21
TRI-STATE UNIVERSITY Angola, Indiana	210	2.46
TUFTS UNIVERSITY Medford, Massachusetts	91	3.87
TULANE UNIVERSITY New Orleans, Louisiana	81	3.97
TULSA, UNIVERSITY OF Tulsa, Oklahoma	88	3.90
TUSKEGEE UNIVERSITY Tuskegee, Alabama	220	2.33
UNION COLLEGE Schenectady, New York	187	2.78
UNITED STATES AIR FORCE ACADEMY Colorado Springs, Colorado	39	4.43
UNITED STATES COAST GUARD ACADEMY	6	4.81
3+6.2011 New London, Connecticut	8	4.75

Very Strong = 4.51–4.99   Strong = 4.01–4.49   Good = 3.61–3.99   Acceptable Plus = 3.01–3.59   Adequate = 2.01–2.99

INSTITUTIONS (Listed in Alphabetical Order)	Rank	Score
UNITED STATES MERCHANT MARINE ACADEMY Kings Point, New York		TK
UNITED STATES MILITARY ACADEMY West Point, New York	89	3.89
UNITED STATES NAVAL ACADEMY Annapolis, Maryland	42	4.39
UTAH STATE UNIVERSITY Logan, Utah	79	4.01
UTAH, UNIVERSITY OF Salt Lake City, Utah	63	4.17
VALPARAISO UNIVERSITY Valparaiso, Indiana	180	2.87
VANDERBILT UNIVERSITY Nashville, Tennessee	99	3.79
VERMONT, UNIVERSITY OF Burlington, Vermont	170	3.04
VILLANOVA UNIVERSITY Villanova, Pennsylvania	167	3.08
VIRGINIA MILITARY INSTITUTE Lexington, Virginia	188	2.77
VIRGINIA TECH Blacksburg, Virginia	47	4.34
VIRGINIA, UNIVERSITY OF Charlottesville, Virginia	48	4.33
WASHINGTON STATE UNIVERSITY Pullman, Washington	101	3.76
WASHINGTON UNIVERSITY IN SAINT LOUIS Saint Louis, Missouri	28	4.59
WASHINGTON, UNIVERSITY OF Seattle, Washington	34	4.50
WAYNE STATE UNIVERSITY Detroit, Michigan	68	4.12
WEBB INSTITUTE Glen Cove, New York	7	4.77
WEST VIRGINIA INSTITUTE OF TECHNOLOGY Montgomery, West Virginia	211	2.45

Very Strong = 4.51–4.99   Strong = 4.01–4.49   Good = 3.61–3.99   Acceptable Plus = 3.01–3.59   Adequate = 2.01–2.99

INSTITUTIONS (Listed in Alphabetical Order)

INSTITUTIONS	Rank	Score
WEST VIRGINIA UNIVERSITY Morgantown, West Virginia	87	3.91
WESTERN MICHIGAN UNIVERSITY Kalamazoo, Michigan	195	2.70
WESTERN NEW ENGLAND COLLEGE Springfield, Massachusetts	234	2.12
WICHITA STATE UNIVERSITY Wichita, Kansas	145	3.31
WIDENER UNIVERSITY Chester, Pennsylvania	219	2.34
WISCONSIN-MADISON, UNIVERSITY OF Madison, Wisconsin	16	4.74
WISCONSIN-MILWAUKEE, UNIVERSITY OF Milwaukee, Wisconsin	111	3.66
WISCONSIN-PLATTEVILLE, UNIVERSITY OF Platteville, Wisconsin	173	3.01
WORCESTER POLYTECHNIC INSTITUTE Worcester, Massachusetts	128	3.48
WRIGHT STATE UNIVERSITY Dayton, Ohio	122	3.54
WYOMING, UNIVERSITY OF Laramie, Wyoming	109	3.68
YALE UNIVERSITY New Haven, Connecticut	33	4.51
YOUNGSTOWN STATE UNIVERSITY Youngstown, Ohio	204	2.55

Very Strong = 4.51–4.99   Strong = 4.01–4.49   Good = 3.61–3.99   Acceptable Plus = 3.01–3.59   Adequate = 2.01–2.99

Part V

RATING OF UNDERGRADUATE SCHOOLS IN BUSINESS ADMINISTRATION IN THE U.S.

INSTITUTIONS (Listed in Alphabetical Order)	Rank	Score
AKRON, UNIVERSITY OF Akron, Ohio	143	3.04
ALABAMA, UNIVERSITY OF Tuscaloosa, Alabama	60	3.95
ALABAMA-BIRMINGHAM, UNIVERSITY OF Birmingham, Alabama	79	3.71
APPALACHIAN STATE UNIVERSITY Boone, North Carolina	225	2.09
ARIZONA STATE UNIVERSITY Tempe, Arizona	44	4.25
ARIZONA, UNIVERSITY OF Tucson, Arizona	33	4.42
ARKANSAS STATE UNIVERSITY State University, Arkansas	228	2.05
ARKANSAS, UNIVERSITY OF Fayetteville, Arkansas	71	3.79
ARKANSAS-LITTLE ROCK, UNIVERSITY OF Little Rock, Arkansas	144	3.03
AUBURN UNIVERSITY Auburn University, Alabama	122	3.25
BABSON COLLEGE Babson Park, Massachusetts	170	2.75
BALL STATE UNIVERSITY Muncie, Indiana	214	2.24
BALTIMORE, UNIVERSITY OF Baltimore, Maryland	148	2.97
BAYLOR UNIVERSITY Waco, Texas	80	3.70
BOISE STATE UNIVERSITY Boise, Idaho	198	2.45
BOSTON COLLEGE Chestnut Hill, Massachusetts	69	3.82
BOSTON UNIVERSITY Boston, Massachusetts	48	4.18
BOWLING GREEN STATE UNIVERSITY Bowling Green, Ohio	149	2.96

Strong = 4.61–4.99   Very Good = 4.01–4.59   Good = 3.61–3.99   Acceptable Plus = 3.01–3.59   Adequate = 2.01–2.99

INSTITUTIONS (Listed in Alphabetical Order)	Rank	Score
BRADLEY UNIVERSITY Peoria, Illinois	126	3.21
BRIDGEPORT, UNIVERSITY OF Bridgeport, Connecticut	145	3.02
BRIGHAM YOUNG UNIVERSITY Provo, Utah	97	3.51
CALIFORNIA POLYTECHNIC STATE UNIVERSITY-SAN LUIS OBISPO San Luis Obispo, California	176	2.69
CALIFORNIA STATE UNIVERSITY-BAKERSFIELD Bakersfield, California	200	2.43
CALIFORNIA STATE UNIVERSITY-CHICO Chico, California	183	2.62
CALIFORNIA STATE UNIVERSITY-FRESNO Fresno, California	162	2.83
CALIFORNIA STATE UNIVERSITY-FULLERTON Fullerton, California	150	2.95
CALIFORNIA STATE UNIVERSITY-HAYWARD Hayward, California	197	2.46
CALIFORNIA STATE UNIVERSITY-LONG BEACH Long Beach, California	161	2.84
CALIFORNIA STATE UNIVERSITY-LOS ANGELES Los Angeles, California	139	3.08
CALIFORNIA STATE UNIVERSITY-NORTHRIDGE Northridge, California	96	3.53
CALIFORNIA STATE UNIVERSITY-SACRAMENTO Sacramento, California	168	2.77
CALIFORNIA-BERKELEY, UNIVERSITY OF Berkeley, California	5	4.86
CANISIUS COLLEGE Buffalo, New York	151	2.94
CARNEGIE MELLON UNIVERSITY Pittsburgh, Pennsylvania	8	4.81
CASE WESTERN RESERVE UNIVERSITY Cleveland, Ohio	19	4.65
CENTRAL ARKANSAS, UNIVERSITY OF Conway, Arkansas	227	2.06

Strong = 4.61–4.99   Very Good = 4.01–4.59   Good = 3.61–3.99   Acceptable Plus = 3.01–3.59   Adequate = 2.01–2.99

INSTITUTIONS (Listed in Alphabetical Order)	Rank	Score
CENTRAL FLORIDA, UNIVERSITY OF Orlando, Florida	177	2.68
CENTRAL MICHIGAN UNIVERSITY Mount Pleasant, Michigan	190	2.55
CINCINNATI, UNIVERSITY OF Cincinnati, Ohio	66	3.86
CITY UNIVERSITY OF NEW YORK-BARUCH COLLEGE New York, New York	16	4.70
CLARK UNIVERSITY Worcester, Massachusetts	104	3.43
CLARKSON UNIVERSITY Potsdam, New York	107	3.40
CLEMSON UNIVERSITY Clemson, South Carolina	103	3.44
CLEVELAND STATE UNIVERSITY Cleveland, Ohio	140	3.07
COLORADO STATE UNIVERSITY Fort Collins, Colorado	127	3.20
COLORADO-BOULDER, UNIVERSITY OF Boulder, Colorado	45	4.23
COLORADO-DENVER , UNIVERSITY OF Denver, Colorado	105	3.42
CONNECTICUT, UNIVERSITY OF Storrs, Connecticut	81	3.69
CREIGHTON UNIVERSITY Omaha, Nebraska	121	3.26
DAYTON, UNIVERSITY OF Dayton, Ohio	158	2.87
DELAWARE, UNIVERSITY OF Newark, Delaware	74	3.76
DENVER, UNIVERSITY OF Denver, Colorado	49	4.16
DEPAUL UNIVERSITY Chicago, Illinois	63	3.90
DETROIT MERCY, UNIVERSITY OF Detroit, Michigan	99	3.48

Strong = 4.61–4.99   Very Good = 4.01–4.59   Good = 3.61–3.99   Acceptable Plus = 3.01–3.59   Adequate = 2.01–2.99

INSTITUTIONS (Listed in Alphabetical Order)	Rank	Score
DRAKE UNIVERSITY Des Moines, Iowa	125	3.22
DREXEL UNIVERSITY Philadelphia, Pennsylvania	53	4.08
DUQUESNE UNIVERSITY Pittsburgh, Pennsylvania	152	2.93
EAST CAROLINA UNIVERSITY Greenville, North Carolina	108	3.39
EAST TEXAS STATE UNIVERSITY Commerce, Texas	217	2.19
EASTERN MICHIGAN UNIVERSITY Ypsilanti, Michigan	147	2.98
EASTERN WASHINGTON UNIVERSITY Cheney, Washington	199	2.44
EMORY UNIVERSITY Atlanta, Georgia	31	4.45
FLORIDA ATLANTIC UNIVERSITY Boca Raton, Florida	153	2.92
FLORIDA INTERNATIONAL UNIVERSITY Miami, Florida	163	2.82
FLORIDA STATE UNIVERSITY Tallahassee, Florida	75	3.75
FLORIDA, UNIVERSITY OF Gainesville, Florida	30	4.46
FORDHAM UNIVERSITY New York, New York	65	3.87
FORT LEWIS COLLEGE Durango, Colorado	223	2.12
GEORGE WASHINGTON UNIVERSITY Washington, District of Columbia	29	4.48
GEORGETOWN UNIVERSITY Washington, District of Columbia	64	3.88
GEORGIA INSTITUTE OF TECHNOLOGY Atlanta, Georgia	52	4.10
GEORGIA SOUTHERN UNIVERSITY Statesboro, Georgia	201	2.42

Strong = 4.61–4.99   Very Good = 4.01–4.59   Good = 3.61–3.99   Acceptable Plus = 3.01–3.59   Adequate = 2.01–2.99

INSTITUTIONS (Listed in Alphabetical Order)	Rank	Score
GEORGIA STATE UNIVERSITY Atlanta, Georgia	42	4.28
GEORGIA, UNIVERSITY OF Athens, Georgia	50	4.13
HAWAII-MANOA, UNIVERSITY OF Honolulu, Hawaii	109	3.38
HOFSTRA UNIVERSITY Hempstead, New York	110	3.37
HOUSTON, UNIVERSITY OF Houston, Texas	25	4.56
HOUSTON-CLEAR LAKE, UNIVERSITY OF Houston, Texas	164	2.81
HOWARD UNIVERSITY Washington, District of Columbia	165	2.80
IDAHO STATE UNIVERSITY Pocatello, Idaho	192	2.53
ILLINOIS STATE UNIVERSITY Normal, Illinois	141	3.06
ILLINOIS,URBANA-CHAMPAIGN, UNIVERSITY OF Urbana, Illinois	9	4.80
ILLINOIS-CHICAGO, UNIVERSITY OF Chicago, Illinois	54	4.06
INDIANA STATE UNIVERSITY Terre Haute, Indiana	189	2.56
INDIANA UNIVERSITY NORTHWEST Gary, Indiana	221	2.15
INDIANA UNIVERSITY-BLOOMINGTON Bloomington, Indiana	3	4.90
IOWA, UNIVERSITY OF Iowa City, Iowa	34	4.40
JAMES MADISON UNIVERSITY Harrisonburg, Virginia	154	2.91
KANSAS STATE UNIVERSITY Manhattan, Kansas	128	3.19
KANSAS, UNIVERSITY OF Lawrence, Kansas	46	4.21

Strong = 4.61–4.99   Very Good = 4.01–4.59   Good = 3.61–3.99   Acceptable Plus = 3.01–3.59   Adequate = 2.01–2.99

INSTITUTIONS (Listed in Alphabetical Order)	Rank	Score
KENT STATE UNIVERSITY Kent, Ohio	68	3.84
KENTUCKY, UNIVERSITY OF Lexington, Kentucky	94	3.55
LAMAR UNIVERSITY Beaumont, Texas	206	2.35
LEHIGH UNIVERSITY Bethlehem, Pennsylvania	28	4.50
LOUISIANA STATE UNIVERSITY-BATON ROUGE Baton Rouge, Louisiana	32	4.44
LOUISIANA TECH UNIVERSITY Ruston, Louisiana	204	2.37
LOUISVILLE, UNIVERSITY OF Louisville, Kentucky	111	3.36
LOYOLA MARYMOUNT UNIVERSITY Los Angeles, California	203	2.38
LOYOLA UNIVERSITY NEW ORLEANS New Orleans, Louisiana	166	2.79
LOYOLA UNIVERSITY OF CHICAGO Chicago, Illinois	82	3.68
MAINE, UNIVERSITY OF Orono, Maine	112	3.35
MARQUETTE UNIVERSITY Milwaukee, Wisconsin	83	3.67
MARYLAND-COLLEGE PARK, UNIVERSITY OF College Park, Maryland	37	4.36
MASSACHUSETTS INSTITUTE OF TECHNOLOGY Cambridge, Massachusetts	2	4.92
MASSACHUSETTS-AMHERST, UNIVERSITY OF Amherst, Massachusetts	38	4.34
MEMPHIS, THE UNIVERSITY OF Memphis, Tennessee	93	3.56
MIAMI UNIVERSITY Oxford, Ohio	84	3.66
MIAMI, UNIVERSITY OF Coral Gables, Florida	61	3.94

Strong = 4.61–4.99   Very Good = 4.01–4.59   Good = 3.61–3.99   Acceptable Plus = 3.01–3.59   Adequate = 2.01–2.99

INSTITUTIONS (Listed in Alphabetical Order)	Rank	Score
MICHIGAN STATE UNIVERSITY East Lansing, Michigan	17	4.68
MICHIGAN-ANN ARBOR, UNIVERSITY OF Ann Arbor, Michigan	4	4.88
MICHIGAN-FLINT, UNIVERSITY OF Flint, Michigan	169	2.76
MIDDLE TENNESSEE STATE UNIVERSITY Murfreesboro, Tennessee	178	2.67
MINNESOTA, UNIVERSITY OF Minneapolis, Minnesota	14	4.72
MISSISSIPPI STATE UNIVERSITY Mississippi State, Mississippi	102	3.45
MISSISSIPPI, UNIVERSITY OF University, Mississippi	88	3.61
MISSOURI-COLUMBIA, UNIVERSITY OF Columbia, Missouri	41	4.29
MISSOURI-KANSAS CITY, UNIVERSITY OF Kansas City, Missouri	115	3.32
MISSOURI-SAINT LOUIS, UNIVERSITY OF St. Louis, Missouri	100	3.47
MONTANA STATE UNIVERSITY-BOZEMAN Bozeman, Montana	179	2.66
MONTANA, UNIVERSITY OF Missoula, Montana	136	3.11
MURRAY STATE UNIVERSITY Murray, Kentucky	218	2.18
NEBRASKA-LINCOLN, UNIVERSITY OF Lincoln, Nebraska	43	4.27
NEBRASKA-OMAHA, UNIVERSITY OF Omaha, Nebraska	167	2.78
NEVADA-RENO, UNIVERSITY OF Reno, Nevada	205	2.36
NEW MEXICO STATE UNIVERSITY Las Cruces, New Mexico	188	2.57
NEW MEXICO, UNIVERSITY OF Albuquerque, New Mexico	101	3.46

Strong = 4.61–4.99   Very Good = 4.01–4.59   Good = 3.61–3.99   Acceptable Plus = 3.01–3.59   Adequate = 2.01–2.99

INSTITUTIONS (Listed in Alphabetical Order)	Rank	Score
NEW ORLEANS, UNIVERSITY OF New Orleans, Louisiana	142	3.05
NEW YORK UNIVERSITY New York, New York	7	4.83
NICHOLLS STATE UNIVERSITY Thibodaux, Louisiana	195	2.49
NORTH CAROLINA A&T STATE UNIVERSITY Greensboro, North Carolina	224	2.10
NORTH CAROLINA-CHAPEL HILL, UNIVERSITY OF Chapel Hill, North Carolina	12	4.76
NORTH CAROLINA-CHARLOTTE, UNIVERSITY OF Charlotte, North Carolina	114	3.33
NORTH CAROLINA-GREENSBORO, UNIVERSITY OF Greensboro, North Carolina	137	3.10
NORTH DAKOTA, UNIVERSITY OF Grand Forks, North Dakota	172	2.73
NORTH FLORIDA, UNIVERSITY OF Jacksonville, Florida	116	3.31
NORTH TEXAS, UNIVERSITY OF Denton, Texas	85	3.65
NORTHEAST LOUISIANA UNIVERSITY Monroe, Louisiana	216	2.21
NORTHEASTERN UNIVERSITY Boston, Massachusetts	146	3.01
NORTHERN ARIZONA UNIVERSITY Flagstaff, Arizona	207	2.34
NORTHERN ILLINOIS UNIVERSITY DeKalb, Illinois	118	3.29
NOTRE DAME, UNIVERSITY OF Notre Dame, Indiana	23	4.60
OHIO STATE UNIVERSITY-COLUMBUS Columbus, Ohio	26	4.55
OHIO UNIVERSITY Athens, Ohio	92	3.57
OKLAHOMA STATE UNIVERSITY Stillwater, Oklahoma	213	2.25

Strong = 4.61–4.99   Very Good = 4.01–4.59   Good = 3.61–3.99   Acceptable Plus = 3.01–3.59   Adequate = 2.01–2.99

INSTITUTIONS (Listed in Alphabetical Order)	Rank	Score
OKLAHOMA, UNIVERSITY OF Norman, Oklahoma	56	4.03
OLD DOMINION UNIVERSITY Norfolk, Virginia	117	3.30
OREGON STATE UNIVERSITY Corvallis, Oregon	89	3.60
OREGON, UNIVERSITY OF Eugene, Oregon	36	4.37
PACIFIC LUTHERAN UNIVERSITY Tacoma, Washington	210	2.29
PACIFIC, UNIVERSITY OF THE Stockton, California	173	2.72
PENNSYLVANIA STATE UNIVERSITY-UNIVERSITY PARK University Park, Pennsylvania	22	4.61
PENNSYLVANIA, UNIVERSITY OF Philadelphia, Pennsylvania	1	4.93
PORTLAND STATE UNIVERSITY Portland, Oregon	184	2.61
PORTLAND, UNIVERSITY OF Portland, Oregon	208	2.32
PURDUE UNIVERSITY-WEST LAFAYETTE West Lafayette, Indiana	11	4.77
RENSSELAER POLYTECHNIC INSTITUTE Troy, New York	51	4.12
RHODE ISLAND, UNIVERSITY OF Kingston, Rhode Island	130	3.17
RICHMOND, UNIVERSITY OF Richmond, Virginia	185	2.60
RUTGERS UNIVERSITY-NEWARK COLLEGE OF ARTS & SCIENCES Newark, New Jersey	73	3.77
SAINT CLOUD STATE UNIVERSITY Saint Cloud, Minnesota	211	2.28
SAINT JOHN'S UNIVERSITY Jamaica, New York	106	3.41
SAINT LOUIS UNIVERSITY Saint Louis, Missouri	62	3.93

Strong = 4.61–4.99   Very Good = 4.01–4.59   Good = 3.61–3.99   Acceptable Plus = 3.01–3.59   Adequate = 2.01–2.99

INSTITUTIONS (Listed in Alphabetical Order)	Rank	Score
SAN DIEGO STATE UNIVERSITY San Diego, California	95	3.54
SAN DIEGO, UNIVERSITY OF San Diego, California	180	2.65
SAN FRANCISCO STATE UNIVERSITY San Francisco, California	113	3.34
SAN FRANCISCO, UNIVERSITY OF San Francisco, California	98	3.49
SAN JOSE STATE UNIVERSITY San Jose, California	171	2.74
SANTA CLARA UNIVERSITY Santa Clara, California	77	3.73
SEATTLE UNIVERSITY Seattle, Washington	132	3.15
SETON HALL UNIVERSITY South Orange, New Jersey	138	3.09
SHIPPENSBURG UNIVERSITY OF PENNSYLVANIA Shippensburg, Pennsylvania	226	2.07
SOUTH ALABAMA, UNIVERSITY OF Mobile, Alabama	174	2.71
SOUTH CAROLINA-COLUMBIA , UNIVERSITY OF, Columbia, South Carolina	40	4.30
SOUTH DAKOTA, UNIVERSITY OF Vermillion, South Dakota	159	2.86
SOUTH FLORIDA, UNIVERSITY OF Tampa, Florida	131	3.16
SOUTHERN CALIFORNIA, UNIVERSITY OF Los Angeles, California	20	4.64
SOUTHERN ILLINOIS UNIVERSITY-CARBONDALE Carbondale, Illinois	76	3.74
SOUTHERN ILLINOIS UNIVERSITY-EDWARDSVILLE Edwardsville, Illinois	155	2.90
SOUTHERN METHODIST UNIVERSITY Dallas, Texas	27	4.53
SOUTHERN MISSISSIPPI, UNIVERSITY OF Hattiesburg, Mississippi	160	2.85

Strong = 4.61–4.99   Very Good = 4.01–4.59   Good = 3.61–3.99   Acceptable Plus = 3.01–3.59   Adequate = 2.01–2.99

INSTITUTIONS (Listed in Alphabetical Order)	Rank	Score
STATE UNIVERSITY OF NEW YORK AT ALBANY Albany, New York	78	3.72
STATE UNIVERSITY OF NEW YORK COLLEGE AT BUFFALO Buffalo, New York	24	4.58
STEPHEN F. AUSTIN STATE UNIVERSITY Nacogdoches, Texas	194	2.51
SYRACUSE UNIVERSITY Syracuse, New York	39	4.32
TEMPLE UNIVERSITY Philadelphia, Pennsylvania	57	4.00
TENNESSEE AT CHATTANOOGA, UNIVERSITY OF Chattanooga, Tennessee	181	2.64
TENNESSEE TECHNOLOGICAL UNIVERSITY Cookeville, Tennessee	196	2.48
TENNESSEE-KNOXVILLE, UNIVERSITY OF Knoxville, Tennessee	58	3.98
TEXAS A&M UNIVERSITY-COLLEGE STATION College Station, Texas	10	4.78
TEXAS CHRISTIAN UNIVERSITY Fort Worth, Texas	119	3.27
TEXAS TECH UNIVERSITY Lubbock, Texas	67	3.85
TEXAS-ARLINGTON, UNIVERSITY OF Arlington, Texas	70	3.80
TEXAS-AUSTIN, UNIVERSITY OF Austin, Texas	6	4.85
TEXAS-PAN AMERICAN, UNIVERSITY OF Edinburg, Texas	219	2.17
TEXAS-SAN ANTONIO, UNIVERSITY OF San Antonio, Texas	156	2.89
TOLEDO, UNIVERSITY OF Toledo, Ohio	133	3.14
TULANE UNIVERSITY New Orleans, Louisiana	47	4.20
TULSA, UNIVERSITY OF Tulsa, Oklahoma	86	3.64

Strong = 4.61–4.99   Very Good = 4.01–4.59   Good = 3.61–3.99   Acceptable Plus = 3.01–3.59   Adequate = 2.01–2.99

INSTITUTIONS (Listed in Alphabetical Order)	Rank	Score
UTAH STATE UNIVERSITY Logan, Utah	134	3.13
UTAH, UNIVERSITY OF Salt Lake City, Utah	35	4.38
VALDOSTA STATE UNIVERSITY Valdosta, Georgia	215	2.22
VERMONT, UNIVERSITY OF Burlington, Vermont	120	3.26
VILLANOVA UNIVERSITY Villanova, Pennsylvania	72	3.78
VIRGINIA COMMONWEALTH UNIVERSITY Richmond, Virginia	129	3.18
VIRGINIA TECH Blacksburg, Virginia	55	4.04
VIRGINIA, UNIVERSITY OF Charlottesville, Virginia	15	4.71
WAKE FOREST UNIVERSITY Winston-Salem, North Carolina	90	3.59
WASHINGTON AND LEE UNIVERSITY Lexington, Virginia	187	2.58
WASHINGTON STATE UNIVERSITY Pullman, Washington	91	3.58
WASHINGTON UNIVERSITY IN SAINT LOUIS Saint Louis, Missouri	18	4.67
WASHINGTON, UNIVERSITY OF Seattle, Washington	13	4.74
WAYNE STATE UNIVERSITY Detroit, Michigan	87	3.62
WEST GEORGIA COLLEGE Carrollton, Georgia	212	2.26
WEST VIRGINIA UNIVERSITY Morgantown, West Virginia	135	3.12
WESTERN CAROLINA UNIVERSITY Cullowhee, North Carolina	182	2.63
WESTERN ILLINOIS UNIVERSITY Macomb, Illinois	124	3.23

Strong = 4.61–4.99   Very Good = 4.01–4.59   Good = 3.61–3.99   Acceptable Plus = 3.01–3.59   Adequate = 2.01–2.99

INSTITUTIONS (Listed in Alphabetical Order)	Rank	Score
WESTERN KENTUCKY UNIVERSITY Bowling Green, Kentucky	191	2.54
WESTERN MICHIGAN UNIVERSITY Kalamazoo, Michigan	123	3.24
WICHITA STATE UNIVERSITY Wichita, Kansas	186	2.59
WILLIAM AND MARY, THE COLLEGE OF Williamsburg, Virginia	175	2.70
WINTHROP UNIVERSITY Rock Hill, South Carolina	222	2.14
WISCONSIN-LACROSSE, UNIVERSITY OF LaCrosse, Wisconsin	220	2.16
WISCONSIN-MADISON, UNIVERSITY OF Madison, Wisconsin	21	4.62
WISCONSIN-MILWAUKEE, UNIVERSITY OF Milwaukee, Wisconsin	59	3.96
WISCONSIN-OSHKOSH , UNIVERSITY OF Oshkosh, Wisconsin	209	2.31
WISCONSIN-WHITEWATER, UNIVERSITY OF Whitewater, Wisconsin	202	2.39
WRIGHT STATE UNIVERSITY Dayton, Ohio	193	2.52
WYOMING, UNIVERSITY OF Laramie, Wyoming	157	2.88

Strong = 4.61–4.99   Very Good = 4.01–4.59   Good = 3.61–3.99   Acceptable Plus = 3.01–3.59   Adequate = 2.01–2.99

Part VI

RATING OF PRE-PROFESSIONAL EDUCATION IN THE U.S.

RATING OF PRELEGAL EDUCATION

INSTITUTION	Rank	Score
HARVARD AND RADCLIFFE COLLEGES	1	4.93
YALE UNIVERSITY	2	4.92
COLUMBIA UNIVERSITY	3	4.91
MICHIGAN-ANN ARBOR, UNIVERSITY OF	4	4.90
CALIFORNIA-BERKELEY, UNIVERSITY OF	5	4.89
CHICAGO, UNIVERSITY OF	6	4.88
PRINCETON UNIVERSITY	7	4.86
CORNELL UNIVERSITY	8	4.84
STANFORD UNIVERSITY	9	4.83
CALIFORNIA-LOS ANGELES, UNIVERSITY OF	10	4.80
DUKE UNIVERSITY	11	4.79
NOTRE DAME, UNIVERSITY OF	12	4.78
PENNSYLVANIA, UNIVERSITY OF	13	4.77
NORTHWESTERN UNIVERSITY	14	4.76
MASSACHUSETTS INSTITUTE OF TECHNOLOGY	15	4.74
ILLINOIS,URBANA-CHAMPAIGN, UNIVERSITY OF	16	4.73
JOHNS HOPKINS UNIVERSITY	17	4.72
WISCONSIN-MADISON, UNIVERSITY OF	18	4.70
DARTMOUTH COLLEGE	19	4.69
MINNESOTA, UNIVERSITY OF	20	4.67
GEORGETOWN UNIVERSITY	21	4.65
BROWN UNIVERSITY	22	4.63
NEW YORK UNIVERSITY	23	4.62
NORTH CAROLINA-CHAPEL HILL, UNIVERSITY OF	24	4.61
VIRGINIA, UNIVERSITY OF	25	4.60
INDIANA UNIVERSITY-BLOOMINGTON	26	4.59
VANDERBILT UNIVERSITY	27	4.58
WASHINGTON, UNIVERSITY OF	28	4.56
WASHINGTON UNIVERSITY IN SAINT LOUIS	29	4.54
IOWA, UNIVERSITY OF	30	4.53
OHIO STATE UNIVERSITY-COLUMBUS	31	4.51
PITTSBURGH, UNIVERSITY OF	32	4.50
ROCHESTER, UNIVERSITY OF	33	4.48
TEXAS-AUSTIN, UNIVERSITY OF	34	4.46
GEORGE WASHINGTON UNIVERSITY	35	4.43
RUTGERS UNIVERSITY, NEW BRUNSWICK	36	4.41
STATE UNIVERSITY OF NEW YORK COLLEGE AT BUFFALO	37	4.38
CALIFORNIA-DAVIS, UNIVERSITY OF	38	4.36
UNITED STATES AIR FORCE ACADEMY	39	4.34
CALIFORNIA-SANTA BARBARA, UNIVERSITY OF	40	4.32
MICHIGAN STATE UNIVERSITY	41	4.30
BRANDEIS UNIVERSITY	42	4.27
CASE WESTERN RESERVE UNIVERSITY	43	4.25

INSTITUTION	Rank	Score
CALIFORNIA-RIVERSIDE, UNIVERSITY OF	44	4.22
KANSAS, UNIVERSITY OF	45	4.20
UTAH, UNIVERSITY OF	46	4.18
CLAREMONT MCKENNA COLLEGE	47	4.17
TULANE UNIVERSITY	48	4.15
TUFTS UNIVERSITY	49	4.12
EMORY UNIVERSITY	50	4.11

RATING OF PREMEDICAL EDUCATION

INSTITUTION	Rank	Score
HARVARD AND RADCLIFFE COLLEGES	1	4.93
JOHNS HOPKINS UNIVERSITY	2	4.92
YALE UNIVERSITY	3	4.91
CORNELL UNIVERSITY	4	4.90
CALIFORNIA-BERKELEY, UNIVERSITY OF	5	4.88
CALIFORNIA-LOS ANGELES, UNIVERSITY OF	6	4.87
STANFORD UNIVERSITY	7	4.86
ILLINOIS,URBANA-CHAMPAIGN, UNIVERSITY OF	8	4.84
COLUMBIA UNIVERSITY	9	4.82
MICHIGAN-ANN ARBOR, UNIVERSITY OF	10	4.80
CHICAGO, UNIVERSITY OF	11	4.79
NOTRE DAME, UNIVERSITY OF	12	4.78
PRINCETON UNIVERSITY	13	4.76
WISCONSIN-MADISON, UNIVERSITY OF	14	4.73
NORTHWESTERN UNIVERSITY	15	4.72
DUKE UNIVERSITY	16	4.70
BROWN UNIVERSITY	17	4.68
MASSACHUSETTS INSTITUTE OF TECHNOLOGY	18	4.66
DARTMOUTH COLLEGE	19	4.64
PENNSYLVANIA, UNIVERSITY OF	20	4.62
CALIFORNIA INSTITUTE OF TECHNOLOGY	21	4.61
NEW YORK UNIVERSITY	22	4.60
WASHINGTON UNIVERSITY IN SAINT LOUIS	23	4.58
MINNESOTA, UNIVERSITY OF	24	4.57
INDIANA UNIVERSITY-BLOOMINGTON	25	4.55
VANDERBILT UNIVERSITY	26	4.53
CALIFORNIA-SAN DIEGO, UNIVERSITY OF	27	4.52
RICE UNIVERSITY	28	4.50
GEORGETOWN UNIVERSITY	29	4.48
WASHINGTON, UNIVERSITY OF	30	4.46
NORTH CAROLINA-CHAPEL HILL, UNIVERSITY OF	31	4.43
IOWA, UNIVERSITY OF	32	4.42
CALIFORNIA-DAVIS, UNIVERSITY OF	33	4.40
VIRGINIA, UNIVERSITY OF	34	4.38
TUFTS UNIVERSITY	35	4.37
UNITED STATES AIR FORCE ACADEMY	36	4.36
ROCHESTER, UNIVERSITY OF	37	4.33
BRANDEIS UNIVERSITY	38	4.32
CALIFORNIA-RIVERSIDE, UNIVERSITY OF	39	4.30
CASE WESTERN RESERVE UNIVERSITY	40	4.28
TEXAS-AUSTIN, UNIVERSITY OF	41	4.27
CALIFORNIA-IRVINE, UNIVERSITY OF	42	4.26
EMORY UNIVERSITY	43	4.23
STATE UNIVERSITY OF NEW YORK COLLEGE AT BUFFALO	44	4.22

INSTITUTION	Rank	Score
PITTSBURGH, UNIVERSITY OF	45	4.21
PENNSYLVANIA STATE UNIVERSITY-UNIVERSITY PARK	46	4.20
MICHIGAN STATE UNIVERSITY	47	4.19
TULANE UNIVERSITY	48	4.18
BAYLOR UNIVERSITY	49	4.17
UTAH, UNIVERSITY OF	50	4.16
OHIO STATE UNIVERSITY-COLUMBUS	51	4.15
COLORADO-BOULDER, UNIVERSITY OF	52	4.14
LOMA LINDA UNIVERSITY	53	4.13
OREGON, UNIVERSITY OF	54	4.12
BOSTON UNIVERSITY	55	4.11
KANSAS, UNIVERSITY OF	56	4.09
CALIFORNIA-SANTA BARBARA, UNIVERSITY OF	57	4.07
MARQUETTE UNIVERSITY	58	4.06

Part VII
RATING OF UNIVERSITY ADMINISTRATIVE AREAS

Administrative

Alumni Associations

Athletic-Academic Balance

Comparative Competition for Fellowships/Scholarships

Counseling Centers

Curriculum

Intercollegiate Athletic Departments

Libraries

Public Relations

Trustees/Regents (Private)

RATING OF ADMINISTRATION

INSTITUTION	Rank	Score
HARVARD AND RADCLIFFE COLLEGES	1	4.86
CHICAGO, UNIVERSITY OF	2	4.82
PRINCETON UNIVERSITY	3	4.80
MASSACHUSETTS INSTITUTE OF TECHNOLOGY	4	4.75
MICHIGAN-ANN ARBOR, UNIVERSITY OF	5	4.74
CORNELL UNIVERSITY	6	4.72
DARTMOUTH COLLEGE	7	4.69
CALIFORNIA INSTITUTE OF TECHNOLOGY	8	4.67
JOHNS HOPKINS UNIVERSITY	9	4.64
RICE UNIVERSITY	10	4.61
BROWN UNIVERSITY	11	4.58
NOTRE DAME, UNIVERSITY OF	12	4.57
DUKE UNIVERSITY	13	4.53
NORTHWESTERN UNIVERSITY	14	4.49
YALE UNIVERSITY	15	4.47
COLUMBIA UNIVERSITY	16	4.43
NORTH CAROLINA-CHAPEL HILL, UNIVERSITY OF	17	4.40
ILLINOIS,URBANA-CHAMPAIGN, UNIVERSITY OF	18	4.39
PENNSYLVANIA, UNIVERSITY OF	19	4.37
PITTSBURGH, UNIVERSITY OF	20	4.35
VANDERBILT UNIVERSITY	21	4.33
CARNEGIE MELLON UNIVERSITY	22	4.31
ROCHESTER, UNIVERSITY OF	23	4.30
UNITED STATES AIR FORCE ACADEMY	24	4.29
BRANDEIS UNIVERSITY	25	4.27
UNITED STATES MILITARY ACADEMY	26	4.25
WILLIAMS COLLEGE	27	4.23
WASHINGTON UNIVERSITY IN SAINT LOUIS	28	4.22
SWARTHMORE COLLEGE	29	4.14
HAVERFORD COLLEGE	30	4.13
TUFTS UNIVERSITY	31	4.11
UNITED STATES NAVAL ACADEMY	32	4.08
GEORGIA INSTITUTE OF TECHNOLOGY	33	4.06

RATING OF ALUMNI

INSTITUTION	Rank	Score
HARVARD AND RADCLIFFE COLLEGES	1	4.93
PRINCETON UNIVERSITY	2	4.92
YALE UNIVERSITY	3	4.91
MICHIGAN-ANN ARBOR, UNIVERSITY OF	4	4.90
STANFORD UNIVERSITY	5	4.89
NOTRE DAME, UNIVERSITY OF	6	4.88
DUKE UNIVERSITY	7	4.83
PENNSYLVANIA, UNIVERSITY OF	8	4.81
CORNELL UNIVERSITY	9	4.79
MASSACHUSETTS INSTITUTE OF TECHNOLOGY	10	4.77
CHICAGO, UNIVERSITY OF	11	4.72
DARTMOUTH COLLEGE	12	4.71
NORTHWESTERN UNIVERSITY	13	4.69
CALIFORNIA-LOS ANGELES, UNIVERSITY OF	14	4.66
MINNESOTA, UNIVERSITY OF	15	4.62
WISCONSIN-MADISON, UNIVERSITY OF	16	4.59
RICE UNIVERSITY	17	4.54
CALIFORNIA INSTITUTE OF TECHNOLOGY	18	4.52
MICHIGAN STATE UNIVERSITY	19	4.51
NORTH CAROLINA-CHAPEL HILL, UNIVERSITY OF	20	4.47
GEORGIA INSTITUTE OF TECHNOLOGY	21	4.46
BROWN UNIVERSITY	22	4.42
ILLINOIS,URBANA-CHAMPAIGN, UNIVERSITY OF	23	4.40
COLUMBIA UNIVERSITY	24	4.38
OHIO STATE UNIVERSITY-COLUMBUS	25	4.37
PURDUE UNIVERSITY-WEST LAFAYETTE	26	4.36
NEBRASKA-LINCOLN, UNIVERSITY OF	27	4.34
TEXAS A&M UNIVERSITY-COLLEGE STATION	28	4.31
SOUTHERN CALIFORNIA, UNIVERSITY OF	29	4.30
TULANE UNIVERSITY	30	4.29
TEXAS-AUSTIN, UNIVERSITY OF	31	4.27
VANDERBILT UNIVERSITY	32	4.25
OBERLIN COLLEGE	33	4.23
PENNSYLVANIA STATE UNIVERSITY-UNIVERSITY PARK	34	4.22
IOWA, UNIVERSITY OF	35	4.19
CALIFORNIA-BERKELEY, UNIVERSITY OF	36	4.18
INDIANA UNIVERSITY-BLOOMINGTON	37	4.17
PITTSBURGH, UNIVERSITY OF	38	4.16
TENNESSEE-KNOXVILLE, UNIVERSITY OF	39	4.15
BRANDEIS UNIVERSITY	40	4.13
LOUISIANA STATE UNIVERSITY-BATON ROUGE	41	4.12
OKLAHOMA, UNIVERSITY OF	42	4.11
MISSOURI-COLUMBIA, UNIVERSITY OF	43	4.10
KANSAS, UNIVERSITY OF	44	4.08
VIRGINIA, UNIVERSITY OF	45	4.07
JOHNS HOPKINS UNIVERSITY	46	4.06
ROCHESTER, UNIVERSITY OF	47	4.03
WILLIAMS COLLEGE	48	4.02

RATING OF ATHLETIC–ACADEMIC BALANCE

THE GOURMAN REPORT evaluated and ranked all Division I, II and III schools. For this report one hundred twenty-six schools with scores in the 1.00-4.95 range, in rank order, were selected.

Rating Categories	Numerical Range
Good	4.70-4.95
Acceptable Plus	4.40-4.69
Acceptable	3.60-3.85
Marginal	2.00-2.98
Unsatisfactory	1.00-1.99

STATEMENT

The overemphasis and the abuse of intercollegiate athletics have plagued higher education for many decades. In spite of fulminations of faculty members and administrators, "sanity codes" and other attempted reforms, the evil persists.

THE GOURMAN REPORT adopted a comprehensive agenda and set priorities for the study of collegiate athletics. An institutional file for all colleges and universities participating in athletics was created. In addition, THE GOURMAN REPORT has collected massive amounts of information and has a consistent database that permits unit cost comparison.

ACCREDITING STANDARDS

Academic Advising
Academic Standards
Administration
Admissions
Athletic Director and Office
Athletic Staff
Budget/Revenue/Expenses
Degree Program (Quality of)
Faculty Athletic Representation
Financial Aid (4 Year Institutions)
Graduation Rate

Image Perception
Percentage of Athletes Graduate
Professional Schools
Post Graduate School Scholarships
Public Relations
SAT Scores
Scholarships (4 Year Institutions)
Sports Information
Transcripts (Summary)
Transfer Students (Jr./Community Colleges)
Transfer Students (4 Year Institutions)

ATHLETIC–ACADEMIC BALANCE (CONTINUED)

INSTITUTION	Rank	Score
HARVARD AND RADCLIFFE COLLEGES	1	4.92
PRINCETON UNIVERSITY	2	4.91
YALE UNIVERSITY	3	4.90
CORNELL UNIVERSITY	4	4.89
PENNSYLVANIA, UNIVERSITY OF	5	4.88
BROWN UNIVERSITY	6	4.87
DARTMOUTH COLLEGE	7	4.86
COLUMBIA UNIVERSITY	8	4.85
STANFORD UNIVERSITY	9	4.84
NOTRE DAME, UNIVERSITY OF	10	4.83
DUKE UNIVERSITY	11	4.82
MICHIGAN-ANN ARBOR, UNIVERSITY OF	12	4.81
NORTHWESTERN UNIVERSITY	13	4.80
UNITED STATES NAVAL ACADEMY	14	4.79
RICE UNIVERSITY	15	4.78
VIRGINIA, UNIVERSITY OF	16	4.75
UNITED STATES AIR FORCE ACADEMY	17	4.73
UNITED STATES MILITARY ACADEMY	18	4.72
VANDERBILT UNIVERSITY	19	4.68
WISCONSIN-MADISON, UNIVERSITY OF	20	3.90
RUTGERS UNIVERSITY, NEW BRUNSWICK	21	3.89
GEORGIA INSTITUTE OF TECHNOLOGY	22	3.84
MIAMI UNIVERSITY OF OHIO	23	3.82
CALIFORNIA-LOS ANGELES, UNIVERSITY OF	24	3.80
CALIFORNIA-BERKELEY, UNIVERSITY OF	25	3.79
IOWA, UNIVERSITY OF	26	3.76
INDIANA UNIVERSITY-BLOOMINGTON	27	3.74
OREGON, UNIVERSITY OF	28	3.73
UTAH, UNIVERSITY OF	29	3.70
PITTSBURGH, UNIVERSITY OF	30	3.68
MISSOURI-COLUMBIA, UNIVERSITY OF	31	3.66
TULSA, UNIVERSITY OF	32	3.65
BRIGHAM YOUNG UNIVERSITY	33	3.62
PURDUE UNIVERSITY-WEST LAFAYETTE	34	2.85
SYRACUSE UNIVERSITY	35	2.83
OREGON STATE UNIVERSITY	36	2.82
SOUTHERN METHODIST UNIVERSITY	37	2.80
BOSTON COLLEGE	38	2.74
PENNSYLVANIA STATE UNIVERSITY-UNIVERSITY PARK	39	2.73
NORTH CAROLINA-CHAPEL HILL, UNIVERSITY OF	40	2.70
COLORADO STATE UNIVERSITY	41	2.66
OHIO UNIVERSITY	42	2.65
MINNESOTA, UNIVERSITY OF	43	2.63
WYOMING, UNIVERSITY OF	44	2.59

Good = 4.70–4.95   Acceptable Plus = 4.40–4.69   Acceptable = 3.60–3.85   Marginal = 2.00–2.98   Unsatisfactory = 1.00–1.99

ATHLETIC–ACADEMIC BALANCE (CONTINUED)

INSTITUTION	Rank	Score
NORTH TEXAS, UNIVERSITY OF	45	2.55
TEMPLE UNIVERSITY	46	2.52
BAYLOR UNIVERSITY	47	2.48
NEVADA-RENO, UNIVERSITY OF	48	2.45
HAWAII-MANOA, UNIVERSITY OF	49	2.41
UTAH STATE UNIVERSITY	50	2.37
WESTERN MICHIGAN UNIVERSITY	51	2.31
BOWLING GREEN STATE UNIVERSITY	52	2.26
IDAHO, UNIVERSITY OF	53	2.25
WASHINGTON, UNIVERSITY OF	54	1.90
TEXAS-AUSTIN, UNIVERSITY OF	55	1.88
MARYLAND-COLLEGE PARK, UNIVERSITY OF	56	1.86
WASHINGTON STATE UNIVERSITY	57	1.85
ARIZONA, UNIVERSITY OF	58	1.83
NEBRASKA-LINCOLN, UNIVERSITY OF	59	1.80
FLORIDA, UNIVERSITY OF	60	1.78
CLEMSON UNIVERSITY	61	1.77
OKLAHOMA, UNIVERSITY OF	62	1.76
KANSAS, UNIVERSITY OF	63	1.73
TEXAS A&M UNIVERSITY-COLLEGE STATION	64	1.72
ARIZONA STATE UNIVERSITY	65	1.69
SOUTHERN CALIFORNIA, UNIVERSITY OF	66	1.66
ILLINOIS,URBANA-CHAMPAIGN, UNIVERSITY OF	67	1.62
KENTUCKY, UNIVERSITY OF	68	1.61
OHIO STATE UNIVERSITY-COLUMBUS	69	1.60
GEORGIA, UNIVERSITY OF	70	1.59
MICHIGAN STATE UNIVERSITY	71	1.58
LOUISIANA STATE UNIVERSITY-BATON ROUGE	72	1.56
TULANE UNIVERSITY	73	1.55
ALABAMA, UNIVERSITY OF	74	1.52
WEST VIRGINIA UNIVERSITY	75	1.49
SOUTH CAROLINA-COLUMBIA , UNIVERSITY OF,	76	1.48
AUBURN UNIVERSITY	77	1.46
CINCINNATI, UNIVERSITY OF	78	1.44
NEW MEXICO, UNIVERSITY	79	1.42
IOWA STATE UNIVERSITY	80	1.40
TENNESSEE-KNOXVILLE, UNIVERSITY OF	81	1.37
NORTH CAROLINA STATE UNIVERSITY	82	1.36
MISSISSIPPI STATE UNIVERSITY	83	1.35
HOUSTON, UNIVERSITY OF	84	1.34
KANSAS STATE UNIVERSITY	85	1.33
VIRGINIA TECH	86	1.30
ARKANSAS, UNIVERSITY OF	87	1.29
TEXAS TECH UNIVERSITY	88	1.28

Good = 4.70–4.95   Acceptable Plus = 4.40–4.69   Acceptable = 3.60–3.85   Marginal = 2.00–2.98   Unsatisfactory = 1.00–1.99

ATHLETIC–ACADEMIC BALANCE (CONTINUED)

INSTITUTION	Rank	Score
COLORADO-BOULDER, UNIVERSITY OF	89	1.27
OKLAHOMA STATE UNIVERSITY	90	1.26
SOUTHWESTERN LOUISIANA, UNIVERSITY OF	91	1.25
LOUISIANA TECH UNIVERSITY	92	1.24
NEW MEXICO STATE UNIVERSITY	93	1.23
TEXAS-EL PASO, UNIVERSITY OF	94	1.22
FLORIDA STATE UNIVERSITY	95	1.21
NEVADA-LAS VEGAS, UNIVERSITY OF	96	1.20
MIAMI, UNIVERSITY OF (FLORIDA)	97	1.19
CALIFORNIA STATE UNIVERSITY-FRESNO	98	1.18
CALIFORNIA STATE UNIVERSITY-SANDIEGO	99	1.17
CALIFORNIASTATE UNIVERSITY-SAN JOSE	100	1.16
MRSHALL UNIVERSITY	101	1.15
NORTHERN ILLINOIS UNIVERSITY	102	1.14
EASTERN MICHIGAN UNIVERSITY	103	1.13
TOLEDO, UNIVERSITY OF	104	1.12
KENT STATE UNIVERSITY	105	1.11
EAST CAROLINA UNIVERSITY	106	1.12
ARKANSAS STATE UNIVERSITY	107	1.11
SOUTHERN MISSISSIPPI, UNIVERSITY OF	108	1.10
CALIFORNIA STATE UNIVERSITY-NORTH RIDGE	109	1.09

Good = 4.70–4.95   Acceptable Plus = 4.40–4.69   Acceptable = 3.60–3.85   Marginal = 2.00–2.98   Unsatisfactory = 1.00–1.99

RATING OF COMPARATIVE COMPETITION FOR FELLOWSHIPS/SCHOLARSHIPS BY STUDENTS

INSTITUTION	Rank	Score
HARVARD AND RADCLIFFE COLLEGES	1	4.90
PRINCETON UNIVERSITY	2	4.89
YALE UNIVERSITY	3	4.87
MICHIGAN-ANN ARBOR, UNIVERSITY OF	4	4.84
STANFORD UNIVERSITY	5	4.80
PENNSYLVANIA, UNIVERSITY OF	6	4.78
CORNELL UNIVERSITY	7	4.77
CHICAGO, UNIVERSITY OF	8	4.75
MASSACHUSETTS INSTITUTE OF TECHNOLOGY	9	4.74
WISCONSIN-MADISON, UNIVERSITY OF	10	4.70
CALIFORNIA-BERKELEY, UNIVERSITY OF	11	4.67
CALIFORNIA-LOS ANGELES, UNIVERSITY OF	12	4.63
COLUMBIA UNIVERSITY	13	4.61
NOTRE DAME, UNIVERSITY OF	14	4.58
DUKE UNIVERSITY	15	4.56
DARTMOUTH COLLEGE	16	4.54
NORTHWESTERN UNIVERSITY	17	4.53
CALIFORNIA INSTITUTE OF TECHNOLOGY	18	4.52
CALIFORNIA-SAN DIEGO, UNIVERSITY OF	19	4.50
BROWN UNIVERSITY	20	4.47
INDIANA UNIVERSITY-BLOOMINGTON	21	4.45
MICHIGAN STATE UNIVERSITY	22	4.42
JOHNS HOPKINS UNIVERSITY	23	4.40
MINNESOTA, UNIVERSITY OF	24	4.37
NORTH CAROLINA-CHAPEL HILL, UNIVERSITY OF	25	4.33
UNITED STATES AIR FORCE ACADEMY	26	4.32
ILLINOIS,URBANA-CHAMPAIGN, UNIVERSITY OF	27	4.30
IOWA, UNIVERSITY OF	28	4.26
BRANDEIS UNIVERSITY	29	4.25
TEXAS-AUSTIN, UNIVERSITY OF	30	4.23
OHIO STATE UNIVERSITY-COLUMBUS	31	4.21
VANDERBILT UNIVERSITY	32	4.19
ROCHESTER, UNIVERSITY OF	33	4.17
SWARTHMORE COLLEGE	34	4.16
NEW YORK UNIVERSITY	35	4.14
WASHINGTON UNIVERSITY IN SAINT LOUIS	36	4.12
WILLIAMS COLLEGE	37	4.10
TULANE UNIVERSITY	38	4.09
POMONA COLLEGE	39	4.08
OBERLIN COLLEGE	40	4.06
HAVERFORD COLLEGE	41	4.02
RICE UNIVERSITY	42	4.01

RATING OF COUNSELING CENTERS

INSTITUTION	Rank	Score
CHICAGO, UNIVERSITY OF	1	4.81
PURDUE UNIVERSITY-WEST LAFAYETTE	2	4.79
PENNSYLVANIA, UNIVERSITY OF	3	4.75
BOSTON UNIVERSITY	4	4.74
MICHIGAN STATE UNIVERSITY	5	4.73
WAYNE STATE UNIVERSITY	6	4.72
MINNESOTA, UNIVERSITY OF	7	4.68
NEW YORK UNIVERSITY	8	4.66
BRANDEIS UNIVERSITY	9	4.65
PRINCETON UNIVERSITY	10	4.63
OHIO STATE UNIVERSITY-COLUMBUS	11	4.62
ILLINOIS,URBANA-CHAMPAIGN, UNIVERSITY OF	12	4.61
KANSAS, UNIVERSITY OF	13	4.59
DUKE UNIVERSITY	14	4.57
ROCHESTER, UNIVERSITY OF	15	4.53
NORTHWESTERN UNIVERSITY	16	4.52
STATE UNIVERSITY OF NEW YORK COLLEGE AT BUFFALO	17	4.51
PENNSYLVANIA STATE UNIVERSITY-UNIVERSITY PARK	18	4.50
INDIANA UNIVERSITY-BLOOMINGTON	19	4.49
BAYLOR UNIVERSITY	20	4.48
DARTMOUTH COLLEGE	21	4.46
MICHIGAN-ANN ARBOR, UNIVERSITY OF	22	4.44
CORNELL UNIVERSITY	23	4.43
WISCONSIN-MADISON, UNIVERSITY OF	24	4.41
TEMPLE UNIVERSITY	25	4.40
STANFORD UNIVERSITY	26	4.38
DENVER, UNIVERSITY OF	27	4.37
CALIFORNIA-BERKELEY, UNIVERSITY OF	28	4.36
CITY UNIVERSITY OF NEW YORK-CITY COLLEGE	29	4.35
BROWN UNIVERSITY	30	4.33
YALE UNIVERSITY	31	4.31
CATHOLIC UNIVERSITY OF AMERICA, THE	32	4.30
NORTH CAROLINA-CHAPEL HILL, UNIVERSITY OF	33	4.29
RICE UNIVERSITY	34	4.27
TULANE UNIVERSITY	35	4.25
CALIFORNIA-LOS ANGELES, UNIVERSITY OF	36	4.23
CASE WESTERN RESERVE UNIVERSITY	37	4.22
RUTGERS UNIVERSITY, NEW BRUNSWICK	38	4.21
VANDERBILT UNIVERSITY	39	4.20
UNITED STATES NAVAL ACADEMY	40	4.18
IOWA, UNIVERSITY OF	41	4.17
TUFTS UNIVERSITY	42	4.16
WASHINGTON UNIVERSITY IN SAINT LOUIS	43	4.15
PITTSBURGH, UNIVERSITY OF	44	4.14
JOHNS HOPKINS UNIVERSITY	45	4.11
CARNEGIE MELLON UNIVERSITY	46	4.09
OBERLIN COLLEGE	47	4.08
CALIFORNIA-RIVERSIDE, UNIVERSITY OF	48	4.05
CALIFORNIA-SANTA BARBARA, UNIVERSITY OF	49	4.03

RATING OF CURRICULUM

INSTITUTION	Rank	Score
PRINCETON UNIVERSITY	1	4.92
HARVARD AND RADCLIFFE COLLEGES	2	4.91
MICHIGAN-ANN ARBOR, UNIVERSITY OF	3	4.90
YALE UNIVERSITY	4	4.88
STANFORD UNIVERSITY	5	4.84
CALIFORNIA-BERKELEY, UNIVERSITY OF	6	4.78
CHICAGO, UNIVERSITY OF	7	4.76
WISCONSIN-MADISON, UNIVERSITY OF	8	4.74
CALIFORNIA-LOS ANGELES, UNIVERSITY OF	9	4.72
PENNSYLVANIA, UNIVERSITY OF	10	4.70
JOHNS HOPKINS UNIVERSITY	11	4.68
COLUMBIA UNIVERSITY	12	4.65
MINNESOTA, UNIVERSITY OF	13	4.62
MASSACHUSETTS INSTITUTE OF TECHNOLOGY	14	4.61
NORTHWESTERN UNIVERSITY	15	4.60
CORNELL UNIVERSITY	16	4.57
DARTMOUTH COLLEGE	17	4.54
NOTRE DAME, UNIVERSITY OF	18	4.52
INDIANA UNIVERSITY-BLOOMINGTON	19	4.50
DUKE UNIVERSITY	20	4.47
BROWN UNIVERSITY	21	4.45
NEW YORK UNIVERSITY	22	4.43
ILLINOIS,URBANA-CHAMPAIGN, UNIVERSITY OF	23	4.41
STATE UNIVERSITY OF NEW YORK COLLEGE AT BUFFALO	24	4.39
NORTH CAROLINA-CHAPEL HILL, UNIVERSITY OF	25	4.37
WASHINGTON, UNIVERSITY OF	26	4.35
CALIFORNIA-SAN DIEGO, UNIVERSITY OF	27	4.33
TEXAS-AUSTIN, UNIVERSITY OF	28	4.31
IOWA, UNIVERSITY OF	29	4.30
OHIO STATE UNIVERSITY-COLUMBUS	30	4.29
RUTGERS UNIVERSITY, NEW BRUNSWICK	31	4.28
WASHINGTON UNIVERSITY IN SAINT LOUIS	32	4.27
RICE UNIVERSITY	33	4.26
PURDUE UNIVERSITY-WEST LAFAYETTE	34	4.25
PENNSYLVANIA STATE UNIVERSITY-UNIVERSITY PARK	35	4.24
ROCHESTER, UNIVERSITY OF	36	4.23
CALIFORNIA-SANTA BARBARA, UNIVERSITY OF	37	4.22
VIRGINIA, UNIVERSITY OF	38	4.21
CARNEGIE MELLON UNIVERSITY	39	4.20
TULANE UNIVERSITY	40	4.19
CASE WESTERN RESERVE UNIVERSITY	41	4.18
PITTSBURGH, UNIVERSITY OF	42	4.17
CALIFORNIA-DAVIS, UNIVERSITY OF	43	4.14
BRANDEIS UNIVERSITY	44	4.12

CURRICULUM (CONTINUED)

INSTITUTION	Rank	Score
TUFTS UNIVERSITY	45	4.11
WAYNE STATE UNIVERSITY	46	4.10
VANDERBILT UNIVERSITY	47	4.08
MICHIGAN STATE UNIVERSITY	48	4.07
UTAH, UNIVERSITY OF	49	4.05
CALIFORNIA-RIVERSIDE, UNIVERSITY OF	50	4.04
KANSAS, UNIVERSITY OF	51	4.03
UNITED STATES AIR FORCE ACADEMY	52	4.01

RATING OF INTERCOLLEGIATE ATHLETIC DEPARTMENTS

THE GOURMAN REPORT evaluated and ranked all Division I, II, and III schools. For this report 122 schools with scores in the 1.0-4.99 range, in rank order, were selected.

INSTITUTION	Rank	Score
MICHIGAN-ANN ARBOR, UNIVERSITY OF	1	4.85
STANFORD UNIVERSITY	2	4.84
NOTRE DAME, UNIVERSITY OF	3	4.83
DUKE UNIVERSITY	4	4.81
PRINCETON UNIVERSITY	5	4.79
PENNSYLVANIA, UNIVERSITY OF	6	4.76
RICE UNIVERSITY	7	4.72
HARVARD AND RADCLIFFE COLLEGES	8	4.70
DARTMOUTH COLLEGE	9	4.68
CORNELL UNIVERSITY	10	4.63
UNITED STATES AIR FORCE ACADEMY	11	4.61
YALE UNIVERSITY	12	4.58
UNITED STATES MILITARY ACADEMY	13	4.55
NORTHWESTERN UNIVERSITY	14	4.53
UNITED STATES NAVAL ACADEMY	15	4.50
VIRGINIA, UNIVERSITY OF	16	4.46
BROWN UNIVERSITY	17	4.42
VANDERBILT UNIVERSITY	18	4.41
COLUMBIA UNIVERSITY	19	4.40
WISCONSIN-MADISON, UNIVERSITY OF	20	4.30
RUTGERS UNIVERSITY, NEW BRUNSWICK	21	4.24
COLGATE UNIVERSITY	22	4.21
NORTH CAROLINA-CHAPEL HILL, UNIVERSITY OF	23	4.16
GEORGIA INSTITUTE OF TECHNOLOGY	24	4.14
CITADEL, THE	25	4.12
VIRGINIA MILITARY INSTITUE	26	4.11
MIAMI UNIVERSITY (OHIO)	27	4.08
WILLIAM AND MARY, THE COLLEGE OF	28	4.02
WAKE FOREST UNIVERSITY	29	3.78
CALIFORNIA-BERKELEY, UNIVERSITY OF	30	3.75
IOWA, UNIVERSITY OF	31	3.72
CALIFORNIA, LOS ANGELS, UNIVERSITY OF	32	3.68
INDIANA UNIVERSITY-BLOOMINGTON	33	3.66
OREGON, UNIVERSITY OF	34	3.62
UTAH, UNIVERSITY OF	35	3.57
PITTSBURGH, UNIVERSITY OF	36	3.54
MISSOURI-COLUMBIA, UNIVERSITY OF	37	3.52
TULSA, UNIVERSITY OF	38	3.51
BRIGHAM YOUNG UNIVERSITY	39	3.46
PURDUE UNIVERSITY-WEST LAFAYETTE	40	3.40

Good = 4.40–4.95   Acceptable Plus = 4.01–4.39   Acceptable = 3.00–3.99   Marginal = 2.00–2.99   Unsatisfactory = 1.00–1.99

INTERCOLLEGIATE ATHLETIC DEPARTMENTS (CONTINUED)

INSTITUTION	Rank	Score
NORTH CAROLINA-CHAPEL HILL, UNIVERSITY OF	41	3.28
OREGON, UNIVERSITY OF	42	3.24
SOUTHERN METHODIST UNIVERSITY	43	3.20
TEXAS CHRISTIAN UNIVERSITY	44	3.15
SYRACUSE UNIVERSITY	45	2.91
PENNSYLVANIA STATE UNIVERSITY-UNIVERSITY PARK	46	2.88
BOSTON COLLEGE	47	2.85
COLORADO STATE UNIVERSITY	48	2.79
OHIO UNIVERSITY	49	2.75
MINNESOTA, UNIVERSITY OF	50	2.72
WYOMING, UNIVERSITY OF	51	2.71
NORTH TEXAS, UNIVERSITY OF	52	2.68
TEMPLE UNIVERSITY	53	2.66
BAYLOR UNIVERSITY	54	2.60
NEVADA-RENO, UNIVERSITY	55	2.55
HAWAII, MANOA, UNIVERSITY OF	56	2.51
UTAH STATE UNIVERSITY	57	2.46
AKRON, UNIVERSITY	58	2.43
WESTERN MICHIGAN UNIVERSITY	59	2.39
BOWLING GREEN STATE UNIVERSITY	60	2.33
CENTRAL MICHIGAN UNIVERSITY	61	2.27
BALL STATE UNIVERSITY	62	2.25
WASHINGTON, UNIVERSITY OF (SEATTLE)	63	2.18
SOUTHERN CALIFORNIA, UNIVERSITY OF	64	1.87
TEXAS-AUSTIN, UNIVERSITY OF	65	1.85
MARYLAND-COLLEGE PARK-UNIVERSITY	66	1.83
WASHINGTON STATE UNIVERSITY	67	1.82
ARIZON, UNIVERSTIY OF	68	1.80
NEBRASKA-LINCOLN, UNIVERSITY OF	69	1.79
FLORIDA, UNIVERSITY OF	70	1.78
CLEMSON UNIVERSITY	71	1.77
OKLAHOMA, UNIVERSITY OF	72	1.75
KANSAS, UNIVERSITY OF	73	1.74
TEXAS A&M UNIVERSITY-COLLEGE STATION	74	1.70
ARIZONA STATE UNIVERSITY	75	1.68
LOUISVILLE, UNIVERSITY	76	1.63
ILLINOIS, URBANA-CHAMPAIGN, UNIVERSITY OF	77	1.61
KENTUCKY STATE UNIVERSITY	78	1.59
OHIO STATE UNIVERSITY-COLUMBUS	79	1.58
GEORGIA, UNIVERSITY OF	80	1.57
MICHIGAN STATE UNIVERSITY	81	1.56
LOUISIANA STATE UNIVERSITY-BATON ROUGE	82	1.55
TULANE UNIVERSITY	83	1.54
ALABAMA, UNIVERSITY OF	84	1.53

Good = 4.40–4.95   Acceptable Plus = 4.01–4.39   Acceptable = 3.00–3.99   Marginal = 2.00–2.99   Unsatisfactory = 1.00–1.99

INTERCOLLEGIATE ATHLETIC DEPARTMENTS (CONTINUED)

INSTITUTION	Rank	Score
WEST VIRGINIA UNIVERSITY	85	1.52
SOUTH CAROLINA-COLUMBIA, UNIVERSITY OF	86	1.51
AUBURN UNIVERSITY	87	1.49
CINCINNATI, UNIVERSITY OF	88	1.48
TEXAS TECH UNIVERSITY	89	1.47
MEMPHIS, THE UNIVERSITY OF	90	1.46
IOWA STATE	91	1.44
MISSISSIPPI, UNIVERSITY OF	92	1.42
TENNESSEE-KNOXVILLE, UNIVERSITY OF	93	1.41
NORTH CAROLINA STATE UNIVERSITY	94	1.40
MISSISSIPPI STATE UNIVERSITY	95	1.39
HOUSTON, UNIVERSITY OF	96	1.38
KANSAS STATE UNIVERSITY	97	1.37
VIRGINIA TECH & STATE UNIVERSITY	98	1.36
ARKANSAS, UNIVERSITY OF	99	1.35
NEW MEXICO, UNIVERSITY OF	100	1.34
COLORADO-BOULDER, UNIVERSITY OF	101	1.33
OKLAHOMA STATE UNIVERSITY	102	1.32
SOUTHERN MISSISSIPPI, UNIVERSITY OF	103	1.31
SOUTHWESTERN LOUISIANA, UNIVERSITY OF	104	1.30
LOIUSIANA TECH UNIVERSITY	105	1.29
NORTHERN ILLINOIS UNIVERSITY	106	1.28
EASTERN MICHIGAN UNIVERSITY	107	1.27
NEW MEXICO STATE UNIVERSITY	108	1.26
KENT STATE UNIVERSITY	109	1.25
TOLEDO, UNIVERSITY OF	110	1.24
EAST CAROLINA UNIVERSITY	111	1.22
TEXAS-EL PASO, UNIVERITY OF	112	1.20
ARKANSAS STATE UNIVERSITY	113	1.19
MARSHALL UNIVERSITY	114	1.17
CALIFORNIA STATE UNIVERSITY-SAN DIEGO	115	1.15
GEORIGIA SOUTHERN UNIVERSITY	116	1.14
CALIFORNIA STATE UNIVERSITY-SAN JOSE	117	1.12
CALIFORNIA STATE UNIVERSITY-FRESNO	118	1.11
FLORIDA STATE UNIVERSITY	119	1.09
NEVADA-LAS VEGAS, UNIVERSITY OF	120	1.06
MIAMI, UNIVERSITY OF	121	1.04
CALIFORNIA STATE UNIVERSITY-NORTHRIDGE	122	1.02

Good = 4.40–4.95   Acceptable Plus = 4.01–4.39   Acceptable = 3.00–3.99   Marginal = 2.00–2.99   Unsatisfactory = 1.00–1.99

RATING OF LIBRARIES

INSTITUTION	Rank	Score
HARVARD AND RADCLIFFE COLLEGES	1	4.94
YALE UNIVERSITY	2	4.91
ILLINOIS,URBANA-CHAMPAIGN, UNIVERSITY OF	3	4.89
COLUMBIA UNIVERSITY	4	4.85
CORNELL UNIVERSITY	5	4.83
MICHIGAN-ANN ARBOR, UNIVERSITY OF	6	4.81
CALIFORNIA-BERKELEY, UNIVERSITY OF	7	4.77
WISCONSIN-MADISON, UNIVERSITY OF	8	4.74
STANFORD UNIVERSITY	9	4.73
CALIFORNIA-LOS ANGELES, UNIVERSITY OF	10	4.70
CHICAGO, UNIVERSITY OF	11	4.67
MINNESOTA, UNIVERSITY OF	12	4.64
INDIANA UNIVERSITY-BLOOMINGTON	13	4.62
OHIO STATE UNIVERSITY-COLUMBUS	14	4.60
TEXAS-AUSTIN, UNIVERSITY OF	15	4.58
PRINCETON UNIVERSITY	16	4.57
NORTHWESTERN UNIVERSITY	17	4.52
PENNSYLVANIA, UNIVERSITY OF	18	4.51
NOTRE DAME, UNIVERSITY OF	19	4.50
DUKE UNIVERSITY	20	4.45
NEW YORK UNIVERSITY	21	4.42
JOHNS HOPKINS UNIVERSITY	22	4.38
VIRGINIA, UNIVERSITY OF	23	4.37
WASHINGTON, UNIVERSITY OF	24	4.36
LOUISIANA STATE UNIVERSITY-BATON ROUGE	25	4.35
NORTH CAROLINA-CHAPEL HILL, UNIVERSITY OF	26	4.32
MICHIGAN STATE UNIVERSITY	27	4.30
SYRACUSE UNIVERSITY	28	4.26
RUTGERS UNIVERSITY, NEW BRUNSWICK	29	4.23
IOWA, UNIVERSITY OF	30	4.22
BROWN UNIVERSITY	31	4.18
UNITED STATES AIR FORCE ACADEMY	32	4.15
PITTSBURGH, UNIVERSITY OF	33	4.12

RATING OF PUBLIC RELATIONS

INSTITUTION	Rank	Score
HARVARD AND RADCLIFFE COLLEGES	1	4.87
PRINCETON UNIVERSITY	2	4.86
CALIFORNIA INSTITUTE OF TECHNOLOGY	3	4.85
NOTRE DAME, UNIVERSITY OF	4	4.84
DUKE UNIVERSITY	5	4.79
NORTHWESTERN UNIVERSITY	6	4.75
RICE UNIVERSITY	7	4.73
CORNELL UNIVERSITY	8	4.72
DARTMOUTH COLLEGE	9	4.68
MASSACHUSETTS INSTITUTE OF TECHNOLOGY	10	4.65
MICHIGAN-ANN ARBOR, UNIVERSITY OF	11	4.63
BRANDEIS UNIVERSITY	12	4.58
JOHNS HOPKINS UNIVERSITY	13	4.55
YALE UNIVERSITY	14	4.52
UNITED STATES NAVAL ACADEMY	15	4.51
PENNSYLVANIA, UNIVERSITY OF	16	4.49
CHICAGO, UNIVERSITY OF	17	4.45
ILLINOIS,URBANA-CHAMPAIGN, UNIVERSITY OF	18	4.40
VANDERBILT UNIVERSITY	19	4.38
ROCHESTER, UNIVERSITY OF	20	4.35
COLUMBIA UNIVERSITY	21	4.34
NORTH CAROLINA-CHAPEL HILL, UNIVERSITY OF	22	4.31
NEW YORK UNIVERSITY	23	4.27
TUFTS UNIVERSITY	24	4.25
GEORGETOWN UNIVERSITY	25	4.23
BROWN UNIVERSITY	26	4.22
STATE UNIVERSITY OF NEW YORK COLLEGE AT BUFFALO	27	4.19
GEORGIA INSTITUTE OF TECHNOLOGY	28	4.18
WASHINGTON UNIVERSITY IN SAINT LOUIS	29	4.17
CARNEGIE MELLON UNIVERSITY	30	4.15
UTAH, UNIVERSITY OF	31	4.13
OBERLIN COLLEGE	32	4.11
UNITED STATES AIR FORCE ACADEMY	33	4.10
HAVERFORD COLLEGE	34	4.08
SWARTHMORE COLLEGE	35	4.07
RENSSELAER POLYTECHNIC INSTITUTE	36	4.06
EMORY UNIVERSITY	37	4.05

Part VIII
RATING OF CANADIAN COLLEGES AND UNIVERSITIES

INSTITUTION	Rank	Score
McGILL UNIVERSITY	1	4.64
UNIVERSITY OF TORONTO	2	4.61
THE UNIVERSITY OF BRITISH COLUMBIA	3	4.22
McMASTER UNIVERSITY	4	3.89
UNIVERSITY OF ALBERTA	5	3.63
YORK UNIVERSITY	6	3.61
CARLETON UNIVERSITY	7	3.58
SIMON FRASER UNIVERSITY	8	3.55
THE UNIVERSITY OF MANITOBA	9	3.50
UNIVERSITY OF OTTAWA	10	3.45
THE UNIVERSITY OF CALGARY	11	3.39
UNIVERSITÉ DE MONTRÉAL	12	3.38
UNIVERSITY OF NEW BRUNSWICK	13	3.37
UNIVERSITÉ LAVAL	14	3.36
UNIVERSITY OF WINDSOR	15	3.34
THE UNIVERSITY OF WESTERN ONTARIO	16	3.32
THE UNIVERSITY OF WINNIPEG	17	3.31
MEMORIAL UNIVERSITY OF NEWFOUNDLAND	18	3.30
UNIVERSITÉ DE SHERBROOKE	19	3.29
UNIVERSITY OF SASKATCHEWAN	20	3.28
QUEEN'S UNIVERSITY AT KINGSTON	21	3.27
UNIVERSITY OF WATERLOO	22	3.26
UNIVERSITY OF VICTORIA	23	3.25
DALHOUSE UNIVERSITY	24	3.24
CONCORDIA UNIVERSITY	25	3.23
UNIVERSITY OF GUELPH	26	3.20
THE UNIVERSITY OF REGINA	27	3.18
LAKEHEAD UNIVERSITY	28	3.16
LAURENTIAN UNIVERSITY OF SUDBURY	29	3.15
UNIVERSITÉ DE MONCTON	30	3.14
BRANDON UNIVERSITY	31	3.13
BISHOP'S UNIVERSITY	32	3.12
ROYAL MILITARY COLLEGE OF CANADA	33	3.11
TRENT UNIVERSITY	34	3.10
WILFRID LAURIER UNIVERSITY	35	3.09
ACADIA UNIVERSITY	36	3.08
BROCK UNIVERSITY	37	3.07
TECHNICAL UNIVERSITY OF NOVA SCOTIA	38	3.06
MOUNT ALLISON UNIVERSITY	39	3.05
MOUNT SAINT VINCENT UNIVERSITY	40	3.04
THE UNIVERSITY OF LETHBRIDGE	41	3.03
UNIVERSITY OF PRINCE ISLAND	42	3.02
UNIVERSITÉ DU QUEBEC (Montreal)	43	3.01
ATHZBASCA UNIVERSITY	44	2.99
SAINT MARY'S UNIVERSITY	45	2.97
ST. THOMAS UNIVERSITY	46	2.95

INSTITUTION	Rank	Score
UNIVERSITÉ DUQUÉBEC À TROIS-RIVIÈRES	47	2.92
RYERSON POLYTECHNIC UNIVERSITY	48	2.90
UNIVERSITÉ DUQUÉBEC À CHICOUTIMI	49	2.85
UNIVERSITY OF ST. MICHAEL'S COLLEGE	50	2.84
TRINITY WESTERN UNIVERSITY	51	2.82
UNIVERSITÉ DE QUÉBEC À HULL	52	2.80
UNIVERSITÉ DU QUÉBEC À RIMOUSKI	53	2.77
NOVA SCOTIA AGRICULTURAL COLLEGE	54	2.73
UNIVERSITY COLLEGE OF CAPE BRETON	55	2.70
UNIVERSITÉ DU QUÉBEC EN ABITIBI-TÉMISCAMINQUE	56	2.69
ST. FRANCIS XAVIER UNIVERSITY	57	2.65
UNIVERSITÉ SAINTE-ANNE	58	2.60
UNIVERSITY OF KING'S COLLEGE	59	2.53
SAINT PAUL UNIVERSITY	60	2.47

Part IX
RATING OF CANADIAN ENGINEERING SCHOOLS AND PROGRAMS

INSTITUTION	Rank	Score
UNIVERSITY OF TORONTO	1	4.85
McGILL UNIVERSITY	2	4.83
UNIVERSITY OF BRITISH COLUMBIA	3	4.80
McMASTER UNIVERSITY	4	4.78
POLYTECHNIQUE ECOLE (Université de Montréal)	5	4.75
UNIVERSITY OF SASKATCHEWAN	6	4.72
UNIVERSITY OF ALBERTA	7	4.70
UNIVERSITY OF MANITOBA	8	4.67
LAVAL UNIVERSITÉ	9	4.65
QUEEN'S UNIVERSITY	10	4.61
NOVA SCOTIA TECHNICAL UNIVERSITY	11	4.58
UNIVERSITY OF CALGARY	12	4.56
UNIVERSITY OF OTTAWA	13	4.53
UNIVERSITY OF NEW BRUNSWICK	14	4.50
ROYAL MILITARY COLLEGE OF CANADA	15	4.47
MEMORIAL UNIVERSITY OF NEWFOUNDLAND	16	4.45
UNIVERSITY OF WINDSOR	17	4.42
UNIVERSITY OF WESTERN ONTARIO	18	4.40
UNIVERSITY OF WATERLOO	19	4.34
CARLETON UNIVERSITY	20	4.30
UNIVERSITÉ DE SHERBROOKE	21	4.26
UNIVERSITY OF GUELPH	22	4.20
UNIVERSITÉ DE MONCTON	23	4.15
CONCORDIA UNIVERSITY	24	4.10
LAKEHEAD UNIVERSITY	25	4.04
UNIVERSITÉ DU QUÉBEC (Trois-Rivères)	26	3.80
UNIVRESITY OF REGINA	27	3.50
UNIVERSITÉ DU QUÉBEC (Chicoutimi)	28	3.40
LAURENTIAN UNIVERSITY	29	3.37
SIMON FRASER UNIVERSITY	30	3.15
UNIVERSITY OF VICTORIA	31	3.06

INSTITUTION (Listed in Alphabetical Order)	Program	Score
UNIVERSITY OF ALBERTA Edmonton, Alberta	Agricultural Engineering	4.76
	Chemical Engineering	4.69
	Civil Engineering	4.70
	Computer Engineering	4.67
	Electrical Engineering	4.72
	Engineering Physics	4.30
	Metallurgical Engineering	4.80
	Mineral Engineering	4.81
	Petroleum Engineering	4.83
UNIVERSITY OF BRITISH COLUMBIA Vancouver, British Columbia	Agricultural Engineering	4.84
	Bio-Resource	4.77
	Chemical Engineering	4.82
	Civil Engineering	4.80
	Electrical Engineering	4.81
	Engineering Physics	4.83
	Geological Engineering	4.86
	Mechanical Engineering	4.79
	Metallurgical Engineering	4.84
	Metals and Materials Engineering	4.76
	Mineral Engineering	4.88
UNIVERSITY OF CALGARY Calgary, Alberta	Chemical Engineering	4.62
	Civil Engineering	4.72
	Electrical Engineering	4.71
	Geomatics	3.80
	Mechanical Engineering	4.70
	Surveying	4.66
CARLETON UNIVERSITY Ottawa, Ontario	Aerospace Engineering	4.27
	Civil Engineering	4.54
	Computer Systems	4.53
	Electrical Engineering	4.55
CONCORDIA UNIVERSITY Montreal, Québec	Building Engineering	4.47
	Civil Engineering	4.30
	Computer Engineering	4.46
	Electrical Engineering	4.44
UNIVERSITY OF GUELPH Guelph, Ontario	Agricultural Engineering	4.50
	Biological Engineering	4.46
	Engineering Systems & Computing	3.88
	Environmental Engineering	3.82
LAKEHEAD UNIVERSITY Thunder Bay, Ontario	Chemical Engineering	4.49
	Civil Engineering	4.40
	Electrical Engineering	4.46
	Mechanical Engineering	4.42

INSTITUTION (Listed in Alphabetical Order)	Program	Score
LAURENTIAN UNIVERSITY Sudbury, Ontario	Extractive Metallurgical Engineering	3.39
	Extractive Metallurgy	3.35
	Mining Engineering	3.32
LAVAL UNIVERSITI Quebec, Quebec	Chemical Engineering	4.65
	Civil Engineering	4.68
	Electrical Engineering	4.69
	Engineering Physics	4.70
	Geological Engineering	4.80
	Mechanical Engineering	4.75
	Metallurgical Engineering	4.81
	Metallurgy and Materials Science	4.69
	Mining Engineering	4.76
	Rural Engineering	4.63
	Systems Engineering	4.55
MANITOBA, UNIVERSITY OF Winnipeg, Manitoba	Agricultural Engineering	4.85
	Civil Engineering	4.65
	Computer Engineering	4.64
	Electrical Engineering	4.70
	Geological Engineering	4.77
	Industrial Engineering	4.63
MCGILL UNIVERSITY Montreal, Québec	Agricultural Engineering (Macdonald College)	4.82
	Chemical Engineering	4.88
	Civil Engineering	4.83
	Computer Engineering	4.66
	Electrical Engineering	4.82
	Metallurgical Engineering	4.86
	Mining Engineering	4.87

INSTITUTION (Listed in Alphabetical Order)	Program	Score
MCMASTER UNIVERSITY Hamilton, Ontario	Ceramic Engineering	4.81
	Ceramic Engineering and Management	4.87
	Chemical Engineering	4.73
	Chemical Engineering & Management	4.70
	Civil Engineering	4.79
	Civil Engineering & Computer Systems	4.68
	Civil Engineering & Engineering Mechanics	4.78
	Civil Engineering & Management	4.75
	Computer Engineering	4.71
	Computer Engineering & Management	4.66
	Electrical Engineering	4.80
	Electrical Engineering and Management	4.76
	Engineering Physics	4.65
	Engineering Physics & Management	4.74
	Manufacturing Engineering	4.67
	Materials Engineering	4.45
	Materials Engineering and Management	4.72
	Mechanical Engineering & Management	4.83
	Metallurgical Engineering	4.86
	Metallurgical Engineering and Management	4.77
MEMORIAL UNIVERSITY OF NEWFOUNDLAND St. John's, New Foundland	Civil Engineering	4.61
	Electrical Engineering	4.58
	Mechanical Engineering	4.57
	Naval Architecture	4.50
	Shipbuilding	4.59
MONCTON, UNIVERSITÉ DE Moncton, Nouveau-Brunswick	Civil Engineering	3.48
	Industrial Engineering	3.50
	Mechanical Engineering	3.10
UNIVERSITY OF NEW BRUNSWICK Fredericton, Nouveau-Brunswick	Chemical Engineering	4.67
	Civil Engineering	4.64
	Electrical Engineering	4.68
	Forest Engineering	4.60
	Geological Engineering	4.61
	Mechanical Engineering	4.66
	Surveying	4.63

INSTITUTION (Listed in Alphabetical Order)	Program	Score
NOVA SCOTIA TECHNICAL UNIVERSITY Halifax, Nova Scotia	Agricultural Engineering	4.76
	Chemical Engineering	4.65
	Civil Engineering	4.67
	Electrical Engineering	4.66
	Engineering Physics	4.62
	Industrial Engineering	4.77
	Mechanical Engineering	4.69
	Metallurgical Engineering	4.68
	Mining Engineering	4.78
OTTAWA, UNIVERSITY OF Ottawa, Ontario	Chemical Engineering	4.68
	Civil Engineering	4.65
	Computer Engineering	4.10
	Electrical Engineering	4.66
POLYTECHNIQUE ECOLE (UNIVERSITÉ DE MONTRÉAL) Montréal, Québec	Chemical Engineering	4.71
	Civil Engineering	4.66
	Electrical Engineering	4.70
	Engineering Physics	4.80
	Geological Engineering	4.75
	Industrial Engineering	4.79
	Materials Engineering	4.50
	Mechanical Engineering	4.72
	Metallurgical Engineering	4.81
	Mining Engineering	4.83
	Systems Engineering	4.16
QUEEN'S UNIVERSITY Kingston, Ontario	Chemical Engineering	4.61
	Civil Engineering	4.74
	Electrical Engineering	4.72
	Engineering Physics	4.70
	Geological Engineering	4.81
	Materials and Metallurgical Engineering	4.68
	Mathematics and Engineering	4.76
	Mechanical Engineering	4.69
	Metallurgical Engineering	4.75
	Mining Engineering	4.78
QUÉBEC, UNIVERSITÉ DU Chicoutimi, Québec	Engineering/General	3.38
	Geological Engineering	3.40
	Systems Engineering	3.14
QUÉBEC, UNIVERSITÉ DU Trois-Rivières, Québec	Chemical Engineering	3.26
	Electrical Engineering	3.81
	Industrial Engineering	3.80
	Mechanical Engineering & Manufacturing	3.79

INSTITUTION (Listed in Alphabetical Order)	Program	Score
REGINA, UNIVERSITY OF Regina, Saskatchewan	Electronic Information Systems	3.49
	Environmental Systems	3.46
	Industrial Systems	3.48
	Systems Engineering	3.51
ROYAL MILITARY COLLEGE OF CANADA Kingston, Ontario	Chemical and Materials Engineering	4.57
	Chemical Engineering	4.60
	Civil Engineering	4.63
	Computer Engineering	4.59
	Electrical Engineering	4.65
	Engineering and Management	4.62
	Engineering Physics	4.66
	Fuels and Materials	4.58
UNIVERSITY OF SASKATCHEWAN Saskatoon, Saskatchewan	Agricultural Engineering	4.85
	Chemical Engineering	4.69
	Civil Engineering	4.71
	Electrical Engineering	4.70
	Engineering Physics	4.77
	Geological Engineering	4.80
	Mechanical Engineering	4.66
	Mining Engineering	4.78
SHERBROOKE, UNIVERSITÉ DE Sherbrooke, Québec	Chemical Engineering	4.55
	Civil Engineering	4.50
	Electrical Engineering	4.46
	Mechanical Engineering	4.45
SIMON FRASER UNIVERSITY Burnaby, British Columbia	Engineering Science	3.06
UNIVERSITY OF TORONTO Toronto, Ontario	Chemical Engineering	4.81
	Civil Engineering	4.85
	Computer Engineering	4.73
	Electrical Engineering	4.86
	Engineering Science	4.84
	Geological and Mineral Engineering	4.81
	Industrial Engineering	4.77
	Metallurgical Engineering and Materials Science	4.76
	Metallurgy and Materials Science	4.79

INSTITUTION (Listed in Alphabetical Order)	Program	Score
UNIVERSITY OF VICTORIA Victoria, British Columbia	Computer Engineering Electrical Engineering	2.98 2.99
WATERLOO, UNIVERSITY OF Waterloo, Ontario	Chemical Engineering Civil Engineering Computer Engineering Electrical Engineering Geological Engineering Mechanical Engineering Systems Design	4.59 4.53 4.08 4.55 4.50 4.51 4.52
WESTERN ONTARIO, UNIVERSITY OF London, Ontario	Chemical and Biochemical Engineering Chemical Engineering Civil Engineering Electrical Engineering Materials Engineering Mechanical Engineering	4.58 4.53 4.55 4.56 4.54 4.50
UNIVERSITY OF WINDSOR Windsor, Ontario	Chemical Engineering Civil Engineering Electrical Engineering Engineering Materials Environmental Engineering Geological Engineering Industrial Engineering Mechanical Engineering	4.56 4.53 4.50 4.57 4.49 4.62 4.59 4.51

RATING OF
INTERNATIONAL UNIVERSITIES

RATING OF CURRICULUM (Effectiveness of Program)

(BIOLOGICAL SCIENCES, ENGINEERING, HUMANITIES, PHYSICAL SCIENCES AND SOCIAL SCIENCES)

INSTITUTION	Country	Rank	Score
UNIVERSITÉ PARIS (ALL CAMPUSES)	France	1	4.94
UNIVERSITY OF OXFORD	United Kingdom	2	4.93
UNIVERSITY OF CAMBRIDGE	United Kingdom	3	4.92
UNIVERSITY OF HEIDELBERG	Germany	4	4.91
UNIVERSITÉ LYON I, II, III	France	5	4.90
TECHNICAL UNIVERSITY OF MUNICH	Germany	6	4.89
UNIVERSITÉ MONTPELLIER I, II, III	France	7	4.88
UNIVERSITY OF VIENNA	Austria	8	4.84
EDINBURGH UNIVERSITY	Scotland	9	4.83
UNIVERSITY OF GENEVA	Switzerland	10	4.82
FREE UNIVERSITY OF BRUSSELS	Belgium	11	4.80
UNIVERSITY OF GÖTTINGEN	Germany	12	4.78
UNIVERSITY OF ZURICH	Switzerland	13	4.77
UNIVERSITÉ D'AIX-MARSEILLE I, II, III	France	14	4.76
MCGILL UNIVERSITY	Canada	15	4.75
UNIVERSITÉ BORDEAUX I, II, III	France	16	4.73
UNIVERSITÉ NANCY I, II	France	17	4.71
UNIVERSITY OF TUEBINGEN	Germany	18	4.69
UNIVERSITY OF ERLANGEN-NURNBERG	Germany	19	4.68
UNIVERSITY OF TORONTO	Canada	20	4.67
UNIVERSITÉ DE GRENOBLE I, II, III	France	21	4.64
UNIVERSITY OF MARBURG	Germany	22	4.63
UNIVERSITÉ CATHOLIQUE DE LILLE I, II, III	France	23	4.57
UNIVERSITY OF COLOGNE	Germany	24	4.56
UNIVERSITÉ DE DIJON	France	25	4.55
UNIVERSITÉ DE RENNES I, II	France	26	4.54
UNIVERSITÉ TOULOUSE I, II, III	France	27	4.53
UNIVERSITY OF LONDON	United Kingdom	28	4.52
UNIVERSITÉ CLERMONT-FERRAND	France	29	4.48
UNIVERSITY OF BONN	Germany	30	4.47
UNIVERSITY OF FRANKFURT	Germany	31	4.44
UNIVERSITÉ DE POITIERS	France	32	4.42
UNIVERSITÉ DE NICE	France	33	4.38
HEBREW UNIVERSITY OF JERUSALEM, THE	Israel	34	4.34
CATHOLIC UNIVERSITY OF LEUVEN	Belgium	35	4.19
STOCKHOLM UNIVERSITY	Sweden	36	4.18
UNIVERSITY OF COPENHAGEN	Denmark	37	4.15
UNIVERSITY OF MUNSTER	Germany	38	4.14
UNIVERSITY OF WÜRZBURG	Germany	39	4.13
UNIVERSITY OF MAINZ	Germany	40	4.11
UNIVERSITY OF AMSTERDAM	Netherlands	41	4.10
UNIVERSITÉ DE ROUEN	France	42	4.08
UNIVERSITY OF BOLOGNA	Italy	43	4.07
UNIVERSITY OF MADRID	Spain	44	4.05

RATING OF FACULTY

INSTITUTION	Country	Rank	Score
UNIVERSITÉ PARIS (ALL CAMPUSES)	France	1	4.94
UNIVERSITY OF OXFORD	United Kingdom	2	4.93
UNIVERSITY OF CAMBRIDGE	United Kingdom	3	4.92
UNIVERSITY OF HEIDELBERG	Germany	4	4.90
TECHNICAL UNIVERSITY OF MUNICH	Germany	5	4.89
UNIVERSITÉ MONTPELLIER I, II, III	France	6	4.88
UNIVERSITÉ LYON I, II, III	France	7	4.87
UNIVERSITÉ CATHOLIQUE DE LILLE I, II, III	France	8	4.86
EDINBURGH UNIVERSITY	Scotland	9	4.85
UNIVERSITY OF VIENNA	Austria	10	4.81
UNIVERSITY OF GENEVA	Switzerland	11	4.80
UNIVERSITY OF GÖTTINGEN	Germany	12	4.78
UNIVERSITY OF ZURICH	Switzerland	13	4.76
UNIVERSITÉ D'AIX-MARSEILLE I, II, III	France	14	4.75
UNIVERSITÉ BORDEAUX I, II, III	France	15	4.72
FREE UNIVERSITY OF BRUSSELS	Belgium	16	4.71
UNIVERSITÉ DE DIJON	France	17	4.68
UNIVERSITÉ NANCY I, II	France	18	4.65
UNIVERSITY OF TUEBINGEN	Germany	19	4.62
UNIVERSITY OF TORONTO	Canada	20	4.60
UNIVERSITY OF ERLANGEN-NURNBERG	Germany	21	4.59
UNIVERSITÉ DE GRENOBLE I, II, III	France	22	4.58
UNIVERSITY OF MARBURG	Germany	23	4.50
MCGILL UNIVERSITY	Canada	24	4.48
UNIVERSITÉ DE RENNES I, II	France	25	4.46
UNIVERSITÉ TOULOUSE J, II, III	France	26	4.44
UNIVERSITY OF LONDON	United Kingdom	27	4.43
UNIVERSITÉ CLERMONT-FERRAND	France	28	4.39
UNIVERSITY OF COLOGNE	Germany	29	4.34
UNIVERSITY OF BONN	Germany	30	4.33
UNIVERSITÉ DE ROUEN	France	31	4.31
UNIVERSITÉ DE NICE	France	32	4.30
UNIVERSITY OF FRANKFURT	Germany	33	4.28
HEBREW UNIVERSITY OF JERUSALEM, THE	Israel	34	4.22
STOCKHOLM UNIVERSITY	Sweden	35	4.18
CATHOLIC UNIVERSITY OF LEUVEN	Belgium	36	4.16
UNIVERSITY OF MUNSTER	Germany	37	4.14
UNIVERSITY OF MAINZ	Germany	38	4.13
UNIVERSITY OF WÜRZBURG	Germany	39	4.12
UNIVERSITY OF AMSTERDAM	Netherlands	40	4.11
UNIVERSITÉ DE BESANÇON	France	41	4.10
UNIVERSITÉ DE CAEN	France	42	4.09
TOKYO UNIVERSITY	Japan	43	4.08
UNIVERSITY OF BOLOGNA	Italy	44	4.07
UNIVERSITÉ DE NANTES	France	45	4.06
UNIVERSITÉ D'ORLEANS	France	46	4.05
UNIVERSITY OF COPENHAGEN	Denmark	47	4.04
UNIVERSITÉ DE POITIERS	France	48	4.03
UNIVERSITY OF MADRID	Spain	49	4.02

RATING OF ACADEMIC QUALITY

INSTITUTION	Country	Rank	Score
UNIVERSITÉ PARIS (ALL CAMPUSES)	France	1	4.95
UNIVERSITY OF OXFORD	United Kingdom	2	4.93
UNIVERSITY OF CAMBRIDGE	United Kingdom	3	4.92
UNIVERSITY OF HEIDELBERG	Germany	4	4.91
UNIVERSITÉ MONTPELLIER I, II, III	France	5	4.90
TECHNICAL UNIVERSITY OF MUNICH	Germany	6	4.89
UNIVERSITÉ LYON I, II, III	France	7	4.88
UNIVERSITÉ CATHOLIQUE DE LILLE I, II, III	France	8	4.86
EDINBURGH UNIVERSITY	Scotland	9	4.85
UNIVERSITY OF VIENNA	Austria	10	4.84
UNIVERSITÉ D'AIX-MARSEILLE I, II, III	France	11	4.83
UNIVERSITY OF GÖTTINGEN	Germany	12	4.82
UNIVERSITY OF GENEVA	Switzerland	13	4.81
UNIVERSITY OF ZURICH	Switzerland	14	4.80
UNIVERSITÉ BORDEAUX I, II, III	France	15	4.78
FREE UNIVERSITY OF BRUSSELS	Belgium	16	4.77
UNIVERSITÉ DE DIJON	France	17	4.75
UNIVERSITÉ NANCY I, II	France	18	4.73
UNIVERSITY OF TUEBINGEN	Germany	19	4.70
UNIVERSITY OF ERLANGEN-NURNBERG	Germany	20	4.69
UNIVERSITÉ DE GRENOBLE I, II, III	France	21	4.68
UNIVERSITY OF MARBURG	Germany	22	4.64
UNIVERSITÉ DE RENNES I, II	France	23	4.62
UNIVERSITÉ TOULOUSE I, II, III	France	24	4.61
UNIVERSITY OF LONDON	United Kingdom	25	4.60
UNIVERSITÉ CLERMONT-FERRAND	France	26	4.59
UNIVERSITY OF BONN	Germany	27	4.55
UNIVERSITY OF COLOGNE	Germany	28	4.54
UNIVERSITÉ DE NICE	France	29	4.52
UNIVERSITÉ DE ROUEN	France	30	4.51
UNIVERSITY OF FRANKFURT	Germany	31	4.49
HEBREW UNIVERSITY OF JERUSALEM, THE	Israel	32	4.42
CATHOLIC UNIVERSITY OF LEUVEN	Belgium	33	4.40
UNIVERSITY OF MUNSTER	Germany	34	4.33
STOCKHOLM UNIVERSITY	Sweden	35	4.32
UNIVERSITY OF MAINZ	Germany	36	4.30
UNIVERSITY OF WÜRZBURG	Germany	37	4.28
UNIVERSITÉ DE BESANÇON	France	38	4.26
UNIVERSITY OF AMSTERDAM	Netherlands	39	4.24
UNIVERSITÉ DE CAEN	France	40	4.22
TOKYO UNIVERSITY	Japan	41	4.21
UNIVERSITÉ DE NANTES	France	42	4.18
UNIVERSITY OF BOLOGNA	Italy	43	4.16
UNIVERSITÉ D'ORLEANS	France	44	4.15
UNIVERSITY OF COPENHAGEN	Denmark	45	4.09
UNIVERSITÉ DE POITIERS	France	46	4.07
UNIVERSITY OF MADRID	Spain	47	4.06

Part XI
APPENDICES

Appendix A: List of Tables

Appendix B: International Institutions of Higher Learning

Appendix C: Selected University Administrations/Regents/Trustees

APPENDIX A: LIST OF TABLES
TABLE 1: RATING OF 140 UNDERGRADUATE PROGRAMS IN THE UNITED STATES

FIELD OF STUDY	Selected Number of Institutions Granting Degree	Total Number of Programs (Curriculum) Evaluated	Total Number of Areas of Study Evaluated	Total Number of Faculty Areas Evaluated	Institutions Listed In Part I
Accounting	631	631	25,810	1,114	41
Aerospace Engineering	46	46	3,612	999	44
Agricultural Business	110	110	826	103	10
Agricultural Economics	70	70	640	97	21
Agricultural Engineering	45	45	2,419	990	37
Agriculture	120	120	8,688	2,111	46
Agronomy	121	121	6,815	1,915	45
American Studies	80	80	1,910	561	33
Animal Science	64	64	2,380	433	35
Anthropology	102	102	1,521	738	50
Applied Mathematics	51	51	1,936	541	16
Arabic	17	17	496	98	9
Architectural Engineering	10	10	430	66	8
Architecture	94	94	1,495	380	39
Art	490	490	8,800	3,001	42
Art History	60	60	4,085	630	41
Asian/Oriental Studies	27	27	1,330	412	13
Astronomy	40	40	1,951	655	25
Astrophysics	25	25	1,162	784	10
Atmospheric Sciences	22	22	751	220	8
Bacteriology/Microbiology	219	219	4,670	1,014	37
Behavioral Sciences	50	50	994	114	9
Biochemistry	312	312	2,699	900	32
Bioengineering/Biomedical Engineering	42	42	2,830	940	16
Biology	630	630	13,224	2,401	48
Biophysics	60	60	1,866	739	13
Botany	173	173	2,985	819	31
Business Administration	730	730	34,720	3,010	45
Cell Biology	40	40	1,100	458	19
Ceramic Art/Design	48	48	1,120	647	14
Ceramic Engineering	15	15	418	83	11
Chemical Engineering	120	120	2,215	843	53
Chemistry	555	555	15,221	2,170	53
Child Psychology	164	164	1,014	467	17
Chinese	50	50	961	112	14
Civil Engineering	144	144	2,961	896	55
Classics	60	60	1,815	688	23
Communication	333	333	8,973	1,615	19
Comparative Literature	65	65	996	455	28
Computer Engineering	36	36	1,762	871	22
Computer Science	260	260	9,875	1,760	57
Dairy Sciences	43	43	412	66	11
Dietetics	127	127	1,273	454	15
Drama/Theatre	401	401	6,222	1,117	46
Earth Science	49	49	1,941	652	12
East Asian Studies	44	44	933	150	11
Ecology/Environmental Studies	151	151	1,020	406	13
Economics	627	627	10,730	3,696	46
Electrical Engineering	170	170	4,422	1,366	62

TABLE 1: RATING OF 140 UNDERGRADUATE PROGRAMS IN THE UNITED STATES

FIELD OF STUDY	Selected Number of Institutions Granting Degree	Total Number of Programs (Curriculum) Evaluated	Total Number of Areas of Study Evaluated	Total Number of Faculty Areas Evaluated	Institutions Listed In Part I
Engineering/General	22	22	1,210	639	10
Engineering Mechanics	21	21	854	352	6
Engineering Physics	17	17	761	139	8
Engineering Science	52	52	1,316	160	10
English	826	826	12,775	3,951	41
Entomology	55	55	1,122	495	26
Environmental Design	46	46	997	217	14
Environmental Engineering	33	33	1,104	366	11
Environmental Sciences	78	78	1,266	512	12
Farm/Ranch Management	20	20	788	152	9
Film	94	94	1,004	261	9
Finance	666	666	10,281	3,302	44
Fish/Game Management	51	51	1,645	724	12
Food Sciences	100	100	851	196	18
Food Services Management	72	72	666	122	12
Forestry	50	50	1,244	832	30
French	430	430	8,746	1,866	30
Genetics	30	30	884	298	13
Geography	83	83	2,300	647	30
Geological Engineering	18	18	777	144	12
Geology/Geoscience	115	115	5,549	1,090	25
Geophysics/Geoscience	47	47	733	169	28
German	301	301	3,901	988	30
Greek	77	77	995	183	16
Hebrew	50	50	388	104	20
History	690	690	15,360	5,431	46
Home Economics	177	177	1,790	798	30
Horticulture	77	77	1,071	312	36
Hotel, Restaurant, Institutional Management	132	132	843	95	22
Industrial Engineering	86	86	2,269	712	34
Information Science	60	60	995	228	10
International Relations	62	62	1,273	469	15
Italian	58	58	1,001	345	22
Japanese	43	43	394	96	14
Journalism and Mass Communications	73	73	3,141	954	31
Labor and Industrial Relations	82	82	792	255	10
Landscape Architecture	39	39	663	105	33
Latin	49	49	1,117	307	11
Latin American Studies	51	51	655	96	16
Linguistics	62	62	1,185	489	30
Management	280	280	4,490	1,128	47
Manufacturing Engineering	7	7	133	34	4
Marine Biology	76	76	1,461	488	7
Marine Sciences	37	37	846	130	6
Marketing	531	531	9,766	2,481	41
Materials Engineering/Materials Science Engineering	38	38	1,303	186	32
Mathematics	166	166	17,829	2,696	58
Mechanical Engineering	200	200	10,814	2,998	58

TABLE 1: RATING OF 140 UNDERGRADUATE PROGRAMS IN THE UNITED STATES

FIELD OF STUDY	Selected Number of Institutions Granting Degree	Total Number of Programs (Curriculum) Evaluated	Total Number of Areas of Study Evaluated	Total Number of Faculty Areas Evaluated	Institutions Listed In Part I
Medieval Studies	44	44	872	116	10
Metallurgical Engineering	40	40	1,799	465	18
Meteorology	41	41	917	272	10
Mining and Mineral Engineering	24	24	1,303	654	17
Molecular Biology	33	33	1,885	746	22
Music	760	760	10,145	4,672	30
Natural Resource Management	68	68	837	222	15
Naval Architecture & Marine Engineering	11	11	449	111	6
Near/Middle Eastern Studies	24	24	583	100	17
Nuclear Engineering	30	30	1,377	435	22
Nursing	507	507	7,278	1,131	39
Nutrition	218	218	1,644	722	28
Occupational Therapy	72	72	1,666	705	32
Ocean Engineering	8	8	450	86	6
Operations Research	40	40	971	230	10
Ornamental Horticulture	24	24	722	210	7
Parks Management	69	69	1,123	401	17
Petroleum Engineering	25	25	1,207	438	17
Philosophy	112	112	2,691	488	21
Physical Therapy	106	106	2,666	1,001	24
Physics	160	160	9,788	3,078	35
Political Science	427	427	9,595	3,130	50
Portuguese	33	33	414	88	12
Poultry Sciences	26	26	416	89	13
Psychology	365	365	17,121	6,219	30
Radio/Television Studies	85	85	1,129	620	9
Religious Studies	104	104	3,860	894	21
Russian	83	83	1,161	760	20
Russian/Slavic Studies	91	91	1,488	490	18
Scandinavian Languages	16	16	281	73	8
Slavic Languages	24	24	999	154	17
Social Work/Social Welfare	221	221	1,670	485	17
Sociology	505	505	15,200	8,141	19
South Asian Studies	10	10	240	56	9
Southeast Asian Studies	10	10	239	54	9
Spanish	479	479	11,714	6,212	36
Speech/Rhetoric	307	307	8,690	2,120	14
Speech Pathology/Audiology	106	106	2,601	954	28
Statistics	70	70	2,370	722	25
Systems Engineering	14	14	310	74	13
Urban and Regional Planning	41	41	864	114	13
Wildlife Biology	33	33	851	110	12
Zoology	129	129	2,822	923	19

APPENDIX A: LIST OF TABLES (CONTINUED)

TABLE 2: RATING OF PRELEGAL EDUCATION IN THE UNITED STATES[1]

Selected Number of Institutions Evaluated   1,726

Quality Prelegal Education: Institutions Listed in the Gourman Report   50

Total Number of Curriculum Fields Evaluated   203,006

Explanatory Note: [1]The rating is evaluated and derived from data for 1,726 undergraduate institutions with reference to curriculum, instruction and "pre-law" programs. The quality of the curriculum and instruction is fundamental to the attainment of legal competence.

TABLE 3: RATING OF PREMEDICAL EDUCATION IN THE UNITED STATES[1]

Selected Number of Institutions Evaluated   1,726

Quality Premedical Education: Institutions Listed in the Gourman Report   58

Total Number of Curriculum Fields Evaluated   202,035

Explanatory Note: [2]The rating is evaluated and derived from data for 1,726 undergraduate institutions with reference to curriculum, instruction and premedical education programs. The quality of the curriculum and instruction is fundamental to the attainment of medical competence.

TABLE 4: RATING OF TEN UNIVERSITY ADMINISTRATIVE AREAS

ADMINISTRATIVE AREAS	Selected Number of Institutions Evaluated	Institutions Listed in the Gourman Report	Total Number of Areas Evaluated
Administration	1,726	35	119,888
Alumni Associations	1,726	50	10,001
*Athletic-Academic Balance			
Comparative Competition for Fellowship/Scholarships	931	43	6,255
Counseling Centers	722	50	30,033
Curriculum	1,726	52	211,646
**Intercollegiate Athletic Departments			
Libraries	1,726	33	80,533
Public Relations	1,726	39	8,444
Institutions	1,726	1,277	215,222
Trustees/Regents (Public and Federal)	860	0	6,131
Trustees/Regents (Private)	489	92	2,660

* See Table 5.
**See Table 6.

TABLE 5: A Rating of Athletic–Academic Balance

Selected Number of Institutions Evaluated	906
Institutions Listed in the Gourman Report	126
Total Number of Areas Evaluated	14,099

TABLE 6: A Rating of Selective Intercollegiate Athletic Departments

Selected Number of Institutions/Athletic Departments Evaluated	906
Institutions/Athletic Departments Listed in the Gourman Report	127
Total Number of Areas Evaluated	7,665

TABLE 7: A Rating of Undergraduate Schools in Business Administration on the Approved List of the Gourman Report

Selected Number of Institutions/Business Administration Departments Evaluated	849
Institutions/Business Administration Departments Listed in the Gourman Report	228
Total Number of Areas Evaluated	32,070

TABLE 8: A Rating of Undergraduate Schools in Engineering on the Approved List of the Gourman Report

Selected Number of Institutions/Engineering Departments Evaluated	272
Institutions/Engineering Departments Listed in the Gourman Report	245
Total Number of Areas Evaluated	37,007

TABLE 9: A Rating of International Universities

ACADEMIC AREAS	Selected Number of Institutions Evaluated	Institutions Listed in the Gourman Report	Total Number of Areas Evaluated
Curriculum	761	44	92,046
Faculty	761	48	16,799
Institutions	761	49	96,049

APPENDIX B: INTERNATIONAL INSTITUTIONS INCLUDED IN THE 10TH EDITION

LISTED BELOW ARE THE INSTITUTIONS INCLUDED IN PART X OF THE TENTH EDITION

COUNTRY AND SCHOOL

AUSTRIA
University of Vienna

BELGIUM
Free University of Brussels
Catholic University of Louvain

CANADA
McGill University
University of Toronto

DENMARK
University of Copenhagen

FRANCE
University of Provence (Aix-Marseilles I)
University of Aix-Marseilles II
University of Aix-Marseilles III
University of Besancon
University of Bordeaux I
University of Bordeaux II
University of Bordeaux III
University of Caen
University of Clermont
University of Dijon
Scientific and Medical University (University of Grenoble I)
University of Social Sciences (Grenoble II)
University of Social Sciences (Grenoble II)
University of Languages and Literature (Grenoble III)
University of Sciences (Lille I)
University of Law and Health Sciences (Lille II)
University of Human Sciences, Literature and Arts (Lille III)
University Claude-Bernard (Lyons I)
University of Lyons II
University of Jean Moulin (Lyons III)
University of Montpellier I
Languedoc University of Sciences (Montpellier II)

COUNTRY AND SCHOOL

Paul-Valery University (Montpellier III)
University of Nancy I
University of Nancy II
University of Nantes
University of Nice
University of Orleans
University of Paris I (Pantheon-Sorbonne)
University of Law, Economics, and Social Sciences (Paris II)
University of Paris III
University of Paris IV
University Rene Descartes (Paris V)
University of Paris VI
University of Paris VII
University of Paris VIII
University Paris-Dauphine (Paris IX)
University of Paris-Nanterre (Paris X)
University of Paris XI
University of Paris XII
University of Paris-Nord (Paris XIII)
University of Poitiers
University of Rennes I
University of Haute-Bretagne (Rennes II)
University of Rouen
University of Social Sciences (Toulouse I)
University of Toulouse-le Mirail (Toulouse II)
University Paul-Sabatier (Toulouse III)

GERMANY
Rhemish Friedrich-Wilhelm University of Bonn
University of Cologne
Friedrich Alexander University of Erlangen-Nüremberg
Johann Wolfgang Goethe University of Frankfurt
Georg August University of Göttingen
Rupert Charles University of Heidelberg
Johannes Gutenberg University of Mainz
Philipps University of Marburg
Ludwig Maximilian University of Munich
University of Munster

COUNTRY AND SCHOOL

Eberhard Karl University of Tubingen
University of Würzburg

ISRAEL
The Hebrew University of Jerusalem

ITALY
University of Bologna

JAPAN
The University of Tokyo

NETHERLANDS
University of Amsterdam

SPAIN
University of Madrid

SWEDEN
University of Stockholm

SWITZERLAND
University of Geneva
University of Zürich

UNITED KINGDOM
University of Cambridge
University of Edinburgh
University of London
University of Oxford

THE CALIFORNIA STATE UNIVERSITY

INSTITUTION	Gourman Overall Administration Rating Administration Leadership Management	Academic-Athletic Balance[1]	Curriculum[2] (Overall Disciplines)	Faculty[3] (All Disciplines)	Faculty Morale
Bakersfield	1.53	Division II Omitted	3.04	3.19	1.72
Chico	1.41	Division II Omitted	3.05	3.18	1.70
Dominguez Hills	1.45	Division II Omitted	3.17	3.25	1.68
Fresno	1.46	1.08	3.25	3.30	1.73
Fullerton	1.40	1.06	3.24	3.29	1.74
Hayward	1.44	Division II Omitted	3.05	3.14	1.39
Humboldt	1.47	Division II Omitted	3.07	3.13	1.66
Long Beach	1.48	1.37	3.31	3.32	1.80
Los Angeles	1.50	Division II Omitted	3.28	3.31	1.73
Northridge	0.60	1.01	3.08	3.21	1.10
Pomona	0.70	Division II Omitted	3.11	3.17	1.30
Sacramento	1.61	1.41	3.19	3.28	1.67
San Bernardino	1.39	Division II Omitted	3.16	3.27	1.65
San Diego	0.61	1.13	3.18	3.33	1.11
San Francisco	1.60	Division II Omitted	3.20	3.34	1.64
San Jose	1.62	1.10	3.22	3.35	1.71
San Luis Obispo	3.15	1.61	3.48	3.50	1.98
San Marcos	2.02	No Athletics	3.01	3.03	1.97
Sonoma	1.43	Division II Omitted	3.14	3.16	1.68
Stanislaus	1.42	Division II Omitted	3.15	3.20	1.60

[1] BA/BS degrees in education not approved and excluded from *The Gourman Report*
[2] Department of Education undergraduate curriculum not approved and excluded from *The Gourman Report*
[3] Faculty members of the Department of Education not approved and excluded from *The Gourman Report*

Strong = 4.41–4.99   Good = 4.01–4.40   Adequate = 3.01–3.99   Marginal = 2.01–2.99   Unsatisfactory = 0.01–1.99

THE CALIFORNIA STATE UNIVERSITY

INSTITUTION	Faculty Salaries	Image of Institution	Public Relations	Standards (Academic)
Bakersfield	Marginal	None—0.01	None—0.01	3.12
Chico	Marginal	None—0.01	None—0.01	3.13
Dominguez Hills	Marginal	None—0.01	None—0.01	3.17
Fresno	Marginal	2.01	2.12	3.19
Fullerton	Marginal	2.04	2.14	3.21
Hayward	Marginal	None—0.01	None—0.01	3.10
Humboldt	Marginal	None—0.01	None—0.01	3.09
Long Beach	Marginal	2.10	1.80	3.20
Los Angeles	Marginal	None—0.01	None—0.01	3.16
Northridge	Marginal	None—0.01	None—0.01	1.99
Pomona	Marginal	None—0.01	None—0.01	3.14
Sacramento	Marginal	2.11	2.13	3.22
San Bernardino	Marginal	None—0.01	None—0.01	3.18
San Diego	Marginal	2.19	1.71	3.28
San Francisco	Marginal	2.18	2.16	3.29
San Jose	Marginal	2.25	2.18	3.27
San Luis Obispo	Marginal	3.30	3.22	3.52
San Marcos	Marginal	None—0.01	None—0.01	3.01
Sonoma	Marginal	None—0.01	None—0.01	3.11
Stanislaus	Marginal	None—0.01	None—0.01	3.10

Strong = 4.41–4.99   Good = 4.01–4.40   Adequate = 3.01–3.99   Marginal = 2.01–2.99   Unsatisfactory = 0.01–1.99

THE UNIVERSITY OF CALIFORNIA

INSTITUTION	Gourman Overall Administration Rating Administration Leadership Management	Academic-Athletic Balance[1]	Curriculum[2] (Overall Disciplines)	Faculty[3] (All Disciplines)	Faculty Morale
Berkeley	2.14	3.79	4.39	4.56	1.91
Davis	2.28	Division II Omitted	4.37	4.54	1.88
Irvine	1.55	3.04	4.20	4.30	1.86
Los Angeles (UCLA)	2.08	3.80	4.38	4.53	1.84
Riverside	2.20	Division II Omitted	4.29	4.32	1.87
San Diego	2.27	Division III Omitted	4.36	4.52	1.90
San Francisco	3.18	No Athletics	4.35	4.55	1.87
Santa Barbara	2.02	3.02	4.33	4.34	1.78
Santa Cruz	2.12	Division III Omitted	4.24	4.27	1.77

[1] BA/BS degrees in education not approved and excluded from *The Gourman Report*
[2] Department of Education undergraduate curriculum not approved and excluded from *The Gourman Report*
[3] Faculty members of the Department of Education not approved and excluded from *The Gourman Report*

INSTITUTION	Faculty Salaries	Image of Institution	Public Relations	Standards (Academic)
Berkeley	Adequate	4.12	4.15	4.64
Davis	Adequate	4.10	4.16	4.62
Irvine	Adequate	3.09	3.08	4.38
Los Angeles (UCLA)	Adequate	4.09	3.89	4.61
Riverside	Adequate	4.02	3.71	4.40
San Diego	Adequate	4.11	3.73	4.60
San Francisco	Adequate	4.14	3.76	4.63
Santa Barbara	Adequate	3.19	4.05	4.59
Santa Cruz	Adequate	3.18	3.60	4.58

Strong = 4.41–4.99   Good = 4.01–4.40   Adequate = 3.01–3.99   Marginal = 2.01–2.99   Unsatisfactory = 0.01–1.99

CITY UNIVERSITY OF NEW YORK (CUNY)

INSTITUTION	Gourman Overall Administration Rating Administration Leadership Management	Academic-Athletic Balance[1]	Curriculum[2] (Overall Disciplines)	Faculty[3] (All Disciplines)	Faculty Morale
Bernard M. Baruch College	2.15	Division III Omitted	4.01	4.12	1.64
Brooklyn College	2.14	Division III Omitted	3.38	3.46	1.62
City College	2.13	Division III Omitted	3.39	3.43	1.50
Herbert H. Lehman College	2.12	Division III Omitted	3.28	3.20	1.48
Hunter College	2.11	Division III Omitted	3.37	4.02	1.49
Queens College	2.07	Division III Omitted	3.36	3.45	1.47

[1] BA/BS degrees in education not approved and excluded from *The Gourman Report*
[2] Department of Education undergraduate curriculum not approved and excluded from *The Gourman Report*
[3] Faculty members of the Department of Education not approved and excluded from *The Gourman Report*

INSTITUTION	Faculty Salaries	Image of Institution	Public Relations	Standards (Academic)
Bernard M. Baruch College	Marginal	3.70	3.12	3.20
Brooklyn College	Marginal	3.60	3.10	3.15
City College	Marginal	3.55	3.08	3.14
Herbert H. Lehman College	Marginal	3.50	3.06	3.13
Hunter College	Marginal	3.69	3.11	3.17
Queens College	Marginal	3.68	3.09	3.12

Strong = 4.41–4.99   Good = 4.01–4.40   Adequate = 3.01–3.99   Marginal = 2.01–2.99   Unsatisfactory = 0.01–1.99

STATE UNIVERSITY OF NEW YORK (SUNY)

INSTITUTION	Gourman Overall Administration Rating Administration Leadership Management	Academic-Athletic Balance[1]	Curriculum[2] (Overall Disciplines)	Faculty[3] (All Disciplines)	Faculty Morale
Albany	2.10	Division III Omited	3.95	3.98	1.85
Binghamton	2.14	Division III Omited	3.97	3.99	1.84
Buffalo	2.16	1.81	4.28	4.34	1.92
Stony Brook	2.01	Division III Omited	4.27	4.33	1.93

[1] BA/BS degrees in education not approved and excluded from *The Gourman Report*
[2] Department of Education undergraduate curriculum not approved and excluded from *The Gourman Report*
[3] Faculty members of the Department of Education not approved and excluded from *The Gourman Report*

INSTITUTION	Faculty Salaries	Image of Institution	Public Relations	Standards (Academic)
Albany	Adequate	None—0.01	None—0.01	4.35
Binghamton	Adequate	None—0.01	None—0.01	4.34
Buffalo	Adequate	3.40	3.05	4.38
Stony Brook	Adequate	3.45	3.07	4.39

Strong = 4.41–4.99   Good = 4.01–4.40   Adequate = 3.01–3.99   Marginal = 2.01–2.99   Unsatisfactory = 0.01–1.99

RUTGERS – THE STATE UNIVERSITY OF NEW JERSEY

INSTITUTION	Gourman Overall Administration Rating Administration Leadership Management	Academic-Athletic Balance[1]	Curriculum[2] (Overall Disciplines)	Faculty[3] (All Disciplines)	Faculty Morale
Rutgers – Camden	2.07	Division III Omitted	3.60	3.63	1.79
Rutgers – Newark	2.06	Division III Omitted	3.62	3.64	1.78
Rutgers – New Brunswick	1.95	3.89	4.03	4.26	1.65

[1] BA/BS degrees in education not approved and excluded from *The Gourman Report*
[2] Department of Education undergraduate curriculum not approved and excluded from *The Gourman Report*
[3] Faculty members of the Department of Education not approved and excluded from *The Gourman Report*

INSTITUTION	Faculty Salaries	Image of Institution	Public Relations	Standards (Academic)
Rutgers – Camden	Good	None—0.01	None—0.01	3.40
Rutgers – Newark	Good	None—0.01	None—0.01	3.42
Rutgers – New Brunswick	Good	4.32	3.50	4.35

Strong = 4.41–4.99   Good = 4.01–4.40   Adequate = 3.01–3.99   Marginal = 2.01–2.99   Unsatisfactory = 0.01–1.99

NOTES

NOTES

NOTES

MORE EXPERT ADVICE

from

THE PRINCETON REVIEW

We help hundreds of thousands of students improve their test scores and get into college each year. If you want to give yourself the best chances for getting into the college of your choice, we can help you get the highest test scores, the best financial aid package, and make the most informed choices with our comprehensive line of books for the college-bound student. Here's to your success and good luck!

CRACKING THE SAT & PSAT 1998 EDITION
0-679-78405 $18.00

CRACKING THE SAT & PSAT WITH SAMPLE TESTS ON DISK 1998 EDITION
0-679-78404-7 • $29.95 with Mac and Windows compatible disks

CRACKING THE SAT & PSAT WITH SAMPLE TESTS ON CD-ROM 1998 EDITION
0-679-78403-9 • $29.95 Mac and Windows compatible

SAT MATH WORKOUT
0-679-75363-X • $15.00

SAT VERBAL WORKOUT
0-679-75362-1 • $16.00

INSIDE THE SAT BOOK/CD-ROM
1-884536-56-5 • $34.95
(Windows/Macintosh compatible interactive CD-ROM)

CRACKING THE ACT 1998-99 EDITION
0-375-75084-3 • $18.00

CRACKING THE ACT WITH SAMPLE TESTS ON CD-ROM 1998-99 EDITION
0-375-75085-1 • $29.95 Mac and Windows compatible

COLLEGE COMPANION
Real Students, True Stories, Good Advice
0-679-76905-6 • $15.00

STUDENT ADVANTAGE GUIDE TO COLLEGE ADMISSIONS
Unique Strategies for Getting into the College of Your Choice
0-679-74590-4 • $12.00

PAYING FOR COLLEGE WITHOUT GOING BROKE 1998 EDITION
Insider Strategies to Maximize Financial Aid and Minimize College Costs
0-375-75008-8 • $18.00

BEST 311 COLLEGES 1998 EDITION
The Buyer's Guide to College
0-679-78397-0 • $20.00

THE COMPLETE BOOK OF COLLEGES 1998 EDITION
0-679-78398-9 • $26.95

FIND US...

International

Hong Kong
4/F Sun Hung Kai Centre
30 Harbour Road, Wan Chai,
Hong Kong
Tel: (011)85-2-517-3016

Japan
Fuji Building 40, 15-14
Sakuragaokacho, Shibuya Ku,
Tokyo 150, Japan
Tel: (011)81-3-3463-1343

Korea
Tae Young Bldg, 944-24,
Daechi- Dong, Kangnam-Ku
The Princeton Review- ANC
Seoul, Korea 135-280,
South Korea
Tel: (011)82-2-554-7763

Mexico City
PR Mex S De RL De Cv
Guanajuato 228 Col. Roma
06700 Mexico D.F., Mexico
Tel: 525-564-9468

Montreal
666 Sherbrooke St.
West, Suite 202
Montreal, QC H3A 1E7 Canada
Tel: (514) 499-0870

Pakistan
1 Bawa Park - 90 Upper Mall
Lahore, Pakistan
Tel: (011)92-42-571-2315

Spain
Pza. Castilla, 3 - 5º A, 28046
Madrid, Spain
Tel: (011)341-323-4212

Taiwan
155 Chung Hsiao East Road
Section 4 - 4th Floor,
Taipei R.O.C., Taiwan
Tel: (011)886-2-751-1243

Thailand
Building One, 99 Wireless Road
Bangkok, Thailand 10330
Tel: (662) 256-7080

Toronto
1240 Bay Street, Suite 300
Toronto M5R 2A7 Canada
Tel: (800) 495-7737
Tel: (716) 839-4391

Vancouver
4212 University Way NE,
Suite 204
Seattle, WA 98105
Tel: (206) 548-1100

National (U.S.)
We have over 60 offices around the U.S. and
run courses in over 400 sites. For courses and locations
within the U.S. call 1 (800) 2/Review and you will be
routed to the nearest office.

Free!

Did you know that The Microsoft Network gives you one free month?

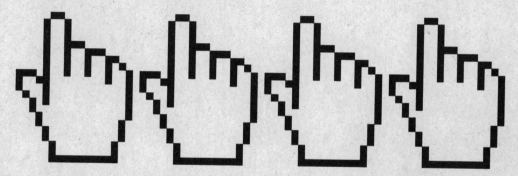

Call us at 1-800-FREE MSN. We'll send you a free CD to get you going.

Then, you can explore the World Wide Web for one month, free. Exchange e-mail with your family and friends. Play games, book airline tickets, handle finances, go car shopping, explore old hobbies and discover new ones. There's one big, useful online world out there. And for one month, it's a free world.

Call **1-800-FREE MSN,** Dept. 3197, for offer details or visit us at **www.msn.com**. Some restrictions apply.

Microsoft® Where do you want to go today?®

MSn™
The Microsoft Network